LINCOLN CHRISTIAN UNIVERSITY

P9-DET-757

Trust wholeheartedly in Yahweh,
put no faith in your own perception. . . .
Do not congratulate yourself on your own wisdom,
fear Yahweh and turn your back on evil.

PROVERBS 3:5, 7 NJB

---

What I spoke and proclaimed
was not meant to convince
by philosophical argument,
but to demonstrate the convincing power
of the Spirit,
so that your faith should depend not
on human wisdom
but on the power of God.

1 CORINTHIANS 2:4-5 NJB

---

For faith has eyes by which it sees
that that is somehow true
which it does not yet see;
it certainly sees that
it does not yet see
what it believes.

AUGUSTINE

---

Revelation is its own donor,
without preconditions,
and alone has the power to place in reality.
From God to reality,
not from reality to God,
goes the path of theology.

DIETRICH BONHOEFFER

---

*Other books by Donald G. Bloesch*

CENTERS OF CHRISTIAN RENEWAL
THE CHRISTIAN LIFE AND SALVATION
THE CRISIS OF PIETY
THE CHRISTIAN WITNESS IN A SECULAR AGE
CHRISTIAN SPIRITUALITY EAST AND WEST *(coauthor)*
THE REFORM OF THE CHURCH
THE GROUND OF CERTAINTY
SERVANTS OF CHRIST *(editor)*
THE EVANGELICAL RENAISSANCE
WELLSPRINGS OF RENEWAL
LIGHT A FIRE
THE INVADED CHURCH
JESUS IS VICTOR! KARL BARTH'S DOCTRINE OF SALVATION
THE ORTHODOX EVANGELICALS *(coeditor)*
ESSENTIALS OF EVANGELICAL THEOLOGY, VOL. 1: GOD, AUTHORITY, AND SALVATION
ESSENTIALS OF EVANGELICAL THEOLOGY, VOL. 2: LIFE, MINISTRY, AND HOPE
THE STRUGGLE OF PRAYER
FAITH AND ITS COUNTERFEITS
IS THE BIBLE SEXIST?
THE FUTURE OF EVANGELICAL CHRISTIANITY
CRUMBLING FOUNDATIONS
THE BATTLE FOR THE TRINITY
A HERMENEUTICS OF ULTIMACY: PERIL OR PROMISE? *(coauthor)*
FREEDOM FOR OBEDIENCE
THEOLOGICAL NOTEBOOK VOL. 1
THEOLOGICAL NOTEBOOK VOL. 2

·CHRISTIAN FOUNDATIONS·

# A THEOLOGY OF WORD & SPIRIT

## AUTHORITY & METHOD IN THEOLOGY

### DONALD G. BLOESCH

Lincoln Christian
University Library

INTERVARSITY PRESS
DOWNERS GROVE, ILLINOIS 60515

© 1992 by Donald G. Bloesch

All rights reserved. No part of this book may be reproduced in any form without written permission from InterVarsity Press, P.O. Box 1400, Downers Grove, Illinois 60515.

InterVarsity Press is the book-publishing division of InterVarsity Christian Fellowship, a student movement active on campus at hundreds of universities, colleges and schools of nursing in the United States of America, and a member movement of the International Eellowship of Evangelical Students. For information about local and regional activities, write Public Relations Dept., InterVarsity Christian Fellowship, 6400 Schroeder Rd., P.O. Box 7895, Madison, WI 53707-7895.

Scripture quotations, unless otherwise noted, are from the Revised Standard Version of the Bible, copyright 1946, 1952, 1971 by the Division of Christian Education of the National Council of the Churches of Christ in the U.S.A. and are used by permission. All rights reserved.

Cover illustration: Guy Wolek

ISBN 0-8308-1411-6

Printed in the United States of America ∞

**Library of Congress Cataloging-in-Publication Data**

Bloesch, Donald G., 1928-
  A theology of word and spirit: authority and method in theology/
Donald G. Bloesch.
    p.    cm.—(Christian foundations; vol. 1)
    ISBN 0-8308-1411-6
    1. Theology, Doctrinal.  I. Title.  II. Series.
  BT75.2.B568  1992
    230'.01—dc20                     92-20688
                                       CIP

17  16  15  14  13  12  11  10  9  8  7  6  5  4  3  2
06  05  04  03  02  01  00  99  98  97

*Dedicated to John S. Baird*

# Acknowledgments

I am indebted to the following persons for their contributions to the writing of this volume: my wife, Brenda, whose research skills have proved exceedingly valuable; my friend, former student and now colleague Elmer Colyer, whose insights on narrative theology have been immensely helpful; Joel Samuels, the librarian of the University of Dubuque and Wartburg Seminary, who has pointed me to some very relevant books; Arthur Cochrane, professor emeritus of Dubuque Theological Seminary, on whose wisdom I have drawn in this study; Arthur Holmes of Wheaton College, who has given me pertinent information on foundationalism and presuppositionalism; Mary C. Trannel, whose careful typing made this book ready for publication; Lance Wonders, an evangelical pastor, former student and friend, with whom I have had extensive dialog on this important subject; and Robert Johnston of North Park Seminary and Gabriel Fackre of Andover-Newton Seminary, whose letters of recommendation enabled me to receive a grant from the Association of Theological Schools, which made this research and writing possible.

# Abbreviations for Biblical Translations

| | |
|---|---|
| RSV | Revised Standard Version |
| NRSV | New Revised Standard Version |
| KJV | King James Version |
| NKJ | New King James Version |
| ASV | American Standard Version |
| NASB | New American Standard Bible |
| NEB | New English Bible |
| GNB | Good News Bible |
| NJB | New Jerusalem Bible |
| JB | Jerusalem Bible |
| NIV | New International Version |

# Foreword

This volume on theological method and authority represents a new venture of mine in systematic theology. It is the first of seven volumes scheduled to appear within the next eight to ten years that deal in depth with specific theological issues. The next in the series will be an investigation of the pivotal doctrine of Holy Scripture, which has become such a bone of contention in recent years. Whereas my *Essentials of Evangelical Theology* was basically an overview of theological themes that belong to the evangelical tradition, this latest venture will be an in-depth analysis of theological issues that are endemic to Christian theology. Some slight changes in my theological perspective will become apparent as this work progresses.

In a time when theology is being reduced to reflection upon human experience, we should heed Martin Buber's prescient warning to Protestants of "a conceptual letting go of God." The disquieting reality today is that the object of faith is being emptied of its conceptual or rational content, and theology is left without any indicators or criteria to gauge the truthfulness of its assertions.

We are living in an age when faith is being divested of its metaphysical import, and attention is focused on the language and psychology of faith rather than its veracity and universal normativeness. Emil Brunner has astutely observed: "Christian belief stands or falls with the assertion that the Word of God is something other than ethics, metaphysics, or religion, something different in its source as well as in its content."[1] While this observation is undoubtedly true, it could create an erroneous impression that Christian faith has no metaphysical implications or that it lacks an ethical dimension or that it can exist apart from a religiocultural incarnation.

Christian faith cannot be reduced to metaphysics, but it contains a metaphysic of its own that challenges other metaphysical claims. The God of the Bible is not the God of metaphysics, but metaphysics can be employed in expounding the nature and actions of this God. The human mind cannot be metaphysically neutral; it will eventually gravitate toward a metaphysical stance that is in the service of either faith or unbelief.

Because of the relativistic milieu in which the church finds itself, there is increasing confusion in theological circles concerning the meaning of the gospel. The older liberal theologians (Adolf von Harnack, Walter Rauschenbusch) blithely envisioned the gospel as "the brotherhood of man" under "the fatherhood of God."[2] In existentialist theology the gospel is the breakthrough into freedom or the recovery of authentic existence. For liberation theologians the gospel becomes the call to solidarity with the disinherited and the oppressed. For process theologians the gospel is the availability of the power of creative transformation. For the celebrated neo-Catholic theologian Hans Küng, who unabashedly makes an effort to accommodate to higher criticism, the gospel is the life and work of Jesus as grasped by historical research and investigation.

In sharp contrast to the above voices, I see the gospel as an irreversible revelation from God that transcends every human formulation but is nonetheless inseparable from the New Testament kerygma or evangelical proclamation. The gospel cannot be uncovered by a historical analysis of biblical texts, though such analysis throws much light on the historical and cultural background of the text. Nor can the gospel be reduced to universal ethical values or transcendental ideals. The gospel is the surprising movement of God into the human history recorded in the Bible culminating in the life, death and resurrection of Jesus Christ and the corresponding movement of God in the personal history of those who believe. The gospel is the divinely given interpretation of the eternal significance of the teaching and work of Jesus Christ, an interpretation that must be given anew to every one of us as we struggle for a fuller understanding of the New Testament accounts of God's act of redemption in Jesus Christ.

The challenge that presently confronts us is to discover a new way of doing theology that will establish its continuity with the catholic tradition, especially as this tradition has come alive in the Protestant Reformation. Friedrich Schleiermacher proposed a theology of religious experience. Paul Tillich advocated a theology of cultural relevance, involving the correlation of the answer of faith with the creative questions of the age. Karl Barth propounded a theology of the Word of God, by which he meant the living Word, Jesus Christ, to whom both Bible and church bear witness.

While standing much closer to Barth than to either Schleiermacher or Tillich, I suggest a theology of Word and Spirit, signifying the unity of truth and power evident in both the Incarnation of God in Jesus Christ and the biblical rendition of this event. The word that proceeds from the mouth of God is filled with the power of the Spirit, bringing life and renewal to those dead in sin. By the action of the Spirit it is communicated to us through the gospel proclamation—found first of all in the Bible and then in the church commentary on the Scriptures.

If the Word of God is taken to mean essentially or primarily the Scriptures, then there is a real question whether we should not speak of a theology of Spirit and Word, since the Spirit takes precedence over the Bible—the divinely inspired but still palpably human witness to the revelation of God in Jesus Christ. Indeed, it is the Spirit who makes the Bible efficacious, though the message the latter provides is indispensable for the Spirit in his work of conviction and persuasion. At the same time, the Spirit was the ultimate author of the Bible and is the ongoing interpreter of the biblical message to the church in every age. How the Spirit speaks to the church does not contradict what the Spirit has already revealed to the prophets and apostles of old, but it may go beyond their specific witness as the Word of God is related to a new situation.

It will become obvious that my theological approach is strikingly similar to that of the magisterial Reformers (especially Luther and Calvin), who always saw the Word and Spirit together, never one apart from the other. The Word derives its efficacy from the Spirit, and the Spirit teaches what he has already disclosed in the word of Scripture. At times the Reformers gave the impression that the role of the Spirit is simply to ratify the word of Scripture rather than to bring new light to bear upon this word, but the latter note can also be detected in their writings. The Reformers' understanding of the relationship of Word and Spirit continued in early Protestant orthodoxy, although in later orthodoxy the paradoxical unity of Word and Spirit was sundered, being replaced by an objectivism of the Word.

When I speak of the Word and Spirit, I am not thinking primarily of a book that receives its stamp of approval from the Spirit, though I affirm the decisive role of the Spirit in the inspiration and illumination of Scripture. I am thinking mainly of the living Word in its inseparable unity with Scripture and church proclamation as this is brought home to us by the Spirit in the awakening to faith. It is not the Bible as such but the divine revelation that confronts us in the Bible that is the basis and source of spiritual authority. The Spirit as our heavenly teacher unfolds the fuller meaning of Scripture to the believing community and seals this meaning in our hearts. Scripture in this way is the Word of God to those with the eyes to see and ears to hear, as is also church proclamation that is based on Scripture.[3]

To speak of a theology of Word and Spirit or Spirit and Word is to reintroduce into theology the critical role of the experience of faith, which is qualitatively different, however, from ordinary human or even religious experience. In faith our experience of life and the world is transformed and redirected. To affirm a theology of Word and Spirit is to affirm that the experience of faith is correlative with God's self-revelation in Jesus Christ. Since faith is a work of the Spirit in the interiority of our being, the truth of the gospel is not only announced from without but also confirmed from within. In the theology presented here both revelation and salvation have to be understood as objective-subjective rather than fundamentally objective (as in evangelical rationalism) or predominantly subjective (as in existentialism and mysticism).

I shall be grateful if this book and the subsequent volumes help to overcome barriers that presently divide evangelicals as well as lay the groundwork for an animated and salutary dialog that includes evangelicals, mainline Protestants, Roman Catholics and Eastern Orthodox. It is my hope that my writings will be used by the Spirit of God to promote Evangelical-Catholic unity, encompassing the churches of the East as well as of the West. With Augustine I affirm a hermeneutics of love in which the fuller understanding of the text remains hidden until Christians learn to live in unity and love with one another.

# ·ONE·

# INTRODUCTION

Things now past I revealed long ago, they issued from my mouth,
I proclaimed them; suddenly I acted and they happened.
ISAIAH 48:3 NJB

There can be no other foundation beyond that which is already laid;
I mean Jesus Christ himself.
1 CORINTHIANS 3:11 NEB

We refuse to bow to the spirit of the age, but we ought
at least to speak the language of that age, and address it from the Cross
in the tone of its too familiar sorrow.
P. T. FORSYTH

The truthfulness of theological statements . . . depends not on
the truthfulness of their intention but on a participation
in the Truth which God alone can give.
THOMAS F. TORRANCE

This book can aptly be described as an exercise in what has come to be known as fundamental theology, in which we explore the foundations of Christian faith. It will involve an investigation of theological method, a definition of basic concepts and a reappraisal of the enigmatic relationship between theology and philosophy.

One of the salient needs in academic theology today is to combat the ideal of an undogmatic theology, a theology free from the constraint of biblical or confessional norms. Currently the emphasis is not on the *truth* of the gospel but on the *wonder* of the gospel or on the *experience* of the gospel. It is not the normativeness of Christian faith but the edification of the human psyche or the broadening of the human imagination that commands our attention. Here perhaps we can detect the influence of the philosopher Richard Rorty: "It is pictures rather than propositions, metaphors rather than statements, which determine most of our philosophical convictions."[1] For philosophers like Rorty language is no longer a mirror of metaphysical reality but a tool for edification and aesthetic enrichment.

Significantly, in narrative theology, which is increasingly in vogue today, the theological task is seen as primarily descriptive rather than ontologically normative.[2] It is said that through pondering and analyzing the biblical narrative we glean insights that deepen our awareness of our place in history. Through the story we gain a sense of who we are in relation to the mystery of transcendence that impinges on us.

The strength of narrative theology is its focus on Scripture rather than on abstract philosophical concepts. Its weakness lies in its tendency to obscure or downplay the metaphysical implications of the faith. The Bible is accorded a mainly functional rather than ontological significance.[3] Theology is *descriptive* of a particular tradition of faith or *evocative* in the sense that it draws us more deeply into this tradition rather than *explanatory* of the nature of ultimate reality. In some narrative theologians (e.g., Gabriel Fackre), focusing on the biblical story provides a vision of the humanization of the world that enables us to participate in the contemporary struggles for human liberation.[4] In other theologians (e.g., Paul van Buren), this position takes the form of vicariously reliving the experiences of the people of God with whom we identify, either as Jews or as Christians.[5] In still others (e.g., Ronald Thiemann), it takes the form of a disguised rationalism in which a critical analysis of the narrative yields perduring insights concerning the divine promise for personal and social renewal.[6]

Theology cannot afford to jettison the metaphysical claims of the faith, for this would reduce it to an investigation of human consciousness. A theology that makes no room for metaphysical speculation, however limited, invariably becomes privatistic and subjectivistic. Its focus is no longer on the God who speaks but on the human person who struggles to find meaning and identity in the midst of chaos. Its task is no longer to elucidate the truth claims of the faith but to rekindle the memory of the community of faith by retelling the story of the ancient people of faith. But does not this story reveal to us something about the cosmos and about the divine creator of the cosmos that has bearing on the way we confess the faith in the face of its intellectual adversaries? Should not theology seek to interpret not only the story of faith but also the whole of reality in the light of this story? Theology will necessarily use philosophical concepts as well as biblical imagery in fulfilling this task.

This brings us to the pivotal question: To what extent is theology dependent on philosophy for its intelligibility? Both Origen and Thomas Aquinas maintained that the water of Greek philosophy could be transformed through revelation into the wine of Christian theology.[7] This is ideal in theory, but what so often happens is that theology itself becomes transformed into another philosophy of religion.

Theology must not be confounded with philosophy. The latter represents a search for a comprehensive picture of the world, whereas the former consists in a faithful exposition of what God has revealed in Holy Scripture. Theology is founded upon the concrete speech of the living God as we hear this in the witness of the prophets and apostles of biblical history. Philosophy is based on the universal aspiration of a searching humanity to penetrate the mystery of human existence. The emphasis in theology is not on the omnicompetence of reason (as in rationalistic philosophy) but on the omnipotence of grace. Its goal is not to bring all of reality under the domain of understanding but to bring understanding into submission to the Word of God. Whitehead has defined philosophy as "the critique of abstractions."[8] Theology might be defined as the critique of human pretensions in the light of God's gracious condescension in Jesus Christ.

Yet while theology has a different basis and goal than philosophy, it is nevertheless compelled to employ the abstract concepts of philosophy in order to make its message intelligible and coherent to both the church and the world. Theology may use philosophy, but it must not strive to bring the insights of faith into alignment with cultural wisdom, for this can only end in a diminution and subversion of the truth of faith.

## Reclaiming Dogma

In this era when propositional or conceptual truth is being sacrificed for existential and emotive truth, it is incumbent on theology to reaffirm the conceptual side of divine revelation. Theology is based not on feeling but on dogma, though this dogma is mediated by experience.

Dogma might be defined as a propositional truth that is grounded in and inseparable from God's self-revelation in Christ and communicated to the interiority of our being by the Spirit of God.[9] It signifies the divinely given interpretation of revelation. A doctrine is a propositional affirmation that represents the church's continuing reflection on the dogmatic norm of faith. The doctrines of the church will not become one with the dogma of revelation until the eschaton—when we will know even as we are known.

Dogmatics is the articulation of the dogma of revelation in the light of the biblical and apostolic witness and in the light of the interpretation of this revelation by the fathers and doctors of the church through the ages. Consequently, dogmatics is always provisional, whereas dogma is abiding.

Two perils are to be sedulously avoided: dogmatism and mysticism. Dogmatism signifies the codification of dogma, and mysticism the dilution of the dogmatic or rational substance of the faith. The truth of revelation is made an object of our understanding in the divine-human encounter, but it never remains an object of our understanding like other truths. We must seek for it ever again in faith and obedience. We know it only as we obey it. We have it only as we are grasped by it. The dogma of revelation consists in the unity of logos and praxis.

Dogma is not a product of our superior reasoning as Christians but an announcement of divine grace that exposes the poverty of our understanding. Dogma is not what we claim to have discovered by ourselves: it is God's claim on us. It is a transrational truth that comes to us in the form of concrete speech.[10] It is impressed on the understanding but never absorbed by the understanding, because it is the speech of God. It is enveloped in mystery, but meaning shines through this mystery. It is not an abstract, theoretical truth akin to the metaphysical truths of rationalistic philosophy.

In the sense in which I use the term, dogma is not just an external truth but an internal truth. It must take root in one's inner being. It appeals not just to the mind but to the whole person. It is not simply a propositional truth but a living, dynamic truth that takes the form of propositions, to be sure, but also other forms, for example, symbolic acts or prayerful entreaty. It includes but is not exhausted by propositions.

An evangelical dogmatics is based on the supposition that God's Word is at the same time God's act. This Word is both conceptual and personal, propositional and existential. It confronts us in the form of concrete speech, but it must penetrate to the core of our being if it is to bring meaning and power to our lives. To Jeremiah the Word of God was like fire in his bones, and this is why he was constrained to make it known (Jer 20:9).

The God of the Bible is not a God who is discovered in the depths of nature or uncovered in human consciousness. Nor is he a God who is immediately discernible in the events of history, even of sacred history, for he is a God who hides himself even in his revelation (cf. Is 45:15; Prov 25:2; Rom 11:33). For the living God to be known, he must make himself known, and he has done this in the acts and words recorded in Scripture. Yet the significance of what has been revealed continues to elude us until our minds are illumined by God's Spirit, who comes and goes as he wills (Jn 3:8).

### Toward the Recovery of Biblical, Evangelical Theology

The world of theology is in confusion today because theology is uncertain regarding its scope and mission. It looks to philosophy or to the social or natural sciences for its understanding of truth and meaning. We need to be reminded that theology has its own distinct method as well as its unique goal, because it is grounded in a definitive revelation in history that confounds rather than confirms human wisdom, that overturns rather than builds upon human experience.

For purposes of clarification it is necessary to establish lines of demarcation between a theology of revelation and theologies that are dependent on cultural wisdom for their veracity and credibility. Theology must be free not from dogma or confessions but from the pressures of the world to conform to its standards and values.

The position I am advocating must not be confounded with *revelational positivism,* in which the fact of revelation is simply acknowledged and upheld as true apart from the confirmatory interior witness of the Spirit, which makes this fact concrete and meaningful in our lives.[11] Nor can it be identified with *presuppositionalism,* in which we begin with postulates concerning ultimate reality that are unprovable but provide the key to explaining the whole of reality (Cornelius Van Til, Gordon Clark).[12] Nor can it be equated with *foundationalism,* in which we begin with a priori assumptions impressed on the mind by their intrinsic power to convict and persuade,[13] assumptions that are indubitably true, having intuitive certainty (Descartes, Leibniz, Thomas Reid).[14] Nor does it fall under the rubric of *evidentialism,* which appeals to empirically demonstrable certainty (J. W. Montgomery, Stuart Hackett, R. C. Sproul).[15] Nor is it to be confused with *coherentism,* in which we try to justify our position by showing the cohesive unity of our beliefs (Kant, Arthur Holmes).[16]

Instead, I would call my position a *fideistic revelationalism,* in which the decision of faith is as important as the fact of revelation in giving us certainty of the truth of faith.[17] The revelation is not simply assented to but is existentially embraced as the truth or power of salvation. Certainty of its truth becomes ours only in the act of decision and obedience by which the external truth becomes internalized in faith and life. This is not fideism in the narrow or reductionist sense because our faith has a sure anchor and basis in an objective revelation in history. It is not a positivism of revelation because we do not claim a rationally demonstrable or apodictic certainty nor even an intuitive or axiomatic certainty; instead, we have a practical or moral certainty that is ever more fully realized in a life of repentance and obedience.[18]

A theology of Word and Spirit could easily be confused with foundationalism because it presupposes an indefeasible criterion outside ourselves that becomes the infallible standard for faith and practice. Yet this criterion or authority does not consist in a priori assumptions or universal principles or transcendental ideals that are impressed on the mind by divine grace or reside in the mind by the constitution of human nature. God's Word can never be identified with assumptions or principles generally available to human reason, for God's Word is always new and unexpected, even though it stands in unmistakable continuity with what God has declared in the past through the mouths of his prophets and apostles. Foundationalism tries to anchor one's thought in basic premises that are beyond all possible doubt (indubitable) and beyond any need of correction (incorrigible).[19] In a theology of Word and Spirit we receive or hear the concrete speech of God, which makes an indelible impression on the human soul but can never be fully assimilated by the human mind. To know the full import of what is revealed, we must act in obedience to what we presently ascertain to be the will of God.

The knowledge of God in a theological context has an eschatological thrust that is irreconcilable with the self-evident axioms of foundationalism, which are more akin to natural theology. We look forward to the public revelation of the mystery of God's marvelous condescension in Jesus Christ at the end of the age rather than look within to innate ideas or universal truths that have only to be drawn out into the open. Theology is grounded not so much in noninferential beliefs as in the living God himself, whose credibility is not guaranteed by foundational presuppositions but by his actual speaking to us day by day in our life and work.[20] God proves himself to us again and again as we believe and obey. Only as we increase in love do we become able to discriminate between the true and the false (Phil 1:9-10 NEB).

It is fashionable in current theology to acknowledge that certain beliefs and practices can be normative for Christians, who belong to a particular tradition and community, but to be noncommittal regarding the universal validity or ontological veracity of these beliefs. Theology, it is said, consists basically in a phenomenological analysis of Christian experience rather than in an affirmation of Christian truth. Against those who envision theology as essentially *descriptive* (George Lindbeck[21]) or as *constructive* (Schubert Ogden[22]), I contend that theology is fundamentally *prescriptive,* for its case rests upon truth claims that have metaphysical import. The essence of theological work is not the recital of narrative or the elucidation of religious or generally human experience but the promulgation of a gospel that is both the truth and the power of salvation.

This does not mean that I wish to resurrect a kind of evangelical triumphalism that arrogantly dismisses the searching questions of outsiders and shuts out self-critical inquiry. We do not have the truth in its ultimacy, but we know the One who is the truth, and our task is to point others to this One who alone can resolve their difficulties and bind their wounds. Faith is a humble acknowledgment that the truth of the Word of God resides outside us and that it becomes ours only when we take up the cross and follow Christ in lowly discipleship. Faith does not furnish axiomatic certainty, but it is a process of continually becoming sure as we return again and again to the wellspring of life and meaning—the Word of God, which is both hidden and revealed in Holy Scripture as well as in the broken yet relatively dependable witness of the fathers and mothers of the church through the ages.

I am not calling for a return to an enervating orthodoxy but for the rediscovery of an enlivening and liberating orthodoxy, the faith that nurtured and sustained the prophets and saints throughout Christian history. True orthodoxy must always be carefully distinguished from what Edward J. Carnell aptly calls "cultic orthodoxy"—the tenacious clinging to theological or creedal formulas out of desperation and insecurity.[23] True orthodoxy is a perpetual abiding in the faith with joyful confidence in the reign of the Spirit. Cultic orthodoxy springs from the unwholesome desire for a security blanket to maintain one's inner equilibrium. True orthodoxy is a willingness to make oneself vulnerable for the sake of the gospel.

The church is unable to resist the infiltration of cultural ideology because it expends its energies in trying to make the faith relevant to the culture rather than in discovering the abiding relevance in the message of faith. Its trumpet emits an uncertain sound (1 Cor 14:8) because it seeks to win the approbation of the centers of learning, wisdom and power in the culture.

In this day it is not enough to know the truth—we must speak and live this truth if it is to make its way into the hearts and minds of those around us. The task of a biblically based theology is to equip the church to make a powerful and compelling witness to God's self-revelation in Jesus Christ as we find this in Holy Scripture. Our witness should take the form of deeds as well as words, but it cannot be reduced to deeds. We cannot commit ourselves to the truth of the gospel unless we understand this truth, and we will never understand it unless it is explained to us by those who have tasted its power and experienced its efficacy. This truth must finally be taught us by the Spirit of God himself as he uses his ambassadors and heralds to bring enlightenment to those who grope in the darkness that engulfs the world and power to those who sense their helplessness in the face of the pseudogods that hold the world in subjection. It is the Spirit who converts and convicts (Jn 16:8), but he does so through human instrumentality. He does not need our aid, but he grants us the privilege of being covenant partners with him in making known the truth that alone can bring meaning to those who drift in aimlessness, and peace and joy to those crippled by depression and fear. Theology's task is to prepare the way for the kingdom of God by celebrating the advent of the Son of God in the power of the Spirit of God given to the church at Pentecost.

# ·TWO·

# THE
# THEOLOGICAL
# MALAISE

Why do you not understand my language?
It is because my revelation is beyond your grasp. . . .
You are not God's children; that is why you do not listen.
JOHN 8:43, 47 NEB

Let none offer the seekers a system making exclusive claims
to truth, but let each man offer his characteristic, individual presentation.
FRIEDRICH SCHLEIERMACHER

There are fewer and fewer intellectual objections to the
legitimacy or possibility of treating a classic, whether religious or
nonreligious, as a perspicuous guide to life and thought.
The only question is whether one is interested and can make it work.
GEORGE LINDBECK

Religious special claims cannot be allowed in the University,
even—or perhaps especially—in its Divinity School. . . . It is the task
of the Divinity School within this University to increase our understanding
of religious belief in all its diversity.
JAMES W. LEWIS

The incontrovertible triumph of the Enlightenment over both the Reformation and the Counter-Reformation has sapped the spiritual vitality of modern Western civilization. Since the eighteenth century, humanity rather than God has become the focal point of theology and philosophy. Trust in human reason has slowly but surely displaced trust in divine revelation as the infallible guide for life and thought. Though the omnicompetence of reason has been sharply challenged, faith in its practical efficacy still holds sway over the centers of knowledge and power in society. Kant sought to limit reason to the phenomenal world, and the baneful result was an abysmal dichotomy between religious and historical truth, which still wreaks havoc in both biblical and theological studies.[1]

The modern age has also witnessed the palpable erosion of transcendence as evidenced in the rise of naturalistic and idealistic monisms.[2] Whereas traditional Christian faith has stoutly affirmed the reality of the living God who created both mind and matter, the modern trend is to treat one of these as the all-encompassing reality, thereby making it tantamount to God.[3] The irrefragable triumph of immanentism is dramatized in the precipitous movement from theism to deism to pantheism and panentheism. Some theologians have endeavored to preserve a transcendence within immanence; Schleiermacher referred to "the infinite in the finite" and Bultmann to "the unconditional in the conditional." Moderns are also open to the idea of an epistemological transcendence in which reality in itself exceeds the compass of human reason, but this is not the ontological transcendence of traditional faith, which could speak of an infinite qualitative distinction between God and humanity (Kierkegaard).[4]

With the rise of the technological society the sacred has acquired a new locus—scientific mastery and technical accomplishment. Instead of the Bible, the church and the sacraments of traditional Christianity or the inner light of conscience or reason venerated by the Enlightenment, post-Enlightenment society celebrates technology as the spiritual hope and goal of human endeavor.[5] In biblical studies it is now commonplace to assume that the truth of faith is procured by hermeneutical method rather than by divine disclosure. In the disciplines of worship and spirituality one often gains the impression that contact with the sacred depends on liturgical technique or sacramental performance rather than on the free movement of the Spirit in the preaching and hearing of the Word of God. We appear to have succumbed to the arrogance of our own expertise.

The overriding concern in the technological society is rational efficiency, and human values are subordinated to this end. Technical reason, which measures truth by its practical efficacy, supplants contemplative reason, with its focus on truth that holds meaning for human existence. The ruling philosophy is positivism, which seeks the domination of the object by the subject. Reality is reduced to the empirically observable and the scientifically explicable.

The technocratic mentality values performance, not prayerful reflection. It admires and rewards the producer rather than the saint or the savant. The goal is to gain power over the world rather than the wisdom that teaches us how to live in the world as brothers and sisters with a common origin and destiny. A preoccupation with things and gadgetry crowds out a vision of a spiritual reality that transcends the world of natural phenomena.

Hand in hand with the idolatry of technique is the emergence of a new mysticism, which finds the locus of the sacred in nature. Here one perceives a flight from reason and an enthronement of human feelings and instinctual drives. A new romanticism threatens to usurp the hegemony of a deadening rationalism. For Nietzsche the criterion for truth lay in an intensification of power rather than in the contemplation of transcendental ideals. Heidegger asserted that "thinking only begins at the point where we have come to know that Reason, glorified for centuries, is the most obstinate adversary of thinking."[6] The New Age movement heralds the advent of a neopaganism that depreciates the rational and elevates the mystical and irrational.[7]

Mysticism is not wholly averse to technological values, however, and a synthesis of the new mysticism with technological supremacy is conspicuous in such seminal thinkers as Teilhard de Chardin, Joseph Campbell, Theodore Roszak and Fritjof Capra. The devotees of the Age of Aquarius appreciate mysticism as a technique for gaining access to the creative power immanent in the universe and waiting to be harnessed for human expansion and domination.

In the postmodern climate in which we live, traditional values as well as universal moral norms have become problematic. Even God is more of a question than a certitude. Language becomes a game to control one's destiny or gain power over nature rather than a pathway to truth. Truth is no longer universal and ontological but efficacious and enriching, not informative so much as transformative. In Christian circles the story of salvation is increasingly seen as a projection of human hopes and dreams upon the plane of history rather than a divine intervention into history.

Lessing contended that the necessary truths of reason can never depend on the accidental truths of history. Now these necessary truths of reason are being broadly questioned, and the only criterion for human life is what brings personal satisfaction to the human soul or what best serves human advancement. Lindbeck puts it well: "Ours is again an age when old foundations and legitimating structures have crumbled. Even the defenders of reason think it unreasonable to ask anything more than that they be followable of philosophies and religions . . . which give them richness, comprehensiveness, and stability."[8]

## The Slide into Relativism

The age of ecumenism is slowly but surely giving way to the age of religious pluralism, in which objective truth claims are being shelved for crosscultural analyses of the creative role of religion in cultural life. The focus is not so much on whether religions are true but whether they serve the human spirit in its search for meaning and fulfillment.

Historicism, which depicts human knowledge as a product of historical and cultural relationships, has contributed in no small way to the modern mood of relativism.[9] According to its celebrated proponent Ernst Troeltsch, "History has no place for absolutes." When historical method is applied to biblical study, he maintained, it becomes a "leaven that transforms everything, and finally shatters the whole framework of theological method as this has existed hitherto."[10] Gordon Kaufman, who writes from a historicist perspective, confesses that "we can see no way in which we will ever be able to plumb the true meaning of human life—or whether there even is such a thing."[11] For him, the questions of meaning, the good and the salvation of the human spirit are ultimately unknown and unknowable. In this kind of theology the divine reality becomes an "inscrutable mystery" that opens us to a future containing both promise and peril.

The historicist mentality is also noticeable in liberation theology, which speculates that our ideas of God and morality can be adequately understood only in their historical and cultural matrix. Thus the liberationist Ismael Garcia frankly acknowledges that "no theological formulation can claim any more permanence, certainty, or universality than any other form of human reflection."[12]

The principle of relativity is even more integral to process theology and philosophy, which explain the mystery of life in terms of historical and cosmic evolution. God is no longer a being who stands apart from the evolutionary process but one element, however important, in this process. God is the creative force or power of transformation that directs the world process from within by luring all things toward a higher level of integration and intensity.

In the theology of religions, associated with John Hick, W. Cantwell Smith, Leonard Swidler, Raimundo Panikkar and Paul Knitter, among others, revelation becomes the breakthrough into a higher form of consciousness, and God becomes the creative ground and depth of all being or the cosmic unity that holds all things together.[13] Religion is celebrated as the human quest for identity and meaning rather than the service of the glory of God. What distinguishes the person of faith is no longer a decisive commitment to the will and work of God manifested in Jesus Christ but an openness to the truth immanent in the human soul. Hick favors a theocentric perspective, which holds that God reveals himself equally in all religions, over an ethnocentric perspective, which views only one religious tradition as normative.[14] With similar audacity, some theologians of religions vigorously contend that a distinctly Christian consciousness needs to give way to a global consciousness that allows for truth to unfold itself in myriad ways and experiences (Panikkar, Ewert Cousins).

In narrative theology, doctrines become communally authoritative rules of discourse and action rather than either truth claims or expressive symbols (Lindbeck). What is most important in transmitting a religioethical heritage is not the propositional truths we affirm but the kind of vocabulary we employ.[15] To speak of Jesus as Lord makes sense only in the community of faith, where people experience his liberating power. Theology becomes a phenomenological analysis of a particular religious tradition rather than an exposition of a definitive divine revelation that calls into radical question all human claims to truth and authenticity. The proposals Lindbeck offers in his groundbreaking book *The Nature of Doctrine* are "meant to be ecumenically and religiously neutral."[16]

Narrative theologians frequently appeal to Barth, who, they say, saw the unity of the Bible in an overarching story suggesting a "vast, loosely-structured, non-fictional novel,"[17] but they fail to give due recognition to his firm insistence on the historical basis of the Christian faith. A cogent argument can be made that in volume 4 of his *Church Dogmatics* Barth prepared the way for narrative theology by focusing on the analysis of the text as narrative rather than on the text as the bearer of intrinsic, quasi-metaphysical meaning. But the later volumes must surely be read in the light of the earlier ones, in which Barth definitely set forth ontological truth claims.[18]

The so-called postmodern hermeneutics also bears poignant witness to the deleterious effects of a relativist mentality. Edgar McKnight argues that just as the structures of literature change, so the Bible too is always changing.[19] Every time we read the Bible the text itself has changed, and we too have changed. Everything, it seems, proceeds from change and leads to change. Becoming is celebrated over being to such an extent that relativism verges toward nihilism, creating a vacuum in meaning that yearns for a sure anchor for faith in the midst of an allencompassing chaos.

It is too seldom recognized that the God of pluralism and inclusivism can be a jealous God, one that refuses to countenance any deviation from the pluralistic ideal. If all truth is relative, then any claim to ab-

solute truth must be denounced as an expression of tribalism or eth-
nocentrism—or fundamentalism. Pluralism itself becomes a new absolute that can tolerate no rival gods. James W. Lewis, dean of students
of the Divinity School of the University of Chicago, has tersely expressed
this absolutist version of the new faith: "Religious special claims cannot
be allowed in the University, even—or perhaps especially—in its Divinity
School. . . . It is the task of the Divinity School within this University to
increase our understanding of religious belief in all its diversity."[20]

## A New Church Conflict?

As mainstream academic theology veers ever more toward the left, a
reaction is ineluctably setting in, sounding the clarion call to restoration.
We see this reaction in the frantic efforts in conservative circles to preserve patriarchalism, biblical inerrancy and confessional integrity.
Among ultraconservative Catholics there is also a passionate concern
for papal supremacy, magisterial authority, Marian veneration and the
restoration of the Latin Mass.

A protest against the leftist perversions of the faith is understandable
and welcome, but we need to remember that there are heresies on the
right as well as on the left. The antidote to a humanistic version of
Christianity is not repristination, which could consign the faith to cultural irrelevance. What is required is the recovery of a centrist position
standing thoroughly in the tradition of orthodoxy but not averse to
articulating the faith in new ways that relate creatively to the contemporary situation. A centrist position must not be misconstrued as a
middle-of-the-road position that tries to hold opposing camps in dialectical tension; instead, its goal is to drive beyond the theological polarity to a synthesis that negates the misconceptions of both sides but
at the same time fulfills their legitimate hopes and concerns.

Not surprisingly, Hans Küng has proposed Erasmus as a theological
model for our time, a person, he claims, who admirably avoided both
the biblicistic rigidity of Luther and the dogmatic inflexibility of the
Counter-Reformation.[21] Yet Erasmus proved to be a mediating theolo-

gian whose determined irenicism became suspect to both sides as it appeared (perhaps wrongly) that he was simply straddling the fence.

Paul Tillich looked to Schelling and Schleiermacher as worthy guides in theological reconstruction. But in all three thinkers one can detect an illicit accommodation to the cultural ethos rather than a renewed dedication to the apostolic commission, and the result has been a lamentable diffusion of the biblical thrust of the faith.

My principal mentors have been Luther, Calvin, Forsyth and Barth, all of whom championed the biblical integrity of the faith but were at the same time remarkably and sometimes daringly innovative in their restatement of the faith. Barth has been especially helpful in the modern discussion, since he ably delineated the biblical erosion endemic to cultural Protestantism[22] and proposed a viable alternative anchored in Scripture and tradition. Yet we must not remain with Barth but go beyond him if we are to speak with an equally fresh voice as new challenges to the faith emerge.

The battle lines today are increasingly not between denominations but across denominations. The conflict is in no small part ideological, for various theological positions have become inextricably intertwined with ideological stances that advance special interest groups in society.[23] I am firmly convinced that the church must refrain from aligning itself with any side in the ideological conflict, that it must speak resolutely to all sides, pointing them to the One who alone can bring reconciliation and peace to both the church and the world.

The paramount issue in the church today is idolatry. New gods are appearing, new faiths are blooming, and these alien faiths have infiltrated the inner sanctuary of the church. There is a pressing need today for sound instruction, for Christians to be educated concerning what is really happening. As the church becomes painfully aware of the depth of apostasy in its midst, a new church conflict *(Kirchenkampf)* may well be on the horizon.[24] When the church speaks, it should speak with a resolute and unequivocal voice, but it cannot do so unless it becomes thoroughly cognizant of both the sources and the implications of the heretical imbalances in its time.

We are living in an era of the confusion of tongues. We are confronted by the rise of theological schools that no longer share a common parameter, that are disturbingly incapable even of engaging in meaningful dialog with one another because of the wide disparity in criteria and goals. Has the church become a new tower of Babel that in its effort to storm the heavens has contributed to an appalling breakdown in communication among its own people? May we be ready to make a bold confession of faith when the moment of truth arrives, but in the meantime let us prepare for the coming battle by educating ourselves on what true theology is and by steeping ourselves in prayer to the holy God who alone can keep theology on the right path, who alone can preserve his church from its own sorry failures and pitiful illusions.

# ·THREE·

# FAITH &
# PHILOSOPHY

---

See to it that no one takes you captive through philosophy and
empty deception, according to the tradition of men, according to the
elementary principles of the world, rather than according to Christ.

COLOSSIANS 2:8 NASB

---

Should one say that knowledge is founded on demonstration by
a process of reasoning, let him hear that first principles are incapable of
demonstration; for they are known neither by art nor sagacity. . . .
The first cause of the universe can be apprehended by faith alone.

CLEMENT OF ALEXANDRIA

---

If you are not able to know, believe that you may know.
Faith precedes; the intellect follows.

AUGUSTINE

---

I believe though I do not comprehend,
and I hold by faith what I cannot grasp with the mind.

BERNARD OF CLAIRVAUX

---

*Causa sui* [the self-caused] is the right name for the God of philosophy.
But man can neither pray nor sacrifice to this God. Before the *causa sui,*
man can neither fall to his knees in awe, nor can he play
music and dance before this God.

MARTIN HEIDEGGER

---

The theological ambivalence in the church today is due in no small
part to the uncritical assimilation of cultural and philosophical
wisdom by sincere but misguided Christians who wish to make
the faith relevant and palatable to its cultured critics and despisers. The
church is in crisis because it has lost its confidence in the power of the
Word of God to make its own way in the world. By seeking to undergird
the Word of God with philosophical argument and recast it in a new

language and symbolism, the church has offered a message that is virtually indistinguishable from that of reasonable men and women of good will. We need to ponder the disturbing picture presented in the New Testament of Christ and culture in irrevocable conflict as well as the divided witness of the church on this critical question. Only when we come to the realization of the utter incompatibility of God's self-revelation in Christ with the creative imagination of human culture can we determine how the biblical message bears upon the pressing issues that presently bedevil supposedly liberated human beings come of age.

**Faith and Reason**

Probably the single most important issue in a theological prolegomenon is the enigmatic relation between faith and reason. Does reason have a role prospectively as well as retrospectively with regard to faith? Can reason prepare the way for faith as well as confirm the truths of faith? Theologians in the church have been divided on this question from the very beginning of church history.

No single approach was dominant among the church fathers. The apologists, such as Justin Martyr and Clement of Alexandria, saw a positive role for reason in leading those on a philosophical quest to the truth of revelation. Tertullian, though also involved in the apologetic task, held that the gospel "is believable because it is absurd . . . it is certain because it is impossible."[1] From a decidedly different perspective, Augustine contended that we cannot believe until we first understand; at the same time, we cannot fully or truly understand until we first believe. Reason has a role in preparing the way for faith and then elucidating the truth of faith after we have assented to this truth.[2]

The same tensions are noticeable in the Middle Ages. Standing in the Augustinian tradition, Anselm placed the emphasis on faith seeking understanding: we begin with faith and then try to understand as much as possible in the light of faith. In the twelfth century Abelard taught that before we believe we must have an adequate intellectual grasp of what is to be believed. This led him to regard faith as an opinion rather than an unshakable assurance of God's promises. A century later, Bonaventure argued that philosophy by itself can lead only to error, not to faith. Thomas Aquinas held that in principle the "natural man" could arrive at a valid knowledge of God and so could stand at the threshold of faith, but in practice natural reason is in nearly all cases mixed with error.[3]

The Catholic mystics increasingly questioned the scholastic synthesis of faith and reason. They held that we can know God only by love, which surpasses rational knowledge. Eckhart warned against fondly imagining that "thy reason can grow to the knowledge of God; that God shall shine in thee divinely no natural light can help to bring about; it must be utterly extinguished and go out of itself altogether."[4] John of the Cross could even say that it is by faith alone that "God manifests Himself to the soul in Divine light, which passes all understanding."[5] At the same time, the mystics contended that we could prepare the way for faith by rational examination and inward purification.

It remained for the Protestant Reformers, Luther and Calvin, to question the human capacity to make contact with divine revelation. While acknowledging that all people are inescapably related to God and endowed with an innate sense of his infinite power and moral order, they were nonetheless insistent that because sin so utterly defaces the imago Dei we are rendered incapable of laying hold of God's redeeming revelation in Jesus Christ apart from a special illumination of the Holy Spirit. Reason needs not to be cultivated but converted; then faithful reasoning can throw light upon the mysteries of the faith but can never exhaust them. Calvin remarked: "If we would comprehend God's wisdom, we must expect to be confounded and dazzled by it, because it is infinite."[6]

Confidence in the power of human reason to validate the claims of faith was much more conspicuous in Protestant orthodoxy,[7] though this movement, at least in its earlier phases, retained the reservations of the Reformers about human capacity in coming to faith. Indeed, the truth of revelation "is not imparted to man by flesh and blood, but solely by the Spirit of grace, who opens a man's eyes and directs his heart, that he may achieve a certain knowledge of revealed fact."[8]

In the twentieth century Karl Barth and Wolfhart Pannenberg represent the two poles in Christian theology on this question. Barth, who has certain affinities with fideism,[9] stresses the priority of faith over understanding, whereas Pannenberg calls for a new appreciation of the open rationality of the Enlightenment. He insists that religious assertions "must positively prove themselves worthy of belief if they are to be able to claim universal relevance."[10] "Every theological statement must prove itself on the field of reason, and can no longer be argued on the basis of unquestioned presuppositions of faith."[11]

It is appropriate at this juncture to define reason and faith. Reason is here understood as any human cognitive faculty or capability. I am using it in the widest sense to include mystical intuition as well as philosophical insight and intellectual comprehension. Faith in this context indicates an inward awakening to the infinite mercy of God revealed in Christ that gives rise to a commitment of the whole person to the claims of Christ. It is not mere opinion but an inward knowledge based on the illumination of the Spirit in conjunction with the hearing of the gospel. Yet it is acknowledgment more than rational understanding, for it involves a venture of trust and obedience that goes beyond what reason is able to guarantee. It is not simply assent *(assensus)* to the truth of revelation but trust *(fiducia)* in the Giver of revelation. Faith also involves experience, for how could we believe unless we experienced the transforming reality that is the object of faith? Faith contains an inward certainty of the trustworthiness of the promises of God, but this is not the same as rational certainty. Reason cannot prove the validity of faith's commitment, but it can explicate faith's claims. It cannot guarantee the truth of the articles of faith, but it can serve this faith.

Faith provides an existential security more than a rational certainty. It rests on the assurance of the heart rather than the conclusions of the intellect. As Pascal said, "The heart has its reasons of which reason knows nothing."[12] Faith boldly ventures into the darkness in the confidence that the light of God's truth shines in this darkness.

Revelation is not the outcome of human reasoning, but it must be explicated by reason. Not a logical conclusion of human thought, it never-theless brings about the liberation and transformation of human thought.

Barth has rightly observed that the knowledge of the gospel is "not a predicate with which one might adorn and characterize human con-structs."[13] On the contrary, it is an event in which human subjectivity is confronted by divine subjectivity, an event that touches us but does not yet wholly govern our lives. Revelation intrudes into human reason-ing and redirects this reasoning, even reversing it in some cases. It does not lie at the end of the human quest but instead overthrows this quest, setting it on a new foundation. Faith is simply the acknowledgment of the miracle of revelation in the chaos and darkness of human life.

### Theology and Philosophy

Just as reason is not completed but overturned by revelation, so philos-ophy, the very human attempt to fathom ultimate reality, finds itself in tension if not in conflict with theology, the faithful explication of God's self-revelation in the sacred history mirrored in Holy Scripture.[14]

Philosophy might be defined as the attempt to bring all of reality under the domain of understanding. Even those philosophies that preach skepticism nonetheless seek to give an intelligible and coherent explanation of reality. They use reason to demonstrate the limitations of reason.

Theology, on the other hand, is the systematic endeavor to render a compelling and faithful witness to the truth of divine revelation. It is addressed primarily to the believing community with the intention of enabling that community to bring all of its thought and action into conformity with the will of God as revealed in Jesus Christ. It neverthe-less takes into consideration the thought and plight of the world outside the church, for its ultimate aim is to bring the whole world into submis-sion to Jesus Christ.

Philosophy focuses upon the salient themes and foundational ques-tions that shape the cultural ethos. It therefore mirrors both the spirit and the unrest of the times (Hegel).[15] It represents culture reflecting upon itself rather than culture in submission to God. Theology focuses on the gospel, which confronts the culture as a question that sharply challenges cultural wisdom. It exposes our persistent questioning as a futile endeavor to hide ourselves from God. Philosophy is the creative thought of a particular age that reflects on the aspirations and questions of that age. Theology is the creative thought of the church that explores the questions that God addresses to a particular age. Philosophy signifies the creative probings of a particular age. Theology signifies the redemptive witness of the church to a particular age.

Philosophy is the attempt to see all things whole, in a unified perspective. Theology is the attempt to see all things in the light of God's self-revelation in Jesus Christ. At the same time, theology confesses that only God has the synoptic vision of the whole of reality and that our understandings will always be limited and incomplete.

Unlike philosophy, theology is not so much a perspicacious probing into the meaning of existence as a faithful witness to the redemption of existence through what God has done for us in Jesus Christ. It is a witness born out of concerted reflection on both the biblical revelation and the human quest for wisdom through the ages.

The task of theology is to acquire not observational knowledge about God (as in naturalistic empiricism) or conceptual mastery of him (as in idealistic rationalism) but an understanding of his will and purpose disclosed in Jesus Christ, an understanding that eventuates in obedience. What characterizes theology is not the comprehension of divine mysteries nor the apprehension of human possibilities but fidelity to the Word of God, which involves acknowledging human limitations but also confessing the gift of divine illumination in the midst of these limitations.

Theology can never be definitive, for it is always a contemporary exposition of the definitive biblical word. It does not precede proclamation in the form of prediscussion but follows it in the form of reflection (Thielicke).

The method of theology might be said to be a posteriori, beginning from data furnished by a revelation in history, rather than a priori, beginning from metaphysical first principles. At the same time, it is a posteriori only in a qualified sense: it yields the truth of revelation only when the Spirit illumines these facts in the light of the transcendent criterion of the gospel of God.

From the evangelical perspective, our knowledge of God is neither synthetic nor analytic in the purely philosophical sense.[16] We do not take the way of idealism, seeking to analyze the individual parts of a comprehensive unified picture of reality.[17] Nor do we take the way of empirical rationalism, striving for a unified vision of the various facets of experience. Instead, our task is simply to reiterate or reaffirm what is given in revelation, humbly listening to God's Word and then endeavoring to translate this Word into human thoughts, words and actions. At the same time, we try as best we can to arrive at a coherent or comprehensive picture of reality by interpreting the whole of experience in the light of God's Word. This picture will always be incomplete and open-ended, however, since the total vision of reality lies beyond the compass of human reason, even one informed by faith.

The criterion in philosophy is what lies within the purview of human possibilities—what is accessible to human reason or what resides within the inner recesses of our being. Protagoras spoke for most philosophers when he declared that "man is the measure of all things." According to Kant, "All our knowledge begins with the senses, proceeds then to the understanding, and ends with reason," which provides "the purposive unity of things."[18] For Whitehead, "Ultimately nothing rests on authority; the final court of appeal is intrinsic reasonableness."[19] Philosophy is necessarily anthropocentric or homocentric. Even when a place is made for God, God is there to crown the human quest for wisdom and security.

Theology's criterion is the will and purpose of God as demonstrated in the life, death and resurrection of Jesus Christ, attested in Holy Scripture. The focus of theology is neither on divine essence nor on human existence but on divine existence in humanity as we see this in Jesus Christ. Philosophy is inclined to champion autonomy, trusting in the self for direction and certainty, as opposed to heteronomy, submission to an external standard or power alien to the self (Kant).[20] Theology presents a case for theonomy, in which the self submits to an authority beyond the self that is at the same time its ground and goal.[21]

In philosophy reality signifies either mind or matter, or an underlying unity between them, such as force or energy. In theology the prime reality is the living God, who brings the world of temporality and materiality into being and creates the energy that vitalizes this world. Moreover, this living God is not reducible to mind or thought but instead constitutes a dynamic unity of will and intelligence, of being and action. He is the self-existing and self-sustaining One *(Causa sui)* whose knowledge encompasses all human perceptions and conceptions but at the same time infinitely transcends them.

A dogmatic maxim of the church fathers was *Deus semper maior* (God is always greater), which catches the spirit of the prohibition of images. For theology, God does not belong to a genus. He infinitely transcends the principles and categories of human thought. He is not to be subsumed under either being or becoming, but he is the One who causes the worlds to be and to become. God is not static, universal being but a particular being in action; he is not universal will but a particular will to love.

God is not a being besides others nor simply the depth and ground of being but the self-revealing and self-communicating Lord of being (Emil Brunner). Being belongs to God rather than God to being.[22] Being can be predicated of God but only analogously, not univocally.[23] The same can be said of such perfections as love, justice, truth and power.

The God of Christian faith is neither the transcendental universal (Plato) nor the concrete universal (Aristotle). Instead, he is the absolutely singular, the One out of whom universals arise.[24] He is not the "chief exemplification" of "all metaphysical principles" (Whitehead)[25] but the supreme metaphysician who concocts such principles. He can be equated neither with essence nor with existence, but he constitutes the dynamic unity of essence and existence.

Philosophers in general downplay the significance of history, whereas theologians see divine revelation occurring in particular events in history. Aristotle regarded poetry as much more important than history, "for poetry tends to express the universal, history the particular."[26] Plotinus depicted historical events as so many incidents in a play, not to be compared to the spiritual reality encountered in the interior life. History interested Hegel only because it signified the realization of the Idea of Spirit, the unfolding of what was already implicit in logic. In Marxism what is decisive is not particular historical events but the dialectic principle operating within history.[27] For Heidegger history is a "being unto death"; truth is the timeless being of ontology.[28] Emil Fackenheim sagaciously observes that "philosophic thought seeks radical universality, and the truths to which it lays claim transcend history even if they encompass not eternity but merely all time or all history."[29]

Theology, on the other hand, sees truth revealed not in universal concepts nor even in universal history[30] but in particular events in history—above all the event of God becoming man in Jesus Christ. It is this scandal of particularity that constitutes an offense to philosophical reason, which seeks to absorb the particular in the universal. Yet it is a mistake to imply that history is the source or matrix of revelation. Faith involves going beyond the bare facts of history to see the hand of God at work in history. Faith does not bypass the witness of history but perceives this witness in the light of eternity. The focus of faith is not on history as such, not even on biblical history, but on eternity breaking into history at a particular time and place.

Parallel to philosophy's disdain for the historical is its inclination to elevate the conceptual over the symbolic. What is sought is knowledge that is comprehensive and univocal.[31] The language of faith is relegated to the realm of poetry (Spinoza, Hegel), and the task is to translate this into the language of truth, which is philosophy. In contrast, theology regards the language of faith as closer to reality than the language of abstract thought. Theology contends that we have at the most an analogical language of God but never one that is univocal or literal.

In theology, the pivotal questions are, How can we be justified before a holy God? Where can we find God? What does God require of us? In philosophy they are, What does it mean "to be"? What is truth? How can I know? Who am I?[32] Theologians do not ignore such questions, but they now see them in the light of the divine act of redeeming a lost human race. Theology focuses on the creation of meaning, whereas philosophy is occupied with the meaning of meaning. Theology does speak to the question that concerned Kant—What ought I to do? It places the emphasis, however, not on universal law but on God's commandment, which is personally addressed to each one of us in the situation in which we find ourselves.

Tillich argues with some cogency that philosophy is oriented about the structure of being and theology about the meaning of being for us. But one can show that for a great many philosophers the ontological is subordinated to the soteriological. One can also show that theology is compelled to investigate questions relating to ontology in the light of its overriding soteriological concern. Tillich acknowledges that "every creative philosopher is a hidden theologian" gripped by his own ultimate concern of faith.[33] Indeed, "ontology presupposes a conversion, an opening of the eyes, a revelatory experience."[34]

I contend that every philosophy represents a rationalization for a false theology or religion and that true theology necessarily excludes philosophy—not its concerns, not even its language, but its world view, its metaphysical claims. In contradistinction to Tillich, I hold that theology and philosophy are not simply two ways of approaching reality, but they speak fundamentally of two different realities. I agree with Pascal that the God of the philosophers is something other than the God of Abraham, Isaac and Jacob. It is the difference between an idol created by the imagination and the experience of the true God.[35] The relation between theology and philosophy is not one of synthesis or correlation but one of conflict and contradiction.

The passionate concern of theology is "God's search for man," not "man's quest for God" (Barth). Our knowledge of God is based on God's gracious initiative toward us, not on our perceptivity or striving. For Plato we reach the ultimate principle of unity by "pure intelligence." For Plotinus we reach this principle by inward purification and ecstatic self-transcendence. For Kant we reach it by practical reason or moral will. For the theologian we receive it when we are confronted by the living Christ in the awakening to faith.

### Faith and Metaphysics

This brings us to a consideration of the relationship between faith and metaphysics. Metaphysics might be defined as the investigation of the ultimately real. It is, obviously, the core and soul of philosophy. Descartes aptly defined philosophy as a tree whose root is metaphysics.[36] Metaphysics is closely associated with ontology, the theory of being.

Theology is not metaphysics, but it must relate to metaphysics. Its intention and scope are different from that of metaphysical philosophy, but it is constrained to use metaphysical concepts. Theology necessarily has a metaphysical dimension, for it must speak to the problem of the structure of being, even though its primary concern is the revelation of the New Being in sacred history.

Whitehead has observed that Christianity is "a religion seeking a metaphysic" whereas Buddhism is "a metaphysic generating a religion."[37] This is only partly true, for biblical religion already contains a metaphysic, albeit more implicit than explicit. It is a metaphysic oriented about eternity breaking into history rather than one focused on an abstract eternity or solely on a concrete history.

There have been sporadic attempts in the history of philosophy to transcend metaphysics, to focus on human needs rather than on reality itself. For example, the positivist philosopher Auguste Comte averred that humanity is now entering the positive stage of history (as opposed to the earlier theological and metaphysical stages), where the concern is no longer with explaining metaphysical abstractions but now with observing and verifying empirical facts.[38] In his system philosophy is reduced to sociology, although it can be shown that his whole enterprise is grounded in a particular conception of what reality is. Kant saw metaphysics as the science of the boundaries or limits of human reason. He rejected metaphysics as a construction of a priori theoretical principles but made a place for a metaphysics of moral consciousness. We cannot attain valid or certain knowledge of supersensible reality, but we can produce reasoned positions for such a reality.

In theology, too, efforts have been made to rise above metaphysical concerns. Albrecht Ritschl sought to ground the Christian religion in ethics rather than metaphysics, preferring to regard the statements of theology as value judgments based on historical perception instead of metaphysical affirmations. We can know God's effect upon us but not what God is in himself. H. R. Mackintosh argued against Ritschl that "faith must always be metaphysical, for it rests upon convictions which, if true, must profoundly affect our whole view of the universe and the conduct befitting us within it. In this important sense, a metaphysical import belongs to every judgment concerning Ultimate Reality."[39] Yet he hastened to point out that "the belief or judgment in question need not have been reached by way of metaphysical argument, and in point of fact no essential Christian belief has ever been so reached, although metaphysical argument may later have been employed to defend it."[40]

It has been fashionable in modern theology since Ritschl, Herrmann and Harnack to bemoan the biblical-classical synthesis that combined Hebraic ideas with the thought-world of Hellenism and reinterpreted the teachings of Jesus in the light of classical philosophy.[41] While it would be a mistake to try to expurgate all Hellenistic elements from Christian theology in order to get back to the simple faith of Jesus, we need to recognize that a general transformation of Christianity did take place because of a too heavy dependence on Hellenistic categories in the explication of the faith.

In both patristic and medieval theology the Hellenistic conception of God as the impassible Absolute frequently overshadowed the biblical depiction of God as the gracious heavenly Father who condescends to share in our tribulation and ignominy. God became the all-knowing

Intellect or pure actuality rather than the One who loves. The God of the Bible is not Absolute Mind, not thought thinking upon thought (Aristotle), but the Acting Subject who encounters us in the moment of decision. It is the difference between the Idea of the Good and the living God who wills the good.

The meaning of love was likewise altered in theological speculation. Whereas the *agape* of the New Testament signifies a love that is outgoing, sacrificial and unconditional, the *caritas* upheld by Augustine and Aquinas, and by the Catholic mystical tradition in general, was much closer to the *eros* of Greek religion and philosophy, which is self-seeking and self-serving.[42] Agape is not based on the value of the one loved but instead creates value; eros is attracted to what has greatest value. Agape is a descending love that goes out to the forsaken and downtrodden; eros is an ascending love that seeks the perfection of the self in possession of the supreme good (i.e., absolute being). The *caritas* of the biblical-classical synthesis made a place for both descent and ascent, but the emphasis was on the latter. By the aid of grace, Anselm said, a person can begin and complete the ascent to the perfect good.[43]

To their credit, process theologians have been alert to the compromise represented by the biblical-classical synthesis, though they have not recoiled from offering a compromise of their own—a biblical-modern synthesis. They forcefully remind us that the self-contained Absolute of Hellenistic thought is a far cry from the God of tender and loving mercy who empathizes with our sufferings. They rightly fault the openness of past theologians to the Greek idea of perfection as self-sufficiency, an idea not easily reconciled with the biblical view of perfection as boundless compassion. Yet by aligning Christian faith with the philosophy of emergence and process, they have lost sight of the infinity and omnipotence of God. God becomes the "fellow sufferer who understands" (Whitehead)[44] rather than the almighty Lord who takes the form of a servant in the redemption of his people. In the biblical view God does not simply empathize with our suffering: he overcomes the powers of sin and death by taking the penalty of sin upon himself in the person of his Son. God does not aspire to his own self-fulfillment (as in the process view) but willingly makes himself vulnerable to suffering in order to rescue a despairing humanity. Despite their emphasis on modernity, process theologians remain heavily indebted to classical thought.[45] Thus Hartshorne can justifiably call his position a neoclassical theism.

Against the temptations to gain support from either antiquity or modernity, Christian faith presents a picture of God that both shocks antiquity and overturns modernity. The God it upholds is not a substance in the sense of an unchanging substratum hidden beneath the changing phenomena of the world. Nor is this God a creative process in the world with which we necessarily interact in our struggle for fulfillment. Instead, this God is a personal being in action who descends into our midst from the beyond, confronting us in our misery and liberating us for service in his name.

The Christian revelation transcends both its Hebraic matrix and the Hellenistic ethos. At the same time, it preserves the abiding values of Hebraic religion as well as the valid insights of Hellenistic philosophy, but it places these in a new context. It subordinates them to a new vision that drastically calls into question all human wisdom and goodness.

Christian faith cannot say with Fichte that "it is the metaphysical element alone, and not the historical, which saves us."[46] Even so, faith does not jettison the metaphysical concern, nor does it see history as itself redemptive. History is the field in which the living God who alone redeems meets us. Moreover, this God is not a construct or principle but the One who acts to reconcile and redeem a lost world. In our elucidation of the mighty works of God, we are constrained to make use of metaphysical concepts, but these concepts never encompass or contain the reality of which they purport to speak. Instead, they function as indicators or symbols of a reality that is hidden from sight and understanding until this reality makes itself known.

Christian faith must not be confused with either idealism or naturalism. In idealism the object is transposed into a subject. In naturalism the subject is reduced to an object. But faith is also not mysticism, in which the subject-object relationship is totally transcended. Instead, faith transfigures this relationship so that the divine object is at the same time a subject who meets us in the divine-human encounter.

Nor should faith be aligned with either monism or dualism. In monism all reality is reduced to one substance such as mind or matter; in dualism ultimate reality is conceived to be two things—mind and matter, or intelligence and force. Faith instead speaks of a supernatural creationism in which there are two realities—God and the world—but only the first is unconditional and absolute; the second is conditional and derivative. Supernatural creationism is not a philosophical possibility, however, since it entails a leap of the imagination on the basis of faith in the living God.

Can faith enter into an alliance with a particular metaphysics in order to make the truth of the gospel more intelligible to the contemporary mind? Here I agree with Pannenberg, who does not always follow his own advice: "Christian theology can effect a link-up with the philosophical concept of God only when it undertakes a penetrating transformation of the philosophical concept right down to its roots. Wherever philosophical concepts are taken over, they must be remolded in the light of the history-shaping freedom of the biblical God."[47]

One can show that the New Testament itself employed philosophical concepts, but they are now set in a new context and given a new meaning. They have been baptized into the service of the gospel. For example, *doxa* in classical Greek meant opinion or having a good opinion. In the New Testament it means the glory and praise of God. The word *truth (alētheia)* in Hellenistic philosophy signified eternal being, whereas in the biblical vision truth is the historical fact of God becoming man in Jesus Christ. In Aristotle's philosophy *telos* is the immanent aim of the life process; in the New Testament it signifies the end of the ages. It has an eschatological rather than an ontological character. In this same philosopher *kairos* is the good in the category of time; in the New

Testament time itself has a *kairos,* a fulfillment. Many other examples can be given to show that philosophy can be used by theology but must not operate in a magisterial way.[48]

In short, our approach to metaphysics and philosophy must be utilitarian. We are permitted to use concepts and imagery drawn from the wisdom of the culture, but we are not allowed to bow down before them and let them determine our thinking.[49] Philosophy is neither a preparation for theology nor a handmaid of theology (views entertained by various medieval thinkers). Nor is it the heir of theology, as in so much liberal theology. Instead, it is a potential rival of theology, for it represents a world view that must invariably conflict with the biblical view of God and the world. Yet it is not necessarily an enemy of theology, for the Spirit of God works in the world as well as in the church. The partial truths that it stumbles upon can be brought into the service of theology.

The deepest threat to faith lies not in philosophy but in the eagerness with which theologians rush to claim philosophical support for the claims of faith. Philosophy should generally be seen as an advocate of humanity rather than an instrument of the devil. It represents the pinnacle of natural human wisdom and as such should be respected. But we must scrupulously avoid an amalgamation of philosophy and theology. Let there be an ongoing dialog, but dialog will not be fruitful unless each side remains true to the criteria and values that shape its perspective on life and the world.

## Faith and Religion

If philosophy constitutes an ever-present source of temptation to Christianity, there is also a more subtle threat. Martin Buber has sagaciously observed that modernity is hostile to faith but surprisingly open to religion.[50] Faith—dependence on the high and holy God who judges cultural values and aspirations—certainly contradicts what commonly passes for religion—the methodical cultivation of spiritual potential. Yet faith does not exist apart from a religious framework, and religion is not purified and thereby transcended unless it is informed by a living faith.

Religion might be defined as an enterprise by which human beings seek to make contact with the spiritual power within them and beyond them. Faith represents the intrusion of the Spirit of God into the human soul awakening us to our predicament and moving us to cleave to Jesus Christ as our only Savior. Religion is humanity trying to ascend to God; faith is a work of divinity confronting the human soul in its creature-liness and sinfulness.

Tillich sees all religions as being rooted in the mystical a priori that prompts all people to seek for God. The Christian revelation is the answer to the human quest, which is basically a religious quest. In contrast, Barth sees religion as the endeavor to use divinity in order to ensure ourselves from harm or advance ourselves in the world. According to him, God's self-revelation in Jesus Christ overturns rather than fulfills our religious yearnings and aspirations. The gospel is not an answer to the questions that religion induces but the question that exposes our questions as rationalizations for self-seeking and self-loving. Biblical Christianity does not deny that all people have an immediate awareness of God in that God may and does speak to people in a direct as well as an indirect manner. Yet it insists, against mysticism, that we do not have an adequate knowledge of God apart from his self-revelation in the sacred history culminating in Jesus Christ. While acknowledging a mystical dimension in faith, it insists that the mystical experience is not sufficient for either cognition or salvation.

Religion is rooted not only in our sense of separation from the God who is the source of our existence but also in the desire to possess this God, even to make ourselves God. Faith fulfills the deep-seated human yearning for the God of the Bible, but it negates the sinful desire to be as God. It overthrows religion as a tower of Babel that tries to storm the gates of heaven. But it re-establishes religion as the vehicle for faith making its own way in the world. Religion is the garment of faith, but a garment that tends to suppress and distort faith unless it is constantly being purified and reformed by divine grace.

Religious experience is not to be confused with the awakening to faith, and yet faith involves experience just as it involves cognitive apprehension. Faith comes to us in the form of both knowledge and experience, but because this knowledge is human knowledge and this experience is human experience, we cannot depend on these things but must always go to the source of both our knowledge and experience—the revealed Word of God, Jesus Christ. Religious experience is the medium but not the norm or source of theology.

Jacques Ellul makes an interesting comparison between faith and belief. The former he associates with revelation and the latter with religion. He advances the view that "revelation and faith in revelation . . . run totally contrary to religion."[51] "Belief is reassuring. People who live in the world of belief feel safe; God is their protector. On the contrary, faith is forever placing us on the razor's edge. Though it knows that God is the Father, it never minimizes his power, and so it fills us with fear and even dread."[52] In contrast to religion, "revelation destabilizes. It turns the game upside down; all bets are off. It makes a shambles of foresight and probabilities. It brings an imponderable, unexpected, incalculable element into our policies and contrivances."[53]

Representing a quite different orientation, Carl Jung maintains that "no matter what the world thinks about religious experience, the one who has it possesses the great treasure . . . that has provided him with a source of life, meaning and beauty."[54] In my opinion, the religiosity that Jung promotes poses a more dire threat to the integrity of the faith than the irreligion of Marxist socialism. Religion is not the same thing as revelation, nor is mystical spirituality the same thing as biblical piety.

In this discussion we must avoid two errors. The first is to separate faith from religion, which means that faith is then divorced from ritual, sacraments, even congregational worship and prayer. But faith cannot live except in the fellowship of the church. Faith cannot thrive apart from cultic rites and communal celebrations. The second error is to identify faith with religious experience or with outward acts of piety. Religion is then seen as the seedbed of faith, or the giver and sustainer of faith. But the church is only an instrument in the hand of the living

God, just as visions and dreams are only channels of the Spirit of God. We must not confuse the external trappings with the redeeming reality itself. Faith has need of a credo to express its truth, but it cannot be frozen into a dogmatic formula, which would stifle its truth. It has need of sacraments to celebrate its message, but its truth can never be objectified in sacraments, for this would substitute the veneration of images for the adoration of the living God.

Today it is fashionable in ecumenical circles to press for dialog among the great world religions. Attempts are being made to water down the exclusive claims of Christian faith in order to facilitate interfaith understanding. For example, according to John Hick the great world faiths constitute bona fide ways to salvation that should command our respect, though not necessarily our agreement. For Hans Küng, the truths in other religions add to rather than subtract from the truth of Christian faith. According to Karl Rahner, genuine seekers after truth in other religions are already Christians—though anonymous ones. John Macquarrie thinks that the revelation of true humanity is to be discerned not only in Jesus but also in luminaries of other religious traditions, such as Buddha and Confucius.[55]

In my view, which is close to that of Barth and Kraemer, the revelation of Jesus Christ stands in judgment over all religions, including institutional Christianity.[56] The beliefs and experiences in all religions need to be purified and tested by God's self-revelation in Jesus Christ. The way to truth and salvation lies not in deepening our own religious sensibilities, even if these be Christian sensibilities, but in being converted by the Spirit of God to the One who is himself the way, the truth and the life (Jn 14:6). It is not a question of maintaining the superiority of the Christian religion over other religions but of fully recognizing the inadequacies and ambiguities in all religious life and experience even while expressing appreciation for those things in religious life that make for psychic wholeness and social cohesion. Religion is both culture transforming and culture destroying, but it is not redemptive. The ambassador of Christ will point people beyond their religious experience to the One who uproots our religious and cultural attachments in order to place us on a new foundation. The vision that Christian faith brings stands in contradiction to the spiritual vision of the culture in which that faith is proclaimed.

It is possible to speak of the hidden Christ in the world's cultures and religions, but this Christ will invariably be misunderstood and confused with the idols of human imagination. We meet the hidden Christ as the Judge of our ambitions and achievements, but we do not know him as Lord and Savior until we meet him as the manifest Christ, the Christ to whom the Scriptures testify.

True piety, true religion, does exist, but it is piety and religion constantly being reformed and transformed by the searing and purifying grace of a holy God. Biblical piety does not rest content with its own expression but always points beyond itself to the God who saves despite our pieties and rituals. Biblical piety takes us out of ourselves, out of our vain endeavors to make something of ourselves religiously, and focuses our attention not on what we can do for God but on what God has done for us in his reconciling and atoning work in the cross and resurrection of Jesus Christ. We are called to testify not to the sublimity of our worship nor to the virtue of our moral achievements but to the God who redeems us from the sin in our worship and morality. We are justified neither by spirituality nor by morality but only by the vicarious, forgiving love of God as revealed and fulfilled in Jesus Christ.

**Faith and Ethics**

It is not sufficient simply to dwell on the gift of faith: we must also give serious attention to the obedience of faith. Faith remains barren unless it is united with love, and we are sanctified by faith working through love. Dogmatics necessarily involves ethics, just as ethics presupposes dogmatics.

Not surprisingly, philosophy and theology diverge not only in the area of metaphysics but also in that of ethics.[57] In philosophy ethics is oriented about the idea of the good; in theology the focus is on the Author of the good—the living God. In philosophy the ultimate criterion is the principle of the good in the mind of God or the good as a transcendent ideal or abiding value; in theology it is the commandment of God. It is not simply what God thinks but what God wills that determines the meaning of the good for us. Theological ethics is an ethics of grace; philosophical ethics tends to be an ethics of duty or law.[58] Ethics in the Christian sense is neither the firm adherence to universal rules (Kant) nor the intelligent "foresight of consequences" (John Dewey),[59] but the faithful response to God's gracious initiative.

Classical humanism, which was reborn in the Enlightenment, teaches an ethics of eudaemonia or happiness as the goal of human existence;[60] theology emphasizes blessedness (from the Greek *makarios)*, which is qualitatively different from its worldly counterpart. While happiness means the fulfillment of the self, the realization of our dreams and desires, blessedness means the crucifixion of the self for the sake of the glory of God and the service of our neighbor. While happiness signifies a life free from discord and misery, blessedness involves taking suffering on oneself in order to rescue the perishing and dying. Happiness is dependent on the circumstances of life; blessedness is contingent on the outpouring of the Holy Spirit, which may occur even when life's circumstances are most dismal and hopeless.

Correspondingly, while philosophical ethics is generally oriented about eros—the love that seeks its own perfection in union with the highest[61]—theological ethics focuses on agape—the love that sacrifices what is dearest to us in order to help the despairing and needy.[62] Eros is the desire to enjoy and possess. Agape is the willingness to sacrifice for the good of others. Eros is illustrated in Plato's ladder to heaven, whereby love ascends to that which is supremely beautiful. Agape is most graphically depicted in the descending love of God to humanity in the Incarnation of Jesus Christ.

Philosophy, representing the creative thinking of the natural person, makes a prominent place for self-love. According to Berkeley, "Self-love being a principle of all others the most universal, and the most deeply engraven in our hearts, it is natural for us to regard things as they are fitted to augment or impair our own happiness, and accordingly we denominate them *good* or *evil.*"[63] The Enlightenment philosopher Helvétius (d. 1771), in whom we see a confluence of ethical egoism and hedonism, contended that "self-love is the universal basis of human conduct, and self-love is directed to the acquisition of pleasure."[64] It has often been said that if we love ourselves truly we will learn to love others because we see in them a reflection of ourselves or the mirror of the universal self. Rousseau was insistent that self-love is capable of developing into the love of humanity and the promotion of the general happiness that are of concern to every virtuous person.[65] Theologians seeking to accommodate to the humanistic understanding hold that God too is characterized by self-love and that he loves humanity only insofar as it reflects his own goodness and wisdom.

In the biblical perspective self-love is not something to be encouraged or celebrated but rather overcome. When Jesus called us to love our neighbor as ourselves (Mt 22:39), he was not commanding self-love but only recognizing that self-love is part of our nature and that we should love others with the same power or force with which we love ourselves.[66] Christian faith makes a place for self-respect and self-affirmation, but it does so on the basis of the fact that we are the objects of God's infinite love. Because we are elected by God to be his sons and daughters, we can celebrate our new status by trying to become in fact what we are called to be by grace.

Philosophy presupposes humanity's innate ability to pursue the good, even to discover the good. According to idealism, because we are free and intelligent beings and because we are in contact with Universal Intelligence, we can progress toward the good, the true and the beautiful. Fichte said: "Luther has freed us from the mediation of human priests, but he failed to realize that we do not need a mediator at all because the human soul carries the divine spark within itself."[67] Indeed, "no one is our master, and no one can become our master. We carry our charter of freedom, given and sealed by God, deep in our bosom."[68]

In modern naturalism the good is determined by whether it promotes human welfare according to the wisdom garnered from the natural and social sciences.

Whereas classical humanism encourages the cultivation of human virtue, meaning human capacity for the good, evangelical theology prefers to speak of graces that are worked in us by the Spirit of God as we seek to do the divine will. To become virtuous is to become morally worthy. To become gracious is to become a sign of the passion and victory of our Lord Jesus Christ.

The goal in theological ethics is to give glory to God by serving an oppressed and ailing humanity. Philosophical ethics is much more anthropocentric than theocentric. It seeks the realization of human potential through moral discipline and knowledge. Aristotle said the practice of virtue is what makes us virtuous. Christianity says that serving our neighbor in need makes us transparent to the goodness of God.

Theology recognizes that natural humanity can know something of the justice of God simply through reason and experience but will invariably misunderstand it. The philosopher David Hume acknowledged such a reality as justice but saw it as an artifice or invention having its basis in felt utility. Plato tried to ground justice in intelligible reality, but his ideal state countenanced such things as slavery, banishment of the aged to the country and willful neglect of the incurably ill. Karl Jaspers comments that because of such notions "Plato negates what even in antiquity was known as *philanthropia* and *humanitas.*"[69]

The righteousness of the kingdom of God transcends even while it negates the classical conception of justice, for it speaks of a grace that forgives our sins and does not requite us according to our iniquities (Ps 103:8-13). Justice rewards the deserving, but grace goes out to the undeserving. Our righteousness is law-abiding and conforming; God's righteousness is creative and liberating. Our task is to celebrate and witness to his righteousness, which alone redeems from sin. We must certainly include in our witness, however, works of justice and mercy, which are human works, to be sure, but nonetheless give credibility to our commitment to the coming righteousness of his kingdom.

## Beyond Fideism and Rationalism

Theology is constantly deceived into supposing that the only two options are fideism and rationalism. Certainly these are obvious viable possibilities, but they are not the only ones. We need today a reaffirmation of a theological method that goes beyond and overcomes this polarity.

Rationalism is evident in many of the theological luminaries of the past, especially in those who would be classified as philosophical theologians or even Christian philosophers. John Scotus Erigena argued that reason is prior to authority and that true authority is simply "the truth found by the power of reason and handed on in writing by the Fathers for the use of posterity."[70] John Locke insisted that the truths of revelation must be shown by reason to be in fact revealed before we can be expected to accept them by faith. Propositions that are contrary to reason cannot form a part of divine revelation.[71] In our day Norman Geisler finds "the law of noncontradiction" reigning "sovereignly and universally over all *thinking* and *speaking* about God."[72] Either logic "controls all our thoughts about reality all the time or we are left with some thoughts and statements about reality that are contradictory."[73] According to Gordon Clark, when we believe, we freely choose a view that satisfies our intellect according to the laws of logic.[74] Pannenberg is convinced that revelation must be open to "general reasonableness" and that the truth of revelation must be demonstrable to natural reason.

While a fideistic thrust can be discerned in a number of theologians through the ages—Tertullian, Luther, Pascal, Hamann, Kierkegaard[75] and the early Barth—an unvarnished variety of fideism is most prominent today in the writings of Jacques Ellul. Ellul speaks of faith as "an illogical venture" in which there is "no road from belief to faith."[76] Indeed, faith is even "without a trace of [intellectual] belief."[77] In stark contrast to both Calvin and Luther, Ellul insists that faith "incorporates doubt as part of itself."[78] To have faith is to realize that "the only thing

I know is that I don't know anything."[79] Ellul sees faith rooted in the divine summons to obedience rather than in the impartation of knowledge.[80]

While rationalism holds to *credo quia intelligo* (I believe because I understand) and fideism to *credo quia absurdum est* (I believe because it is absurd), evangelical theology in the classical tradition subscribes to *credo ut intelligam* (I believe in order to understand). In this last view faith is neither a blind leap into the unknown (Kierkegaard) nor an assent of the will to what reason has already shown to be true (Carl Henry), but a venture of trust based on evidence that faith itself provides. We do not believe without our reason, but we also do not believe on the basis of reason. Faith entails thinking and examining. In order to come to a mature faith we need to search and examine the Scriptures as well as the tradition of the church.

Faith is not an act of the will in which reason is suspended but a rational commitment. It is not against reason but above reason. Reason is involved in faith at the very beginning, but it is not the foundation of faith. Augustine is right that we must understand the words of the gospel before we can commit ourselves to him who is the content of the gospel, but this is not true understanding, only external apprehension. We do not truly understand until our inward eyes are opened by the Spirit of God to discern the depth of meaning contained in the gospel.

Prior to faith our reasoning is distorted by sin. We use our reason to rationalize our self-interest rather than to come to the truth. The natural person does not seek for God but tries to hide from God (cf. Ps 14:2-3; 53:1-3; Rom 3:11). Once our will is converted by the Spirit of God to the service of the gospel, however, our reason, too, becomes a salutary instrument of faith. We now use our reason to understand our faith more fully and to serve the gospel in obedience to the Great Commission. Luther makes an important distinction between "reason" and "faithful reasoning"—only the latter gives glory to God.

The theological method I affirm is "faith seeking understanding," which goes back to Augustine and Anselm. We begin with faith's apprehension of divine revelation and then endeavor to explore the ramifications and implications of this for daily life. I agree wholeheartedly with Anselm: "I do not seek to understand that I may believe, but I believe in order to understand. For this also I believe—that unless I believed, I should not understand."[81] Our starting point is God's self-revelation in Jesus Christ, which creates faith within us. This is not fideism because we begin not with our act of faith but with God's action toward us. It is also not rationalism because what we are led to affirm is not the conclusion of reason as such but the outcome of grace opening our inward eyes to a truth beyond our thoughts and imagination.

Faith does not supply its own content but apprehends the content objectively given in the Word. This Word does not contradict the structure of reason, but it does contravene the direction of our reasoning prior to the act of faith. Faith is neither irrational nor simply rational but suprarational in that it directs us to a truth that transcends human imagination and perception.

Theology could not say with the existentialist philosopher Martin Heidegger that "thinking only begins at the point where we have come to know that Reason, glorified for centuries, is the most obstinate adversary of thinking."[82] Against philosophical irrationalism theology contends that it is sin, not reason, that constitutes the major obstacle to true understanding. Against rationalism theology says that it is not reason but divine grace that brings us into contact with ultimate reality.

Psychologically, faith might legitimately be described as a leap in the dark, but theologically faith is an awakening to the light, which is not accessible to either human perception or human conception. We believe what cannot be comprehended by human reason, but the eyes of faith can nevertheless see dimly what is beyond reason's compass. As Augustine put it, "Faith has eyes by which it in some way perceives to be true that which it does not yet see, and by which it very surely perceives that it does not yet see what it believes."[83]

Human reason cannot grasp the mystery of divine revelation, but it can witness to this mystery. It cannot encompass this mystery, but it can make contact with this mystery, though not on the basis of any power within itself.

Can reason confirm the truth of revelation after this truth encounters us? I prefer to say that the Holy Spirit confirms the truth of faith to reason. Reason receives and acknowledges what the Spirit offers, but in and of itself it cannot validate or substantiate the claims of faith.

Faith brings spiritual certitude but not rational certainty. It cannot guarantee by rational means that the events recorded in the Bible actually happened as described; yet it can give compelling witness to the truth of the gospel story as the Spirit brings home to us this story's redeeming power.[84] Nor can it guarantee the credibility of its conclusions or the perfect reliability of its experiences; nevertheless it clings to the One in whom it trusts with the unshakable assurance of hope.[85] What we derive from faith is a certainty of the heart, an inward peace and confidence, which neither rational demonstration nor empirical verification can provide.

The object of faith is neither true propositions (as in rationalism) nor an experience of the ineffable (as in mysticism) but the living Word of God who is revealed as well as hidden in the mystery of his self-disclosure in biblical history. In mysticism reason is overwhelmed by mystery. In rationalism logic prevails over mystery.[86] In biblical faith meaning shines through mystery.

In contrast to philosophy, theology is necessarily eschatological, since our understanding of the mysteries of faith will always remain broken and deficient. Faith is not yet sight, and this means that we know not so much by rational demonstration as by trustful commitment. We can "know in part" because we are already known by God (1 Cor 13:12; Gal 4:9), and this state of being apprehended and confronted by the living God is the final basis for theology.

I oppose both the Kantian view that faith is a moral attitude devoid of rational content and the Leibnitzian view reaffirmed by Francis Schaeffer that there are "good and sufficient reasons" for believing in the truth of the Bible.[87] Faith knows of whom it speaks, but this knowledge is not available to the person outside the circle of faith. God's Word is true and dependable, but this fact is credible only to those who are grasped by this Word in the decision of faith.

My position is probably closer to fideism than to rationalism; yet it is not really fideism, for it is based not on a venture into the unknown, necessarily fraught with uncertainty, but on the divine-human encounter, which expels all doubt. We know really and truly because we are known by God. We can live without agonizing doubt and fear because Jesus Christ has overcome all doubt and fear through his cross and resurrection triumph. The light shines in the darkness and the darkness has not overcome it (Jn 1:5). We are still not free from doubt and fear, for sin lingers on even in those who are most sanctified. Yet doubt is not a property of faith, as Tillich and Ellul erroneously allege, but rather belongs to the domain of sin, which is already passing away as the kingdom of God advances in human history.

Against philosophical theology I maintain that revelation must not be absorbed into a rational system, but reason must be taken into revelation. Reason can be a useful tool in the service of faith, but it cannot supply the substructure for faith (as in Thomism). Revelation enlightens reason, and reason can celebrate and testify to the truth of revelation. The relationship of faith and reason is not either-or but both-and; yet we must never fail to give priority to the first. And when we uphold faith it is not the act of faith but the object of faith that should command our primary attention. For it is the object of faith that convicts us of our sins and convinces us of its truthfulness and credibility. And the object of faith is not a propositional formula or a rational, ethical ideal but the living, redeeming God incarnate in Jesus Christ, attested nowhere more decisively than in Holy Scripture.

## Appendix A: Kierkegaard
Perhaps no one more than that brilliant and enigmatic nineteenth-century Danish philosopher Søren Kierkegaard has made fideism a solid

theological option for our time.[1] For Kierkegaard the truth of faith is not only above reason but also against reason. It is an "objective uncertainty" that can be held to only by the passion of inwardness. It requires a leap into the darkness of the unknown rather than rational supports; indeed, when the latter are introduced the act of faith, in which we risk everything for our eternal happiness, is subverted. "To believe against the understanding," he says, "is martyrdom; to begin to get the understanding a little in one's favor, is temptation and retrogression."[2] Because God is "the absolutely different," we cannot grasp him rationally, but we can nevertheless commit ourselves to him by a supreme act of the will. While the freedom to choose the highest is not a general possibility, it becomes a possibility in the moment of visitation by God's Spirit.[3]

In this perspective, truth is not an abstract doctrine or an intuitive apprehension but the transformative reality of the incarnate Word making contact with us in a paradoxical encounter. It is basically God's self-communication to those who have been gripped by the passion of faith.[4] It is the opening up of a new horizon for those who have been confronted by the living God.

Faith involves the crucifixion of intelligence, but once faith takes root in personal life it enables us to make sense of our predicament. In the irreversible and incomparable event that gives rise to faith we begin to see a light that illumines the darkness that envelops us. The absurdity of the object of faith is replaced by a luminosity that gives meaning and direction to life. Yet because the Christian is never in a state of perfected being but always in the process of becoming, because sin is never simply left behind but continues to intrude in life and thought, the paradoxical character of the moment of God's descent into time reasserts itself, and the need for the leap of faith and abnegation of reason is renewed.[5]

Kierkegaard has made an outstanding contribution with his penetrating and devastating critique of idealism by poignantly reminding us that there is no congruity but only a radical cleavage between thought and an existing subject. The object of faith is not an idea that can be grasped by the mind but the event of eternity entering time, God becoming human in Jesus Christ. This event confronts us as the absolute paradox, which induces wonder but defies comprehension.[6] Kierkegaard's stress on the otherness of God is a welcome antidote to the radical immanentism of the Hegelians, but it too can result in an imbalance—an unrelieved dualism that contravenes the biblical picture of a God who loves and cares for his people to the extent of sharing in their joys and sorrows. This is not to deny that Kierkegaard fully affirmed the God of unbounded love, but he could not entirely extricate himself from the classical idea of God as the impassible, self-contained Absolute, blithely towering above the world of temporality and materiality.[7] The tension between these two conflicting notions is painfully evident when he says, "I know that in Thy Love Thou sufferest with me, more than I, infinite Love—though Thou canst not be changed by that."[8] H. R. Mackintosh makes this astute observation:

On a review of all the data we are justified, I think, in concluding that two conceptions of God . . . were at war within his divided mind—conceptions which it is impossible to reconcile. . . . On the one hand is the thought of God as Holy Love—a conception evoked by the whole redeeming fact of Christ. . . . In the later phases of Kierkegaard's reflection we encounter a sheerly metaphysical contrast between Eternity and time, between a featureless Absolute Substance and the nothingness of man.[9]

Nor is it unjust to accuse Kierkegaard of overemphasizing the hiddenness of God to such an extent that God remains even for the Christian an impenetrable mystery. Against Kierkegaard it is necessary to contend that God is not an "objective uncertainty" but the ground of certainty. He is not the "absolutely unknown" but the One who has made himself truly known in the person of his Son Jesus Christ. In existentialism reason reaches up to the supreme paradox and is then thrown back upon itself. In evangelical theology the absolute paradox breaks into the processes of reason and entirely redirects them. Faith does not leave reason behind but uses reason to demonstrate that the truth of divine revelation lies beyond reason. Kierkegaard can also speak in this way, but for the most part he regards reason as an adversary rather than a useful tool of faith.[10]

For Kierkegaard there is a radical disjunction between faith and reason: "Faith begins precisely where thinking leaves off."[11] I believe, to the contrary, that God is to be found not at the boundary of reason but in the crisis of history where God became man in Jesus Christ,[12] whose presence and power are communicated to us by his Spirit in the event of the preaching and hearing of God's Word. Faith comes by hearing (Rom 10:17), and hearing is a rational event. Faith involves the turning around of reason but not its crucifixion,[13] for in faith we make contact not with the nothingness but with the Logos, the supreme rationality who brings meaning into a world otherwise palpably absurd and meaningless.[14] Some of Kierkegaard's names for God—"the absolutely unknown," "the Limit," and "the sheerly unqualified Being"—are more reminiscent of mysticism than of biblical faith, but Kierkegaard maintains continuity with evangelical tradition by his firm insistence that divine grace is necessary for the miracle of faith and that the truth comes to us from without, not from within. His affinity to Lutheran Pietism is evident when he speaks of the need to prepare ourselves to receive faith by recognizing and deploring our helplessness and guilt.[15] Thus to despair of oneself becomes a virtual precondition of faith.[16]

Reflecting the accent on a *theologia viatorum* in his Lutheran and Pietistic heritage, Kierkegaard postulated stages on life's way which the pilgrim travels in order to satisfy the human yearning for infinity—the aesthetic, the ethical and the religious. Just as the law is prior to the gospel, so the aesthetic and ethical are prior to the religious.[17] And this means that apologetics plays a role before dogmatics, although a negative one—exposing the contradictions and antinomies in human existence and reasoning. Kierkegaard offered an indirect communication of the gospel, which was designed to prod people to seek an answer to life's ultimate questions outside themselves. He began with the misery and predicament of human beings and then sought to lead them to the outer limits of reason where they could be confronted by the infinite abyss. He nevertheless recognized that rational dialectic must be superseded by direct witnessing if people are ever to enter the domain of faith.[18] Dialectics can lead a person to the Absolute,[19] but only a power outside the self can cause anyone to place confidence and trust in the Absolute.

Karl Barth broke with Kierkegaard and existentialism when he realized that we cannot really know the extremity of our need until we are first awakened to faith by the love of God shown forth in Jesus Christ. Kierkegaard allowed that the person in despair could have a faint intimation of his or her existential need for God, though not a true understanding. For Barth only on the basis of faith can we effectively engage in the ethical task of combating the powers of the world. Only as people of faith can we truly enjoy the pleasures of life. The aesthetic life is not to be left behind but to be appropriated anew in the light of the free grace given to us by God, which restores rather than annuls creation. Whereas Barth was firmly convinced that despite human perfidy and obstinacy culture could be transformed and renewed by divine grace, Kierkegaard came to the sobering conclusion that cultural pursuits had to be renounced in the interest of securing eternal happiness.[20]

Despite the bleakness that now and again clouded his vision, particularly in his later years, we remain indebted to Kierkegaard for his insightful and timely warning against a Christianity that capitulates to modernity. He saw himself as a knight of faith upholding the uncompromising demands of the gospel in the midst of a corrosive secularism. He freely used philosophical terminology in order to make an indirect witness to the God hidden and revealed in Jesus Christ, a witness that, he hoped, might have an impact on the intelligentsia. It was Kierkegaard who through the use of an existential dialectic and the language of paradox helped to safeguard the reality of mystery and transcendence in Christian faith in a time when rationalism and immanentism practically reigned supreme in both philosophy and theology. Yet by focusing so much on the infinite distance between God and humanity, he failed to do justice to the indwelling Christ and the sanctifying and illumining work of the Holy Spirit, which leads one into a deeper appreciation of the truth of the Christian message.

If we followed Kierkegaard all the way, we would end in a truncated Christianity. But this does not mean that we cannot learn from his many profound insights, which are ultimately rooted in a living faith in the God of Abraham, Isaac and Jacob. We would do well to take seriously his trenchant observation that when the passion of faith is weakened, the truth of faith will become steadily more dim and will ineluctably take on the character of offense and absurdity. And nothing weakens the passion of faith more than the sorry attempt to make the truth of faith respectable and reasonable,[21] thus undercutting the necessity for a life-and-death decision. The theology of paradox needs to be superseded by a theology of Word and Spirit in which the light of God's truth breaks through our present darkness, so that paradox does not simply mark the limitations of reason but facilitates the appropriation of the wisdom and power of Christ by the company of the committed.[22]

# ·FOUR·

# THEOLOGICAL
# LANGUAGE

---

To whom can God be compared?
How can you describe what he is like?

ISAIAH 40:18 GNB

---

Perhaps not even John spoke the reality as it was, but as he could;
for he, a human being, was speaking of God.

AUGUSTINE

---

Language or speaking stands in correlation to hearing,
understanding, and obeying.

KARL BARTH

---

We understand in and through language. We do not invent
our own private languages and then find a way to translate our
communications to others. We find ourselves understanding
in and through particular languages.

DAVID TRACY

---

The basic problem . . . is that language about God has become
detached from the Reality of God, and a conceptuality arising out of our
own consciousness has been substituted for a conceptuality
forced upon us from the side of God Himself.

THOMAS F. TORRANCE

---

Through the centuries theologians of the church have been poignantly aware of the signal differences between the language of abstract thought and that of faith. Many of the Christian mystics said that God transcends the purview of our perception and imagination and therefore cannot really be known conceptually. Gregory of Nyssa remarked that "concepts create idols, only wonder comprehends anything."[1] The mystical goal was a "knowledge beyond discourse" and a "vision beyond images."[2] Thomas Aquinas, on the other hand, maintained that we could know something of God by discerning the similarity between God and his creatures in the midst of an even greater dissimilarity. For Thomas analogy was a middle way between univocity (literal knowledge) and equivocity (uncertain knowledge). Still other scholars, such as Eunomius and Duns Scotus, claimed that we can have a univocal or exact knowledge of God based on the fact that we are created in his image.

In our day conservative evangelicals like Gordon Clark, Edward J. Carnell, Carl Henry, Ronald Nash and Roy Clouser argue for the possibility of a univocal knowledge of God. Gordon Clark maintains that human logic and knowledge are identical with that of God, even to the point where "God and logic are one and the same first principle."[3] According to Carnell, there is a "univocal point of identity between time and eternity."[4] He allowed for analogical knowledge of God, but such knowledge has a univocal element. We can really know what is the true, the good and the beautiful because these human conceptions have their metaphysical status in God. As human beings we have a point of contact with divinity, in whom we see the perfection of these ideals. Carnell even deemed it proper to contend that "God is perfectly held by standards that hold an upright man imperfectly."[5] For Norman Geisler the situation is simple: "In the Bible the main things are the plain things, and the plain things are the main things."[6] Human logic and reason are capable of penetrating the enigma of the mystery of God (though not exhaustively).

On the other end of the spectrum are those theologians, usually of a mystical or existentialist bent, who regard human language as wholly inadequate for giving us real knowledge of God. Both Karl Jaspers and Fritz Buri believe that words serve merely as ciphers of transcendence because God cannot be objectified. Paul Tillich, here reflecting the philosopher Immanuel Kant, allows that humans can have a "symbolic awareness" of God but not theoretical knowledge.[7] The American pragmatist Eugene Fontinell considers revelation basically noncognitive, the language of revelation merely serving to stimulate people of faith to create goals and ideals for themselves. Feminist theologians generally call us to construct a new language about God based on the modern consciousness of a holocentric world—in which every aspect of reality is seen as part of an organic whole. For Sallie McFague we can have at the most intimations of transcendence that can best be grasped by metaphors.[8] Pannenberg maintains that our language about God is little more than equivocal and must wait for its fulfillment until the eschaton, when both equivocity and analogy are transcended.[9]

Karl Barth follows Aquinas in affirming an analogical relation between God and humanity. Barth rejects, however, the approach of natural theology in which we assign to God the perfections of human attributes. Instead, we begin with the divine perfection and then try to understand human imperfections in this light. The analogical relation can be properly discerned only on the basis of faith *(analogia fidei)* in the triune God, not on the basis of a knowledge of God that belongs to our human nature *(analogia entis)*. What Barth offers is not so much an analogy as a catalogy, an analogy from above *(analogia gratiae)*.[10]

For Barth the veracity of human speech about God lies not in human ability to discern analogical relationships, however, but in God's free act of condescension to our weakness and imperfection.

> By the grace of God we shall truly know God with our views and concepts, and truly speak of God with our words. But we shall not be able to boast about it, as if it is our own success, and we have performed and done it. It is we who have known and spoken, but it will always be God and God alone who will have credit for the veracity of our thinking and speaking.[11]

Against a reactionary strand of biblical orthodoxy, Barth contends that simply returning to the biblical mode of speech about God does not guarantee that we will truly hear the Word of God. Even the language of ecclesiastical dogma and the Bible is not exempt from the crisis of the limitation of all human language in conveying real knowledge of God. Even the words "Father, Creator, Lord, Sovereign—and even the word God itself—are not in themselves and as such identical with the ineffable name by which God calls Himself and which therefore expresses His truth; and therefore they cannot in themselves express His truth."[12] Yet because God has chosen to meet us in the lowly form of the biblical witness, that is where we should seek him and where he may be found.

A similar approach to the problem of God-language is taken by Thomas F. Torrance, who argues that "theological knowledge and theological statements participate sacramentally in the mystery of Christ as the Truth."[13] He acknowledges that "all true theological concepts and statements inevitably fall far short of the God to whom they refer, so that their inadequacy, as concepts and as statements, to God must be regarded as essential to their truth and precision."[14] Yet our concepts can nonetheless communicate the divine truth of who God is through their capacity to reflect the divine light that is the source of their illumination. The human forms of thought and speech found in the Scriptures "are unable of themselves to convey the Word of God," but "they are nevertheless grounded and structured through the incarnation in the very Logos who inheres eternally in the Being of God and are the vehicles of his address to mankind."[15]

Torrance warns against the mystics and existentialists who speak of a noncognitive and nonconceptual language about God. He is adamant that there can be no knowledge of God, no faith, which is not basically conceptual, or conceptual at its very root, and therefore there is no non-conceptual gap between God's revealing of himself and our knowing of him. Far from meaning that knowledge of God in his eternal Being is captured within the grasp of our creaturely concepts, this means that the human concepts which arise in faith under the creative impact of the speech of God are grounded beyond themselves in the *ratio veritatis* of the divine Being.[16]

### The Enigma of Faith-Language

The Bible's language about God and his relationships to humankind is for the most part symbolic or mythopoetic. A symbol in this context indicates any imaginative description that points beyond itself to a reality that somehow eludes immediate perception and conceptual mastery. I include in this general category such forms of speech as analogy and metaphor. An analogy refers to a partial resemblance between things fundamentally distinct, whereas a metaphor signifies a word or phrase ordinarily used of one thing that is applied to another. A metaphor yields impressions but not real knowledge. An analogy conveys partial but not complete knowledge. That the Bible uses both analogical and metaphorical language cannot be denied, but this does not mean that we therefore lack real knowledge of God. A metaphor can serve to sharpen our apprehensions of God's mighty acts just as an analogy can throw light upon these acts while still falling short of presenting a full understanding of them.[17]

Symbolic knowledge contrasts with conceptual knowledge, which tends to be univocal or exact. While a symbol is a pictorial term that brokenly reflects what it is intended to signify, a concept is an abstract term that roughly corresponds to what it purports to signify. Whereas a symbol directs the mind to what can only be imperfectly understood, a concept is immediately apprehensible by the mind. Its meaning can be rationally determined; the meaning of a symbol can at the most be only intuitively grasped.[18] The symbol always seeks more precise meaning, but thought becomes removed from experience unless it remains anchored in the symbol. According to Paul Ricoeur, "The symbol gives rise to thought," but thought always returns to and is informed by the symbol.[19] In order to gain deeper understanding of the mystery of God's self-revelation in the history of Israel culminating in Jesus Christ, we need to translate our symbols into concepts, but this does not necessarily bring us closer to the truth. Something is lost in the process of translation; for this reason we must always return to the mythopoetic language of Canaan in order to maintain contact with the noetic roots of our faith. As Macquarrie has rightly observed, "The symbol lights up for us levels of meaning and of reality in ways that perhaps conceptual language could not do, above all, if it is an abstract language."[20] In the words of Avery Dulles, "Christian doctrines are never so literal that they cease to participate in the symbolic. They live off the power of the revelatory symbols."[21]

I have difficulty with Henry Wieman and other philosophical theologians who maintain that concepts are the meaning of symbols.[22] Concepts are an attempt to elucidate the meaning already in symbols, but the concept as an abstraction is actually further from the reality that the symbol describes and that is itself the source and ground of the meaning in both concept and symbol. Against both Tillich and Gilkey I maintain that the symbolic language of faith cannot be made intelligible or credible by translating it into a modern ontology.[23] The meaning-content of faith is inseparable from the symbolic language in which faith comes to us, and this meaning-content is the criterion in judging both the truth and the untruth in an ontological system. Ontological concepts can be used to explicate the meaning of the language of the gospel and dogma, but these concepts are then baptized into the service of the gospel. The concepts themselves then become metaphors that do not yield theoretical knowledge but only impressionistic intimations of the reality that the symbols describe. In other words, such graphic terms for God as "Father," "King" and "Lord" are closer to the divine reality than such abstract terms as "ground of being," "creative process" or "power of creative transformation." The latter terms can be used to supplement the graphic or imaginative language of faith, but they do not give us real or univocal knowledge of who God is.

Spinoza aptly stated the attitude of philosophical theologians: "The sole aim of philosophy is truth: the sole aim of faith obedience and piety."[24] On the contrary, faith alone lays hold of the truth of God, and in so doing it may utilize philosophical concepts, but this truth is discerned only partially. The discernment of faith is not to be confused with the language of sight or univocity. It is not controlling knowledge but receiving knowledge. It is not univocal but dialogical; that is, it is dependent on the initiative and speaking of God.

We must keep in mind that "symbol" itself is an ambiguous term, and

I am not using it in the Tillichian sense of a sign that points beyond itself to an ineffable or nonobjective reality. A symbol in that sense would be an image that mediates divinity to us rather than a word that is used by divinity to encounter us both rationally and experientially.

The symbolic language of Scripture has its source not in religious experience (as Schleiermacher, Tillich and Gilkey suppose) but rather in a divine revelation that breaks into cultural and religious experience from the beyond. If the symbols have their genesis in certain primal experiences, they will invariably change, since our "cultural experience and forms of reflections on that experience change."[25] When symbols cease to function in shaping our actual lived experience, the implication is that they can be discarded for new symbols.[26] In my perspective the symbolic language of biblical faith that bears witness to God's self-revelation in Jesus Christ is effectual in conveying meaning only when seen in the light of this revelation, that is, only when people of faith under the impact of the Spirit have their inner eyes opened to the significance of what God has done for us in Christ. The capacity of this language to bear meaning does not lie in the vicissitudes of cultural experience or history but in the action of the Spirit of God, who infinitely transcends human culture and history even while he moves upon and within them.

Christianity is not a religion that points beyond itself by means of symbols to a transphenomenal and undefinable reality but a religion that celebrates the intervention of a transcendent God into the phenomenal and historical world. This divine intervention can only be described in mythopoetic language, but it must be interpreted in conceptual language, which remains, however, always open-ended and tentative. The gospel is not a symbol that directs us to a higher spiritual world but a report of the saving deeds of God in the empirical world in which we find ourselves. Yet this report invariably makes use of symbolic or pictorial language, for how else can realities that transcend human perception and conception be described?

It is fashionable in liberal circles to try to get beyond the anthropomorphic language of the Bible into the more impersonal or supraper-sonal language of a modern ontology. Yet the language of Scripture is best understood as theanthropomorphic rather than simply anthropo-morphic, for its focus is not on human experience or self-understanding but on the divine-human existence that we see in Jesus Christ. Its concern is not with humanity seeking to find itself through religion but with God confronting humanity caught in the web of religious idolatry.

Torrance trenchantly observes that in theology we proceed from *my-thos* to *logos,* from "thinking projectively in pictures and images to thinking in terms of structured imageless relations."[27] We already discern this kind of translation in Scripture, particularly in the writings of Paul, whose language Ricoeur regards as "semi-conceptual."[28] Against Bultmann, who contends that true understanding of the biblical narrative is available to us only when we proceed to demythologize this story, I maintain that the Word of God can be known only in its mytho-poetic garb, and that while we need to go beyond this original language of faith, we can never supplant it because by the power of the Spirit it contains the divine criterion of faith apart from which we would be lost in a morass of subjectivism and relativism.

Biblical faith is to be distinguished from both rationalism, which reduces mystery to logic, and mysticism, in which rationality is eclipsed. In the biblical view, the language of faith is translucent to its object, that is, it conveys partial light of what it purports to signify. In the mystical view the language of faith is virtually opaque to its object. We know the true God not by reason but only by love. He can be described basically only by negation, by what he is not rather than by what he is *(via negativa).* In the rationalist view the language of faith is transparent to its object, that is, it presents a clear and distinct picture of who God really is and of what he has done. Faith-language in the biblical view is analogical, for it is a language of proportionality. In the mystical view our language about God is metaphorical, for its function is to raise us to a higher consciousness rather than give real knowledge. In the rationalist view it is univocal, for the human concepts and phrases that

Scripture uses exactly correspond to what they signify. As opposed to both mystical ineffability on the one hand and rational transparency on the other, I uphold the way of revelational translucency.

Philosophy by its very nature tends toward univocity or the language of identity. John Stuart Mill here speaks for many philosophers: "Unless I believe God to possess the same moral attributes which I find, in however inferior a degree, in a good man, what ground of assurance have I of God's veracity? All trust in a Revelation presupposes a conviction that God's attributes are the same, in all but degree, with the best human attributes."[29] Biblical faith, on the contrary, maintains that, largely because of human sin, there is a cleavage between thought and being and that the test of truth is neither rational clarity nor pragmatic efficacy but fidelity to the promises and commandments in Holy Scripture.

While the language of faith can at most be analogical or parabolic, faith looks forward to the time when the veil will be lifted and we shall see God face to face. This is why faith itself is something provisional; only love is eternal. "Now we see through a glass, darkly; but then face to face" (1 Cor 13:12 KJV). Jesus said, "These things I have spoken to you in figurative language; but the time is coming when I will no longer speak to you in figurative language, but I will tell you plainly about the Father" (Jn 16:25 NKJ). In the eschatological denouement of history, there will be a restoration to the peoples of a "pure language" so that "they all may call on the name of the LORD" (Zeph 3:9 NKJ).

Again, it must be emphasized that the mystery of revealed truth is not encapsulated in any human language, not even the language of sacred Scripture. Instead, the truth of this mystery is bestowed on this language as a gift in the awakening to faith. We know not through an exploration into the symbolic roots of the faith[30] but through a divine-human encounter, which illumines both the symbols and concepts of faith while at the same time underlining their rudimentary and limited character. Symbols in and of themselves yield neither participatory awareness of a higher level of reality nor tacit knowledge of such a reality; yet under the impact of the Spirit they can communicate real knowledge of reality in itself, knowledge that cannot build a system of being (as in Hegel) but can direct us to the pathway to salvation.

## Dialectic and Paradox

In addition to analogy the key components in theological language are dialectic and paradox. Theology shares with philosophy a deep-seated respect for the canons of logic, but it insists that in describing the mystery of divine revelation in human history, we have to make use of forms of thought and procedure that transcend the limitations of general human discourse.

The concept of dialectic has a venerable philosophical tradition. It originally meant a method of argumentation that took the form of dialog. In Socrates it was the art of question and answer in which truth latent within us would be brought into the open. In Aristotle it signified a pattern of logical reasoning. In medieval theology it consisted in the pairing of contrasting opinions followed by an attempt to reconcile them. In Hegel it was the dynamic process of universal reality through thesis, antithesis and synthesis, reflected in history. In Kierkegaard it was a method of holding together affirmations that are diametrically antithetical.

Modern dialectical theology (Barth, Brunner) is based on the view that there is neither an identity between thought and being (as in Platonic idealism) nor a direct correspondence (as in realism), but instead a cleavage, which is the result not of finitude per se but of sin. This cleavage is overcome in the paradoxical entry of eternity into time, that is, in the Incarnation of the infinite God in Jesus of Nazareth. All contradictions in human thinking concerning God and his relationship to us have their center in this absolute paradox (Kierkegaard), which is incomprehensible to human reason. Dialectical theology, says Brunner, is

> seeking to declare the Word of the Bible to the world. . . . What the Word of God does is to expose the contradiction of human existence, then in grace to cover it. . . . It is only by means of the contradiction between two ideas—God and man, grace and responsibility, holiness

and love—that we can apprehend the contradictory truth that the eternal God enters time, or that the sinful man is declared just. Dialectical theology is the mode of thinking which defends this paradoxical character, belonging to faith-knowledge, from the non-paradoxical speculation of reason, and vindicates it against the other.[31]

In his earlier period Barth envisaged a philosophical dialectic that proceeds by question and counterquestion to a synthesis that is never actualized in time. In place of the classical theological methods of gaining knowledge of God (the *via affirmativa,* the *via negativa* and the *via eminentiae)* he presented the *via dialectica,* in which polar pairs are held together in the response of faith—infinity and finitude, eternity and time, judgment and grace. In Barth's view the knowledge of God is not a direct apprehension of revelation but of ourselves being known in the experience of faith.[32] Barth was poignantly aware that this position leads to agnosticism regarding God unless it is drastically modified or reformulated.

As Barth progressed in his thinking he veered away from philosophical dialectics, in which we move toward God by the art of affirmations and negations, to a theological dialectic, in which we explore the implications of God's coming to us in Jesus Christ. Barth became convinced that dialectic of itself was ineffectual to bring the believer real knowledge of God, that God himself must break into our dialectic and turn it around before we can begin to know God in the mystery of his revealedness and hiddenness.[33] The theological dialectic is based on an event in time, which is the center around which question and answer constantly revolve and cannot move away.

Some critics allege that Barth abandoned dialectical theology for analogy after he began the *Church Dogmatics.*[34] But they overlook the fact that Barth regarded theological dialectics as necessary to theological reasoning even when he came to appreciate the concept of analogy as giving us positive knowledge of God. Barth acknowledged that dialectics "may still try to set up a system, to close the circle, or to think it has closed the circle, when in fact all it can ever do is to draw out

---

radii continually from the center."[35] "The dialectic still remains on our part: yet not in such a way that we are still in the grip of that dialectic; rather in such a way that the dialectic is directed and controlled from the side of the event which is God's part."[36]

I agree with Barth and Brunner that dialectical reasoning is necessary in the theological enterprise because the paradox of the eternal God dramatically entering the stream of human history in Jesus Christ can be grasped only through holding together aspects of the truth about God and his plan of salvation that seem contradictory to human reason. We cannot conceive of the unity between the two natures of Christ and the two sides of salvation (divine predestination and the human decision), but we can believe in this unity and try to explicate it as best we can. Torrance makes the trenchant point that the Spirit is the "act of God upon us which keeps our concepts or cognitive forms open, so that our thought and speech are stretched out beyond themselves toward the inexhaustible nature of the divine Being. . . . If we close these concepts in order to give them the kind of precision apposite only to concepts we develop in knowledge of determinate realities, then we smother knowledge of God and evade His Reality."[37]

Ellul has forcefully argued that dialectic is anchored in revelation itself, for the dynamics of revelation necessitates a method of reasoning designed to hold together polar opposites— grace and freedom, divine law and human law, Christ and culture.[38] Unlike philosophical thinking, theological dialectic refuses to resolve contradictions; instead, it strives to keep them in creative tension with each other.

Dialectical theology is an open-ended theology, whose formulations are ever tentative. The synoptic vision or final synthesis belongs only to God, but we can bear witness to this through our approximate formulations. The Word of God is not broken or refracted, but our theological formulations must remain so, and this means that we dare not presume to pronounce absolutely the last word (Barth).

Theological dialectics is based on the dialog between the creature and its Creator, not on reason dialoging with itself. In this enterprise we are led by the Spirit to a higher unity, but always one that reminds us that our theology is a *theologia viatorum* (theology of wayfarers), not a *theologia beatorum* (theology of the blessed in heaven).

As already indicated, dialectics in the theological sense is closely associated with paradox. Genuine evangelical theology will not only be dialectical but also paradoxical. In its Greek derivation *paradox* means contrary to opinion or expectation. It is not a logical contradiction as such but a new creation that interrupts logical thinking and disturbs the flow of rational discourse. It does not so much contradict the canons of logic as overturn them—but only to the finite mind. In the mind or Logos of God, all contradictions are resolved. This means that a paradox does not indicate any bifurcation in reality, for reality is ultimately intelligible. In theology paradox functions as "a juncture or intersection for mystery."[39] It is not a logical riddle but a new reality that cannot be fully grasped by finite reason.

According to Kierkegaard there is only one absolute paradox, the event of God assuming human flesh in Jesus Christ.[40] All other paradoxes in Christian faith are derivative from or reflective of this one great paradox, which can be grasped not by reason but only by faith. Yet Kierkegaard maintained that while faith removes the absurdity of the paradox, the mystery remains.

Like dialectic, paradox keeps our theology humble, forcing us to acknowledge that the reality of which we speak cannot be mastered by human reasoning. In the words of Ellul, "Paradox, always related to the word springing up as something new, prevents thought from closing up and reaching completion. Paradox prevents the system from accounting for everything, and does not allow a structure to mold everything."[41]

It was Barth's conviction that "the Word of God alone fulfills the concept of paradox with complete strictness, whereas in all other thinkable 'paradoxes' the opposition between communication and form is such that it can be dissolved from some superior point of vantage."[42] Yet he urged more sparing use of this concept in theology because it can easily cause confusion rather than strengthen understanding.[43]

Indeed, as his theology developed, Barth moved away from both dialectics and paradox without jettisoning these concepts. This perhaps accounts for the fact that he began to lapse into objectivism, thereby failing to hold together the polar opposites of grace and faith, predestination and obedience, heaven and hell.[44] Dialectical theology at its best maintains the object-subject antithesis, and once this antithesis is overcome the paradoxical character of the faith is subverted. Tillich departed from a theology of paradox when he sought for a God beyond the God of the divine-human encounter, for a unity that dissolved the object-subject antithesis.

The predilection of philosophy is to overcome the polarities and ambiguities of life by arriving at a synthesis that perfects and crowns human reasoning. It cannot tolerate anything that defies rational comprehension, for this is to acknowledge a surd in human existence.[45]

On the other hand, mysticism gives up the quest for rational understanding and is content to remain in the darkness of faith, preferring to leave God wrapped in mystery and obscurity. With profound satisfaction Dionysius the Pseudo-Areopagite could describe God as "the dazzling Darkness" and "the super-essential Darkness." Mystics do not claim to have a theoretical knowledge of God but only a sense of God's presence. Gerald Heard is typical: "Silence and darkness are almost essential conditions for a practical man's deepest worship. For his knowledge of himself, which is not slight but intuitional, teaches him where his reason must stop and he with it wait, while the metareason does its work."[46]

The biblical theologian contends that our knowledge of God is neither clear and distinct (as in rationalism) nor abstruse and recondite (as in mysticism) but dialectical and paradoxical. It is a knowledge that is on the way to comprehension rather than one that claims comprehension.

Orthodoxy acknowledges that the divine content of faith is more true than plain, whereas heresy sees it as more plain than true (Richard Hooker). Heresy in its effort to gain rationality ends by dissolving mystery. Orthodoxy humbly recognizes that God's self-revelation in Christ is characterized neither by mystical ineffability nor by rational clarity but by paradoxical intelligibility. Thus it can be known but only partially, because "human words and concepts can never fully echo God's inexhaustible Word and Wisdom."[47]

**The Divine Names**

While the human words and concepts employed by the Holy Spirit in the formation of the Scriptures fall short of bringing us univocal knowledge of God, they nevertheless give us vital information that we neglect only at our peril. There is no meaning without words: the pathway to the transcendent source and ground of meaning lies through the medium of words.

Evangelical theology holds that the primal symbols that describe God in the Bible are not ciphers pointing beyond themselves to imageless transcendence but *names* by which Transcendence discloses its innermost being to us. A name in the Bible reveals the character and personality of the subject. The name and being of God are often used in parallelism with one another, thereby inferring their practical identity (cf. 1 Kings 8:16; Ps 18:49; 68:4; 74:18; 86:12; 92:1; Is 25:1; Mal 3:16).[48]

When we name something we have power over it. By naming the animals, Adam was given dominion over them (Gen 2:19-20; cf. 2 Sam 12:28). But we cannot name God because God is hidden from our sight and understanding. God must name himself, and he has done so in Holy Scripture. He reveals himself as the "One who is" or "I am who I am" or "I am He who is" (Ex 3:13-14; 6:2-3).[49] This name is usually pronounced *Yahweh*, though the original pronunciation was lost in the postexilic period.[50] Because of the increasing sanctity associated with the proper name of God, it was often rendered as *Adonai* (in the Hebrew, meaning "my great Lord"). This social title for God came to be used more and more in common worship.

Besides the proper or personal name for God, *Yahweh*, generic names for God in Old Testament history include *Elohim, Eloah, El Shaddai* ("God the Almighty"), *El Elyon* ("God Most High"), *El Berith* ("God of the Covenant") and *El Olam* ("God of Eternity"). *Yahweh Sabaoth* ("Lord of

Hosts"), which depicts God as the commander of armies, and *Yahweh Elohim* are compound names for God that carry the power and intimacy of a proper name. *El Shaddai* and *El Elyon* are sometimes paired with *Yahweh* and thereby share some of the personal flavor and warmth of that name (cf. Ps 21:7; 91:9-10).[51]

In the New Testament God reveals himself as Lord *(Kyrios),* Father *(Patēr)* and *Abba* (the Aramaic word for "dear Father").[52] The latter term, which Jesus and the apostles used in invoking God in prayer, indicates special warmth and intimacy (Mk 14:36; Rom 8:15; Gal 4:6). The designation of God as Father was already evident among the Old Testament prophets (cf. Deut 32:6; Is 63:16; 64:8; Jer 3:19; Ps 89:26), though not all that common.

God is also given the Trinitarian name—Father, Son and Spirit (Mt 28:19; 3:16-17; 2 Cor 13:14; 1 Pet 1:2). Some scholars (e.g., Robert Jenson) argue convincingly that this Trinitarian name came to function as the proper name for God in the apostolic church, equivalent to *Yahweh* in the Old Testament.[53] "Father, Son and Spirit" indicates not simply different roles that the one God assumes in relationship to his creatures (the heresy of modalism) but ontological distinctions within God himself—the mystery of one God in three persons or agencies of consciousness. The formula now in favor in avant-garde circles— "Creator, Redeemer, Sustainer"—fails to do justice to the concern of the church fathers that God is an ontological and not merely an economic Trinity.

In addition, God reveals himself under the name of Jesus, God incarnate. The Hebrew form is *Joshua* or *Jehoshua,* which means "Yahweh saves" or "Yahweh is salvation." The apostolic claim was that salvation is only in this name (Acts 4:12; cf. Ps 9:10; 54:1; 124:8; Mt 1:21; Jn 3:18). In John 8:58 Jesus identifies himself with the Tetragrammaton of Exodus 3:14: "I AM WHO I AM." Jesus is *Yahweh* in human flesh, the preexistent Son of God made man.

The name for God in the Bible is a unique symbol that reveals the inner character of God. It is a symbol that is at the same time a title,[54] and yet it is more than either of these: it mirrors the reality to whom we pray and for whom we hope. The name of God reveals who he is, not primarily how he acts or relates to the world. As soon as the faithful can pronounce the divine name, they are permitted through the power of this name to share in the glory of Yahweh.[55]

At the same time, the names for God are still analogical, not univocal, for there is a residue of mystery in these names. They reveal but do not exhaust the mystery of divinity. God is hidden even in the revelation of his name.

The name of God not only points to the divine reality but also encompasses this reality. Yet it does not exhaust this reality. Nor is its power resident within itself: its source is in the reality of God. The divine name is an extension of the divine presence, but only as an instrument or vehicle. The reality of God transcends our feeble articulation of this name.

To pronounce the name of God correctly does not guarantee access to the throne of God. We reach God only when we utter his name in the spirit of faith and penitence, acknowledging that our ability to name God in the right way rests on the movement of the Spirit of God within us. The reality of God cannot be seized, even by uttering his name; but once we are grasped by the divine reality we are then set free to confess his name as an act of faith and obedience.

Against the mystical type of religion, which seeks for a God beyond names and titles, Barth rightly maintains that "God is not anonymous. He has a name. He has made himself a name. He has made it known as his holy name. He has already hallowed it. He has already invested it with honor, validity, radiance, and glory."[56]

We do not accurately portray the God of the Bible simply by calling him "Father" or "Lord." The Greeks called Zeus "Father," though he was regarded only as the genitor of the gods, as first among equals, not as Creator. "Father" does not fully assume the character of a personal name until we acknowledge him as the Father of our Lord Jesus Christ.[57] He is to be envisaged not as a solitary Absolute nor simply as the primal source of all things but as the first person of the holy Trinity, as the

Father in unity with the Son and Holy Spirit in a fellowship of love.

"Father" is not an indefinite name for the divine essence (as in Arianism) but a personal name for God in his dynamic relatedness.[58] Indeed, God's essence is not a reality behind his relatedness, but it consists precisely in his relatedness as Father, Son and Spirit. God is not a solitary being utterly removed from the world but a divine Thou who addresses us in personal encounter.

It is not the idea of generation that gives significance to the Christian use of "Father" but the idea of election.[159] We are elected and adopted into the family of God as his sons and daughters, and this is why we acknowledge him as our Father in heaven.[60] Because we are elected to be conformed to the image of Jesus Christ, both true God and true man, he becomes our elder brother, "the first-born among many brethren" (Rom 8:29).

Evangelical theology argues against neoliberal and radical theologies that the names applied to God in the Bible represent God's own self-designation and therefore cannot be altered or revised. The name for God is a product of divine revelation, not a metaphor or symbol drawn from human experience and then applied to God.[61] Emil Brunner expresses it well:

> The mysterious God, whom the world neither knows nor shows, whom I do not know and whom the inner man does not reveal, must reveal his mystery to the world—must tell his own name—by "piercing" into the world. He must assert himself over against the world as a being who is not-world, not-ego; who reveals his true name, the secret of his unknown will which is opposed to the world.[62]

Idealistic philosophy envisages a God who cannot be encompassed in a name, for this signifies a constriction or narrowing of our conception of God.[63] Fichte exulted: "Sublime and Living Will! named by no name, compassed by no thought! I may well raise my soul to Thee, for Thou and I are not divided. Thy voice sounds within me, mine resounds in Thee; and all my thoughts, if they be but good and true, live in Thee also."[64]

Symbols that are merely symbols die when cultural understanding changes. But God's naming of himself never changes, since God cannot be other than who he is in his eternal being. Symbols in and of themselves are lifeless, but the name of God is filled with power, for it is the peculiar vehicle of the Spirit of God. This is why it is an abomination to take the name of the Lord in vain (Ex 20:7; Deut 5:11).

## Resymbolizing God

It is fashionable in modern theology to treat the language of the Bible as archaic and the names for God as anthropomorphisms that reflect a patriarchal and backward culture. Theology, it is said, needs to search for a new language concerning God (Altizer, Cobb), a new conceptuality that is more inclusive and less naive than the biblical imagery.

Feminists complain that the Bible is hopelessly immersed in a patriarchal culture that relegates women to an inferior status. In order to make the message of the Bible credible to the new world-consciousness we must therefore proceed to desex and depatriarchalize the language of the Bible. Our task, they say, is to seek a more inclusive language for God that takes into consideration the feminine as well as the masculine dimension of the sacred. We should welcome new symbols for God such as "Womb of Being," "Womb and Birth of Time," "Primal Matrix," "Empowering Matrix" and "Immanent Mother."

Existentialists of the Bultmannian variety argue that the language of the Bible is palpably mythological and that the task of theology is to demythologize this language in order to uncover its universal meaning for human existence. People today, says Bultmann, can no longer believe in a world of spirits and miracles, and the mythical garb of the text therefore presents a serious obstacle to faith in the crucified and risen Lord.

Tillich complains that the language of the Bible is burdened with supernaturalism and anthropomorphism, and we are therefore obliged to deliteralize or desupernaturalize the biblical witness. For Tillich, Christ is a symbol that is more universal than the historical Jesus. Our faith is not in Jesus as the incarnate Son of God but in the Christ Spirit or New Being that appeared in Jesus but also in other spiritual masters in history.

Process theologians relegate the Bible to the realm of poetry and therefore plead for a new conceptualization of biblical faith. The traditional symbolism of faith, they tell us, must be put in the framework of a modern ontology if it is to speak to people today. To call God "Father" is anthropomorphic, whereas to envisage God as the Creative Process or as the power of creative transformation is to understand who or what God really is.

The German Christians, that segment within the church who felt led to accommodate the faith to the ideology of National Socialism in the 1930s, also sought a new language for divinity.[65] They objected to the Judaic character of the Bible and were determined to de-Judaize the language of faith. Instead of "the people of Israel" they spoke of "the people of God." The liturgy and hymnody of the church were purged of Judaic expressions like "Amen" and "Hallelujah." In the more radical groups God was referred to as "Eternal Creative Power," "Eternal Divine Force" or "Great Mother." Yahweh, the God of the Old Testament, they insisted, is remote and fearful, whereas the God of German spirituality is present in the depths of the human soul. Jesus was no longer King of the Jews but now the flower or prototype of a new humanity.

It is well to note in the light of the present controversy over inclusive language that the German Christians were also seeking a more inclusive language for God. God, they said, must not be restricted to biblical history but must now be seen as revealing himself in universal history. Ernst Bergmann envisioned God as bisexual, not as exclusively masculine. According to Emanuel Hirsch, one of the more perspicacious German Christian theologians, Jesus saw God "as the God of humanity, so his is a universal, eternal religion," while the Jews addressed their prayers to a God of the Jews only.[66]

Against the German Christians and the Nazi ideology, the Barmen Declaration was drawn up in 1934 by concerned churchmen, both

Lutheran and Reformed, who were intent on maintaining the integrity of the gospel in a time of theological ambivalence and dissolution. The Barmen Declaration rejected "the false doctrine that the church could and should acknowledge as a source of its proclamation, beyond and besides this one Word of God, yet other events and powers, figures and truths, as God's revelation."[67] It also repudiated "the false doctrine that the church could have permission to abandon the form of its message" in order to bring it into accord with "currently reigning ideological and political convictions."[68] Barmen speaks directly to the theological situation today, when the language of the Bible is being replaced by language informed by ideological movements in the culture and when an appeal is made to new revelations in our national history or in universal human history that supersede or correct the biblical revelation.

In the history of Christian thought, the Gnostics and the Neoplatonic mystics introduced a more inclusive language for God against traditional Christian piety, which they considered hopelessly naive. The Gnostics envisaged God as bisexual; the feminine element represented the Eternal Silence and the masculine the Primal Depth (Bythos).[69] God is not a Trinity but an androgynous unity in which masculine and feminine elements are perfectly balanced and harmonized. Thus, to call God "Father" is to make God parochial. The Gnostics pressed for a God beyond fatherhood—an "Eternal Silence" or "Primal Ground" or "Incomprehensible One." God cannot be named because he is "the totally different, the other, the unknown."[70] Gnostic themes are conspicuous in our time in the philosophy of Carl Jung, who has had a decided impact on New Age spirituality.[71]

Among the Christian mystics we discern a similar attempt to rise to the "God above God," the undifferentiated unity beyond personality, temporality and individuality. For Dionysius God "is a Unity which is the unifying Source of all unity and a Super-Essential Essence, a Mind beyond the reach of mind and a Word beyond utterance, eluding Discourse, Intuition, Name, and every kind of being."[72] "When the mind has stripped away from its idea of God the human modes of thought and inadequate conceptions of the Deity, it enters upon the 'Darkness of Unknowing.' "[73] Nicholas of Cusa envisaged a God beyond all human designations: "This alone I know, that I know not what I see, and never can know. And I know not how to name Thee because I know not what Thou art, and did anyone say unto me that Thou wert called by this name or that, by the very fact that he named it, I should know that it was not Thy name. For the wall beyond which I see Thee is the end of all manner of signification in names."[74] For Meister Eckhart God was "the Secret Silence," "the Source," "the Abyss," "the One" and "Absolute Existence."

Eckhart's images would be entirely acceptable to Paul Tillich, in whose theology one can detect a synthesis of classical mysticism, gnosticism and the dynamic process mysticism of the modern age. God is resymbolized as "the infinite abyss," "the infinite ground and depth of all being," "the Spiritual Presence," "the Eternal Now," "the unconditional" and "Being-itself." Tillich seeks for a God beyond "the divine-human encounter," a "God above God," a God of the depths rather than a God of the heights. This is a God of whom we can have only a participatory awareness, not a theoretical knowledge. This is a God who can be described only by symbols but not truly known by any revealed name. Tillich's thought provides a philosophical basis for neognostics and feminists today as they press for a more inclusive language for God. But God then becomes an impersonal or suprapersonal ground or source of being rather than a divine being in action who encounters and dialogs with us as persons.

I think it can be shown that the quest for a new language about God is prompted by a change in the cultural understanding of God. Ever since the Enlightenment the picture of God as a moral agent, as a supernatural being who intervenes in history, has fallen into disrepute. In its place has arisen a God who is not above the universe as its sovereign Lord and Creator but a part of the universe as its ground and source of vitality. A monistic perspective has supplanted the metaphysics of supernatural creationism. The deepest within the universe and within ourselves is now seen as divine. In order to worship this God, immanent in nature and history, we therefore seek new names, new symbols that speak to the religious imagination.

It is my contention that when we change the language about God we are basically moving into another religion. To resymbolize is to redeify, it is to fashion a new God more in accord with our cultural context and experience.[75] To see God as a creative process (process theology), or the power of the future (liberation theology) or the Womb of Being (feminist theology) is no longer to view God as Father, Son and Holy Spirit. Rosemary Ruether quite candidly admits that a shift to inclusive language amounts to the creation of a new God: "A new God is being born in our hearts to teach us to level the heavens and exalt the earth and create a new world without masters and slaves, rulers and subjects."[76]

Feminist theologians in particular are inclined to view "Father" as merely a metaphor for God drawn from patriarchal culture and experience. They therefore see no problem in calling God "Mother," a metaphor they find more congruous with woman's experience. Against this position I maintain that "Father" in the context of the believing community is not a metaphor based on cultural experience but an ontological symbol describing the relationship of the first person of the Trinity to the Son and then to the Spirit.[77] It is God's designation of himself in relationship to Jesus Christ first of all and then to the members of Christ's body. Our human conceptions of fatherhood are judged and transformed in the light of God's self-revelation as Father. In coming to know God as the loving, heavenly Father we are then obliged to question patriarchal conceptions that portray father as tyrannical ruler and wife and children as his subjects. It is from the fatherhood of God that all human fatherhood is named, not vice versa (cf. Eph 3:15).

Pannenberg presents a convincing argument that when "Father" is replaced by another symbol, "there can be no warrant anymore that we are talking about and addressing the same God Jesus did." In Jesus' teaching and prayer "the word 'Father' came to function as a name, not a mere symbol. . . . Only in that way of addressing God and of relating

to him did the unspeakable divine mystery acquire personal quality."
According to Pannenberg the personal character of the God whom
Christians worship is inseparably bound up with the word "Father" as
used by Jesus.

> The word "Son" as indicating a second "person" in the trinity is
> derived from "Father" as a personal name for God, and it is only in
> relation to the Father and the Son that the Spirit could be considered
> as personal too. Hence the personal concreteness of God, at least in
> the Christian tradition, depends on the name "Father.". . . The ex-
> change of this name inevitably results in turning to another God.[78]

It should be kept in mind that the fatherhood of God includes his moth-
erhood. He is a Father in whom the motherly traits of birthing and nurturing are exemplified.[79] Indeed, a number of passages in both Testa-
ments describe God's activity in motherly terms (Deut 32:11; Job 38:29;
Ps 131:2; Is 49:14-15; 42:14-15; 66:13; Mt 23:37). Yet God is nowhere
addressed as mother, nor is God ever depicted as primarily female, as
was the case with the Canaanite religions that Israelite monotheism
sought to replace.[80] In contrast to the gods of the Canaanites, Yahweh
has no consort, for he utterly transcends all natural and biological processes. It is the church as the bride and wife of Yahweh that becomes his
consort. We ourselves as the community of believers assume the role of
the feminine in relation to God, who confronts us in the mode of the
masculine. Gerd Theissen points to this transcendent quality in the God
of the Hebrews: "Because the one God is imagined without wife, sexuality and procreation, he is thought of independently of the basic biological processes. His power is not the power of fertility. His love is not
a sexual bond. He stands outside procreation and birth, sexuality and
death, beyond 'biological evolution' and the sphere of the 'flesh,' as the
Bible calls it."[81]

To be sure, the mother goddess tried again and again to make a
comeback, and the whole history of Israel is the story of the struggle
between the Sky Father and the Earth Mother.[82] In the Wisdom literature Wisdom becomes the spiritualized form of the mother goddess, but

Wisdom is not an independent person alongside God. Rather, "she is a hypostasis of a divine characteristic, a personification of his gracious side which is turned towards the world."[83] Wisdom in this sense is wholly compatible with the claims of monotheistic faith.

The God of the Bible completely transcends sexuality, but he includes gender within himself. He is neither male nor female, but he chooses to relate to us in the form of the masculine—as Father, Son and Holy Spirit. But there is a feminine dimension of the sacred as well—God returning to himself in the form of the church, the mystical body of Christ.[84] The feminine side of God is hidden in the masculine, and we ourselves experience this mothering activity of God as we are nurtured and embraced by the Spirit incarnate in the church as the gathered community of believers. Yet it does not follow that we should call God "Mother" or think of God as female, for this is to return to goddess spirituality, the very thing condemned by the Hebrew prophets and later by the fathers of the church when it resurfaced in the form of Gnosticism.[85] Elizabeth Achtemeier rightly says: "As soon as God is called female, the images of birth, of suckling, of carrying in the womb and, most importantly, the identification of the deity with the life in all things becomes inevitable, and the Bible's careful and consistent distinction between Creator and creation is blurred and lost."[86]

This does not mean, however, that we should therefore think of God as primarily or exclusively male, for God is neither male nor female, even though he chooses to relate to us as Father, Son and Spirit.[87] Hosea warns that God is God and "not man" (Hos 11:9), and it is to be acknowledged that this prophetic warning was often eclipsed when the church came to take on the trappings of the surrounding patriarchal culture.[88] God is not the "Man upstairs" but sovereign Lord, yet one who chooses to exercise his lordship in the form of a servant. He is not simply a provider and protector of his family but a Savior who lays down his life for his sons and daughters. If we call God "Father" out of a patriarchal bias, thereby conveying the impression that God is a petty tyrant or arbitrary ruler rather than the fount of mercy and grace, then we are praying to an idol even though it bears the name of Father. The father-hood of God in biblical perspective does not ratify but instead calls into radical question every patriarchal conception of fatherhood.[89]

In the shift to a new language for God in the modern church, we must be alert to ideological factors that constantly intrude in theological spec-ulation. David Tracy rightly underlines the need for "ethical and political criticism of the hidden, even repressed, social and historical ideologies in . . . all language as discourse, and, above all, in all interpretations."[90] The patriarchal background of the biblical texts must be fully acknowl-edged, but what feminists do not always see is that this patriarchal imagery is utilized and transformed in the light of a criterion that over-turns both patriarchy and matriarchy.[91] The language of patriarchy was nonetheless chosen by God for his self-revelation in Jesus Christ be-cause, as Barth says, it preserves the biblical principle of an above and below, a before and after. Hierarchy is not to be jettisoned in favor of a democratic egalitarianism but is to be reinterpreted in the light of God's self-condescension in the form of the suffering servant.

The ideological complexion of modern theologies is beyond dispute for those who have made a serious investigation of this dimension in theological discourse. Feminist theology can be shown to be integrally tied to the movement of modern women for equality and autonomy; this is especially evident in the economic sphere of life, where mobility and independence are required for advancement on the corporate ladder. Process theology is organically related to the ideals of democratic egal-itarianism with the result that God is portrayed not as king or lord but as "the fellow-sufferer who understands" (Whitehead).[92] Liberation theology is unabashedly ideological in its commitment to the struggle of oppressed peoples for economic and political justice.[93] Not surprisingly, God is resymbolized as the "courage to struggle" and the "event of self-liberating love."

This is not to deny that new language about God can be used wher-ever appropriate as a supplement to the language of Canaan or the language of Zion. God can indeed be regarded as the power of creative transformation, but not to the exclusion of his proper name—Father, Son and Spirit. God the Holy Spirit is indeed God in action, and this entails transformative creativity. God can legitimately be referred to as the ground of being, since he is the source and goal of our life. But he is ground of being only in his role as sovereign Creator; he is not a mystical depth of being that simply upholds us in our struggle for fulfillment.

Some designations gravely distort the true nature of the Godhead. There is no way in which God can rightly be called the "Womb of Being" or "Primal Matrix," for here God is portrayed as fundamentally immanent whereas the God of the Bible is transcendent before he is immanent. His action in bringing the world into being precedes his omnipresence in the world.

The temptation today is to discard the biblical forms of expression on the grounds that they are the product of a patriarchal or Judaic culture.[94] But this is precisely the language in which God has chosen to reveal himself, and we cannot discard it without losing sight of the God who is symbolized in it. Form and content belong together, and when the content is placed in a new form it is invariably altered, sometimes dramatically. I take vigorous exception to Sallie McFague's asseveration that "religious language in the Judeo-Christian tradition excludes us all, for it is largely biblical language," whose concerns are not ours.[95] We should bear in mind that the language of the gospel is both a stumbling block to the Jews and foolishness to the Greeks (1 Cor 1:23). It continues to be an obstacle to our self-understanding until the self is crucified and a new self is created by the Holy Spirit.

Jacques Ellul expresses well my own sentiments: "People no longer understand Christian vocabulary, so we must change it. This is both true and false. It is much more serious than a simple matter of vocabulary; a different choice of words cannot really change the situation. What people do not understand is not certain words but the word itself."[96] Ellul acknowledges that we need to supplement the biblical language, but he warns against abandoning it.

We are here face to face with the mystery of faith. We cannot really know Jesus Christ until our inward eyes are opened in the moment of decision. Apart from this miracle of grace Christ will remain both an enigma and an offense to us. But once our eyes are opened we will then recognize him as the Christ of the Scriptures, the Christ who is the preexistent Son of God and Lord of the universe, who is God himself together with the Father and the Holy Spirit. We cannot have Christ or know Christ apart from the Scriptures, and this also means apart from the language of the Scriptures. The mythopoetic language of Scripture does not need to be superseded but is to be treated with the utmost seriousness as the divinely elected garb in which the Spirit of God meets us and speaks to us.

From my perspective, theological language does not impute to God values drawn from human experience but relays to humanity the transvaluation of the world's values as we see this embodied in Jesus Christ. It is language in the service of a theology of the cross, which finds God only in the servant form of the crucified Christ and in the earthen vessel of the biblical witness to Christ. A theology of glory craves a direct, immediate knowledge of God that is not constricted by human thoughtforms and earthbound imagery. Evangelical theology humbly recognizes that only in God's gracious act of condescension in Jesus Christ as attested in Scripture can we gain knowledge of him, knowledge adequate for a pilgrimage of faith but not for comprehensive understanding. We apprehend God only in the sign, veil and work of his self-humiliation, in the historical particularity of his self-revelation. The sign is not the reality, but we have the reality only in the sign; thus a vital theology will always be characterized by reverence for the proclamation of Scripture as well as obedience to the Lord of Scripture.

## Words and Images

Christianity is a religion of the word rather than a religion of images. In fact, the commandment against making graven images (Ex 20:4; Deut 5:8; cf. Is 40:18-20) is an integral part of the moral foundation of biblical faith, and most commentators see this commandment as being directed against representations of God constructed not only by human hands but also by the human mind. Idolatry can take place in the imagination as well as in ritual practice, and the Bible warns against idolatry in all its sinister forms. Second Isaiah points to the inability of images to describe or represent God accurately: "To whom can you compare God? What image can you contrive of him?" (Is 40:18 NJB).[97] Paul warns that we are never to suppose that God's nature "is anything like an image of gold or silver or stone, shaped by the art and skill of man" (Acts 17:29 GNB). One can argue that the more lifelike and realistic the symbol, the more easily it can become an occasion for idolatry. Scripture insists that faith comes not by focusing first on symbolic representations of God, not by gazing at a great work of art, as Schleiermacher and Tillich suggest, but by hearing the word of God (Is 55:11; 66:5; Jn 5:24; 6:63; Rom 10:17; 1 Cor 1:21; 15:1-2; 2 Cor 5:20; Col 1:5). The psalmist implores his God: "Avert my eyes from pointless images, by your word give me life" (Ps 119:37 NJB). The organ of revelation in biblical faith is not the eye but the ear, though the former may direct us to the latter. "In order to see God," said Luther, "we must learn to stick our eyes in our ears."

An image in this discussion is understood as a representation of divinity that is designed to lead the human subject to a knowledge of divinity. An image need not be idolatrous. It can simply be a symbol that points beyond itself to a reality that exceeds the reach of human perception and imagination. Or it can be regarded as encompassing the divine presence so that it virtually becomes a mediator of divinity. This is when we begin to encounter the evil of idolatry.

We must avoid the temptation to think of God in terms of either imageless transcendence (as in philosophical idealism) or images that encompass or actualize transcendent reality (as in religious idolatry). Images and symbols can be used to direct us to God, but they must never be regarded as being in themselves transparent to God. Between the image, including the imagistic word, and the living God there is an infinite qualitative difference (cf. 2 Cor 4:17-18). In the last analysis it is not the symbol that leads us to God but it is the Spirit of God who makes use of the symbol to come to us. God descends into our language and our worship, thereby giving them meaning and power, but in themselves they have no power to bring us into contact with God.[98]

Of particular relevance to our study is Jacques Ellul's provocative *Humiliation of the Word,* in which he commends Paul Ricoeur's essay on proclamation versus manifestation.[99] Proclamation, which involves interpretation, is an act of speech. Manifestation is a showing forth of the sacred, as we find in the Greek mystery religions. In that type of religion the divine presence is contingent on the act of seeing or vision, but in Hebraic religion it is communicated through speaking and hearing.[100] In the mystery religions worship is a silent spectacle imposed on language, whereas in biblical religion worship is gathering to hear the Word of God. Ricoeur acknowledges that in the church there is a continual alternation between iconoclastic proclamation and symbolic manifestation. The latter can never be discarded, but the danger accrues when the symbol crowds out the word, "which is less concrete, less evident, more austere and demanding."[101] "In all periods of Church history," Ellul observes, "we find a renewed triumph of the image in statues, stained-glass windows, monuments, crucifixes, and relics. Although we cannot separate sight and language, only the Incarnation of Jesus shows us the correct equilibrium or synthesis, as we wait in hope for the fullness of the Kingdom."[102]

Ellul has some telling criticisms of the liturgical movement, which he accuses of substituting a religion of sight for faith in the Word of God. The word is present in the services of worship but "no longer is it a word that bears meaning. The Word is excluded and replaced by liturgical gestures, colors, changes of clothing, incantations, and litanies."[103]

In my judgment Ellul is perhaps too iconoclastic, seeking to expel all symbolism in worship. We must remember that our Reformed fathers also referred to the visible Word, the Word demonstrated in the celebration of baptism and the Lord's Supper. Yet they were adamant that the sacraments are ineffectual apart from the Word, written and proclaimed, and must therefore always be subordinated to the Word. The sacraments in and of themselves have no saving efficacy. They do not contain the sacred but instead witness to the sacred, which is invisible and wholly spiritual. In the sacrament we experience the breaking into our time and space of a higher reality that is inaccessible to sight and unamenable to reason. There is never an identity between the real presence of Christ and the elements of bread and wine, but the latter can be instruments by which we are grasped by the divine presence. They are not humanly contrived means by which we visually mount up to God but earthly signs by which God descends into our midst and speaks audibly to our hearts.

Among the three widely recognized types of religion—the mystical, the ritualistic and the prophetic—it is the last that emphasizes the sovereignty of hearing over sight and ipso facto the priority of language over images. Martin Luther here reflects the distinctive quality of prophetic faith: "A Christian . . . is not guided by what he sees or feels; he follows what he does not see or feel. He remains with the testimony of Christ; he listens to Christ's words and follows Him into the darkness."[104] In this kind of religion God remains unknown until he himself takes the initiative and reveals his will and purpose through the mouth of an ambassador or herald.

Ritualistic religion aspires to control the spiritual presence by tying it to outward rites and symbols. Sacraments are valued for their seeming capacity to relay divine power; supposedly they work *ex opere operato,* by the mere fact of being performed. The constant repetition of certain key words or phrases is believed to raise human consciousness to a higher spiritual plane. Litanies and processions are designed to put the worshiper in the proper spiritual mood. What is important is not the *content* but the *form* of prayer. Friedrich Heiler in his brilliant and controversial study on prayer delineates the notable contrast between ritualized prayer and the prophetic prayer of the heart, which is marked by spontaneity and directness.[105]

The biblical ideal of worship in spirit and truth is characterized not by pomp and ceremony but by the retelling of God's mighty deeds of judgment and mercy and rededication to the service of his glory. It is not the sacrifices of burnt offerings but the sacrifices of a broken spirit that are acceptable before the holy and righteous God (cf. Ps 51:16-17; 1 Sam 15:22; Jer 7:21-23; Hos 6:6). In biblical understanding sight is related to covetousness; what we see we can master or control.[106] Hearing, on the other hand, is associated with faith, for we are then wholly dependent on the speaker and our condition is one of waiting rather than strategic planning.

Like ritualistic religion, mysticism also emphasizes the priority of sight over hearing, though this is an inward or direct seeing. Outward symbols are helpful in guiding us on our mystical quest, but what we eventually see is beyond the compass of our senses.[107] Gerald Heard describes the "peacemaking Children of God" as those "purified of any wish but one—they have a single desire which has taken up their whole life and heart—to see God."[108] Nor, says Gregory of Nyssa, should one ever be satisfied with this desire: "One must always, by looking at what he can see, rekindle his desire to see more."[109] In mystical religion God is often depicted as the Supreme Beauty that we can contemplate and thereby be transfigured and perfected.

Prophetic religion also speaks of the vision of God, but this is understood as a meeting with God face to face in the eschatological fullness of time when we enter into a deeper and more intimate fellowship with him. It is not a contemplation of the essence of God in which we lose consciousness of ourselves or of our fellow humanity. The goal in religion is not contemplative bliss or ecstatic rapture but a fellowship of love (koinonia) that embraces the whole company of the saints.

The gulf between mystical and prophetic religion is similarly striking in the way they conceive of prayer. In mysticism prayer is rising above petition in order to gain an immediate apprehension of the beauty or goodness of God. It is not the pouring out of the soul before God (as in biblical spirituality) but contemplating the divine being. For Gerald Heard prayer is "a method of empirical discovery, a technique for contacting and learning to know Reality."[110] For the prophets prayer is baring the soul to God, struggling to bring our requests before him. It involves submitting to his will, to be sure, but only after striving to change his will so that our needs and desires are brought into the searing light of his presence.[111]

Mysticism of a practical bent is evident in Schleiermacher, whose religion was oriented much more about sight than hearing with faith.[112] He contended that religion thrives best in the "more familiar conversation of friendship . . . where glance and action are clearer than words."[113] More than anything else "the sight of a great and sublime work of art" awakens one to the depth and grandeur of the Universe.[114] What is central in his theology is not Jesus Christ, the God-man, but the *Urbild* or the image of Christ as "essential man."

A similar thrust is discernible in both Herrmann and Tillich, who show an unmistakable affinity to mystical spirituality, though the ethical note is also conspicuous. According to Herrmann we come to know the reality of Christ by focusing on the image *(Bild)* of Christ.[115] In Tillich what is decisive for Christian faith is the picture of Christ presented in the New Testament rather than the historicity of Jesus of Nazareth.[116] It is not the kerygmatic proclamation of what God has done for us in Christ but the reality of the New Being that appears in Jesus, rekindling our sense of the all-encompassing presence of God. In this perspective Christ is a symbol of a higher reality rather than the Word made flesh in a particular person in history.

It is important to note that words or doctrinal formulas can also become images. That is, they may lose their power to point beyond themselves and become simply visual representations of transcendent reality. The words themselves may be invested with divine authority, whereas in the biblical view words are carriers of a meaning that has its origin in the Spirit of God. Ellul contends that once the word is written, "it no longer has the sting of truth it had when said by another person—even when the simplest things were said. No one is involved any longer. The truth is reduced to visual signs, which mean nothing in themselves."[117] Language is thus "reduced by being written down. It ceases being multicentered and flowing, evocative and mythological."[118] Yet he acknowledges that even written language can be the bearer of meaning when it is united by the Spirit to God's own word in Christ. It is filled with life "only when it serves as a support and starting point for a word that is spoken, announced, or proclaimed."[119] That is, we do not really know the Word of God until God himself speaks his Word, and he may indeed speak in conjunction with our reading of Holy Scripture or our hearing of the sermon, but his speaking may occur over and above, even against, our hearing and reading.

God is free; though we are bound to the so-called means of grace, he is not so bound. He may choose to encounter us through the words of angels, as Thomas Aquinas admitted, instead of the words of his prophets and apostles, though what the angels proclaim on such occasions would be none other than the gospel attested in Holy Scripture. Could God ever encounter us in an image or symbol created by the church in order to facilitate or stimulate faith? Certainly the Spirit is free to use even images and symbols to his glory, but we must remember that the devil is also at work using such things to direct us away from the Word to our own feelings and experiences. Images do not have to become idolatrous, but they are easily misused in this way, particularly when religious experience is elevated into a criterion of faith on the same level as the gospel. The gospel is more likely to overturn and redirect our reason and experience than to ratify and confirm them.

In a religion focused on images we become spectators. In a religion oriented about the spoken word we are made active participants, for we are then involved in the process of interpretation. Sight bypasses reasoning, whereas the word of proclamation demands interpretation on the part of both pastor and congregation.

The kingdom of God is not coming "with signs to be observed" (Lk 17:20) but with a power and efficacy that breaks through all attempts to visualize and thereby constrict this reality. It is not a visible phenomenon that can be measured but a new reality implanted within us, transcending sight and comprehension. It can be experienced but not mastered, believed but never controlled. The kingdom of God is the work of the Holy Spirit who fills us with the fruits of the resurrection victory of Christ—but never without the Word. It is in hearing the message of the crucified and risen Lord that we come to know the reality and power of his resurrection triumph over the forces of chaos and darkness.

Not surprisingly, the emphasis on hearing over sight is much more conspicuous in the churches of the Reformation, particularly those in the Puritan tradition, than in either Roman Catholicism or Eastern Orthodoxy.[120] Yet this evangelical note can also be detected in the Catholic and Orthodox communions as well. Significantly, Karl Barth cites these words from a sacramental hymn by Thomas Aquinas:

Sight, feeling, taste delude themselves about thee.
By hearing alone is sure faith
given.
Only what God's Son has said
do I believe.
The Word is truth, and what can
be more true?[121]

Another Catholic sacramental hymn affirms:

When the senses fail to discern,
Certainty for the pure heart
Is given by faith alone.[122]

The evangelical distrust of images is less evident in Eastern Orthodoxy, which is unabashedly oriented about "the power of visionary insight."[123] In this tradition religious symbols are believed to be invested with sacramental power and thereby become bearers of the Transcendent.[124] Yet we have this cautionary word from the modern Russian Orthodox spiritual theologian Alexander Yelchaninov:

The mysterious sphere of art—so attractive, so enchanting—affords its servants but little assistance in drawing nearer to what we call truth; their usual characteristics are selfishness, pride, the thirst for fame, often extreme sensuality. In any case—the sphere of art is not spiritual, but is merely psychological. . . . It seems increasingly evident to me that our decorative, pompous rites must end, have already ended, are now artificial and dispensable; they have ceased to nourish the thirsting soul and must be replaced by different, more active and more congenial types of religious communion. . . . How little our rites—with the priest separated from the faithful by the wall of the *iconostase,* with the freezing space of inlaid floor between the faithful and the altar, with the coolness of the "visitors" towards each other, the chalice presented in vain with the stubborn refusal to approach it—how little all this resembles the religious meetings of the age of the Apostles and the martyrs! The religious element fails, while the decorative develops; the flame in the soul diminishes, while the gilded electric lamps grow brighter.[125]

Yelchaninov bemoans the dependence on sight over faith and lauds those who believe "without seeing." "Yet, we may object, our Lord gave Thomas a tangible evidence of His reality. But this would not help a sinful soul: we may see and not believe, as did the Pharisees."[126] Our Lord was certainly not pleased by Thomas's request for a sign.

Unfortunately, in all Christian communions, including Reformation Protestantism, naked dependence on the Word has slowly but surely given way to a fascination with the visual that borders on idolatry. In today's theological climate liturgy more often than not obscures and downplays the Word instead of elevating it. We need a recovery of the pre-eminent role of biblical preaching, joyous hymn singing and free prayer in the worship services of churches that claim to stand on the gospel alone for their power and sustenance.[127] Liturgy and sacraments have a rightful place in evangelical worship, but unless they serve the ministry of the Word they will subvert rather than enhance true devotion.

**Appendix B: On Meaning**
Language has power only because it is the bearer of meaning. In idealistic philosophy meaning is the idea that a word expresses. In empirical

realistic philosophy meaning is the congruence between a word and the object that it designates. In biblical perspective meaning is the intent given to a word by the Spirit of God in order to direct us to the fount of meaning, the Logos or Word of God. The meaning of the language of faith is not *scientia*, knowledge based on empirical analysis, but *sapientia*, the wisdom that comes from knowing the source and goal of human existence.

Wittgenstein has said that the meaning of a word lies in its use. The biblical theologian would say that the meaning of a word lies in its relationship to the ultimate criterion and source of meaning, the wisdom of God. It is not simply how we use words that determines their meaning but how the Spirit guides us in our use of words to their revelatory significance.

The tradition of modern rationalism, what Jerry Gill calls "critical philosophy," defines meaning in terms of a "static, one-to-one relationship between objects and linguistic signs."[1] Reflecting the legacy of Descartes, it regards absolute precision as necessary for the fulfillment of meaning.

In the biblical view meaning does not lie in scientific exactitude or logical precision but in fidelity to Jesus Christ, who alone signifies the fulfillment and perfection of meaning. Existence apart from Jesus Christ ends in meaninglessness or absurdity. The fragmentary meanings we can acquire on our own lead only to confusion unless they are united with the source and goal of all meaning, the divine *sophia*, the wisdom of God. Meaning takes place in discourse between two or more subjects. It denotes the abiding significance of what transpires in the event of discourse. The meaning of a biblical text is revealed only in the act of discourse between the ultimate author, the Holy Spirit, and the reader or hearer who comes to the Scriptures in faith. Meaning in this ultimate sense is therefore a gift, not an achievement. It is something we can hope and pray for, not something we can obtain on the basis of our own ingenuity and diligence.

The key to meaning lies not in our power of perceptivity but in our receptivity to the divine initiative. "To 'see God,' " as Torrance astutely observes, "we must renounce the criterion of perceptibility and learn to 'hear' Him, but hear Him in a mode corresponding to the nature of His Word."[2] To find the will of God for our lives, which alone makes our lives meaningful, we need to be opened to a world of meaning beyond sense impressions. This higher world of meaning breaks into our limited world of meanings in the awakening to faith in the divine Redeemer.

It is interesting to compare the biblical and Platonic views on meaning, for the latter has had a far-reaching influence on Christian theology. In Platonism meaning is the triumph of form over chaos. In biblical religion meaning is the victory of good over evil. In Platonism meaning is participation in the good, the beautiful and the true. In biblical Christianity it is communion with the living God. In Platonism meaning is insight into the realm of ideas of which the phenomenal world is only a pale reflection. In Christianity meaning is a new creation, the opening up of a new horizon by the indwelling Holy Spirit. In Platonism meaning is the dialogic unfolding of truth latent within the human soul. In Christianity meaning is the overthrow of human untruth by the truth of the Word of God, which uproots human existence and places it on a new foundation.

The inescapable fact is that meaning and truth are indissolubly related. Meaning is an awakening to the truth, which is God's will and purpose for our lives. Meaning is truth finding its way into the thinking faculties of human beings. Meaning is truth penetrating human existence and utterly transforming it.

Language is the vehicle by which the truth of God is communicated to the human subject. It is, to give a slight re-rendering of Heidegger, the "house of meaning," for meaning is a rational event, a meeting of minds. Meaning will *eo ipso* be expressed in propositions, but these propositions are open-ended, invariably falling short of the truth they are trying to express.

Meaning is enveloped in mystery, but it is not obfuscated by mystery. Meaning shines through mystery, hence we can truly understand, though only partially and fragmentarily. We know because we are grasped by the meaning of the Word of God as we encounter this Word in Scripture, the sermon and the sacrament. But we know only brokenly because our minds are too limited to take in the breadth and depth of this transcendent meaning. We know brokenly because our sin blinds us to the full intent of the Word of God for our lives.

I agree with Ellul that theological language as such remains incomplete and insufficient. This is why Scripture entrusts us to the Holy Spirit, for "he is the one who takes the written text and transforms it into the Word. He transforms our murky and ambiguous words into something clear and comprehensible, with no ambiguity."[3] But Ellul goes on to say that "this is not an easy solution or an encouragement to laziness: I can hope for the Holy Spirit's action only when I have done all that is possible—even impossible—to testify to the Word of God with all my means, commitment, intelligence, and effort. It is like the multiplication of the bread *beginning with* the disciples' five loaves."[4]

The language of faith breaks through to reality only when we have strained our critical faculties to the utmost to plumb the hidden depths of its meaning, but the miracle of this occurrence—whereby we gain insight and knowledge of heavenly realities—finally rests on the free movement of the Spirit. To be sure, the meaning of a text may seize us when we have not particularly applied ourselves, but then much effort is required to discern its full implications for our lives. Both the Bible and the sermon come alive through the initiative of the divine subject whom they attest, but it is precisely this divine initiative that arouses within the human subject a burning desire to discover and apprehend the truth that is so critical to human existence.

We understand in and through language, but only when this language is illumined by the Spirit do we begin to know the truth that is the all-determining reality, the center and source of all meaning. Truths of fact can be grasped on our own by means of our senses, but the truth of being can be known only when we are grasped by a power beyond ourselves, only when we are lifted out of ourselves, that is, out of our limited vision, into a new world of meaning anchored in the transcendent.

Meaning in the perspective of biblical faith is not simply cognitive but transformative. It is not simply a perception of truth but an infusion of power. It involves not only an understanding of human existence but the conversion of human existence from the way of untruth to the way of truth. Meaning is a vision of the triumph of God over the powers of chaos and darkness. It is a buoyant expectation that all things work together for good for those who love God (Rom 8:28). It is a deep-seated realization that Jesus is victor over the world and that the future belongs to him.

Indeed, meaning in the biblical view is basically an eschatological category. The meaning of life lies in its *telos,* in its goal, which will be revealed only in the eschatological denouement of history. Yet because we already have a foretaste of the glory that lies ahead, because the kingdom is now being realized in the community of faith and hope, we can have a partial understanding, eventually to be superseded by a full understanding in the absolute future toward which all things move.

# ·FIVE·

# T O W A R D  T H E
# R E N E W A L  O F
# T H E O L O G Y

And this is my prayer, that your love may grow ever richer
and richer in knowledge and insight of every kind, and may thus
bring you the gift of true discrimination.
P H I L I P P I A N S  1 : 9 - 1 0  N E B

Let not many of you become teachers, my brethren, for you know
that we who teach shall be judged with greater strictness.
J A M E S  3 : 1

Prayer, meditation, and trial make a theologian.
M A R T I N  L U T H E R

All true knowledge of God is born out of obedience.
J O H N  C A L V I N

Doctrine and life are really two sides of one Christianity;
and they are equally indispensable, because Christianity is living truth.
P . T . F O R S Y T H

The time has come to lodge a protest in the name of purity and
propriety against the corruption of theology which has now been in full
swing so long and which has been brought about by trying to understand
and treat it simply as a branch of humanities in general.
K A R L  B A R T H

The question of the viability and renewal of theology is comprehensible only against the background of its erosion precipitated
by the Enlightenment. There can be no renewal unless we begin
to grasp the startling extent of its subversion and distortion, which

continues to cast a shadow over theological education.

One manifestation of theological subversion is philosophism—the ill-fated confusion of theology with philosophy of religion. Theology in this context becomes the construction of a world view that stands in juxtaposition with other world views. Or it is the herculean attempt to create a new world of meaning on the basis of universal religious experience. Revelation becomes the breakthrough into a higher form of consciousness rather than a divine intervention into a particular human history. As Teilhard de Chardin phrases it, "God never reveals himself to us from outside, by intrusion, but *from within,* by stimulation, elevation and enrichment of the human psychic current."[1] The case for Christianity is made to depend on the coherence it gives to human experience or its correspondence with the facts of human history.

Philosophism is especially conspicuous in the writings of process theologians. "Christian theology is like philosophy," says Schubert Ogden, "not only in *appealing* to historical evidence but in appealing to the *same* evidence—even if in pursuit of its own distinctive task and thus with the aim of showing that such evidence both confirms and is confirmed by the specifically Christian faith it seeks to understand."[2] "The claim of the Christian witness . . . both confirms and is confirmed by the cognate understanding of ultimate reality represented by philosophy and the special sciences."[3] Theology must show that its claim "is credible by the same criteria of truth" to which current philosophy and sciences are subject.[4] For Langdon Gilkey, "Christian theology is understanding, reflection on, and comprehension of our human experience, our being in the world, in terms of the symbols of the Christian tradition."[5]

Closely related is the aberration of experientialism, which reduces the content of faith to the vagaries of religious or simply human experience. It is not objective information about God but the experience of the numinous that becomes the focal point of theological reflection (Rudolf Otto).[6] Revelation is seen as affective rather than cognitive. Schleiermacher put it bluntly: "It matters not what conceptions a man adheres to, he can still be pious."[7] In his opinion theological statements are possible only as statements of Christian self-awareness. Herrmann agreed that all Christian faith is "really a confidence in an event which has taken place in the Christian's own life."[8] In our day James Gustafson envisages theology as "an enterprise that extrapolates from piety, and other affective responses to the world, to say some things about God."[9] Edward Schillebeeckx begins his theology with a phenomenological analysis of human existence or the universal experience of suffering humanity.[10] For Reinhold Niebuhr the experience of God "is not so much a separate experience, as an overtone implied in all experience."[11]

Christian faith in the classical evangelical tradition does not denigrate experience but sees it as the field of revelation rather than its source or criterion. P. T. Forsyth could maintain that "our theology is not a fixed system we must accept but a gracious experience which we must declare."[12] Yet while recognizing that faith takes an experiential form, he was adamant that it does not originate from experience. Its origin is outside ourselves. The gospel does not depend on our experience for its validity but is confirmed in our experience. Indeed, "the more we find the Cross of Christ to be a finished act of reconciliation for us beyond our consciousness, so much the more do we find it the ruling and growing experience of our consciousness."[13] We see this paradoxical relationship between the authority of the gospel and religious experience in Luther, who could declare in one place, "Only experience makes a theologian,"[14] and yet insist in another that our doctrine is certain "because it carrieth us out of ourselves, that we should not lean to our own strength, our own conscience, our own feeling, our own person, and our own works, but to that which is without us, that is to say, the promise and truth of God which cannot deceive us."[15]

If experience is taken to mean "the total human encounter with our environment in its web of interrelationships,"[16] then all truth that affects human existence will be set in an experiential matrix, but this does not mean that it necessarily springs from this matrix. Truth descends into experience, but it does not arise from experience.

Modern evangelicalism has not been immune from the peril of experientialist reductionism. Experience is sometimes seen not only as the criterion but also as the goal of human endeavor. John Piper admits that "what the Christian Hedonist loves best is the experience of the sovereign grace of God filling him and overflowing for the good of others."[17] I contend that what we should love best is the sovereign God himself, whose grace is poured out for the salvation of the world in Jesus Christ.

Another temptation on the theological road is ethicism—finding the essence of religion in moral precepts. Theologians such as Adolf von Harnack and Wilhelm Herrmann frequently distinguished between the teachings of Jesus and the theology of Paul, alleging that Paul's metaphysical speculation corrupted the simple faith of Jesus. Herrmann strove for a doctrinal formulation free from metaphysics, to be understood "only . . . as the expression of new personal life."[18] Harnack regarded dogma "in its conception and development" as "a work of the Greek spirit on the soil of the Gospel."[19] With sadness Carl Braaten concludes that Harnack's view that the gospel is falsified by dogma "epitomizes the modern Protestant dream of an undogmatic Christianity, one that impinges on religious feeling or moral action and abandons the claim of doctrinal truth."[20]

Theology cannot be confined to moral instruction, though it must certainly include an ethical dimension. Its focus should be on God himself, not so much on God in himself but on God's action toward us in Jesus Christ. A statement of Thomas Aquinas frequently cited by Reformed and Lutheran dogmaticians in post-Reformation orthodoxy was *Theologia a Deo docetur, Deum docet, et ad Deum ducit:* "Theology is taught by God, teaches of God, and leads to God."[21]

If ethicism truncates the gospel, historicism comes close to discarding it altogether. This view, presented most cogently by Ernst Troeltsch, is that all Christian teaching must be understood in the context of historical relationships, that every doctrine is shaped and conditioned by history and culture.[22] Brian Gerrish defines theology as a "disciplined reflection on a historically given, historically mobile way of believing."[23]

According to the Catholic ethicist Charles Curran, all moral teachings arise in a specific historical context and can be understood only in the light of this context.[24] As a result, no doctrinal or ethical teaching is exempt from historical and cultural relativity. The kind of theology Letty Russell advocates is one of "constantly revised questions and tentative observations about a changing world, rather than the type of theology described by Thomas Aquinas as a 'science of conclusions.' "[25] Francis Schüssler Fiorenza assures us, "No external standard, be it history or human experience, exists independent of cultural tradition and social interpretation that can provide an independent foundation of either faith or theology."[26]

The truth in historicism is that our understanding and articulation of the faith are indeed shaped by the sociohistorical context in which this faith comes to us. But I contend that the Word of God itself does not arise from the historical-cultural matrix; instead it descends into it. So the truth-content of the faith both transcends and reflects the stream of human history. The affirmations of faith can be better understood in the light of historical consciousness, but the latter in turn must be corrected and purified in the light of the transcendent truth of faith. We are by no means bereft of an external standard, but this standard is divine revelation bursting into the stream of historical reality and deflecting this reality, even while remaining within it.

Errors in theological understanding are not confined to the left. We also encounter the aberration of biblicism, in which the message of faith is reduced to the stories in the Bible or merely to the facts of the New Testament. Sometimes, Forsyth observed, "you will find people . . . who say, 'Let us have the simple historic facts, the Cross and Christ.' That is not Christianity. Christianity is a certain interpretation of those facts."[27] Biblical study, however valuable in its own right, cannot replace theology, which involves both the exposition of the biblical text and its application to the modern world. Forsyth rightly reminds us that "the only Cross you can preach to the whole world is a theological one. It is not the fact of the Cross, it is the interpretation of the Cross, the prime theology of the Cross, what God meant by the Cross . . . that can make or keep a Church."[28] "The Bible is enough for our saving faith, but it is not enough for our scientific theology."[29]

People need to hear the simple story of salvation, but they must also go on to understand the implications of this story for the life of the church and for their own lives in the cultural situation in which they find themselves. They cannot live on milk alone but must be fed solid food, and this means theological interpretation (1 Cor 3:2; Heb 6:1-2). The "simple gospel" can become a simplified gospel unless it is expounded in the light of the whole of Scripture and the tradition of the church, which is an ongoing commentary on Scripture.

We need to recover the view of the Reformers that doing theology may itself be a form of Christian witness and service. Calvin ranked the discipline of study with that of prayer as indispensable to the life of the pastor. According to Herman Bavinck, "To profess theology is to do holy work. It is a priestly ministration in the house of the Lord. It is itself a service of worship, a consecration of mind and heart to the honor of His name."[30] Indeed, Edward J. Carnell described theology as the sanctification of the mind. The quest for holiness entails not only purity of heart but also rectitude in thinking. We are called to bring our thoughts into conformity to the will of God, and this involves disciplined reflection upon the Word of God.

Finally, we come to the aberration of symbolism: here the content of theology is no longer a sure word from God concerning his purpose in the world but symbolic acts and expressions that point beyond themselves to an ineffable reality. Symbolism is closely related to experientialism and may indeed be one variation of it.[31] Avery Dulles holds that dogmatic statements must both express "the faith of those who utter them" and " 'symbolize' in a thematic way the interior states of soul of the believer."[32] They must also "instill or intensify faith in those to whom they are addressed."[33] Theodore Jennings defines theology as reflection on the Christian mythos, "that set of symbols, rituals, narratives, and assertions which, taken together, announce and mediate the presence of the sacred."[34] The object of our reflection is not simply the Bible or the Christian story but the "liturgy, sacraments, and the history of theological reflection which function as mythos."[35] The expression "Christian mythos" appeals to Jennings because it "reminds us that the object of theological reflection is founded in the imagination and thus requests of us that we attend to the specifically symbolic character of its expression."[36] He would have us focus on representations of the sacred in our present world rather than, as I would say, on the ever-new speech of God that overturns our constructions and visualizations of the sacred.

For symbolists the experience that symbols evoke, rather than the revelation that the church proclaims, becomes the theme of theology. Symbolists conceive of faith no longer as knowledge of the new reality of the risen Christ but as an affective response to the presence of the Holy that bears down upon us. The language of faith is seen as doxological rather than explanatory. What is important is not cognitive words but symbolic acts.

The language of theology will certainly be symbolic in the broad sense in that it will include analogy, metaphor and simile. Yet it will not be exclusively symbolic, nor will it remain with the symbol; instead, it will press beyond it to a reality that is literal rather than symbolic. "God speaking" is a literal event, though our depiction of this event will indeed be symbolic.

In the evangelical theology I propose, symbols do not simply direct us to an unfathomable or ineffable reality (as in mysticism) but may serve as the vehicle for the self-disclosure of the personal reality whom we identify as Jesus Christ. God really does reveal himself and name himself, and this revelation bursts through all symbolic forms even while it may utilize such forms in the service of human understanding. The symbol itself is not revelatory, but it may serve revelation if it is used by the Spirit to direct us to the living Christ.

As one can see, several of these categories of theological misunderstanding overlap, but I have tried to draw distinctions for the purpose of clarifying the theological scene. Symbolism may be both a form of experientialism and a form of philosophism. Likewise, historicism may be a kind of philosophism as well as a type of experientialism.

The point I am making is that theology must not be confused with any rival discipline that bases its credibility on religious or human experience, even if that experience is confirmed by scientific verification. Theology is neither philosophy—a description of ultimate reality—nor psychology—an exploration into the inner states of the human mind. Nor should theology be confused with mysticism, which focuses on the *image* of reality contrived by human imagination rather than on the spoken *word* that overturns human imagination. Theology cannot be subsumed under other disciplines of knowledge just as revelation cannot be subordinated to human reason. Theology leads us out of the morass of subjectivity and relativity into knowledge of ultimate being that we could not attain on our own. It witnesses not to an altered state of consciousness but to a personal being beyond us, who condescends to our level, who meets us on our plane of being and understanding. Theology employs language drawn from metaphysics, but it is not itself metaphysics, for its overriding concern is not a comprehensive understanding of reality but the transformation of reality by the Spirit of the living God.

**Theology Defined**
From this perspective, theology is the systematic reflection within a particular culture on the self-revelation of God in Jesus Christ as attested in Holy Scripture and witnessed to in the tradition of the catholic church. Theology in this sense is both biblical and contextual. Its norm is Scripture, but its field or arena of action is the cultural context in which we find ourselves. It is engaged in reflection not on abstract divinity or on concrete humanity but on the Word made flesh, the divine in the human.

This position stands in fundamental conflict with both the old and the new liberalism. Albrecht Ritschl saw the task of theology as "the articulation of a disciplined theoretical defense of the practical certainty of faith in the divine governance of the world."[37] Here the fulcrum of theol-

ogy is not the Incarnation of the Word of God in history but faith's
venture in obedience to the providential reordering of the world.[38] For
the liberation theologian Gustavo Gutierrez theology is "a critical reflection on historical praxis."[39] Praxis in this context means involve-
ment in the class struggle to build a new society. Thus the emphasis is
not on what God has done for us in biblical history but what we can
do to spearhead the coming of the kingdom.

It is commonly said in neoliberal circles that the task of theology is
to construct a new view of the world or forge a new synthesis of meaning in the light of the tremendous changes in human culture since the
Enlightenment. Instead of the grandiose design of creating a meaningful world (the thrust of Gordon Kaufman's constructive theology),[40] I
uphold the more modest agenda of an evangelical dogmatic theology:
to expound the significance of the new creation that has broken into
this world from the beyond. Theology is not an analysis of the vagaries
of universal religious experience nor an exploration of the possibility of
meaning in a meaningless world but an exposition of the particularities
of Scripture that bring meaning to the otherwise desolate landscape of
human existence.

Theology is the diligent and systematic explication of the Word of
God for every age, involving not only painstaking study of the Word of
God but also an earnest attempt to relate this Word to a particular age
or cultural milieu. Theology in the evangelical sense is the faithful interpretation of the biblical message to the time in which we live. It must
struggle to elucidate the relevance of the cross and resurrection victory
of Jesus Christ for our time and place in history, not simply reaffirm past
interpretations or repeat creedal formulas of another era.

Theology is a science not in the sense of natural science but in the
sense of wisdom: it is certain and true. I here side with Duns Scotus,
who followed Aristotle in contrasting science with opinion and conjec-
ture because of its certainty and truth. Yet Scotus denied that theology
is a science in the strict sense, his ideal being mathematical science.
Here he differed from Thomas Aquinas, who saw theology as a specu-

lative science. This does not mean, however, that its doctrines are only moral postulates. Theology endeavors to present a true picture of the activity of divinity that serves to illumine the pilgrimage of faith. Its purpose is not to give abstract knowledge of God but to direct humanity to its spiritual home for the glory of God. God has provided a revelation of himself sufficient for us to think deeply and rightly concerning his will and purpose so that we may implement his plan for the world in faithful service. Yet God has not given us an exhaustive knowledge of the inner workings of his Spirit or a direct perception of the essence of his being. As Scripture says, "The secret things belong to the LORD our God; but the things that are revealed belong to us and to our children for ever, that we may do all the words of this law" (Deut 29:29).

Even though we cannot claim a comprehensive knowledge of God as he is in himself, we must not suppose that God in himself is other than God as he relates himself to us in Jesus Christ. To know God in Christ is to know God in himself, that is, God as he exists in the paradoxical unity of majestic holiness and unbounded love—though this is always a partial and broken knowledge waiting for completion on the day of redemption.

The method of theology is not reason preparing the way for faith (Abelard) but faith seeking understanding (Anselm). This is not the method of correlation (Tillich) but that of faithful explication. Theology is not existential-ontological, proceeding from existents to Being-itself (Macquarrie), but revelational-situational, proceeding from God's self-revelation in Christ to the human existential situation.

The sources of theology are Scripture and tradition, but the first has priority. Scripture is the primary, tradition the secondary, witness to divine revelation. Culture or human experience is the medium of revelation but not its source or norm. I take issue with Schillebeeckx, who sees the sources for faith as the traditional experience of the Judeo-Christian movement and the contemporary human experiences of Christians and non-Christians.[41] I prefer to speak of contemporary human experience as the field of theology but not its source or norm.

Karl Barth has wisely advised Christians to have the Bible in one hand and the daily newspaper in the other—the Bible to give us the criteria for faith and action, the newspaper to give us sufficient knowledge of the current situation to enable us to apply the directives of our faith in a meaningful fashion. We neglect either of these at our peril.

Yet the concern for relevance can be carried too far. Thomas Finger speaks not only of a "kerygmatic norm" for theology but also of a "contextual norm."[42] "The extent to which theology is intelligible within the experience and thought-world of its context is also a standard by which its adequacy may be measured."[43] At the same time, he cautions against judging the truth of theology by the norms of any context. The contextual norm sets the stage for the way we formulate and convey our message. In my opinion this view still gives too much weight to the context in determining the credibility of the Christian message. The gospel gains its credibility only by the power of the Spirit, and though we must employ the language of our day in expressing the truth-content of faith, this truth must never be brought into even partial accord with the criteria for truth entertained by the culture.[44]

In the last analysis liberal theology is fundamentally anthropology. Its focus is on human existence or self-understanding. Here Reinhold Niebuhr reflects his liberal heritage, declaring theology to be not a science of God but "a rational explication of man's faith."[45] Herrmann views faith as confidence in one's own experience as a Christian. Bultmann defines theology as "the conceptual presentation of man's existence as an existence determined by God."[46] Schillebeeckx bases his theology on a phenomenological analysis of human existence or the universal experience of suffering humanity. According to Troeltsch the role of dogmatic propositions is to unfold the contemporary consciousness of the church.

In the evangelical theology I propose, the focus is neither on divine essence nor on human existence but on divine existence in humanity, as we see this in Jesus Christ. Theology is not the verbalization of religious experience (Schleiermacher), even less of common human experience (David Tracy). Instead, it is the articulation of a divine revelation that breaks into our experience from the beyond and transforms it.

The Catholic philosophical theologian Bernard Lonergan has defined theology as "reflection upon conversion in a culture."[47] If this were taken as an exhaustive definition (which Lonergan does not intend) it would end in rank subjectivism, since human conversion takes many forms. The focus should be not on the experience of faith but on its object—its ground and its goal. The basis of our theology can be none other than God's incomparable act of reconciling the world to himself in Jesus Christ.

In the theological method I advocate, we do not adduce true insights from Scripture (Finger), nor do we deduce true propositions from Scripture (Carl Henry). Neither do we infer general truths from Scripture by an investigation of particulars—the way of induction (Charles Hodge). Instead, we discover the truth within Scripture after being confronted by the One who is the Truth—Jesus Christ. We begin not with Scripture as a historical text but with the living Word of God—Jesus Christ—and then try to ascertain how Scripture bears witness to him.[48]

Theology is neither "experiential-expressive"—expressing the universal aspect of human experience (as in Tracy)—nor "cultural-linguistic"—purporting to describe the cultural-linguistic reality of Christian word and life (as in Lindbeck).[49] Instead, it is creative-transforming—seeking to critique the life and symbols of the church as well as the experience of the culture in the light of the new reality of Jesus Christ. It brings a new horizon to both the church and the world that alters, sometimes dramatically, the church's faith-understanding as well as overturning the culture's self-understanding.

I agree with Tillich that theology is neither an "empirical inductive" nor a "metaphysical deductive" science.[50] Nor can we say (and Tillich concurs) that it is simply a combination of both. Yet I take issue with him when he says theological understanding is grounded in the mystical a priori, which transcends the cleavage between subject and object. Theology is a faith-responsive science. God makes himself an object to our understanding in the event of revelation, but this can be perceived only in faith.

## Dogma and Doctrine

Ever since the Enlightenment, dogma has been viewed with suspicion, especially by Protestants. Harnack regarded dogma as the unwelcome intrusion of the Greek spirit into the world of biblical faith.[51] According to Ritschl, our focus should be not on dogmas about God and Christ, which tend to remove faith from history, but on value judgments that are rooted in the experience of the redemptive work of Christ in history.[52]

*Dogma* has undergone variations of meaning through the centuries. In the New Testament, *dogma* referred to a decree, ordinance, decision or command (Lk 2:1; Acts 16:4; 17:7; Eph 2:15; Col 2:14; Heb 11:23). In Greek philosophy it came to mean doctrinal propositions expressing the cardinal beliefs of a particular school of philosophy. In Roman Catholicism it assumed the form of authoritative declarations of the faith by the teaching magisterium of the church on the basis of special illumination granted to it. Because dogma was said to have its source in Scripture and church tradition, the church came to speak of revealed dogmas, bearing the stamp of infallibility. The Protestant Reformers challenged the infallibility of church dogmas, appealing to Scripture alone as the source of authority and revelation. In place of dogmas they drew up confessions of faith that were to be always under the authority of Scripture. In the development of Reformed theology dogma has come to mean an expression of the truth of faith that has achieved official status in the church but is not itself infallible.[53]

For Karl Barth dogma is "the agreement of Church proclamation with the revelation attested in Holy Scripture."[54] It is therefore an eschatological concept, since there will never be perfect agreement between church proclamation and the eschaton until the parousia, when Christ comes again. Unlike Harnack, Barth did not dissolve dogma in the relativities of history, but he saw dogma as the transcendent goal and model of dogmas.

With Barth I see the need to hold onto the concept of dogma but not to confuse dogma with church formulations that always bear the mark of historical and cultural relativity. Dogma is the divinely given content of the faith apprehended and proclaimed by the believer in the act of obedience. It is the revelational meaning of the biblical message given to us in the act of bearing witness to the faith. Dogma is to be associated with God's self-understanding; dogmatics signifies an expression of the believer's reflection about God.

It is important to distinguish between dogma and doctrine. Dogma is the divinely inspired apostolic interpretation of the events of redemption. Doctrine is the systematic affirmation of this divinely inspired interpretation by the theologians of the church. Dogma is what God declares; doctrine is what the person of faith articulates. Doctrine is dogma condensed in a propositional statement accessible to human understanding and *eo ipso* distortion. Dogma is irreversible and irreformable. Doctrine is open to reformation and correction, but its dogmatic content is irrevocable and unalterable. Dogma in the plural is equivalent to doctrines, but in the singular it ordinarily indicates the content of revelation.

When dogma is translated into dogmas or doctrines, it enters the stream of historical relativity and loses its absolute status. In the process of translation, revelational truth—the truth of personal address—is transmuted into a purely propositional truth—the truth of cognitive mastery.[55] Receiving reason is now superseded by controlling reason.

In its fundamental meaning dogma is always alive and dynamic because it is God speaking and the believing subject hearing. Barth rightly asks, "Is the truth of revelation . . . like other truths in the sense that it may be established . . . as the manifestation of something hidden, in human ideas, concepts and judgments, that it may be, as it were, conserved in this restricted and specialized form, that it can be had as truth apart from the event of its being manifested?"[56]

Doctrine represents the crystallization of dogma, the articulation of the truth of revelation in the form of a guiding standard or normative witness. Doctrines can be trustworthy when they are controlled by the dogmatic norm of the law and the gospel. I concur with Avery Dulles that with qualifications, "one may hold that right doctrine, insofar as it accurately mirrors the meaning of the original message, is, in its content, revealed. God's revelation achieves itself through human concepts and words."[57] Doctrine is nonetheless always open to reformulation as more light breaks through from God's Holy Word. Dogma by its very nature cannot be revised, but doctrine is open to revision as we are led into a deeper or fresher understanding of dogma.

I agree with Barth that dogma has an eschatological thrust. Because our apprehension and formulation will never be in total harmony with the divine revelation until Christ comes again, we need to struggle for a fuller understanding of dogma. Our dogmatic formulas are necessarily incomplete, for God is hidden even in his revelation. This does not mean, however, that they are necessarily untrue. Nor can they be regarded as nonbinding so long as they have their source and inspiration in Scripture.

A dogma represents a claim to absolute truth, but it is also a claim to obedience (Brunner). We can have absolute truth, yet only in the act of obedience. Because disobedience always accompanies our obedience, truth becomes mixed with untruth. By the grace of God we can nevertheless make true statements about what God has revealed to us, but our formulations will invariably show the signs of special interests, historical conditioning and cultural limitations. We must therefore constantly return to the source, Holy Scripture, in order to reformulate the content of the truth of revelation for new situations. No doctrinal formulation is ever in and of itself infallible or irreformable. But it can nonetheless bear and communicate infallible truth.

Dogmas and doctrines are necessary because the church must distinguish sound doctrine from unsound doctrine, whatever the cultural pressures to divert it from this task. The church is compelled to articulate the faith more precisely when it is threatened by heterodoxy and heresy. At the same time, the dogmas of the church must never be identified with the Word of God itself. As Barth poignantly says, "The Word of God is above dogma as the heavens are above the earth."[58]

Church dogmas are not revealed propositional truths but human affirmations born out of fidelity to divine revelation. While not an identity, there is a continuity between the dogma of revelation and church dogma. The dogma of revelation is the story of salvation—but as interpreted by the Spirit of God to the church. We can grasp it only as we are grasped by it. We can have it only by returning to it again and again. "Even in the Scriptures," Brunner observed, "the divine dogma is not simply 'given,' but it is given in such a way that at the same time and continually it must be *sought*."[59]

The dogmatic norm in the Bible is the law and the gospel: the law illumined by the gospel and the gospel fulfilled in the law. But as soon as we define what the gospel is, we have the kerygma, not the gospel. The gospel transcends human formulations even while it is reflected in these formulations.[60]

Dogma is not the last word but the beginning word. When our eyes are opened to the revelatory meaning of what God has done for us in Christ, we embark on a pilgrimage of faith that involves a lifetime of striving to understand what the Spirit is teaching us to see. Dogma is therefore not only the ground of our faith-understanding but its goal and culmination.

We can cherish the dogma of the two natures of Christ, as defined by the Council of Chalcedon (A.D. 451), while recognizing it to be an imperfect reflection of the divine mystery of God in Christ. It is binding on the church but not absolutely infallible in the sense of being faultless or undeceiving. It is not in and of itself infallible, but by the illumination of the Spirit it communicates infallible truth, that is, dogmatic truth. It is binding in the sense that it must be taken seriously as a normative statement of the church's faith. Its truthfulness is based on its continuity with the mind of Christ as this is reflected in the church.

The truth of every church dogma and doctrine is ultimately grounded in the revelation that God has given to us in Jesus Christ and that he gives again through the work of his Spirit in the church. Thomas Torrance is indubitably correct when he declares, "The truthfulness of theological statements . . . depends not on the truthfulness of their intention but on a participation in the Truth which God alone can give."[61] They must certainly be guided by "the truth content of the Scriptures, but what must determine theological formulation is the objective truth forced upon the interpreter of the Scriptures by God himself."[62]

In recent years there have been new interpretations of dogma in Roman Catholic circles. Hans Urs von Balthasar regards the propositions of dogma as true "insofar as they are a function and an expression of the Church's understanding of the Christ-mystery, as given to it by the Holy Spirit. They cannot be taken out of this setting; therefore, they do not have any *purely* theoretical (i.e., non-experiential, non-existential) truth."[63] Gerald O'Collins cautions that no "dogmatic statement can ever exhaustively express the mystery of God's self-communication in Christ. Here as elsewhere faith must continue to 'seek understanding' and appropriate new formulations."[64] O'Collins is insistent that dogmas cannot and should not be treated as ultimate norms. "The supreme rule of faith" is found in "the Scriptures, taken together with sacred Tradition."[65]

Karl Rahner here resonates with much of what is being said in this chapter: "The clearest formulations, the most sanctified formulas, the classic condensations of the centuries-long work of the Church in prayer, reflection and struggle concerning God's mysteries: all these derive their life from the fact that they are not end but beginning, not goal but means, truths which open the way to the—ever greater—Truth."[66]

As Catholic theologians come to recognize the relativity of dogmatic formulation and as Protestant theologians begin to sense the need for a confessional or dogmatic norm in theological work, there may be reason to hope for an emerging consensus on this important issue in the whole church. Yet there is also the somber possibility that theology in its eagerness to come to terms with the new historical understanding spawned by the Enlightenment will lose sight of the irrevocable fact that there is an infallible standard transcending and governing history, that God's Word in the form of the gospel and the law is irreformable and irreversible, and that theological study and teaching therefore have an anchor in the transcendent, which cannot be ignored without irreparable harm to the thought and life of the church.

## Dimensions of a Renewed Theology

The kind of theology I advocate is a self-transcending theology, pointing beyond itself to Jesus Christ, to what God has done for us in Christ. It sees itself in the service of the church proclamation of the gospel.

Theologizing, I firmly believe, entails a personal relationship and acquaintance with Jesus Christ, involving a renewal of the mind and heart of the theologian. Theology presupposes regenerate theologians. It is to be done by those who have experienced the Holy Spirit as the interpreter of Scripture. As Luther discovered, "theological knowledge is won by experiencing it."[67]

I assert this against Schubert Ogden's extraordinary contention that "even though faith without theology is not really faith at all, theology without faith is still theology, and quite possibly good theology at that."[68] The crux of the matter is not whether the theologian accepts the answer of the witness of faith but whether he or she reflects on the question to which the answer is addressed. From my perspective, the pivotal question does not arise out of human experience but is itself a gift of revelation and therefore presupposes that the subject has already been grasped by revelation.

It is well to note that Calvin called his *Institutes* not a *summa theologiae* but a *summa pietatis* (a summary of piety). Indeed, according to John McNeill, the secret of Calvin's mental energy "lies in his piety; its product is his theology, which is his piety described at length. His task is to expound . . . 'the whole sum of piety and whatever it is necessary to know in the doctrine of salvation.' "[69]

A renewed theology will be evangelical, that is, centered in the gospel of reconciliation and redemption as attested in Holy Scripture. It will serve the evangelical proclamation and will therefore have a pronounced missionary dimension.

It will also be catholic in the sense that it will be universal in its outreach and stand in continuity with the tradition of the whole church. It will draw on the theological commentary on Scripture in the church through the ages. The Reformers appealed not only to Scripture but also to the church fathers in support of their theses.

In addition, a renewed theology will be Reformed. First, it will be anchored in the Protestant Reformation. It will see the Reformation as the rediscovery of the New Testament gospel of salvation by free grace. Second, it will see itself as always being reformed in the light of the Word of God. Theology in this sense will be a *theologia viatorum* (a wayfarers' theology) or a *theologia in via* (a theology on the way). It will not be a *theologia beatorum* (a theology of the blessed) or a *theologia in visione* (a theology in vision). The theologian will humbly acknowledge that he or she has not yet arrived, that the absolute system, the final synthesis of all theses and antitheses, is the property only of God the Almighty.

This same attitude of dependence on the Lord will lead a renewed theology to be pentecostal, in the sense of being open to the new wind of the Spirit. But this is the Spirit never separated from the Word. Theology acknowledges that God has yet more light to break forth from his Holy Word (John Robinson, d. 1625). This new light, however, is not a new revelation—and certainly not a contradiction of what has gone before—but its amplification and clarification.

Finally, theology will earnestly strive to be orthodox.[70] It will not be slavishly bound to the creedal formulations of the past, but it will respect them. It will make use of creeds in order to go beyond them to a new articulation of the faith that nevertheless stands in continuity with the old.

Theology at its best will be integrally related to practice. "Knowledge of God," Barth pointed out, "is not an escape into the safe heights of pure ideas, but an entry into the need of the present world, sharing in its suffering, its activity and its hope."[71] The goal of theology is holiness in life and thought. The motto of liberation theology has much to commend it: "No one can understand the gospel without the performance of the gospel."[72] This is in accord with the words of the psalmist: "A good understanding have all those who do His commandments" (Ps 111:10 NKJ; cf. 1 Jn 2:3-4; 4:7-8 JB). But we should not overlook the other side of the paradox—that knowledge of God has priority over action in the name of God (cf. Col 1:9-10; 2 Jn 9). It is not until we are awakened to the love of God poured out for us in Jesus Christ that we will be moved to do acts of love out of gratefulness for what God has done for us. It is only when we ourselves practice love that we are enabled to understand the full implications of the gift of faith.

A catholic evangelical theology will be characterized by a high view of Scripture, unabashedly holding to *sola Scriptura,* the watchword of the Reformation. This means not that Scripture is the only source of revelation but that it is the original and primary witness to revelation. Scripture therefore has primacy—over the church, religious experience and reason. Evangelical theology will take strong exception to Ogden's contention that "the locus of the canon . . . cannot be the writings of the New Testament as such but can only be the earliest traditions of Christian witness accessible to us today by historical-critical analysis of these writings."[73] It will firmly resist the call of Rosemary Ruether for a new canon that would widen the Scriptures of the church to include Gnostic writings and literature of goddess spirituality.[74] It will affirm with the church father Jerome that "the bulwark of the Church is that man who is well grounded in Scripture."[75]

Another hallmark of a catholic evangelical theology is its high view of God. The God of theology will *eo ipso* be the God of Scripture, the sovereign Creator and Redeemer of the world. It will not be the finite God of process philosophy (Whitehead) and philosophical personalism (Brightman) but the personal-infinite God attested in the Bible (Francis Schaeffer). This God is not only Savior of humankind but Lord of everything that exists.

With full confidence in the power and mercy of God, evangelical theology will uphold the Reformation principle of the sovereignty of grace. Grace not only saves but also rules. We are not only justified by grace but also kept by grace. Yet grace works not apart from human action but in and through human action. Grace realizes its goal in human life through the cooperation that it itself makes possible. A religion of grace will always be arrayed against a religion of works-righteousness. Christianity is not legalism or moralism but the story of the triumph of grace in the lives of sinful human beings.

Paradoxically, the evangelical theologian will have a high view of humanity, agreeing with Irenaeus that "the glory of God is man fully alive." Humanity is not reduced to nothingness by grace but instead elevated into fellowship with divinity. God's grace does not denigrate the human but sanctifies and restores it to its true purpose.

A catholic evangelical theology will have in addition a high view of the church, not hesitating to call the church "our holy mother" (as Calvin did). The church represents the feminine side of the sacred, the bride of Christ, who cleaves to the One who lays down his life for her (Eph 5:21-33). We are conceived in the womb of the church and nurtured by the tender love of this holy mother. The church is a sacrament of the grace of God in Christ, a visible sign of the invisible grace that is sealed in our hearts by the Spirit of God.

Finally, evangelical theology will be grounded in a personal commitment to Jesus Christ. Theologizing is valid only when done by those who trust in the grace of Christ for their wisdom and who are motivated by the desire to give glory to God in Christ.

Theology in the sense intended here is more than descriptive. It is also prescriptive, for it presents the truth of faith as normative for all human endeavor. Its task is to clarify and interpret the divine dogma communicated to the church by the Spirit. Its purpose is to serve the church proclamation, the heralding of the good news that we are saved only by grace through the atoning sacrifice of Jesus Christ for the sins of the world.

### The Two Sides of Theology

Theology has two sides: the dogmatic and the apologetic. Its mandate is to combat misunderstandings of the faith (polemics and apologetics) and to articulate the true understanding (dogmatics). Apologetics is the conscious endeavor to answer criticisms from the world outside the church. Polemics is the systematic effort to counter misunderstandings within the family of faith.

Apologetics is not the preamble to dogmatics but an activity within dogmatics. The best defense of the faith consists in expounding the message of faith in love. The self-attesting Scripture, not the new world consciousness, is the point of departure for evangelical theology. In other words, the substance of the faith takes priority over the evidence of faith.

The evangelical theologian does not blithely proceed to correlate the creative questions of the culture and the answer of faith (as in Tillichian apologetics). Instead, we are challenged to lead people to ask the right questions, questions that are hidden from sinful humanity until the moment of revelation. We seek neither a correlation of the gospel with secular thought nor a synthesis of the gospel with secular thought but a confrontation of secular claims by the truth of the gospel.

Theology exists to serve the proclamation of the church. It will therefore be a kerygmatic theology, focusing on the message of faith. But it will also have a prophetic dimension, endeavoring to bring the law of God to bear upon both personal and social sin. Finally, it will have an apologetic dimension, for it will make a determined effort to unmask the powers of the world that challenge and attack the church. Yet in fulfilling its apologetic mandate it will not presume that arguments for the faith can ever induce faith in unbelievers, for faith comes only by the hearing of the Word of God (Rom 10:17). At the same time, it nurtures the hope that as it defends the claims of faith before both church and world it might in the process kindle within unbelievers a curiosity regarding these claims that could be used by the Spirit to lead them into a situation where they might be ready to hear the gospel message.

The method of a theology of revelation is faith seeking understanding (Augustine, Anselm). Reason is not the springboard to revelation nor its foundation but its servant in making the truth of revelation clear both to the church and the world. Our task as theologians of the church is to preach not a bifurcated or private gospel but the whole gospel. We are enjoined to proclaim Jesus Christ as Lord of all of life (Francis Schaeffer). This means we will proclaim not simply the message of salvation but the divine commandment that calls for a dramatic reordering of the life of society and of personal life.

Theology as an agency in the renewal of the church strives for a balance of doctrine, life, experience and worship. Doctrine is important, but it becomes lifeless apart from the experience of the Spirit, the life of obedience and the adoration of the true God in prayer and thanksgiving. Philip Spener rightly depicted theology as not a mere science but a *habitus practicus* (a way of life).[76] Theology is integrally related to the trials and pitfalls of life as well as to its joys and hopes. As Luther observed with characteristic forthrightness, "One becomes a theologian by experiencing death and damnation, not by understanding, reading, and speculating."[77]

The emphasis today is on *praxis* over logos and *doxa* (worship) over dogma. This is a sorely needed corrective to the lifeless orthodoxy that has been more constricting than liberating. Yet the corrective itself is liable to create a new imbalance. We must not overlook the perennial need for sound doctrine in the church. Here we see the relevance of the Pastoral Epistles, which urge us to remain true to the faith once delivered to the saints (cf. 1 Tim 4:6; 2 Tim 3:16; Tit 1:9; 2:7, 10). In the current pluralistic climate we should take to heart this Johannine admonition: "Any one who goes ahead and does not abide in the doctrine of Christ does not have God; he who abides in the doctrine has both the Father and the Son" (2 Jn 9).

The more we emphasize *praxis,* the more we run the risk of losing sight of both the propositional and historical dimensions of revelation. Theology has to do with both the living of the Christian life and the knowledge of the true God, of his plan and purpose for the world. Neglect of the latter can only leave us vulnerable to the allurements of the New Age mentality that encourages a counterfeit spirituality.

Theology is an intelligible and articulate explication of the message of Scripture on the basis of an experience of the Lord of Scripture for the purpose of greater obedience to him. This explication entails not only affirming the truth of the gospel but also exposing the untruth that subverts or ignores the gospel. To say yes to Jesus Christ is to say no to the spirit of the antichrist. The ability to say yes has its basis in the illumination and empowering of the Holy Spirit (1 Cor 12:3). The resolve to say no has this same source, for the discernment and power to resist untruth come from divine grace, not from natural human sagacity.

## The Challenge Today

In order to reaffirm orthodoxy we need first to rediscover heresy. Orthodoxy indeed emerges when the church struggles to reclaim the faith in the face of its distortions and misinterpretations. This is not an undertaking for the fainthearted. With his usual perspicacity Luther realized, "If I profess with the loudest voice and clearest exposition every portion of the truth of God except precisely that little point which the world and the devil are at that moment attacking, I am not professing Christ, however boldly I may be professing Christ!"[78]

Heresy signifies a palpable imbalance in the interpretation of the faith so that certain truths are ignored or downplayed. It may also indicate an aberration that strikes at the vitals of the faith. In the first sense it is probably more accurately described as heterodoxy.

Schleiermacher was one of the first modern theologians who tried to take heresy seriously (which did not prevent him from fostering it himself). He saw basically four types of heresy: the docetic and ebionitic, which refer to misunderstandings of the person of Christ; and the Manichaean and Pelagian, which represent misapprehensions in the realm of soteriology.[79] While his analysis has much to commend it, it is woefully inadequate in confronting such perversions of the faith as "German Christianity" and apartheid. Schleiermacher could justly be accused of promoting the heresy of unionism—seeking Christian unity at the price of letting go of doctrinal particularity.[80] The problem arises from a false irenicism in which love is elevated over truth.

Subjectivism is another theological aberration that wreaks havoc in the church, and Schleiermacher's influence is discernible here also. In this misunderstanding, autonomous human reason or experience becomes the determinant for Christian thinking and practice. Thus Gregory Baum denies that the Christian message gives us information about the divine to be rationally assimilated. Instead, it is salvational truth that raises human consciousness and enables one to see the world in a new light.[81]

According to Langdon Gilkey, "authority for all of us has no locus except here in this world, in present experience; and consequently the authorities we recognize must be generated out of experience itself."[82]

The opposite error is objectivism, in which the human mind is called to submit to a purely external authority. Kant aptly referred to this as the peril of heteronomy. We find objectivism in sacramentalism, creedalism and ecclesiasticism, in which the confession of faith or the church is made the final criterion for life and thought. The shadow of heteronomy clouds the vision of Max Thurian, erstwhile theologian of the Taizé community: "We have no better access to the truth contained in Sacred Scriptures and believed in by the whole Church than the trinitarian and Christological dogmas of the first councils. . . . *Theological science is composed of exegesis and of submission to the faith of the councils.*"[83]

Another seedbed of heresy is eclecticism, which draws from various traditions, often conflicting and disparate. The search for a global religion that would in effect supplant institutional Christianity was already noticeable in Schleiermacher, and it has reappeared in Paul Tillich, John Hick and Rosemary Ruether, among others. Ruether is unabashedly eclectic when she says, "The search for usable tradition may widen to pre-Christian, non-Christian, and post-Christian traditions, not simply over against the biblical and Christian traditions, but as a way of placing it in a larger context, which complements and corrects its biases."[84]

Closely related to eclecticism are latitudinarianism and pluralism: here any exclusive or particular claim to truth is frowned upon as a sign of provincialism and fanaticism. Schleiermacher prepared the way for the new mentality: "Let none offer the seekers a system making exclusive claim to truth, but let each man offer his characteristic, individual presentation."[85] He and those who followed in his steps failed to perceive the fanaticism inherent in such a position.

Christians, of course, should acknowledge the pluralism of the modern age in which various religions and ideologies coexist in mutual and sometimes creative tension, but we cannot under any circumstances surrender our claim to a definitive revelation. There can be a relative pluralism in theology, which seeks to interpret the faith for every age, but not in dogma, which is the doctrinal foundation of faith. We are free to elaborate the doctrinal or dogmatic substance of the faith, but we are not free to discard or ignore its core meaning. Dogma is irreformable, but theology must be constantly reformed in the light from almighty God given in Holy Scripture.

The opposite error of eclecticism and latitudinarianism is sectarianism—unduly narrowing the range of Christian experience and elevating marginal doctrines into dogmas. When belief in the premillennial reign of Christ or the pretribulation rapture of the saints becomes part of the message of the gospel, we are trapped in a dangerously sectarian mindset. Sectarianism is the identification of a particular church with the holy catholic church or a particular theology with the wisdom of God. Just as liberals gravitate to eclecticism and latitudinarianism, so conservatives veer in a sectarian direction. Evangelicals and fundamentalists are notorious for majoring in minors.

The primary task of the theologian today is not, as Langdon Gilkey says, "the revision of the Christian message in contemporary terms"[86] in accord with the prevailing philosophies of the culture, but the reaffirmation of a catholic evangelical theology, which celebrates biblical faith kept alive in the universal tradition of the whole church. To this end we must have a faithful rendition of the Christian message both in the language of Canaan and in the language of our day. Nor can we accept with Schubert Ogden that "the ultimate criteria for the truth of any claim can only be our common human experience and reason, however hard their verdict may be to determine."[87] Our ultimate standard must be the gospel of God that brings all human experience and cultural values into radical question.

In some circles today it is fashionable to speak of theology as describing a particular tradition rather than presenting a normative claim to truth competing with other claims. Doctrines, George Lindbeck suggests, specify rules for Christian speech and action rather than norms that have a basis in ultimate reality. But theology is not simply descriptive but also combative. It must expose error in thinking and must call for a decision for the truth. It seeks to persuade as well as to expound, yet basing its appeal not on its own logic but on the metalogic of the cross of Christ, which drives reason beyond itself. Theology does not merely explicate the doctrines of faith for the sake of coherence and meaningfulness but also presents its doctrines as truth claims calling for decision.

With the rise of narrative theology, the emphasis has shifted from exploring the metaphysical implications of the faith to investigating the story of a people on pilgrimage. While reflecting certain biblical concerns, this development is nonetheless fraught with peril. Theology can ill afford to ignore the issue of truth, for it is truth that gives narrative its significance. Revelation brings us not only insight into the human condition but also foresight into the divine plan for the world. The divine incursion into history sets the stage for an excursus in ontology. Theology is certainly more than a generalized description of the faith of the community: it entails a metaphysical probing of how this community is grounded in reality.[88] Christianity is not a religion in search of a metaphysic (as Whitehead erroneously believed);[89] it is a faith that has its own metaphysic, but one that needs to be developed over against the illusory speculations of a humanity that has declared its independence from God.

The overall aim in this kind of exploration is not conceptual mastery or comprehensive understanding but a faithful rendition of the truth-content of divine revelation as this pertains to the whole of reality. Theology is not to seek a place in the sun at the expense of philosophy but to aspire to give all praise to God's glory, humbly recognizing that the perfect or fulfilled system of thought lies only in the mind of God. Our little systems are at the most imperfect reflections and approximations of the absolute system that God alone possesses. Theology's task is to set up signs and parables that point to the perfect wisdom of God, which for the church is an eschatological hope rather than a realized possibility.

### A Venture in Obedience
Theology is a venture in obedience before it is a search for deeper understanding—either of divinity or of humanity. We seek to understand in

order to be fit instruments for service in God's kingdom. In our obedience we will try to build bridges of understanding but also tear down bridges that can only lead to greater misunderstanding. We will be messengers of hope but also prophets of gloom, for our task is to announce the divine judgment on human sin as well as the gospel of God's grace.

In our theological endeavor we have models from the past to guide us. For Luther theology was essentially a battle *(Kampf)*, whereas for Thomas Aquinas it was primarily wisdom *(sapientia)*. This accounts for the often erratic character of Luther's writings and the well-balanced but somewhat boring character of Thomas's works. Yet we need both: rational coherence and the sharpness of polemical combat. Both Luther and Aquinas employed rational analysis and polemical argument, though not to the same degree. Both sought to maintain the mystery and paradox in revelation. This is more evident in the former, but Aquinas too maintained that the truth of faith, though intelligible, is incomprehensible. Both would concur with the apostle Paul: "Now we see in a mirror dimly, but then face to face" (1 Cor 13:12).

Theology is not a *game* in which we share insights or discoveries about ultimate reality in order to gain intellectual stimulation or deeper self-understanding, for this would make it into a sophisticated kind of psychology. Nor is it essentially a *quest* for wisdom, for then it would become just another philosophy. Nor is it basically a *battle* against false belief, for this would reduce it to polemics.[90]

Instead, theology is essentially a *witness* that takes the form of faithful reflection on the truth revealed by God in a particular time and place in history for the purpose of equipping the church in its apostolic task of preaching and teaching. As a witness to the truth revealed by God it will involve exposing falsifications of this truth as well as striving to understand the ramifications of this truth for every aspect of experience.

Theology will include the dimensions of battle and wisdom, but it will exclude any attempt to construe it as simply an intellectual exercise. When theology becomes a game it is bereft of serious commitment and even of serious content. The bona fide theologian will recognize that we have to say an irrevocable no to some beliefs and an equally irrevocable yes to others. We must be charitable but at the same time resolute in our fidelity to the gospel.

Likewise, theology must not be reduced to a phenomenological description of religious experience or of human existence. It is on the contrary an announcement of the good news that a Savior has come into the world who not only promises deliverance to a people enslaved by the powers of darkness but also who aspires to be Lord of all creation. Theology is *reflection* on the meaning and impact of God's intervention in human history but for the purpose of *obedience* to this God as Lord of the universe.

Evangelical theology of the kind I am proposing will be characterized by humility. The theologian will be fully cognizant of the fact that human thoughts are not the same as the thoughts and ways of God and may be a very inadequate way of expressing the truth revealed by God. Thomas Aquinas sardonically commented on his own theology shortly before his death: "It reminds me of straw." Karl Barth wryly followed suit: "The angels will laugh when they read my theology."

A theology rooted in the gospel will also be imbued with the spirit of love. We are obliged always to speak the truth in love. As Thomas Aquinas wisely admonished, "We must love them both, those whose opinions we share and those whose opinions we reject. For both have labored in the search for truth, and both have helped us in finding it."[91]

Finally, evangelical theology will be noted for its daring. It will seek to witness to the truth of God with boldness and resolution, undeterred by pressures from the world. Indeed, holy boldness can be said to be the salient mark of great theology. Yet this boldness must be informed by wisdom, love and humility.

Theology at its best will be a venture of daring love born out of fidelity to the Great Commission to share the gospel with all peoples. It will not try to impose its claims or impress the world with its superior wisdom. It will seek only to serve the incarnate Word of God, its Lord and Master, by announcing the coming of his kingdom with its promise of liberation and transformation for the world.

## Appendix C: Gospel and Kerygma

A distinction I wish to make between the gospel and the kerygma brings out the qualitative difference between revelation and its human articulation. The gospel is the *evangelion,* the good news of salvation through the atoning sacrifice of Jesus Christ and his glorious resurrection from the grave. The phrases "gospel of God," "gospel of Christ" or "gospel of his Son" (cf. Rom 1:1, 9; 15:16; 1 Cor 9:12; 2 Cor 2:12) all carry the implication that Christ or God is both the content and author of the gospel. The gospel is God or Christ speaking through his messengers (2 Cor 10:10-13). Paul declares that he received the gospel through a special illumination of God (Gal 1:16). The gospel, therefore, is not a creation of the human mind but a message revealed by God.

Because the gospel is God's revelation, not a product of theological imagination (1 Cor 2:9; Gal 1:11), it is not an obvious truth for those whom the god of this world has blinded (2 Cor 4:3-4). The gospel is veiled to those who are perishing, but to those who are being saved it is the power and wisdom of God (1 Cor 1:24). It is possible to receive the message of salvation merely as a human word rather than the Word of God (1 Thess 2:13); this means that the gospel itself, Christ for us and in us, cannot be equated with the cultural and religious form in which it comes to us. Apart from the illumination of the Spirit, the gospel is nothing more than the kerygma, the preaching of the gospel. Ideally, the kerygma is the preaching of Christ plus its content, the risen Christ. Yet apart from the descent of the risen Christ into the words of the preacher, the kerygma remains simply an announcement or proclamation devoid of transforming power and existential meaning. When the proclamation is enlivened and illumined by the Spirit of Christ, it then becomes the gospel, the revivifying message of salvation.

It is, of course, a profound mistake to separate the gospel from the apostolic preaching, because form and content belong together in the event of revelation. Just as we cannot separate the divine commandment from the Decalogue and the Beatitudes, so we cannot separate the divine promise from the preaching of Paul and the other apostles. The biblical witness concerning the divine promise and the divine commandment constitutes the objective criterion by which we can distinguish what is truly from God and what is merely from humanity.

Yet the divine commandment is always something more than the moral codes found in the Bible. This commandment is not simply law but "the law of the Spirit of life in Christ Jesus" (Rom 8:2). It is "the law of liberty" (Jas 1:25), the law that liberates for obedience, rather than the law that restricts and condemns. It is not the law of works and condemnation but the law of life and freedom.[1]

Similarly, the divine promise, or the gospel, cannot be reduced to the apostolic preaching, though it is through this preaching that we receive knowledge of the divine promise. The gospel of God is the personal address of God through his messenger calling us to repentance and faith. The gospel of God is God speaking and humanity hearing in the event of decision and faith. Apart from the Spirit the gospel becomes simply "a noisy gong" or a "clanging cymbal" (1 Cor 13:1).

But the gospel is more than the words of the kerygma. It is "the power of God unto salvation" (Rom 1:16 KJV), the word that liberates and revivifies. The kerygma is the historical form in which the gospel comes to us, and the gospel apart from this apostolic witness would be another gospel. Yet the apostolic witness without the Spirit would be simply a historical description of the gospel, not the gospel itself. The gospel is a word that brings release to the captives, recovery of sight to the blind and liberty to the oppressed (Lk 4:18). The gospel is a word that goes out from God and does not return to him empty (Is 55:11). It is a word that remains the property of God, but a word that we can hear and know through the action of the Spirit of God upon us. But once we have heard, we need to hear ever again. The gospel is the water of life that revives those who are dying of spiritual thirst, but this water is not simply available at our behest. It is water that is given only to those who return again and again to the wellsprings of faith in renewed repentance and dedication in order to live in the victory of the power of the Spirit.

Through our rational faculties we can grasp the kerygma but not its

Christological telos and meaning, which are veiled to natural reason and disclosed only to the eyes of faith. This is what makes the gospel truly supernatural—a gift from God, and not at all a human achievement. The gospel is the treasure waiting to be found, the pearl of great price waiting to be discovered (Mt 13:44-46). It is not immediately available either in the pages of Scripture or in the pronouncements of the church, but it is hidden in the witness of Scripture and needs to be dug out through diligent searching and praying.

The gospel is not simply the story of salvation but the power of salvation. It includes but at the same time transcends the kerygma, which is its earthly form of expression. We cannot have the gospel as if it were a conclusion of human reason, because we cannot have conceptual mastery of its divine content—the living Christ. But our eyes can be opened to this heavenly content through the work of the Spirit upon and within us. Our task is not to comprehend the mystery of the gospel but to rejoice in what it promises and to obey what it commands. We are called to freedom in obedience through the power of the new life that comes to us in the awakening to faith in the one Lord and Savior, Jesus Christ.

The core of the gospel, which is also the content of the kerygma, is summed up by Paul: "God was in Christ reconciling the world to himself" (2 Cor 5:19). Yet the impact of these words is lost unless we are at the same time being baptized into the death of Christ (Rom 6:1-14; 1 Cor 15:31-34). The meaning of the gospel is not apprehended apart from an experience of the passion and victory of our Lord Jesus Christ over death and sin. The words of the kerygma are therefore not identical with the Word of God, but there is nevertheless a paradoxical unity between them, a unity hidden from natural reason until we are enlightened by the Holy Spirit. The gospel comes to us in the form of kerygma, and to translate it into another form is tantamount to transforming it into another gospel.

### Appendix D: Orthodoxy
It has been fashionable in theological circles, including the circles of neo-orthodoxy, to downgrade orthodoxy in favor of a faith that is living

and vital. Schleiermacher bewailed the emphasis on dogma and doctrine, contending that the essence of religion is feeling.[1] Barth warned of the peril of dogmatism on the one hand and mysticism on the other and pointed to a third way, the dialectical approach, which holds every opinion as tentative and in need of completion in a synthesis that forever eludes us while we are still in this mortal flesh.[2] Wesley bemoaned the confining and narrowing elements in orthodoxy and sought for a revival that would burst through the constricting thought-forms and biases of the ecclesiastical establishment. The most fierce opponent of Pietism was not liberalism but Lutheran and Reformed orthodoxy, which distrusted any appeal to religious experience that relegated right doctrine to secondary importance.

We need today to recover the apostolic and Reformation principle that doctrine and life belong together and that the object of faith is not simply the personal presence of Jesus Christ or the love of God revealed in Christ but the truth of God personified in Christ. We are called to trust not simply a Person but his promises and affirmations as well. The faith by which we believe *(fides qua creditur)* must not be separated from the faith which is believed *(fides quae creditur)*, the faith once delivered to the saints (Jude 3). Our task is to uphold not only Jesus Christ but also the apostolic interpretation of what God has done for us in Christ. We are to call people not only to share in a vital communion with Christ but also to affirm what the apostles teach concerning Christ. To be sure, saving faith is faith in Christ as Lord and Savior, but saving faith cannot be maintained apart from contending faith, the faith that vigorously upholds the integrity of the gospel against all efforts to embellish it with other gospels.

In this context orthodoxy means firm adherence to the true faith, the faith of the apostles, the fathers and the Reformers. It includes humble trust in the power of the Spirit to illumine and inform but also profound respect for the great confessions of faith that have kept the church on the straight and narrow way through the ages.

Orthodoxy as a faith orientation must not be confused with orthodoxy as a system of truth or as a school of thought. True orthodoxy may well be present in the formulations of creeds and doctrines, but it is not to be confined or reduced to such formulations. Creeds can always be reformed and clarified, but orthodoxy, a firm abiding in the faith once delivered to the saints, can only be confessed and celebrated.

Orthodoxy must also be distinguished from orthodoxism, a tenacious clinging to dogmatic formulations out of a sense of desperation that the truth of faith stands or falls on the basis of our feeble understanding and articulation. Orthodoxism is a warped orthodoxy, even a dead orthodoxy, but orthodoxy as the content and object of a living faith is kept alive by the Spirit of God, who guides the church to a right understanding of the truth (Jn 16:13).

Orthodoxy signifies not the ideological center of the church but its theological center. It is holding in creative tension conflicting emphases and polarities that would otherwise tear the church apart. It is walking the knife-edge between sectarian dogmatism and amorphous eclecticism. It is demonstrating a willingness to do justice to the faint perceptions of truth even in heterodoxy, humbly recognizing that such misunderstandings arise through an imbalance in the church's proclamation and teaching that neglects some valid aspect of scriptural truth.

While orthodoxy is characterized by both zeal and balance, it is not the golden mean between extremes. Instead, it is the golden thread that runs through all extremes. It is the sword that cuts through every faction or party in the church that elevates itself over others, claiming special merit in the sight of God. It is the word from God that stands in judgment over all systems of orthodoxy, all hardened formulations of the faith.

Schleiermacher erroneously believed that the "visible religious society can only be brought nearer the universal freedom and majestic unity of the true church by becoming a mobile mass, having no distinct outlines, but each part being now here, now there, and all peacefully mingling together."[3] Against this latitudinarian stance, I argue that the unity of the church can be maintained only on the basis of truth, meaning here the apostolic, revelatory meaning of the law and the gospel attested in Holy Scripture, in the ecumenical creeds and in evangelical confessions.

At the same time, the truth of the gospel can be perceived only when we practice love toward other people, especially our fellow Christians. We can speak the truth only when we speak it in love.

Orthodoxy, right belief, is intimately related to *orthopraxis*, right action. There can be no apprehension of the gospel apart from obedience to the imperatives of the gospel. Yet we cannot do the truth unless we are in the truth. Being grasped by the truth of the gospel is prior to obeying the gospel, though a fuller or deeper understanding of the gospel comes through obedience.

True orthodoxy is liberating rather than restricting. It frees us to engage in creative dialog with those who hold differing opinions because our eyes have been opened to the grace of God that is intended for all humanity, even in its sin and error. When we see our fellow human beings as both sinners who have lost their way and objects of God's electing grace, we can then enter into dialog in the hope that through dialog the truth of the gospel will manifest itself to those who do not yet believe or who believe falsely. Because we know that the truth of the gospel is God's own truth, we need not fear that it will be overthrown or defeated in the arena of controversy and debate. Truth will vindicate itself and will overpower falsehood, even when this comes to us in the guise of truth.

We should press beyond orthodoxies—rival faith systems—to orthodoxy—a perpetual abiding in the faith once delivered to the saints. We should place our trust not in theologies or creeds, but in him to whom the creeds and doctrines bear witness—the living Lord who speaks his truth to the church in every age. Our task is to proclaim this truth and teach this truth knowing that we can never fully comprehend its mysteries but that through the work of the Spirit its meaning will be communicated to all those who have accepted Christ as their Savior and acknowledge him as their Lord and Master.

We are called not simply to love our neighbor but also to love the truth, declared in the Bible and proclaimed by the church in every age. We are summoned to embrace our Lord who is the Truth and to serve our fellow humanity in the light of this truth. Apart from piety—the fear of God—our service will degenerate into an inglorious attempt to control and manipulate our neighbor for our own ends. But service informed by zeal for the honor of God and love for the truth of God will be spiritually rewarding for all parties involved.

Orthodoxy means fidelity to the promises of God and zeal for his glory. It combines steadfast trust in the reliability of the biblical witness concerning God's truth with an earnest desire to share this truth with others who still wander in the darkness of sin and despair. It also involves purity in worship, for right doctrine cannot be maintained apart from right praise.[4] Orthodoxy in the ideal sense will always be evangelical—grounded in the gospel and emboldened by love to bring the truth of this gospel to a lost and despairing humanity for the greater glory of God.

# ·SIX·

# NATURAL THEOLOGY

---

Canst thou by searching find out God?

JOB 11:7 KJV

---

We cannot see God in nature,
although we can try to see nature in God.

GREGORY OF NYSSA

---

Not only do we know God by Jesus Christ alone,
but we know ourselves only by Jesus Christ.

PASCAL

---

The gospel of grace is superhuman as well as supernatural;
it is as much above natural affection as above natural law.
The central act of grace is as much beyond the human heart
to do as it is beyond the natural reason to explain.

P. T. FORSYTH

---

The battle against natural theology, which is unavoidable
as a theological axiom, is the battle for true obedience in theology.

KARL BARTH

---

One of the ongoing debates in Christian theology is whether the knowledge of God can be acquired through natural reason and general human experience or whether it is secured only through the biblical revelation. All parties concur that the person outside Christ is still in contact with God. They all affirm that there is a general awareness of the power and presence of God in conscience and nature. But is this awareness sufficient for a theology that would tell us valid things about God and morality?

Natural theology was already present among the apologists and fathers of the early church. Some believed the Spirit of God to have been working in Greco-Roman civilization long before the advent of Christ in preparation for the Christ revelation. Augustine regarded the rational knowledge of God before faith as a kind of self-revelation of God to the soul, finding its completion in the full revelation in Christ. In his *Consolation of Philosophy*, Boethius made an elaborate argument for the reality of God entirely on the basis of human reason without any appeal whatsoever to Christ or the Scriptures.[1]

Both the church fathers and the doctors of the medieval church believed that natural theology can take three forms: the way of negation *(via negativa)*, by which we negate attributes of the finite order; the way of affirmation *(via eminentiae)*, by which we affirm positive attributes of God on the basis of creaturely analogy; and the way of causality *(via causalitatis)*, by which we identify divine attributes by means of the relationship of effect to cause. This last method formed the basis for the cosmological and teleological proofs for the existence of God that compelled the mind to acknowledge the reality of God as the first cause, the prime mover or the cosmic designer.

The ontological proof for the existence of God, advanced by Augustine and Anselm, was much more introspective. Every person, they held, has an idea of perfect being that must entail its existence, for otherwise the idea would not be perfect.[2] In the case of Anselm it is a matter of debate among scholars whether this should be understood as a proof convincing to the world or as a rational demonstration that confirms the Christian's understanding of God.[3] Although his method was "faith seeking understanding," Anselm nevertheless seemed to make no distinction between the church and the world in offering his famous proof.

In the thirteenth century Thomas Aquinas tried to bring together natural and revealed theology by conceiving of the first as a preamble to faith in the God of revelation. His synthesis rested on the contention that acceptance of divine revelation logically presupposes knowledge of a God who is capable of revealing himself. Revelation does not overturn the arguments for God that can be advanced by reason but completes and fulfills the quest of reason for certainty and wisdom. Thomas's natural theology was based on the Aristotelian notion of knowledge through the senses. We cannot know the essence of God, but we can infer his existence by examining God's effects in nature.[4]

Bonaventure's approach to the knowledge of God was more akin to Neoplatonic mysticism. In order to arrive at an understanding of the "First Principle," which is spiritual and eternal, we need first to perceive the imprint of eternity in the things of the world accessible to our senses. We then proceed inward in order to find the eternal image that corresponds to the objects of sense perception. Finally we ascend from the multiplicity of images to the unity of the Eternal One, the source and ground of both ideas and things.[5]

Like Thomas, John Duns Scotus affirmed the reality of natural law but contended that it rested on the divine will rather than the divine mind (as in Thomas), and was therefore not absolutely immutable. He held that God's infinite power, his creation ex nihilo and the divine conservation and government of the world can be demonstrated by reason, but this is not true of special providence.

William of Occam (d. 1347) also sought to ground moral order in the will of God, but God's omnipotence, he believed, could not be proved by reason. He roundly criticized the so-called proofs for the existence of God, fully convinced that the existence of an absolute, supreme and infinite being can be affirmed only on the basis of faith. Occam's theology represents a sharp challenge to the natural theology of patristic and medieval tradition.

The belief in the sufficiency of reason to gain knowledge of God and his moral law was also challenged by the Catholic mystics of the fourteenth to sixteenth centuries, who distrusted the subtleties of scholastic reasoning and emphasized the need to walk by the darkness of faith. "If I had a God whom I could understand," Eckhart confessed, "I should never consider him God."[6] John of the Cross warned, "If we rely on other lights, clear and distinct, of the understanding, we have ceased to rely on the obscurity of faith, which has therefore ceased to shine in the dark place of which the Apostle speaks."[7] We are united to God not by rational dialectic but by the passion of love. The break with natural theology was not total, however, since the *via negativa* still played a prominent role in the thought of the mystics.

While stressing the need to journey into the self to find God, the mystics nevertheless recognized that self-knowledge is woefully deficient apart from the knowledge of God as revealed in Jesus Christ. This is strikingly evident in Teresa of Avila: "We shall never succeed in knowing ourselves, unless we seek to know God. By looking at his greatness, we become aware of our own vileness; by looking on his purity, we see our own impurity; by considering his humility, we see how far we are from being humble."[8]

The Reformers of the sixteenth century, Luther and Calvin, also expressed serious reservations about natural theology, but these reservations had much more to do with the folly of human sin than with the finiteness of human understanding. Calvin maintained that "God bestows the actual knowledge of himself upon us only in the Scriptures."[9] Yet Calvin did not deny the fact that the natural person can know something of God and of the moral order apart from faith. This knowledge, however, is sufficient not to redeem us but to condemn us, for it renders us inexcusable in the sight of God. Luther, too, was willing to grant that people naturally know that there is a God, but such knowledge induces idolatry rather than true faith. The most adamant opponent of natural theology was the young Melanchthon, who declared, "The reality of God, the wrath of God, and the mercy of God are spiritual things, and therefore cannot be known by the flesh."[10] According to Hans Engelland, Melanchthon thought through "Luther's doctrine of sin to the final conclusion."[11] In his theological maturity Melanchthon came to a quite different position, and indeed prepared the way for the rationalism endemic in Lutheran orthodoxy.[12]

In the seventeenth century Pascal, while allowing for natural knowledge of God, was keenly aware of the limitations and deceptions of natural theology. God can be truly known only through faith in Jesus

Christ, and only in the light of Christ can we come to a true understanding of ourselves. The philosophical proofs for the existence of God are insufficient to convert "hardened atheists" and prove to be "useless and sterile," since they yield a knowledge of God apart from Christ.[13]

Protestant orthodoxy in its early phases made a place for natural theology within the church, but a natural theology that arose outside the family of faith could only be *theologia falsa,* the speculation of pagan philosophers. Yet as orthodoxy developed, it attached steadily increasing importance to the role of reason in coming to a rudimentary knowledge of God apart from faith.[14] Natural theology came to furnish the substructure that set the stage for revealed theology.[15] Moreover, revelation was held to yield the same kind of knowledge as that procured by natural reason, though the content remains beyond the reach of our natural capacities. This content is nevertheless accessible to human reason, since it is given in Holy Scripture and is therefore plain for all to see.

The Pietists and Puritans were not inclined to offer proofs for the existence of God, but they did posit an inescapable awareness of God that gives rise to a universal yearning for communion with him. Richard Sibbes was convinced that from the "common light of nature which discovereth there is a God, even natural men in extremities will run to God, and God as the author of nature will sometimes hear them."[16]

In the Enlightenment of the late seventeenth and eighteenth centuries natural theology once again came to the fore, with the defenders of traditional faith trying to make the faith credible by appealing to rational demonstrations. For John Locke (d. 1704) "revelation is natural reason enlarged by a new set of discoveries communicated by God immediately; which reason vouches the truth of."[17] Reflecting a more biblical orientation, J. G. Hamann referred to Nature and History as the two great commentaries on the divine Word, but he was insistent that this Word is the only key that unlocks the knowledge of both. He was sharply critical of the proofs for the existence of God: "If it is fools who say in their heart, 'There is no God,' those who try to prove his existence seem to me to be even more foolish."[18] Throughout his life he sought to combat the reduction of faith to rational demonstration.

In the nineteenth century the emphasis was not on proving God by abstract reasoning but on discovering God in religious and even general human experience. In the words of Schleiermacher, "The Universe is ceaselessly active and at every moment is revealing itself to us."[19] Hegel saw God as having two revelations, nature and spirit: "Both manifestations are temples which He fills, and in which He is present."[20] Nature and grace were no longer separate but now brought together in a spiritual unity. "The heavens and the earth alike speak of God," declared Henry Ward Beecher, "and the great natural world is but another Bible, which clasps and binds the written one; for nature and grace are one— grace the heart of the flower, and nature its surrounding petals."[21] The Romantic poet Robert Southey voiced the spirit of the age:

Go thou and seek the House of Prayer!

I to the woodlands wend, and there,

In lovely Nature see the God of Love.[22]

One lonely, prophetic figure who raised his voice against this capitulation to natural theology was Søren Kierkegaard, who attacked the Platonic and Hegelian notion that truth is latent within us. On the contrary, the truth about God and ourselves must be given to us by a Teacher who is at the same time the Savior of the world—Jesus Christ. "Nature, the totality of created things, is the work of God. And yet God is not there; but within the individual man there is a potentiality . . . which is awakened in inwardness to become a God-relationship, and then it becomes possible to see God everywhere."[23] God cannot be discovered in nature, but the imprint of God on nature can be recognized in the light of his incomparable Incarnation in human history.

Immanuel Kant's incisive criticisms of natural theology had a much greater influence on the course of philosophy and theology, at least during the nineteenth and early twentieth centuries. According to Kant, who signals both the culmination and the end of the Enlightenment, reason can form judgments solely in the realm available to human perception; when it tries to penetrate the noumenal realm it becomes involved in insuperable contradictions or antinomies. To try to give a rational demonstration of the existence of God is to make an unwarranted leap from what can be rationally assured to what is rationally unknowable. Kant brilliantly showed that the cosmological and teleological arguments really have their basis in the ontological argument, which postulates a necessary correspondence between thought and being. But for Kant, being is not a predicate of thought. To show that something is logically necessary is not to prove that it exists in reality. The efforts of natural theology are therefore "null and void." This did not prevent him from introducing a moral proof for the existence of God. While God cannot be rationally demonstrated, we still have a basis for believing in God as the author of the moral law, which informs most human law. God is not a valid conclusion of human reasoning, but belief in God can nevertheless give meaning to human existence. God now becomes a postulate not of pure reason but of practical reason, in which ethical conduct rather than metaphysical knowledge is the paramount concern.

In the twentieth century natural theology has been questioned by P. T. Forsyth, Karl Barth, Otto Weber, Arthur Cochrane and Jacques Ellul, whereas it has reappeared in a new form in Emil Brunner, Wolfhart Pannenberg, Paul Tillich, John Cobb, Karl Rahner, Hans Küng and John Macquarrie, among others. Macquarrie voices the new mood: "Traditional natural theology saw the traces of God in his created works. I am suggesting that we can also see him in the work he has left unfinished, in the freedom and openness that remain."[24] Modern thinkers generally no longer rest their case on proofs for the existence of God (though Charles Hartshorne tries to retain the ontological proof); instead, they point to the primal intuitions of God that arise out of existential need, as indicating a higher reality that shapes human existence and directs human history.[25]

## Karl Barth and His Adversaries

The most formidable opponent of natural theology in our century is Karl

Barth, indubitably the most profound and creative theological mind since the Reformation. Barth arrayed himself against what he called "neo-Protestant" theology, associated with Schleiermacher, Ritschl, Herrmann, Troeltsch and other luminaries of Protestant liberal theology. What united all these theologians was their supposition that humanity has within itself the capacity to lay hold of divine revelation. The continuity rather than the discontinuity between God and humanity was their salient emphasis. God is not removed from his creation but instead is immanent in human religious experience and ethical endeavor.

According to Barth, neo-Protestantism resulted in the acculturation and domestication of the faith so that Christianity became transmuted into a culture religion. Against the pillars of neo-Protestant theology Barth declared that there is no way that leads to the event of God's self-revelation in Christ. There is "*no* faculty in man for apprehending it," for "the way and the faculty are themselves new, being the revelation and faith, the knowing and being known enjoyed by the new man."[26]

For Barth the gospel cannot be equated with a religious attitude or reduced to ethical principles. The gospel always remains a word from the beyond that stands in judgment over both human spirituality and human righteousness. "Nothing is so meaningless as the attempt to construct a religion out of the Gospel, and to set it as one human possibility in the midst of others. Since Schleiermacher, this attempt has been undertaken more consciously than ever before in Protestant theology—and it is the betrayal of Christ."[27]

Barth perceived in both Bultmann and Tillich the recrudescence of neo-Protestant immanentalism. Both of them made their appeal to some capability or power within humanity that could lead to faith in God as the power of being. Heidegger's philosophy, Bultmann insisted, could give an accurate picture of the fallenness of humanity, but grace is necessary to enable us to gain deliverance from our guilt and despair. Tillich likewise taught that the natural person can know something of human lostness but can rise above this lostness only by the power of grace. Barth frankly admitted that he was separated from this new form of neo-Protestantism "not only by a different theology but, as in the case of Catholicism, a different faith, or, in humanistic terms, a different feeling for life."[28]

Whereas Tillich advocated building a bridge between the gospel and the world of unbelief, Barth, following Kierkegaard, was more comfortable with the metaphor of the fortress, which challenges the outside world by its very existence. The fortress is invulnerable to attack from without, but once we leave the fortress to battle our opponents on their own terrain we risk being overwhelmed by a superior force, for we now no longer have the gospel as our sole armor and defense.

The gravest threat to the church's preaching and teaching ministry appeared in the German Christians, that congeries of groups within the German church in the late 1920s and 1930s that sought to accommodate the faith to the newly arising ideology of National Socialism. This was bridge building at its worst. Barth astutely perceived in "German Christianity" the culmination of the heresy of neo-Protestantism. The German Christians gained support from a significant number of Christian theologians, including Gerhard Kittel, Paul Althaus, Emanuel Hirsch, Friedrich Gogarten, Otto Weber and Karl Adam.[29] They saw in the National Socialist revolution a revelation of God to the German people that could be harmonized with the revelation in the Bible.

Emanuel Hirsch (surprisingly, a Kierkegaard scholar) considered it parochial to limit God's revelation to the history of only one particular people—the Jews. God is unceasingly revealing himself through the great events that shape the histories of all peoples, including the German people. The knowledge of God is found not only in Scripture but also in the laws that govern the life of a people *(Volksnomos)* or in the spirit of a nation *(Volksgeist)*. For Hirsch the church should be independent of the state, but it should be bound spiritually to the cultural ethos.[30] The overriding temptation of the German Christians was to reinterpret the revelation of God in Scripture in the light of the political upheavals that shook Germany in the 1930s.

It was in opposition to the German Christians that the Confessing

Church emerged in Germany enlisting the support of such luminaries as Karl Barth, Martin Niemoeller, Dietrich Bonhoeffer, Hans Asmussen and many others. The Barmen Declaration, authored principally by Barth, was the catalyst for the ensuing church struggle *(Kirchenkampf)*.[31] Against the German Christian claim to other sources of revelation, the Barmen Declaration insisted that Jesus Christ as presented in Holy Scripture is the only revelation of God that can inform the church's proclamation: "Jesus Christ, as he is being attested for us in Holy Scripture, is the one Word of God which we have to hear and which we have to trust and obey in life and in death."[32]

Interestingly, Paul Tillich refused to lend his support to the Confessing Church, though he was adamantly opposed to Nazism as well as to the German Christians. Tillich, then visiting professor of theology at Union Theological Seminary in New York, had been forced to leave Germany because of his book *The Socialist Decision,* which documented his commitment to ideological socialism.[33] He saw in the Confessing Church the creation of "a new heteronomy, an anti-autonomous and anti-humanistic attitude," which he regarded as "a denial of the Protestant principle."[34] Tillich sought a third way beyond the polarity of "German Christianity" and Barthian supernaturalism—the way of a religio-ethical humanism that would build upon values common to both the Christian ethos and the enlightened segment of secular society.

> Though the intelligentsia came to admire the Church for its stand against nationalistic paganism, they were not drawn to it. The dogma defended by the Church did not and could not appeal to them. In order to reach this group, the Church must proclaim the gospel in a language that is comprehensible to a non-ecclesiastical humanism. It would have to convince both the intellectuals and the masses that the gospel is of absolute relevance for them. But this conviction cannot be imparted by the pointedly anti-humanist paradoxes that are used in confessional theology.[35]

It is in the light of the threat of the German Christians that Barth's break with Emil Brunner has to be understood. Unlike Tillich and Bultmann,

Brunner was passionately committed to biblical, evangelical Christianity and was generally regarded as an ally of Barth in challenging the presuppositions of neo-Protestantism. Yet Brunner believed that theology has in addition to its task of explication and proclamation the task of apologetic persuasion, which necessarily involves some kind of natural theology. In his *Nature and Grace,* published in 1934 soon after the Synod of Barmen, Brunner declared that "it is the task of our theological generation to find the way back to a true *theologia naturalis,*" and that it was to be found "far away from Barth's negation and quite near Calvin's doctrine."[36] Brunner's book was immediately welcomed by the German Christians, who rightly saw this as a challenge to the first article of the Synod of Barmen, which affirmed Christ as the only Word of God. Barth replied to Brunner's thesis with a polemical tract entitled *Nein!* in which he stoutly defended the exclusive character of the biblical revelation and showed that Brunner's theology actually constituted a reversion to Catholicism with its principle of grace perfecting nature.

It was Brunner's contention that humanity has within itself "a capacity for revelation" or "a possibility of . . . being addressed," which enables a person to apprehend and receive God's revelation. Brunner spoke of the need for finding a "point of contact" between reason and revelation, for otherwise revelation would be a sheer mystery to human understanding. He found this point of contact in the universal consciousness of guilt, the realization that our fundamental condition is one of finiteness and despair. "This knowledge of sin is a necessary presupposition of the understanding of the divine message of grace."[37] Barth rightly perceived that Brunner was departing not only from Scripture but also from the Protestant Reformation, which sees human salvation as solely the work of God. A human being can do nothing to prepare the way for this revelation; both faith and the capacity to receive faith come from God.

Barth acknowledged with Calvin that God's glory and power are objectively disclosed in nature, but sin renders us incapable of perceiving that this glory and power originate in the true and living God. For

Brunner the revelation of God in nature is a revelation of his wrath, and it is out of the soil of despair that faith comes. Our encounter with the divine wrath prepares us for faith in the divine mercy. Barth accused Brunner of the Catholic error of the *analogia entis,* by which we seek knowledge of God on the basis of the perfection of human attributes. For Barth the biblical way is the *analogia relationis,* by which we can gain knowledge of ourselves in the light of our relationship to God through Jesus Christ.

As his thought matured, Barth hardened in his resistance to natural theology, for he increasingly recognized the danger of severing the knowledge of God the Creator from the knowledge of God the Redeemer. We can know God the Creator only in the light of his revelation in Jesus Christ as the Redeemer. Moreover, we can know our sin only in the light of the grace of God revealed in Jesus Christ. Human beings caught in the web of sin are not first to be reduced to nothingness by being exposed to God's wrath. Instead, the task of the church is to introduce them to both God's love and wrath by pointing them to Jesus Christ.

Furthermore, just as the knowledge of God's love for us in Christ enables us to appreciate the severity of God's wrath against sin, so it is only in the light of the gospel that we come to know the real meaning and impact of the law of God. Rejecting the Lutheran understanding of the law of God as prior to the gospel, Barth maintained that the gospel is prior to the law, that the divine promise comes before and indeed is the basis for the divine commandment.

Natural theology, Barth observed with increasing disenchantment, can also be a way of avoiding commitment to Jesus Christ. By focusing our theological study on the traces of God that can be gleaned from a study of nature and history, we exempt ourselves from the need for listening to God as the revealing Subject who confronts us in our sin and calls us to obedience.

Barth did not deny the reality of natural theology. Indeed, he regarded it as inevitable, for it represents the human being's attempt to make sense of the mystery of life and of the universe on the basis of human power and ingenuity. It is not something to be combated on its own ground, but "it is undermined, relativized and set aside by the actual knowledge of God mediated through Christ."[38] Natural theology should be respected as sinful humanity's "only hope and consolation in life and death." It would be unkind to try to remove this by an eristical attack on human possibilities and thus reduce our hearers to despair, as Brunner advocated. Instead of expending our energies in demolishing natural theology, we should give the positive antidote to natural theology—the story of salvation through Jesus Christ as delineated in the Bible.

In his later years Barth tried to reassess natural theology in a more positive manner by incorporating its concerns within a theology of revelation *(theologia revelata)*. In addition to the one great light of Jesus Christ, he began speaking of "little lights" in nature and history that reflect the light that is in Christ.[39] Nature is not a source or avenue of revelation, but it may be a sign and witness of the one revelation for those who have eyes to see and ears to hear. What Barth opposed was an independent natural theology, the claim to an autonomous knowledge of God. The truth of God that we find in nature is never self-evident but must always be united with and subordinated to the truth revealed in Jesus Christ. "There is neither natural theology nor natural law, but the omnipotence of God who is acting in all of history. Humanity is never without traces of this action, but there is no natural law which reveals itself as self-evident truth."[40]

Barth could even speak of a third circle of witnesses in addition to the prophets and apostles in the Bible and the fathers and mothers of the faith in the church catholic. That is, we as people of faith can truly hear the voice of God in the secular and in the non-Christian religious world, but we will always recognize this as the voice of the One who spoke decisively and definitively in Jesus Christ, and we shall measure the truthfulness of these other words in the light of the one great word spoken in Christ. Non-Christians too may hear the voice of God in their own cultural and religious matrix, but they will invariably misunderstand it. This voice will only confirm them in their own sinfulness and idolatry rather than open them to the possibility of faith in the one true God—the God of Abraham, Isaac and Jacob, the God who truly and fully disclosed his will and purpose for humankind in the person of his Son, Jesus Christ.

### The New Catholicism

Natural theology has always played a prominent role in Catholic history, though in some important Catholic theologians it has been minimized and relativized (as in Pascal, Maurice Blondel, Henri de Lubac and Romano Guardini). Vatican I canonized the doctrine of natural revelation when it stated with an appeal to Romans 1:20 that God "can be known with certitude by the natural light of human reason from created things," though supernatural revelation is necessary in order that the natural can be known "with no admixture of error."[41]

Since Vatican II (indeed, even prior to it) a new Catholicism has developed that reinterprets the role of natural theology. Theologians of the new Catholicism include Karl Rahner, David Tracy, Bernard Lonergan, Edward Schillebeeckx, Hans Küng, Bernard Cooke, Thomas O'Meara, Charles Curran, Gregory Baum, Donald Goergen and Matthew Fox. Whereas Plato, Plotinus and Aristotle were formative influences in the old Catholicism, Teilhard de Chardin, Martin Heidegger, G. W. F. Hegel, Henri Bergson and Alfred North Whitehead are philosophical mentors for avant-garde Catholicism.

In contrast to the old, the new Catholicism seeks to overcome the dualism between grace and nature. Nature is not supplemented by grace but permeated by grace. Grace does not build upon nature; instead, grace renews nature from within. The new Catholicism speaks no longer of God intervening in history and nature, but now of history and nature being included in the creative, forward movement of God. Instead of a supernatural creationism in which God stands over against nature, it upholds an eschatological panentheism, in which God and the world are interdependent. Instead of a Christology from above in which we begin with the pre-existence of Christ, it espouses a Christology from below, beginning with the humanity of Christ.

Revelation is no longer the impartation of propositional truths but now the breakthrough into a higher consciousness. "The Christian message is not information about the divine, to be intellectually assimilated," Gregory Baum avers. "It is, rather, salvational truth; it raises man's consciousness; it constitutes a new awareness in man through which he sees the world in a new light and commits himself to a new kind of action."[42] Our point of departure is no longer faith in a divine revelation in a particular history but now a "fundamental trust" in our fellow humanity (Küng).[43] The goal of Christian endeavor is not the conversion and salvation of the spiritually lost but the humanization of society. An appeal to historical consciousness, which is "an awareness . . . of a transitory present and a genuinely new future," takes precedence over an appeal to the codified traditions of the past.[44] Vatican II's "growing appreciation for historical consciousness was representative of the emerging insights of a new philosophy of process," a sense that "what is real is not essence but existence, not being but becoming."[45]

Also characteristic of the new Catholicism is pansacramentalism: viewing the whole of creation as revelatory. Because Christ's grace is everywhere present and because this grace employs many different instrumentalities, it is suggested that institutions and structures of secular society may be channels of revelation as well as the church. It is even claimed that "adherents of non-Christian religions are being brought to God through their religious institutions and not independently of them."[46]

Closely associated with the idea of a universal salvific grace is the idea of a cosmic incarnation by which the entry of Christ into the world is seen as the "beginning of the divinization of the world as a whole."[47] Sometimes the incarnation of God is interpreted, as in Hegel, as the self-emptying of God into the world, and human history is viewed as the return of the world to God in the form of *Geist* (Spirit). Teilhard's view of a kingdom of freedom at work in history eventuating in the christi-fication of the universe is also pervasive. The Second Vatican Council's plea for the safeguarding of natural rights and human dignity led Karl Barth to ask if the Council was making an infelicitous accommodation to the spirit of the modern age.[48] According to Barth, the basis for free-dom and justice lies not in inherent natural rights but in the divine elec-tion and calling of all peoples to be ambassadors and witnesses of Jesus Christ. One Catholic scholar's interpretation of the Vatican II statement on human rights lends credence to Barth's uneasiness: "No more can one say that natural rights can be superseded by divine revelation, as if the God of nature and the God of Jesus were not one [and] the same."[49]

Not all Catholic theologians of the contemporary period share the optimism and incipient monism so pervasive among both Catholic and Protestant scholars. Romano Guardini, who was influenced by Pascal and Kierkegaard, leaves no doubt that "revelation is not a subjective experience but simple Truth promulgated by Him Who also made the world."[50] The correct theological procedure, Guardini argues, is to begin with God's movement toward us as we see this in Jesus Christ, not with the searchings of the human spirit for God.

> It is the hallmark of a genuine revelation that it cannot be deduced from any forms or potentialities of this world, but rather is utterly independent of them and, indeed, disrupts them. Revealed truth can only be recognized if we cease to approach it with earthly standards and are prepared to accept it on its own terms. . . . And though, indeed, revelation must be accepted without justification by earthly standards, once accepted, it forthwith throws its light upon this very world, encourages it to ask questions of essential importance to it, and gives answers far exceeding natural wisdom.[51]

Hans Urs von Balthasar, too, is a worthy mentor for both Catholics and Protestants who seek another option on the contemporary theological scene. Von Balthasar opposes the "grandiose subjectivity" characteris-tic of the mystical tradition of the church. He calls for a Christocentric and theocentric theology that does not deny the goodness of creation but perfects and crowns creation. In implicit criticism of much traditional Catholic dogmatics, von Balthasar writes: "If there is to be Revelation, it must move from God to a creation, to a creation that does not include the notion of Revelation in and of itself."[52] Instead of grace building upon nature, and theology upon philosophy, divine revelation brings a completely new understanding of both nature and philosophy. "Theology is not a superstructure built atop philosophy. The relativity of the philosophical necessity is made clear in the fact that it only becomes fully evident when it is set off . . . from the theological contingency."[53] Von Balthasar quotes approvingly from his Catholic colleague Erich Przywara, who also seeks to move beyond the Thomist-Scotist understanding: "The way to God and the image of God is only a shadowy hint of something which is brightly revealed by Christ alone; he is the unique exegesis that makes God visible to us. By his own decision, God is revealed to us nowhere else but in Christ."[54]

Like its Protestant counterpart, Catholic theology is at the crossroads; it remains to be seen whether it will return to some form of natural theology or go forward to a theology of creation (as one facet of a theology of the Word of God), interpreting nature in the light of the one revelation of God in Jesus Christ. We are living in a time when belief in the particularity of the biblical revelation is being supplanted by a view of grace that sees all of nature as revelatory and grace as everywhere active, even in non-Christian religions and secular movements, such as socialism, nationalism and feminism. The hope of theology rests on whether we look for our guidance to such defenders of biblical spirituality as Pascal, Kierkegaard, Barth, Guardini and von Balthasar or to proponents of the new spirituality like Teilhard de Chardin, Kazantzakis, Ralph Waldo Emerson, Schelling, Hegel, Whitehead and Matthew Fox, who are determined to overcome what Kierkegaard called "the infinite qualitative gulf between God and humanity."

## General Revelation
The question of a general revelation in nature and history is inextricably

tied to the question of natural theology. Most proponents of natural theology appeal to the general disclosure of God in nature, conscience and universal history. Is there a biblical basis for such a supposition?

Those who try to make a place for natural religion often appeal to Psalms 19:1-4 and 97, which assert that the heavens proclaim the glory and righteousness of God. Yet it is by no means clear that these Psalms promote the idea of a revelation of God independent from the revelation of God's Word to Israel.[55] In fact, in Psalm 19 the light that comes to us from the heavens is definitely linked with the light that comes to us from the Torah.[56] Psalm 97 says expressly that Zion hears the voice of the heavens and is glad, but the earth "sees and trembles"; it does not discern God's action as grace and mercy but only as judgment and wrath.

While the biblical testimony allows for the fact that all people have some sense of the impact of God's universal working in nature and history, it insists that this knowledge is suppressed by the natural person and is thus rendered deceptive rather than dependable. It provides the occasion for idolatry instead of preparing the way for true worship of God (cf. Ps 97:6-7; Jer 10:14; Is 43:10-17; 44:9).

Jeremiah bemoans the fact that despite the universal display of God's mercy and goodness in creation and history, every person is "senseless and without knowledge" and chooses to worship idols rather than the living God (Jer 10:14 NIV). In the face of God's glorious work in creation and history, "all people stand stupefied, uncomprehending" (NJB).

Ecclesiastes gives voice to the skepticism concerning natural knowledge of God that appears again and again in the Old Testament: "I perceived that God has so ordered it that man should not be able to discover what is happening here under the sun. However hard a man may try, he will not find out; the wise man may think that he knows, but he will be unable to find the truth of it" (Eccles 8:17 NEB; cf. Job 11:7 KJV; Rom 11:33-34).

Paul's statements in Romans 1 and 2 concerning the objective disclosure of the presence and power of God in nature (Rom 1:20; 2:14-15) are often cited by defenders of natural theology. Yet Paul goes on to say that human beings in their sinful folly seek to extinguish this light and are thus prevented from truly knowing what God intends to teach them. Their knowledge is sufficient to condemn them but not to enlighten them. They experience the judgment of God, but fail to recognize the origin and true meaning of their desolation and despair and the hope of their existence. They experience God's wrath but do not truly know this wrath as the anger of God's love, for their minds are darkened. Paul makes clear that the knowledge of God's wrath is intimately tied to the knowledge of Jesus Christ, for it is in him that we truly know our sin and the judgment of God against sin.[57]

Some cite Romans 2:14-16 as evidence that one may be justified before God on the basis of natural revelation. Paul states that "when Gentiles who have not the law do by nature what the law requires, they are a law to themselves, even though they do not have the law." First, it is very unlikely that Paul is speaking of gentile pagans, for it is Christians who have the law written on their hearts through the gift of the Holy Spirit.[58] Second, even if Paul were speaking of non-Christians, he would only be pointing to a theoretical possibility, for he explicitly declares that "all have sinned and fall short of the glory of God" (Rom 3:23).

The Fourth Gospel describes Jesus Christ as the true light that "enlightens every man" (Jn 1:9). The world was made through him, and "yet the world knew him not" (1:10). Although the light has come into the world, "men loved darkness rather than light, because their deeds were evil" (3:19). The "light shines in the darkness," but "the darkness did not comprehend it" (1:5 NKJ).[59]

While Calvin made a place for general revelation, he was adamant that this knowledge is sufficient only to condemn us, not to give us a true understanding of God's will and purpose for our lives. The Canons of Dort interestingly referred not to a general revelation but to "the light of nature." Hendrik Kraemer regards "general revelation" as a "misleading term" in need of purification if it is to continue to be of use in theology.[60] G. C. Berkouwer accepts general revelation but sharply distinguishes it from the revelation of Jesus Christ in the Bible. It cannot form the basis for a natural theology because human sin corrupts our understanding and blinds our senses.[61] Consequently he firmly rejects the Roman Catholic view that human beings have a "capacity for revelation," that in and of themselves they are "capable of knowledge of God."[62]

The confidence that general revelation can give us true though inadequate knowledge of God and can therefore furnish the basis for natural theology is nowhere more evident today than in conservative evangelical circles. Bruce Demarest states what is probably the prevailing view in the conservative Protestant world:

> The law written on the heart informs the creature of his spiritual duties vis-à-vis the Creator and Judge of the world. Only when one is conscious of his guiltiness does the receptivity of grace become a possibility. Only when one sees himself as a sinner before the God of Creation does the offer of reconciliation in the gospel make sense. If intuitional and inferential knowledge of God were not present, God's gracious communication to man in the form of special revelation would remain a meaningless abstraction. Special revelation, then, begins at the point where man's natural knowledge of God ends. Natural theology is properly the vestibule of revealed theology. . . . Special revelation completes, not negates, the disclosure of God in nature, providence, and conscience.[63]

Against Demarest I contend that to posit prior human receptivity to the gospel is to make salvation contingent on the human will as well as on divine grace. And to suggest that we can see ourselves as sinners before we are awakened to the truth of God's reconciliation for us in Christ is to attribute to human beings power that is simply not countenanced by the biblical witness or by the witness of the Reformation. I also disagree that special revelation completes the knowledge of God derived from nature and conscience, for this conveys the misleading impression that the two kinds of knowledge are of the same nature and therefore can be joined together.

The dispensational theologian Herman Hoyt argues that "it is true that Christ is the perfect revelation of God. But there is also a revelation of God in the Scriptures and in nature and in the life and experience of God's people."[64] My difficulty with this position is that it conceives of these "other revelations" as separate from the revelation of Christ. I hold that there is only one revelation of God in Jesus Christ, but this revelation is reflected and attested in Scripture, nature, conscience and experience. If we choose to speak of other revelations besides the one great revelation in Jesus Christ, then they must be conceived as being subordinate to and dependent on God's self-revelation in Christ.

Millard Erickson affirms the reality of a general revelation, but, like Berkouwer, he sees it as an inadequate basis for natural theology because of sin, which seriously impairs our noetic faculties.[65] At the same time, he believes this general revelation furnishes a "point of contact" with the gospel that will bring recognition of the gospel as soon as it is heard. He even allows for the possibility of non-Christians, on the basis of general revelation, despairing of their own righteousness and throwing themselves on the mercy of God and thereby receiving justification, though the ground of justification will still be the atoning sacrifice of Christ of which they are as yet unaware.[66]

Norman Geisler likens general revelation to a flash of lightning in the sky at night and special revelation to the shining of the sun in the daytime.[67] It would be closer to the biblical perspective to see general revelation as simply the reflection in the waters of the lightning in the sky at night. Certainly we cannot compare special revelation to the sustained light in the noonday sun, for this would mean that God's revelation is continually and immediately accessible to Christians, whereas revelation is God's free act of self-disclosure, which must occur again and again if we are to remain in the truth. Geisler's position serves to underplay, if not to deny, the mystery and reality of the *deus absconditus,* the God who is hidden—even in his revelation.

Conservative scholars such as Carl Henry often object to the view of one revelation on the grounds that it allegedly makes revelation correlative with salvation rather than with knowledge. It implies that one cannot know God unless one is a recipient of his saving work and power, which is to deny the biblical truth that revelation results in condemnation as well as salvation. Revelation as I conceive it yields real knowledge of God, but knowledge that is personal and concrete, not speculative and abstract. I agree, moreover, that revelation, even understood as occurring exclusively in Christ, does not necessarily entail the acceptance of salvation, but what it does bring us is the reality of salvation. In the mystery of God's providence and predestination, only some are awakened to faith even when confronted by Christ as Lord and Savior. This is why Paul can speak of the preaching of the gospel as an aroma of salvation to some and an aroma of condemnation to others (2 Cor 2:15-16).

I am coming to agree with Hendrikus Berkhof that "general revelation" is a term that should probably now be abandoned because of its ambiguity and imprecision.[68] If revelation is essentially a personal encounter, general revelation would seem to contradict this essential dimension of revelation. If revelation is defined as God's effectual communication of his will and purpose to humanity, then we have no revelation in nature that can be positively conjoined with the biblical meanings of "unveiling" (apokalypsis) and "manifestation" (from phaneroō).

How then should we understand the spectacular work of God in nature and conscience that renders us inexcusable in his sight? It is probably better to regard this general working of God as an exhibition or display of his power and goodness than as a revelation that effectively unveils or conveys his plan and purpose for our lives. Through his general working in nature and conscience, we are exposed to the mercy of God as well as to his wrath and judgment, but God's light and truth are disclosed to us only in the encounter with Jesus Christ as presented in Holy Scripture.

It is appropriate to speak of a general presence of God in nature and history, but this general presence does not become a revelation of his grace and mercy until it is perceived in the light of Jesus Christ. Only in the light of Christ, Karl Barth contended on the basis of Psalm 39:9, can we properly discern God's general light in nature. Yet the light in nature is a reflected or derivative light. It is not a source of the light of Christ but a witness to it, a witness recognizable only to the eyes of faith. Forsyth likened the relation between these two kinds of light to that between the sun and moon. The moon (nature) has no light within itself, but it does indeed reflect the light of the sun, the one source of light for our world (Jesus Christ).[69]

In short, while the wonders of nature manifest God's deity and power, because of human sin they fail to give us real knowledge. They do bring us a deep-seated awareness of God—sufficient, however, to condemn us, not to save us. Real knowledge of God entails not only objective disclosure but also subjective understanding.

A remaining question concerns the status of revelation in the Old Testament. If revelation in its true sense occurred only in Jesus Christ, does this mean that the saints of the old covenant were deprived of revelation? It is theologically more appropriate here to speak of the Old Testament revelation as a preform of the Christ revelation than as a natural or general revelation. Jesus Christ was present in Old Testament history but hidden, even in his revelation. The revelation of God's power and goodness to the people of Israel was preparatory to the full revelation of his grace and mercy in Jesus Christ. We can speak of the Old Testament revelation as an anticipatory or preparatory revelation rather than revelation in its fullness and glory. In order to understand the light of God's truth in the Old Testament, we must therefore view it from the perspective of the full disclosure of this light in Jesus Christ.[70]

One could argue on the basis of numerous Old Testament passages that the law of God constituted a revelation of his truth to the people of Israel. The law indeed brings light from God, but again and again it was misunderstood by Israel as a code of moral rules regulating the life of the nation instead of the law of spirit and life that moves us to service to the needy and forsaken of the world. Apart from the gospel, the law of the Old Testament becomes a legalistic code that stultifies and kills rather than vivifies and renews. Rabbinic Judaism can appropriately be described as a "covenantal nomism,"[71] "a legal religion emphasizing the deeds of the Law and giving pride of place to what is appropriately termed orthopraxy as contrasted with orthodoxy."[72] What the knowledge of the law brings us, apart from the gospel of the free grace of God, is a misunderstanding rather than a proper or true understanding of God's righteousness, which is at the same time God's justifying grace that goes out to undeserving sinners.[73]

**Natural Morality**

One of the perennial debates in Christian theology is whether there is a natural morality that can be discovered by reason and that is valid for both Christians and non-Christians. The overwhelming testimony of Christian tradition is that natural morality exists, though how it is related to the higher righteousness of the kingdom of God has been vigorously disputed. Calvin spoke for many when he said: "There is no doubt that certain notions of right and justice are innate in the human mind, and that a light of justice shines in them."[74]

Human justice as a rational ideal is reflected in both the Bible and the Apocrypha as well as in Hellenistic thought and culture. In Jeremiah 17:10 we read: "I the LORD search the mind and try the heart, to give to every man according to his ways, according to the fruit of his doings" (cf. Deut 1:16-17; Ps 28:4; Mt 7:2; Gal 6:7). God's justice is to repay "all people as their deeds deserve and human actions as their intentions merit" (Ecclus 35:22 NJB). The *lex talionis* (law of retribution), enunciated in Exodus 21:23-25, Deuteronomy 19:21 and Leviticus 24:17-21, is also found in the Code of Hammurabi and the Assyrian laws. Plato and Aristotle defined justice as giving to every person their due, and this idea was pervasive in the ancient world.

At the same time, in the Hebrew Scriptures the rational ideal of justice is transcended. It is not only fairness and equity that characterize the just person but also compassion and generosity. Justice is not only alloting to people a fair share of the goods, but also bringing people into a right relationship with one another and with God. Zechariah enjoins the covenantal community, "Administer true justice; show mercy and compassion to one another" (Zech 7:9 NIV). The Hebrew word *shalom* means not simply peace but reconciling peace, peace united with justice, though shalom in its fullness is an eschatological hope rather than a present reality (cf. Ps 85:8-13).

Biblical religion also affirms that all our initiatives for human justice, even the best of them, cannot merit eternal salvation. Our trust must be not in our own righteousness but only in God's righteousness. Ezekiel assures us, "The righteousness of the righteous shall not deliver him when he transgresses . . . and the righteous shall not be able to live by his righteousness when he sins. Though I say to the righteous that he shall surely live, yet if he trusts in his righteousness and commits iniquity, none of his righteous deeds shall be remembered; but in the iniquity that he has committed he shall die" (Ezek 33:12-13).

In the sight of God all human righteousness is to no avail (Is 64:6; Ps 143:1-2), though in the sight of nations human righteousness is duly recognized and respected (cf. Deut 1:16-17; Ezek 5:6-8). Human efforts for right living are deficient for justification before God because they are mixed with evil motives. "How," Job asks, "could anyone claim to be upright before God?" (Job 9:1 NJB). Another Wisdom author concludes, "There is not a righteous man on earth who does what is right and never sins" (Eccles 7:20 NIV).

In the biblical perspective, God's righteousness is qualitatively different from what human beings can achieve on their own. God's righteousness is his grace, which forgives sins and does not requite us according to our iniquities (Ps 103:8-10; Rom 1:17). Divine righteousness overturns standards of natural justice, for it consists in overlooking iniquities and justifying those who are unrighteous. "Now to one who works, his wages are not reckoned as a gift but as his due. And to one who does not work but trusts him who justifies the ungodly, his faith is reckoned as righteousness" (Rom 4:4-5). Whereas human justice indicates conformity to law, divine justice signifies liberation for self-giving service.

The nature of divine justice can be understood only in the light of the tension between God's holiness and his love. The holiness of God is his transcendent majesty and purity that cannot tolerate sin. His love is his everlasting pity and compassion that will never let sinners remain in their sins. The Bible sometimes indicates a noticeable tension between God's holiness and his love (Hos 11:8-9; Jas 2:13; cf. Ecclus 16:11-16). At the same time, it also provides firm ground for seeing them in a paradoxical unity so that God's holiness is informed by his love just as his love is informed by his holiness. This means that God's righteousness in its deepest sense can be identified with his grace that forgives iniquity, with his compassion that cancels human debts.

Is it possible in this perspective to speak of a moral law or a natural law that is universally applicable and apprehensible? Because human law has its ultimate ground in the divine will, we can affirm a moral law not in the sense of unchanging rational principles that are self-evident in human nature but in the sense of a divine imperative that impinges on the conscience of every human being. Moral law or natural law is not an immutable moral code that even God cannot alter (as Hugo Grotius maintained), but the variegated expression of God's freedom in manifesting his holiness and righteousness. It has its basis not in humanity but in the divine commandment. It is a law that is always in the process of becoming, always taking new forms, since God's commandment is ever new even while it is ever the same.

In a truly evangelical and biblical theology, natural law or moral law cannot be separated from the mind or will of God. It signifies the inescapable relatedness of humanity to the omnipresent God who addresses us in our conscience. The reality of moral law is the universal sense of the reality of the holy God in whom law and grace are united.

Can the person outside faith arrive at a valid understanding of God's commandment? Here we must say that while every person has some intimation or awareness of God's law, those who are ensnared by their evil inclinations will invariably misunderstand it (Prov 28:5 NIV). The natural person can reflect God's righteousness even in the condition of sin but cannot fathom the source of true justice. Everyone has a sense of justice, but there is no uniform law of justice that commands universal assent. Likewise, everyone has an awareness of God, but there is no uniform idea of God that holds true for every culture.

The natural person has some faint intimation of divine justice but only a confused understanding of divine love. This is because God's love is hidden in his justice, and we can know this love only when it is revealed to us through the cross of Jesus Christ.

The cross of Christ not only tells us what love is but also what justice is. The cross reveals not only God's suffering love for sinful humanity but also the vindication of God's holiness, which judges human sin. It also points to the paradoxical unity of the divine love and the divine holiness. Christ paid the penalty for human sin required by divine law, but he was also motivated by sheer love, not by legal compulsion. Moreover, what he has procured for us through his vicarious death and glorious resurrection far exceeds what law as such demands. God's love goes beyond the requirements of law, for he deigns to regard us not simply as forgiven sinners but as his sons and daughters who are given a share in the priesthood and kingship of Christ.

One can say with Emil Brunner that natural law has a formal content but not a material content that is universally discernible. The formal content is giving to people their just desert, but what this means and how this is applied will differ radically from culture to culture. This is why Christian ethics cannot be grounded in natural law theory but instead must be rooted in the divine promise and the divine commandment as they are disclosed in the biblical revelation.

At the same time, we are not free to disregard the laws of nations, the laws that govern society. Such laws will reflect a measure of the truth of God's commandment because they are anchored in the common grace of God that reaches all people. Such laws, though they can never justify us before God, are nevertheless necessary in the providential plan of God to preserve society from chaos. They do not inspire people to love one another, but they do prevent people from harming one another. Yet if they are divorced from the eternal Giver of law, they will inevitably become stultifying codes that cripple the human spirit. As Christians we should seek to transmute justice as a rational ideal into social righteousness as a concrete reality and thereby set up signs and parables of the coming kingdom of God.

Against the prevailing trend in modern ethical theory, I hold, on the basis of biblical revelation as well as church tradition, that natural morality, the morality of preservation, must never be confused with gospel morality, the morality of redemption. Natural morality or legal justice ensures that people are given their due. The morality of redemption or transforming justice makes people willing to give up what is rightfully theirs for the sake of others. Natural morality depends on force to preserve order and to implement justice in society. The morality of redemption relies solely on the power of the powerlessness of love to overcome evil. By resisting the temptation to retaliate against the one who does evil, we will shame that person into repentance (cf. Rom 12:14-21).

Natural morality has a relative validity, since it reflects the law of God in creation. But because of human sin, there is a fundamental incongruity between natural morality and the morality of redemption. Divine righteousness will always be qualitatively different from human righteousness, but this difference does not mean that the latter can never correspond to the higher righteousness by the grace of God.

It is God himself who establishes true justice in the world. We can point to his justice and celebrate it, but we cannot create it. He will make his righteousness prevail over the nations (Is 51:5). "Faithfully he brings true justice; he will neither waver, nor be crushed until true justice is established on earth, for the islands are awaiting his law" (Is 42:4 JB). His justice is designed not simply to preserve society from disorder but also to bring people into a right relationship with one another and with their Creator and Redeemer.

In rational philosophy justice has its basis in the human need for freedom and for sustenance, both of which enable one to live and prosper in a cruel and demeaning world. In theology justice has its basis in the need for the freedom to realize one's destiny in the world before God. The freedom that rational philosophy speaks of is transposed into a natural right that is self-evident. The freedom that theology upholds is a gift from God to undeserving sinners. This means that in theological perspective justice can only be fulfilled in the love that God pours out on an unjust people.

Natural justice is rooted in the human claim to life, liberty and the pursuit of happiness. Supernatural justice is based on the divine grace that cancels all human debts so that all may have superabundant life—the peace and joy that the world cannot know.

Jacques Ellul has made a signal contribution to this discussion by affirming the *fact* of natural law but not the concept of natural law as this is employed in natural theology.[74] Human reason can never be a source or standard for law, but it can organize and implement the law that is impressed on the conscience of every person. Human laws have a relative validity because God wills to preserve creation from chaos by means of them. Yet these laws are a very imperfect approximation of the spiritual righteousness of the kingdom of God, which alone justifies and liberates. Ellul argues that the basic content of human law is the same everywhere, and here he can be faulted.[76] Nevertheless, it is incontrovertible that human laws again and again reflect the eternal law, which is the will and purpose of God, and they do so not because human beings on their own can discover universal truth by either induction or rational reflection, but because God in his grace relates his law to the human condition even in its sin and dereliction. God establishes his law in the midst of the world's chaos, though the human apprehension and articulation of this law will always fall short of its perfect realization as spirit and life. Human law, Ellul argues, is not autonomous and therefore natural, but it depends entirely on the righteousness of God. God judges human beings according to their own human laws and they are found wanting. For example, the people of Jerusalem are condemned not only for their disobedience to divine law but also for their failure to live up to the law of other nations. "Although inferior to the law of God, this law is still valid, and Jerusalem ought to have submitted to it."[77] Natural law can never be a criterion for justice, but it can be accepted as a reflection of true justice, which is known only in Jesus Christ.

The church is obliged to bring the partial justice that nations can achieve on their own under the scrutiny of the righteousness of God as revealed in Jesus Christ and the Bible. It will acknowledge that even the natural person can be "touched by what God does in preserving and governing the world, in his limiting orderings, which make life possible."[78] But with Berkouwer it will not see in this universal working of God a "receptivity for the Giver of this law and the Originator of these boundaries."[79] Faith arises only when people are brought face to face with the love of God as revealed and fulfilled in Jesus Christ. The church will therefore proclaim not only God's commandment but also God's promise, for it is trust in this promise that motivates people as they exercise their civic responsibilities to press for a higher degree of justice.

There is no observable point of contact between justice as a purely rational ideal and the paradoxical love of the cross, but there is a noticeable point of conflict. Love negates and at the same time fulfills justice. But justice does not of itself lead to love, though love always leads to a refurbished and purified justice. Likewise, the law apart from the gospel does not of itself direct us to the gospel, but the gospel directs us to the law, now illumined and transformed by the grace of the gospel.

Today, liberation theology influenced by Marxism seeks a new understanding of justice. The principle of human need becomes the criterion for justice over the older principle of merit or desert (allegedly espoused in bourgeois liberalism). The liberationist Ismael Garcia defines justice as "distribution according to need."[80] In my view the final criterion for justice is not human need but the divine commandment as we see it embodied in the concrete historical existence of Jesus Christ. Garcia speaks of the need for well-being and freedom but not of the need for reconciliation with God. Love, which is simply the longing for justice, becomes a political force that employs coercion. I hold that in the biblical perspective love is the meekness that overcomes evil by refusing to strike back, by refusing to retaliate in kind.

I concur with both Emil Brunner and Reinhold Niebuhr that the relative justice we are able to achieve in a society chronically tainted by human sin must always be differentiated from the absolute justice, the higher righteousness of the kingdom of God.[81] Relative justice can move toward absolute justice, but we must never confound the two kinds of righteousness. A nation cannot be ruled by love, but love can change a nation as a leaven that permeates the attitudes and consciousness of its people. Justice will remain defective and inequitable unless it is superseded by and united with the love that brings about a transvaluation of values.

Christians are summoned not to the ideal of love, as a transcendent goal, but to the practice of love in the here and now. We are called not toward a perfection beyond this world but to exhibit a perfection of love in the midst of this very imperfect world. This love is not a human power or property, however, but solely the movement of the Spirit in which we may be caught up but which we can never control. We can seek and pray for this love, but in the last analysis it is conditional on the free action of the living God. The kingdom will come in God's own time and way, but we can proclaim it and prepare the way for it by calling people to repentance.

### A Theology of Creation

In place of a natural theology, in which the knowledge of God is based on what we can discover on our own through reason and nature, I propose a theology of creation, in which we analyze nature and conscience in the light of God's self-revelation in Jesus Christ. This means that our investigation of nature already presupposes nature as God's good creation. Similarly, our analysis of the interior state of the human soul presupposes that we are created in the image of God and redeemed through the Incarnation of God in Christ. A theology of creation is one aspect of a theology of the Word of God, which sees creation, reconciliation and redemption as an indissoluble unity.

Scripture tells us that God has not left himself without a witness in human history (Acts 14:17), but this witness is suppressed by human sin. Jesus Christ is the light that enlightens every person (Jn 1:9), but this light is obfuscated by human temerity and presumption. God's saving acts in the history of Israel constitute his vindication in the sight of the nations (Ps 98:2), but the nations interpret these acts not as God's intervention in the world but as the insatiable craving for power by an insolent people.

I agree with Otto Weber that biblical religion does not presuppose an ontological remoteness between God and humankind, for this smacks more of deism than of biblical monotheism.[82] God is nearer to us than hands and feet (Augustine), but God is never part of us. He vicariously identifies with our sorrow and lostness, but his divine inviolability and integrity are never compromised.

An evangelical Christian could not say with John Scotus Erigena and many other mystics that the soul is able to find God because at its center the soul is God. We cannot find God until we are found by God in the event of the awakening to faith.

While all people have some perception of the God whom they do not understand in the mystery of his otherness, only those who are beneficiaries of his saving grace have a genuine knowledge of his mercy and his holiness. While there is a universal consciousness of guilt, only those who have been awakened to the reality of the crucified and risen Savior have a consciousness of sin. While the experience of remorse is common throughout the world, only those who are convicted of sin by the Spirit of God are moved to repentance.

I agree with Barth and Berkouwer over Brunner and Bultmann that there is no natural capacity for the gospel. The general awareness of God is not a steppingstone to the gospel or a point of contact with the gospel, because it is invariably misunderstood. It falsifies rather than illumines the divine reality as well as the human situation. Outside Christ we experience the wrath and judgment of God without realizing that it comes from God. We may also experience the general goodness of God,[83] but attribute our good fortune to fate or to an impersonal divine providence. Only in Jesus Christ do we really know both the severity of God's wrath and the depth of his love. Only in the light of the cross and resurrection of Christ do we perceive the indissoluble unity of God's wrath and love.

In our investigation of the knowledge of God we begin with the revelation of God in Jesus Christ. Then we try to see all other lights, all other revelations, in the light of this one great revelation. Creation can be understood only in the light of redemption, because human sin blocks a right understanding of creation. Creation does not prepare the way for redemption, but redemption restores and elevates creation.

The ultimate, primary source of our knowledge of God is Jesus Christ. Other lights clarify and illumine what God has done for us in Christ, so long as our inward eyes have been opened to Jesus Christ. While affirming the universal presence of God in creation, Paul was adamant that we have no other "knowledge of the glory of God" except "in the face of Christ" (2 Cor 4:6; cf. Rom 11:33-36; Eph 1:15-17). The lights that reflect the glory of God in nature and history are signs of grace more than means of grace, indications of his goodness and mercy rather than their source.

There are reverberations or echoes of the one great revelation in Jesus Christ but not new revelations or "other revelations." These echoes are anticipations and indications of revelation, but they do not constitute revelation except when united with the one great light—God's act of self-disclosure in Jesus Christ. Instead of speaking of general and special revelation, it is theologically more proper to affirm the one revelation of God in Jesus Christ and signs and evidences of this one revelation in nature and history. We should perhaps speak of anticipatory and confirmatory signs of this one revelation.

The knowledge of God and of morality that humans can procure on their own is qualitatively different from the knowledge that the people of God have of these things. The intimations of God and of morality in nature and conscience do not lead to true knowledge of God; instead, they constitute obstacles to such knowledge. They are sufficient to condemn us but not to enlighten us. Jonathan Edwards trenchantly perceived the gulf between the horizons of the "natural man" and the Christian: "The conceptions which the saints have of the loveliness of God, and that kind of delight which they experience, are quite peculiar, and entirely different from anything which a natural man can possess, or of which he can form any proper notion."[84]

A theology of creation will understand creation as the preamble to redemption—not in the sense of something deficient that needs to be perfected but in the sense of a foreshadowing of a still greater perfection that is its telos or goal. Indeed, it will acknowledge that God created the world for the sake of redeeming the world. The forgotten and buried knowledge of God in creation is brought to light in redemption. The law of creation is then seen for what it really is, as the law that proceeds from the gospel and leads to the gospel. It works wrath but only to lead us to grace. It is not simply a pointer to grace but is itself a demonstration of grace, for its author is our Redeemer as well as our Creator.

Instead of trying to see God in nature, a biblical theology of creation will try to see nature in the light of God (Gregory of Nyssa). It will celebrate nature as a creation of God, not as the garment or body of God. It will rejoice in the light that is reflected in nature, but it will not see nature as the source of either light or life. Nature may be designated as our sister but not as our mother.

The knowledge of God through nature and conscience apart from the revelation in Christ is not a true knowledge but a deceptive knowledge. It is not an understanding but a misunderstanding. It is not a saving knowledge but a condemning knowledge. It gives us not a capacity for revelation but an incapacity. Natural revelation is simply a reflection of the light of Christ. It is indirect revelation and therefore revelation in the improper sense. Special revelation is a revelation of the light of Christ itself and therefore revelation in the proper sense.

**Natural Theology Today**

We are presently living in a period marked by the resurgence of natural theology, even of nature religion. This can be seen in feminist theology, process theology and the neomystical theology of the New Age and the New Thought movements. Nature is no longer subordinate to Christ but now supersedes Christ as the locus of the sacred.[85] God is no longer Lord and Creator of the universe but now the creative power of the universe, the Womb of Being, the Life-Force, the Primal Matrix, or "the sensitive Nature within Nature" (Bernard Meland). Elizabeth Achtemeier gives some compelling reasons for rejecting natural theology:

> Because God is not bound up with or revealed through the created world, but is revealed only through his own Word (whose meaning includes his acts), nature's processes and structures are not revelatory of the nature of God. If they were, then we could pretty well conclude that the big gods eat the little gods, that death is as much a part of the divine purpose as is life, and that, judging from the deity's supposed "incarnation" in human beings, God is evil as well as good. The Bible knows better, and so it refuses to identify God with his world. According to the second commandment of the Decalogue, we cannot find him revealed through "anything that is in heaven above, or that is in the earth beneath, or that is in the water under the earth."[86]

George Hunsinger is also sharply critical of the infatuation of contemporary theologians with natural theology. He sees it as presaging the loss of the prophetic dimension of Christian faith, for if there is no God who stands over and against nature and history, then there is no criterion that can judge nature and history. "The Christ of natural theology is always openly or secretly the relativized Christ of culture. The trajectory of natural theology leads from the Christ who is not supreme to the Christ who is not sufficient and finally to the Christ who is not necessary."[87]

The battle against natural theology in our day will cross all denominational and confessional lines. Sad to say, modern conservative evangelical theology is as much in the grip of natural theology as is the new liberal theology. May we rediscover with Karl Barth that there is no way that leads from nature or history to the God who revealed himself in Jesus Christ. There is only God's way to us revealed and fulfilled in Christ. To celebrate God's coming to us as the Sun of righteousness (Mal 4:2) means to let go of confidence in ourselves, in our own powers of perception and conception, and trust only in the light that breaks into our lives from the beyond. We then know only because we are known by God; we then believe only because we are set free to believe by his grace; we then obey only because we are impelled to obey out of the love that is poured into our hearts by Christ Jesus (Rom 5:5).

Natural theology ends in idolatry because it means constructing a God out of human reason and experience. A theology of creation gives glory to God because it entails worshiping God under the name given to us in revelation—Father, Son and Holy Spirit. A natural theology views the world as the source of our knowledge of God and therefore of our power over both nature and God. A theology of creation envisions the world as the theater of God's glory. The knowledge given to us in Christ is not the speculative knowledge of natural theology but the knowledge of personal acquaintance. It brings us not mastery over nature or control over our own destiny but power for service and mission.

### Appendix E: Thomas F. Torrance

Theologians who have benefited greatly from Karl Barth are now reconsidering natural theology. Among the most prominent of these is Thomas F. Torrance, who vehemently rejects natural theology in the old sense—as a prelude to positive or revealed theology *(theologia revelata).*[1] Yet he makes a place for natural theology as the field in which our reflection on God's self-revelation in Christ takes place. Natural theology provides the conceptuality by which we try to make sense of the biblical revelation in the cultural milieu in which we live. Torrance argues forcefully that every theological assertion must have an empirical correlate; the investigation of empirical reality thereby provides us with the framework by which we can make the message of faith intelligible to our contemporaries. The conceptual tools that we derive from modern science must still, of course, be "under the control of God's own intelligible reality" as made known in Jesus Christ.[2]

Torrance by no means favors jettisoning the theological conceptuality that is part of our inheritance—derived from both the Bible and the Hellenistic philosophical tradition. Yet he wishes to bring it into a positive relationship with the thought-world of modern science so that its truth can be effectively communicated to the modern person. He advocates rephrasing the older conceptuality and in some cases translating it into a new conceptual language that speaks to modernity, but God's self-revelation in Jesus Christ as recorded in Scripture—the primary basis of the older conceptuality—must remain our indefeasible criterion.

The question arises whether Torrance is imposing on the Bible a realist theory of knowledge drawn from modern empirical philosophy and the natural sciences that may in fact obscure rather than clarify certain biblical affirmations. He speaks of our relation to God as one of subject to object.[3] But does not the living God infinitely transcend the subject-object polarity, and is not a knowledge of God contingent on God descending into our world of space and time as opposed to our finding God by penetrating through and rising above the world of creaturely reality?[4]

Torrance acknowledges that natural theology, as he understands it, does enable us to give contemporary sense to the knowledge of God derived from the Bible. Roundly criticizing the dualistic mode of thinking, which he claims even left its imprint on Barth,[5] he wishes to substitute a realist, unitary theory of knowledge that overcomes the bifurcation between the noumenal and phenomenal, the spiritual and the material, the intelligible and the sensible—the product of a long and venerable philosophical tradition, including Plato, Augustine, Descartes and Kant. Against the dualist or idealist understanding of a cleavage between God and the world, Torrance sees God as freely interacting with the world, as molding the world according to his own purposes.

Torrance clearly recognizes that natural theology, incomplete in itself, must be fulfilled in revealed theology. My question is whether he is sufficiently alert to the danger of allowing natural theology to become again a separate compartment of theology that sets the stage for revealed theology. It should be seen on the contrary as an integral dimension of the one task of theology—to lay the basis for a compelling and forthright witness to the truth of God disclosed in Jesus Christ to both the contemporary church and world.

Not surprisingly, in view of his empiricist orientation, Torrance is very supportive of the cosmological argument for the existence of God, in which God is deduced as the first cause or prime mover of the world phenomena. Yet within the framework of Torrance's natural theology, this argument is no longer a proof involving a "necessary or logical inference" from a contingent effect but instead a "real explanation of real relations . . . God has established with his creation of the universe."[6] This new statement of the cosmological argument as well as his natural theology in general "is not a rational structure that can be treated as complete and consistent in itself, but only as consistent within the empirical conditions of our actual knowledge of God and of the creation."[7]

I readily acknowledge Torrance as a profoundly creative and discerning biblical theologian of our day who has contributed in no small way to the evangelical renaissance. I sincerely appreciate his bold attempt to maintain continuity with the tradition of the church catholic, his appeal to the church fathers as well as to the doctors of the medieval church and the Reformers. We can learn from his timely admonitions to resist accommodating to theological and cultural fads, to maintain the integrity of the church's witness in a time of mounting latitudinarianism and syncretism.

His reassessment of natural theology also elicits my admiration, but not without some gnawing reservations. I can appreciate his concern to integrate theological and scientific knowledge, to include the cosmos as well as humanity in a genuine theology of the Word of God. Yet can the latest scientific construct of humanity and the universe be taken so seriously that theology must strive to correlate its insights with a particular *Weltanschauung* (world perspective) or even *Weltbild* (world picture)? Can science be trusted to give an abiding insight into the cosmic order that will have permanent validity, especially in the light of the fact that scientific theories have undergone as much revision as theological constructions through the years? Can science or even the philosophy of science be expected to provide theology with a conceptual framework permitting fruitful dialog with modernity?

I respect Torrance's imposing attempt to restore objectivity to the theological enterprise, but must this lead to a new natural theology that is, to be sure, not independent from a theology of revelation (as was the old natural theology) but dependent on theology proper for its efficacy and meaningfulness? Is Torrance speaking, as Barth and I are, of a theology of creation that unites dogmatic and apologetic concerns in the service of the proclamation of the gospel?[8] Or does he have in mind a philosophical theology that seeks a synthesis between the faith affirmations of the apostolic church and the modern world view? Is he committed to the Reformation dictum that divine revelation is self-authenticating and does not need to be transposed into a new symbolic-conceptual framework in order to be meaningful and credible to the modern person? Torrance is still writing, and I am sure that he will resolve some of these questions to our satisfaction.

Significantly, Karl Barth, whom Torrance regards as basically an ally, warned of the danger of expunging all idealism from theology.[9] Against both Rudolf Bultmann and Friedrich Gogarten, who vigorously opposed idealism in any form, Barth contended that anti-idealism can be just as damaging as a biblical-idealistic synthesis.

> Idealism is the antidote to all demonology passing itself off as theology. By stressing God's non-objectivity it reminds us that all human thinking and speaking about God is inadequate. It protects theology's object from being confused with other objects. It directs us to the God who is God only in genuine transcendence. Theology needs this antidote and this modesty.[10]

Barth saw idealism as a positive partner in dialog as well as a potential adversary. Idealism in the service of faith enables us to guard against identifying God as an object of theology with the objects of worldly perception. Yet Barth was also alert to the signal dangers of idealism in which "the Beyond of God" becomes confused with "the Beyond in our own spirit."[11]

The phenomena of nature and history, Barth forcefully reminds us, cannot as such be witnesses and organs of revelation. Revelation is to be found only where God decisively enters nature and history, and he has done so only at one place and time—in the life history of Jesus Christ.

Unlike Barth, Torrance shies away from calling God "the Wholly Other," for fear of allowing the re-entry into theology of a dualistic metaphysics in which divinity is radically disparate from nature.[12] Theology must certainly differentiate itself from a philosophy of dualism, but it cannot deny that the God whom it celebrates dwells in "unapproachable light" (1 Tim 6:16), and that this same God is inaccessible to both human perception and conception. God is not ontologically remote from either humanity or nature, but God is hidden in the world of empirical reality because of the blindness caused by human sin. The heavens declare and reveal the glory of God (Ps 19:1-4), but only those with the eyes and ears of faith can see this light or hear this voice.[13]

Theology, Barth assures us, may employ insights derived from both realistic and idealistic philosophy, but it should not attempt a synthesis that would overcome the dualism between mind and matter, substance and structure, the intelligible and the sensible, the spiritual and the temporal, because this would invariably transmute theology into another philosophy of religion. James Smart, in interpreting Barth, has these words of wisdom:

> For theology, truth and reality are one in God and this synthesis which exists only in God is beyond the grasp of human thought. Theology is *human* thought and as such cannot lay hold upon the unity beyond the antitheses but must move dialectically from the truth in the one to the truth in the other. Its thinking has its source in the hidden unity that philosophy is trying to reach.[14]

I agree with Barth that the church must never expend its energies in bringing its witness into harmony with any philosophy or Weltanschauung, even one based on the latest theories of the natural sciences.[15] We must affirm the objective reality of the empirical world as well as the ontological objectivity of God, but never regard the world as such as the domain in which we come to know this transcendent objectivity. The arena of revelation and salvation is not the world, understood as either nature or history, but the life, death and resurrection of Jesus Christ. The Incarnation of God in Christ as well as the resurrection of Christ to God occurred in history but at the same time beyond history (in superhistory). These events are not to be subsumed under *Historie,* objective, recorded history as such, but under *Geschichte,* the eternal significance of a particular history, which cannot be uncovered by historical research or investigation.[16] The basis of our faith does not lie in empirical reality, even when this empirical reality includes the realm of the "experienced imperceptible and intangible" (as in Torrance).[17] Instead, it lies in eternity breaking into empirical and temporal reality, God descending to our plane of existence, and this event is attested only in the Bible, not in nature or experience as such.[18]

I am at one with Torrance in celebrating a God who moves and acts both in nature and history. This God must be sharply differentiated from the god of deism, who creates the world and then remains detached from it. Our God is ceaselessly acting and moving to bring the world to its completion and fulfillment in the kingdom of God, but this kingdom entails negation as well as fulfillment, for both nature and humanity lie under the shadow of sin and death. I heartily join with Torrance in seeing the coming of the kingdom as the transfiguration of the cosmos as well as the redemption of humanity.

# ·SEVEN·

# RETHINKING
# THEOLOGICAL
# AUTHORITY

Put all your trust in the Lord
and do not rely on your own understanding.
PROVERBS 3:5 NEB

If anyone is prepared to do his will,
he will know whether my teaching is from God or whether
my doctrine is my own.
JOHN 7:17 JB

The real ground of our certitude . . . is the nature of the thing
of which we are sure, rather than the nature of the experience
in which we are sure.
P. T. FORSYTH

The ultimate meaning of Word is not a document;
but the documents were preserved by the ancient Hebrews
and the early church because they testified, they bore witness,
to the force of the Word. The people had experienced it,
and they were transformed by it.
JOSEPH SITTLER

Technically Christianity is not even true because the Bible says so
but rather because God who is the ultimate screen of truth has said so.
OS GUINNESS

The question of authority is indubitably at the center of the tensions and conflict in the churches today. Is authority to be placed in human wisdom or cultural experience, or is it to be located in an incommensurable divine revelation that intrudes into our world from the beyond? Does it lie within the compass of what we can ordinarily discover or conceive, or does it break into our world as a new reality that overturns human imagination and conception? Is it a truth waiting to be uncovered through diligent searching, or is it a word personally addressed to us, calling us to repentance and obedience?

"Authority" comes from the Greek *exousia,* meaning "right" or "power" (cf. Mt 7:29; 8:9; 21:23-27; 28:18; Jn 5:27; Acts 1:7; 9:14; Rom 13:1; Rev 12:10). The Latin *auctoritas* referred originally to "moral weightiness" based on prestige, age or wisdom. It also indicated the right to exercise power in a given sphere. Authority in the biblical sense means the power and right to determine what is true or valid. Authority carries the connotation of both binding force and liberating power. It not only directs and controls us but also sets us free for creative service.

Authority in the theological sense is not to be confused with authority in the sociological sense. It is not simply a right or power invested in an institution or person but a claim that convinces by the freedom and deliverance that it effects. It is thus a gift, not merely a demand; a joy, not a trial. It is liberating more than constricting, renewing more than regulating (cf. Jn 17:2).

Obedience to authority in the theological sense is not servile subjection to an external power or norm but glad acceptance of the message that saves and transforms. It is not placing ourselves under an objective standard or external rule or code (the way of heteronomy) but being grasped by a power that encompasses and penetrates us. Nor is it trust in our own inner resources and wisdom (the way of autonomy). Rather, it means surrender to the living Lord who is at the same time the ground and center of our being (the way of theonomy).[1]

The authority for faith signifies the criterion or norm for faith. It constitutes the ultimate arbiter of truth and morals. It is not a rule or code but a living voice, not a credo or standard but a living person. Jesus Christ himself is the ultimate authority for Christian faith. He unabashedly claimed, "All authority in heaven and on earth has been given to me" (Mt 28:18). The apostle Paul writes to the faithful at Colossae: "You have been given fullness in Christ, who is the head over every power and authority" (Col 2:10 NIV). It is commonly said that the Bible is the authority in Protestantism and the church or the tradition in Roman Catholicism. Yet this is a gross oversimplification of a complex issue and does justice to neither side. When evangelical Protestantism in the classical sense claims the Bible for its authority, it has in mind not simply the book but the Word illumined by the Spirit. The Bible is the formal norm for faith; the gospel or the voice of the living Christ is the material norm. Our indefeasible criterion is not the Bible as a book of rules but the divine promise and the divine command relayed by the Spirit through the Bible.

This ultimate norm—the gospel-law—can only be dimly perceived. It is the rule of faith that determines which parts of the Bible are crucial for faith and life and which are peripheral. It has been stated in various ways: justification by faith, the covenant of grace, the substitutionary atonement, the gospel of reconciliation and redemption, among others. Yet every human formulation falls irremediably short of expressing the plenitude of meaning that is encompassed in the norm of revelation.

This position can be justly accused of presupposing a canon within the canon. Yet taking this route does not mean that our appeal is limited to particular books in the Bible. We must affirm that the gospel or the gospel-law is explicit or implicit in every part of Scripture. It is more appropriate to speak of peaks and planes within the canon, for some parts of the Bible mirror the message of redemption in Christ more poignantly than others.

### Loci of Authority

To hold to Jesus Christ as the absolute norm for faith does not relieve us of the hard task of determining where this norm is to be found. For Karl Barth the norm of faith or basis of authority is outside us *(extra nos)* in the objective self-revelation of God in Jesus Christ. For Rudolf Bultmann the norm is the experience of the new life, the realization of forgiveness that is impressed upon us in our encounter with the preached word of the cross. For Paul Tillich and Reinhold Niebuhr the

RETHINKING THEOLOGICAL AUTHORITY

norm is both subjective and objective, consisting in an objective disclosure in past history and a subjective illumination in present or existential history.[2]

From my perspective, the ultimate norm is the gospel of God based on the mighty acts of God. It can also be thought of as the voice of the living Christ or God's self-revelation in Christ as proclaimed by the apostles of the New Testament. In 1 Peter the gospel is spoken of as the living Word, the good news that is preached (1:23-25). In Hebrews 4:12 it is the revelation of God in Christ and in the Bible. It is given explicit articulation in Romans 1:1-6 and 1 Corinthians 15:1-8. The gospel is not simply the events of salvation history mirrored in the Bible but the illumination of these events to the church in all ages. It is the revelatory significance of what God has done for us in Christ in the sacred history leading up to and including Christ. It is the word of reconciliation and redemption, the message of judgment and grace. It is the announcement that Jesus is the Christ, the Messiah of Israel. It is the proclamation of the imminent coming of the kingdom of God (an emphasis in the synoptic Gospels).

Revelation took place in a particular history in the past, the sacred history that constitutes the content of the Bible. It is this sacred history that can be described as the objective locus of revelation. But the Bible, too, as the record of this history must be included in the objective pole of revelation. The Bible is the original witness to the mighty acts of God. It contains and participates in sacred history, in the dramatic interaction between God and his people.

Because revelation describes the work of God in history and not simply history itself, it should be seen as not merely historical but superhistorical. History is not the foundational source of revelation, but revelation takes place in history. History is the occasion by which we hear the revealed Word of God.

The ultimate or eternal source of revelation is the holy God himself. The Bible or biblical history is the mediate or historical source of revelation. It is not the experiences of the biblical writers but the content of the Word addressed to them by the living God that constitutes the essence of revelation.

The gospel is the story of salvation, but there is a danger in reducing the contents of Scripture to the "Christian story" (as in narrative theology).[3] A story often conveys the pilgrimage of faith of a particular people, but the gospel is not simply the story of the struggle of the soul or of the aspirations of a people but the Word of God addressed to the soul—not directly or immediately as in mysticism but through events that actually happened.[4]

Yet we must not underplay the experiential dimension of revelation and authority. Revelation happened in the decisive intervention of God in past human history, but it also happens in religious experience. The Reformers commonly described this subjective pole as the illumination of the Spirit. It can also be thought of as the awakening to faith, the voice of conscience or the inner light (cf. Rom 9:1; Gal 1:11-12). The Word is not only external but internal in that it comes to reside in the depths of our inner being (Deut 30:14). According to Jeremiah the Word of God was in his heart like "a burning fire" shut up in his bones (20:9 NKJ; cf. Ezek 3:3). Paul testified, "The same God who said, 'Out of darkness let light shine,' has caused his light to shine within us, to give the light of revelation—the revelation of the glory of God in the face of Jesus Christ" (2 Cor 4:6 NEB; cf. Eph 1:17-18).

The experiential pole of faith is also pronounced in the Johannine literature of the New Testament. It is not enough to hear the message of Christ; we must abide in him if we are to know his truth (Jn 14:16-17; 15:1-11). In 1 John we read, "Christ has made this true, and it is true in your own experience" (2:8 NEB). Thus "He who believes in the Son of God has the testimony in himself" (5:10).

The two facets of authority are graphically illustrated in 2 Peter 1:19, where the authority for faith is likened to a "lamp shining in a dark place" (Scripture) and also to the "morning star" rising in our hearts (the Christ within). Here we see the inseparable and dynamic interrelationship of Word and Spirit.

It is indisputable that theological authority has both a historical and a mystical dimension. Scripture needs to be correlated with experience if its content is to be truly known. Scripture without experience is empty, but experience without Scripture is blind (H. Richard Niebuhr). Scripture is the objective norm by which we can measure the validity of our experience. But to be vital and fruitful, this norm must take root in our lives, which means that we must experience the reality of God presented in Scripture.

Yet in addition to the historical and mystical poles, authority also has a sacramental or ecclesial dimension. We receive revelation in the context of the community of faith. We perceive the truth of the gospel through the eyes of the church. It was not until the Ethiopian eunuch was instructed by the missionary Philip that he came to see the messianic and salvific truth in the passage in Isaiah that so perplexed him (Acts 8:26-39).

The ecclesial tradition constitutes the matrix in which revelation comes to us and is interpreted by us. We come to know the love of Jesus not only because "the Bible tells us so" but also because of what we are told by our holy mother, the church. It is no wonder that the apostle could describe the church as "the pillar and bulwark of the truth" (1 Tim 3:15).

Luther, who emphasized the primacy of Scripture, could nevertheless declare: "The word of God cannot be without the people of God, and the people of God cannot be without the word of God. Who would preach or listen to preaching if no people of God were there? And what could or would the people of God believe if the word of God were not present?"[5]

At the same time, Luther was not ready to agree with Augustine that we should not believe the gospel unless moved by the authority of the church. We believe the gospel because the Spirit seals the truth of the gospel in our hearts, and this truth is self-authenticating. The church helps us to understand this truth in the context of the fellowship of love, but it is not the source or origin of this truth.

The church has authority insofar as it submits to the higher authority of the revealed Word of God, Jesus Christ, who is its head and goal. If we speak of the church as "infallible," Karl Barth wisely observed, this is "not because its pronouncements, which are of necessity humanly limited, possess as such inerrancy and perfection; but because by its pronouncements it bears witness to the infallible Word of God and gives evidence that it has heard that Word; because the Church, 'abandoning all its own wisdom, lets itself be taught by the Word of God.' "[6]

If we include the church as a dependable authority for faith, we have in mind not any particular denomination but the holy catholic church, the kingdom of Christ, which crosses all denominational lines. This is the church that in Zwingli's words "depends and rests only upon the word and will of God." This church cannot err, for it is "governed and refreshed by the Spirit of God."[7]

Theological authority is paradoxical in the Barthian sense rather than dialectical in the Tillichian sense. It is not based on a dialectic between the Spirit of God and the human spirit, because this would make the self-understanding of fallen humanity the criterion for the validity of the message.[8] We are not to rely on our own understanding or perception but solely on the Word that comes to us from without (Prov 3:5), a Word that takes root within us, to be sure, but never becomes part of our being. My method is reason grasped by revelation and brought into the service of revelation rather than an independent reason interpreting revelation.

Karl Barth made a helpful distinction between three forms of the Word of God—the revealed Word or living Word (Christ), the written Word (Scripture) and the proclaimed Word (the church).[9] Barth asserted the unity of the one Word of God in these three forms, but the priority of the first over the last two and the priority of the second over the last. There is something like a perichoresis in these three forms of the Word in that the revealed Word never comes to us apart from the written Word and the proclaimed Word, and the latter two are never the living Word unless they are united with the revealed Word.[10]

In relation to Barth's typology, I would add a fourth form—the inner Word (cf. Jn 5:38; 1 Cor 2:16; 2 Cor 11:10; 13:5; Col 1:27; Jas 1:21; 1 Jn 2:14; 5:10). The written Word and the proclaimed Word have no efficacy unless Christ makes his abode within us by his Spirit. It is not only the light that comes to us from the Bible and the church but also the light that shines within us by the indwelling Spirit that convinces us of the truth. This is the light of a reborn conscience, and may also be referred to as the inner light, though not in the Quaker sense.[11] Jesus Christ as the revealed Word of God in past history becomes the living Christ through the experience of being engrafted into his body by the Spirit. Yet this experience is always mediated by external means of grace—the Bible and the sermon.[12]

It is also possible to speak of the visible word (the sacraments) and the embodied word (the Christian life). Yet because the visible word is an extension of the proclaimed word, for the sacraments gain their efficacy from the word of proclamation, and because the embodied word is simply a reflection and manifestation of the power of the inner word, I have chosen to remain with this fourfold typology.[13]

The Bible is the external standard by which we judge the truth of the church and the truth in our own experience. The Bible is dependent on the church not for its truth but for the communication of its truth. The church gives us the Bible, but it also places itself under the authority of the biblical message, the gospel of God. The Bible is dependent on the inner Word for the acceptance of its truth.

The Bible, the church and the light of conscience are all dependent norms. Over these is the transcendent, absolute norm—the revealed Word of God, Jesus Christ. Paul referred to this norm as "the mind of Christ" (1 Cor 2:16). Barth calls it "the dogmatic norm." Jesus Christ is the apex and the foundation of faith and authority, but he chooses to meet us in the encounter with Scripture and the preaching of the gospel in the community of faith.

In 1 John we are introduced to three witnesses—the Spirit, the water and the blood, and these three agree (5:8). If we have the Spirit alone, we end in mysticism or spiritualism. Yet the experience of the Spirit is indispensable for faith and life in Christ. If we have the water (the sacrament) by itself, we are then only under another heteronomy. The blood may be taken to signify the atoning sacrifice of Christ on the cross in biblical history, but this sacrifice must make experiential contact with us to be effectual.[14]

The need for personal experience of Christ is potently illustrated in John 4, where the Samaritans tell one of Jesus' converts: "It is no longer because of your words that we believe, for we have heard for ourselves, and we know that this is indeed the Savior of the world" (4:42). The testimony of God is indeed found in the human heart as well as in a book or in a sermon. Yet in our willingness to make a place for the sometimes disputed role of experience in faith, we must forever be on guard against the heresy of experientialism, in which experience becomes the ruling norm for truth and life. Examples of this aberration are legion. For the German mystic and Anabaptist Hans Denck, the norm is the spirit, not the letter; the living word, not the written word.[15] George Fox, the founder of the Quakers, stressed the priority of the leading of the Spirit over the letter of Scripture. The Quaker theologian Robert Barclay denied that spiritual revelation had to be tested by the Scriptures.[16] In the Oxford Group movement, now known as Moral Re-Armament, the appeal is to the inner voice or guidance of the Spirit, not to the written word.[17] Much is said of the human change effected in us but nothing of the divine change effected in Christ. The Russian Canadian sect the Dukhobors upholds new revelations and new Christs, which render Scripture superfluous.

The experientialist aberration is also conspicuous in Protestant liberal theology. Schleiermacher's appeal was to the "corporate experience" of the people of God rather than to purely private revelations. "The living word in a community and the religious stirrings of a community have a far higher power than the written letter."[18] Dietrich Ritschl finds the criterion for faith in the spiritual presence of Christ in the community, not in "a collection of witnesses and reports from two thousand years ago which in contrast to later texts are given revelatory quality."[19] A more individualist bent can be detected in Carl Rogers, the spiritual father of the modern pastoral care movement: *"Experience is, for me, the highest authority.* The touchstone of validity is my own experience. No other person's ideas . . . are as authoritative as my experience."[20]

A mystical thrust is also evident in the Russian Orthodox philosopher Nicolas Berdyaev: "The criterion of truth is in the subject, not in the object, in freedom, not in authority, the importance of which is merely sociological. The criterion of truth is not in the world and not in society, but in Spirit, and there is no criterion of Spirit outside Spirit itself."[21]

Even in modern evangelicalism the experientialist fallacy remains an omnipresent danger. Jerry Walls, an evangelical Methodist associated with the Good News movement, rightly maintains that experience is basic but nevertheless subordinate to Scripture. Yet he says: "What this points up, clearly enough, is that appeal to the authority of Scripture logically involves a more basic appeal to *experience,* namely, to the experience of the Biblical writers. It is because we have become convinced that the Biblical writers had certain experiences that we appeal to the authority of Scripture."[22] I would argue to the contrary that our faith is grounded not in the experience of the writers of Scripture but in the reality they experienced and in the message they received in their experience.[23]

Evangelical faith affirms the primacy of Scripture over experience but not to the exclusion of experience. If we have the Bible alone—apart from the church and apart from the experience of faith—then we end in the morass of a certain kind of fundamentalism or narrow biblicism. Early scholastic orthodoxy at its best held to the complementarity of Word and Spirit, though the function of the Spirit was simply to ratify the Word rather than to bring new truth via the Word to the church in every age. When the Reformers spoke of *sola Scriptura,* they meant the Bible illuminated by the Spirit in the matrix of the church. *Sola Scriptura* is not *nuda Scriptura* (the bare Scripture). It means that the Bible is our primary authority, not our only authority.

The Reformers always regarded the Bible as an instrument of the Spirit, a tool used by the Spirit to bring the truth of the gospel to the hearts of lost men and women. A case could be made that they also thought of the Bible in the matrix of the church, never divorced from the church. The Bible is the historical or mediate source of revelation but not the only channel of revelation. Our authority is not completely enclosed in the pages of a book, for this would reduce the truth of the Bible to law and also exclude the role of the Holy Spirit.

Biblical authority has a higher place than church authority because it is based on the primary witnesses to revelation, whereas church tradition is anchored in the secondary witnesses to revelation. We affirm the Bible over the church and over religious experience, but at the same time the Bible as exercising authority in the church and in religious experience.

If we have the church or the creeds alone, then we end in a confessional orthodoxy, ecclesiasticism or sacramentalism. This is the perennial temptation in Roman Catholicism. For Cardinal John Henry Newman the supreme arbiter in natural religion is conscience, whereas in revealed religion it is the vicar of Christ, Peter. Karl Rahner regards the church's "awareness of faith" as "a theological supreme court."[24]

Spiritualist theologians like Thomas Müntzer agreed with the Catholic church that the Bible by itself is inadequate without a divinely inspired interpreter. Yet this interpreter is not the church or the pope or the councils but instead the prophet, "the new Elijah, the new Daniel, to whom is given the key of David to open the book sealed with seven seals."[25]

This so-called Catholic temptation is also present in the mainstream Anabaptist tradition. We see it, for example, in Eberhard Arnold, illustrious founder of the Society of Brothers: Christ's truth "bears a new criterion which is decisive for the whole present age, a criterion which proves the purity and unity of the leading light. It is the unanimity of the Church of Christ of all ages."[26]

Classical evangelical theology discriminates between the wheat and the chaff in church tradition. As Luther put it, "What does not teach Christ is not apostolic, even though Peter or Paul teach it; again, what preaches Christ is apostolic even though Judas, Annas, Pilate, and Herod do it."[27]

If we have Christ or the message of Christ alone apart from Scripture, the church and experience, then we end in a historical objectivism, a positivism of revelation, a Christomonism. This has always been the temptation in Barthian circles, though Barth himself never intended to separate the ontological norm, Christ, from its mediation in history and experience.[28] Jesus Christ alone *(solus Christus)* is the sure anchor and foundation of Christian faith. Yet this is not Christ outside history or even Christ in past history but Christ alive in the church through his resurrection, Christ dwelling in our hearts by his Spirit. We come to know Christ as the power of creative transformation only through the experience of his cross and resurrection. We come to participate in the salvation that Christ offers only by being born from above by his Spirit.

**Absolute and Relative Norms**

The absolute norm for Christian faith is the "gospel of God" (Rom 1:1; 1 Tim 1:11), the "gospel of Christ" (2 Cor 9:13; 10:14; Phil 1:27) or the "gospel of the kingdom" (Mt 24:14). It may also be designated as the "law of Christ" (Gal 6:2) or the "mind of Christ" (1 Cor 2:16). Yet this norm is hidden in relative norms. "Relative" in this context does not mean deceptive but dependent. The Bible, the church and conscience are dependent for their efficacy on the living Word of God, Jesus Christ, as he speaks and acts in and through these subordinate norms for faith and life.

The presence of the living Christ in the midst of the faithful must be believed rather than perceived (in the empirical sense). This presence cannot be empirically documented, but it does have empirical reverberations, for the fruits of faith are evident in the lives of those who are indwelt by the Spirit. Yet only the eyes of faith can recognize these fruits as manifestations of the Spirit of God.

Luther at one place described the presence of Christ in the church as "impalpable" and "insensible," though he did not mean to deny the experiential dimension of the faith. We cannot perceive Christ with the visible eye, but we can experience Christ in our heart. We cannot make contact with Christ through any of the senses or by reason, but he makes contact with us in the depths of our being so that we can know even though we cannot comprehend. "The word itself, without any respect for persons, must do enough for the heart, must so grasp and convince one, that, caught up by it, one feels how true and right it would be even if the whole world . . . said otherwise."[29]

Christ is hidden or concealed even within the self in that he is never immediately accessible to us. He is known only as he makes himself known in the crisis of repentance and faith. We were baptized into his death and raised with him to newness of life (Rom 6:1-11), and yet the new life in Christ is something hidden—from ourselves and from others—though it can sometimes be experienced in the form of upwelling joy and outgoing love.[30] Paul says that our "life is now hidden with Christ in God," and when Christ, who is our real life, appears, then we also will "appear with him in glory" (Col 3:3-4 NIV).

When we describe Jesus Christ as the absolute, irreducible norm of faith, we mean not only Christ crucified and risen but also the indwelling Christ. It is not only the transcendent Christ who is the source of our authority and faith but also the incarnate Christ. It is Christ *for* us and *in* us.

We affirm the interdependence of the relative norms—the Bible, the church, conscience—and the independence of the absolute norm—God's self-revelation in Jesus Christ. These relative norms are interdependent, but they are not equal. The church and conscience (or the experience of faith) are dependent on the Bible, which is the original witness and record of divine revelation.

We also do not have the absolute norm except in the form of relative norms. The gospel of God is not given to us directly but comes to us through the Bible and through the church proclamation, insofar as this proclamation rests upon the Bible.[31] The relative norms in and of themselves do not possess the capacity to reveal God in Christ, but by the action of the Spirit they can bear and communicate this revelation. The finite can be a bearer of the infinite, but only when the infinite acts in and upon the finite.

This subtle relationship between the absolute and relative norms of faith can perhaps be made more clear by the illustration of the water, the faucet and the glass. We receive the water of life only through the faucet (the Bible) and the glass (the church). Yet we really have this water only when we ourselves drink from the glass (the experience of faith).

Scripture, the church and the faith experience are instrumental norms, but they are not in themselves the definitive norm of faith. The Bible might be regarded as a regulative norm as well, but it is not in and of itself the absolute norm. Yet by the action of the Spirit it participates in this absolute norm. It is in the Bible that we hear the voice of the living Christ, the revealed Word of God. The Bible is then not only a witness to revelation but revelation itself in human words.

While it is the supreme guardian and definitive expression of the church tradition, the Bible is also included within tradition. It is the embodiment of the apostolic tradition and the criterion and judge of the ecclesiastical tradition. It is likewise the ruling norm and judge of religious experience.

The act of God in giving Scripture and the act in which he makes Scripture his word for us are reciprocal coefficients.[32] The moment of revelation occurred then—in the history of Israel culminating in the Incarnation of Jesus Christ—and this same moment occurs now as the Spirit opens our inward eyes to the eternal significance of this event of redemption.

The relative norms for faith might be regarded as derivative authorities. Their authority is derived from the divine reality to which they point and attest. They have real authority but only when seen in their organic relatedness to the divine Spirit who speaks and acts in and through them. It is this Spirit who is the ultimate author of the Scriptures and the divine center of the church.

The relative norms for faith have both an absolute or divine side and a human side. We see in these norms the divine in the human, not the divine eradicating the human. This means that these subordinate norms are not only relative but in one sense absolute. Yet if they are absolute it is only because of the action of the Spirit of God. They become the living Word of God by a miracle of divine grace. They are made to convey truth that is absolute and irrevocable by the work of the Spirit upon them and also within us.

The Reformers tried to do justice to all the loci of authority. While emphasizing the primacy of Scripture over the church, they never separated Scripture from the church. They focused their attention not on the Bible as a codebook of law but on the Bible as the law of life and freedom. Their trust was not in the Bible as a book of history but in the Bible made alive in the church by the action of the Spirit. While a church or council may sometimes err,[33] the Bible never errs in that it gives us the truth originally intended by the Spirit so long as we search the Scriptures in faith. But our infallible standard for faith is not the Bible in and of itself but the Bible united with the Spirit.

With the Reformers we must take care not to separate the Bible from the experience of faith or the light of conscience. This is not an experience or light independent of Scripture but one informed by Scripture. When Luther declared at the Diet of Worms that he could do no other, it was because his conscience was *bound* to the Word of God.

For neo-orthodoxy, Paul Tillich rightly observed, experience was never a source for systematic theology, since this would imply a norm outside revelation itself.[34] Yet Tillich contended that in one sense, experience can be thought of as a theological source insofar as it is the medium through which the revelation is received: the medium "colors the presentation and determines the interpretation of what it receives."[35] Experience is not an independent source for theology but a dependent medium, which nevertheless shapes theological explication.

In my view, experience is indeed a medium of revelation, but it should never determine the interpretation of revelation, for revelation contains within itself its own interpretation.[36] Our task as theologians is to subordinate our understandings and experiences as much as possible to the new light that comes to us from the Bible. We should not come to the Bible with questions derived from our life experience (as Tillich suggested) but instead allow the Word of God to remold our life experience. It is not our question to God but his question to us that constitutes the point of departure for an evangelical systematic theology (cf. Job 38:1-3).

Whereas the Reformers appealed to the Word and Spirit (meaning here the written Word), Karl Barth's appeal was to the living Word, Jesus Christ, as he speaks to us by the Spirit through the Scripture and the church. My preference is to see the source of authority as the Triune God—Father, Son and Holy Spirit—as he speaks to us through the gospel concerning Jesus Christ, the gospel contained in Scripture and reaffirmed by the church. I would add that this gospel must also be experienced by the faithful as their source of life and renewal in the world. The differences between these positions are minimal, for they all uphold Scripture not in isolation from but in coordination with other sacred authorities. When a position that affirms the complementarity of Word and Spirit or the dependence of Scripture on the gospel is contrasted with the narrow biblicism of evangelical fundamentalism, then the differences become much more significant.

## The Paradoxical Nature of Theological Authority

The criteria of theological authority all have a paradoxical form in that they contain two sides—the divine and the human. Jesus Christ, the absolute criterion, can be apprehended only in the form of paradox—as fully God and fully man in one person. There is no paradox in Christ himself nor in his relation to God, for he is not a surd in reality but the divine rationality that lies at the basis of worldly reality. He is not the "ultimate irrationality" (Whitehead) but the Logos, the power and wisdom of God.

Jesus Christ as the foundational paradox of faith is both God and man. This means that he is both infallible, in the sense of being nondeceiving, and fallible, in the sense of being vulnerable to the limitations and biases imposed by history.[37] Christ is a paradox not in the sense of a logical riddle but in the sense of a new reality (Tillich). The apparent contradiction is due to the limitations of our reason. The offense of the paradox is due to the arrogance of reason.

The Christological paradox is paradigmatic for other paradoxes. But Jesus Christ is sinless, and this means that he alone is the perfect vessel for the divine plan of salvation in the world. He alone is the primal or original sacrament, the visible means of an invisible grace. There is a hypostatic union between the eternal Christ and the Jesus of history, but there is no such union between Christ and the church or between the Word and the Bible. Nor is there such a union between Christ and the individual believer.[38]

The Bible also has a paradoxical authority, for it is both the word of God and the word of human authors. It is both divine revelation and an ineradicably human testimony. It is the Word of God but in a worldly form. It is a dependent norm but also a dependable norm because it is grounded in Jesus Christ. Its authority is delegated or derivative from Christ.

The church, too, has two sides that witness to the mystery of Christ's continuing presence in the world. It is both the kingdom of Christ and an ecclesiastical institution. It is not the incarnation of Christ, but it could be regarded as the divinely appointed vessel of the Spirit of God. Augustine ingeniously referred to the Holy Spirit as the soul of the church.

Just as there is a distinction between the Word of God and the Bible, so there is a distinction between the Spirit and the church. Here I heartily concur with Hans Küng: "For all the links between them there is no identity, but rather a fundamental distinction between the Spirit of God and the human structure of the Church."[39] The church is distinct from what is divine and yet inseparably united with it (Karl Rahner).

The inner light or the light of conscience also reflects the indissoluble mystery of the divine in the human. Conscience is both the voice of Christ and the superego. Only a conscience that is captive to the Word of God (Luther) is absolutely normative for the Christian. Conscience is not so much a criterion as a clarification of the truth of faith (Ellul). Moreover, conscience can be lost with the demise of faith (1 Tim 1:19-20 NIV). Like the church it can be seared and maimed (1 Tim 4:2), but so long as the believer is linked with Christ in the mystery of faith, conscience will always be somewhat of a guide on the pilgrimage of faith.

The Enlightenment severed conscience from faith in the living God, elevating it to an independent criterion that actually opposed the claims of faith. This new understanding is to be found in Rousseau: "Conscience! Conscience! Divine instinct, immortal voice from heaven; sure guide for a creature ignorant and finite indeed, yet intelligent and free; infallible judge of good and evil, making man like to God!"[40] It is also reflected in the idealist philosopher Fichte: "Conscience alone is the root of all truth: whatever is opposed to conscience, or stands in the way of the fulfillment of her behests, is assuredly false."[41]

In assessing the authorities for faith and life, we must be on guard against both the docetic and ebionitic types of heresy. These terms were originally applied to heretical interpretations of the person of Christ. The docetists denied or underplayed the humanity of Christ by envisaging Christ as a transcendent ideal or a purely spiritual reality. The ebionites fully acknowledged the humanity of Christ but failed to relate it adequately to his divinity. For the modern ebionite the Bible is edifying religious literature or the embodiment of the spiritual wisdom of a particular people, but not the inspired Word of God. The church is a socially productive fellowship but not the mystical body of Christ. For the docetist the Bible is a verbal revelation from God, a compilation of divine utterances, but not a human witness that necessarily bears the marks of historical and cultural conditioning. Or the Bible is the visible container of a timeless idea or of an eternal truth. For the docetist the invisible church is the essential church, and the visible church is simply its external form. In trying to clarify the mystery of the two sides of the Bible and the church, both the docetist and the ebionite fail to perceive the ineluctable paradox that we have the divine only in the human; for the present, therefore, we must be content to walk by faith, not by sight.

### The Ground of Certainty

The certainty of faith lies in the inward confirmation of the Spirit concerning the objective validity of the biblical revelation. We are given a spiritual, not a rational, certainty. The mysteries of faith remain incomprehensible, but the Giver of faith works within us a confident trust and assurance.

The basis of certainty is to be found in the unity of the internal and the external. The ground of certainty is Jesus Christ as perceived by faith, not God or the Son of God as he is in himself. The basis of authority lies in the promises of Scripture illumined by the Spirit, not in the Bible simply as a book, that is, in the letter of the Bible. It lies in faith as a work of the Holy Spirit within us, not faith as an act of believing or faith as an experience or feeling. The seat of authority is the faith that gives rise to repentance, but the source of our authority is the living Christ, who implants and nurtures faith by his Spirit.

The basis of certainty is neither subjective nor objective. God, indeed, is transpolar and transhistorical. Divinity transcends the polarity of subjective and objective. God is the Absolute Subject who nevertheless graciously makes himself an object for our understanding by the working of his Spirit. The ground of certainty is God speaking through the objective event and the subjective experience.

That authority does not lie simply in historical knowledge is made abundantly clear by our Lord: "Flesh and blood has not revealed this to you, but my Father who is in heaven" (Mt 16:17). We know Jesus as the Christ not by knowing Jesus according to the flesh but by having our inner eyes opened to the divinity that is hidden in him (Eph 1:17-18). Authority has its locus not in our conscience as such but in the Spirit of Christ working in our conscience. Paul insisted, "I speak the truth in Christ—I am not lying, my conscience confirms it in the Holy Spirit" (Rom 9:1 NIV).

What Christians have is not self-certainty but "soul-certainty" (Forsyth), or even better, God-certainty. It is not the fact of our experience but the fact *which* we experience that shapes and determines Christian faith (Forsyth).[42] What I espouse is not fideism but a faith that is deeper than fideism, for it is anchored in the supreme rationality that constitutes the content and object of faith.

Luther was adamant that true faith takes us out of subjective feelings and experiences and leads us to place our trust and confidence only in Christ. "This is the reason why our theology is certain: it snatches us away from ourselves and places us outside ourselves, so that we do not depend on our own strength, conscience, experience, person, or works but depend on that which is outside ourselves, that is, on the promise and truth of God, which cannot deceive."[43]

Our theology rests upon the living Word of God. Yet this is the Word of God not by itself but as apprehended by faith and interpreted by the church. What Forsyth says is quite sound: "We have not two certitudes about these supreme matters, produced by authority *and* experience, but one, produced by authority *in* experience; not a certitude produced by authority and then corroborated by experience, but one produced by an authority active only in experience, and especially the corporate experience of a Church."[44]

To put it another way, the Holy Spirit is not a second criterion alongside the Word but one aspect of the sole criterion—the Word enlightened by the Spirit or the Spirit illuminating the Word. The Spirit does not simply reveal to us the original meaning of the text but leads us into the deeper truth to which the text bears witness. The Spirit directs us to the divine content of the Bible, which transcends and at the same time fulfills the verbal testimony.

Our authority is revelational-contextual rather than merely biblical or merely historical. It is dynamic and paradoxical, not merely propositional or transparently logical. It is theological, not philosophical or sociological. It is personal and transcendent. In Forsyth's words, "The final authority is not only external, or other, in its action, but personal. It is a relation of persons in holy love."[45]

The authority for faith is certain and dependable because it is anchored not in ourselves, not in the church, not even in the Bible as a book, but in Jesus Christ himself, the eternal God-man, who is the head of the church and the center of the Bible. The testimony of God is greater than the testimony of his messengers (1 Jn 5:9). It is included in the testimony of church tradition, but it is at the same time hidden and concealed in this testimony. It is present in the witness of the church, but it is anchored and grounded in Jesus Christ.

Jesus Christ is the light, the Bible is the lamp and the church is the household of light. The inner light is the eyes of faith, or the eyeglasses that enable us to perceive the light correctly. We can therefore say that the church is under the Bible, and the Bible is under the gospel. The authorities for faith are not equal, but they are all of decisive importance. Religious experience is the medium by which we discern the light and truth of Christ, but it is not the source or norm for this light and truth. Religious experience is dependent on the Bible for its truth, but the Bible in turn is dependent on religious experience for its efficacy.

Jesus Christ is the center of our being, the author of the Bible and the head of the church. Could Christ ever contradict the Bible or the church? Of course, Christ cannot contradict himself, but his Word is not identical with the words of his servants and messengers. The apostle exhorts us to test the spirits to see whether they come from God (1 Jn 4:1; cf. 1 Cor 14:32), and the criterion is always whether the prophet's testimony conforms to the gospel of God, which comes directly from Christ. Only those prophets who clearly confess that Jesus Christ alone is Lord are to be trusted (1 Jn 4:2-3), for such a confession is impossible except by the Holy Spirit (1 Cor 12:3).

The authority of the Word of God is not arbitrary but personal and spiritual. It is not heteronomous but theonomous. It demands not uncritical submission but joyous fidelity. It asks not for blind acceptance but for careful consideration. This authority provides its own evidence. It sets us free to believe and to obey. When this freedom wells up within us, we are made inwardly certain that the message of the gospel indeed comes from God. As our Lord phrases it, "Whoever has the will to do the will of God shall know whether my teaching comes from him or is merely my own" (Jn 7:17 NEB).

Authority is a gift as well as a claim. It claims our allegiance but at the same time imparts the capacity and willingness to adhere to this claim and act upon it. As the law of spirit and life it liberates us for obedience.

Johann Christoph Blumhardt, who had a marked impact on both Karl Barth and Emil Brunner, gave an apt description of theological authority:

> One must have norms, even for the Bible. And in this case it is Christ, as he is presented by the apostles. Wherever in scripture I cannot make that norm fit, then that passage is not for me until I *can* make it fit. Many times, then, I must wait until the teaching comes, until finally it is given to me.[46]

## Mystery and Meaning

As the people of God we have Christ, but only in the sign, veil and work of his redemption. We perceive not Christ in the majesty of his glory but the hidden Christ, who is hidden even in his act of revelation. Our knowledge of God and Christ is indirect, since it is mediated to us through a particular history.

Faith signifies an encounter with the Word of God, but this Word is enveloped in mystery. The person of faith is not, however, overwhelmed by mystery, for meaning shines through mystery.[47] We have in the Christ revelation both the disclosure of meaning and the fulfillment of meaning (Reinhold Niebuhr), but this is a partial disclosure and a partial fulfill-ment. Faith has both mystical and rational elements. Faith consists in an experience that is at the same time united with the word. The object of faith is not an ineffable presence but a spoken message or a living

Subject who speaks a definite word concerning himself.

I cannot agree with the existentialist philosopher Karl Jaspers: "Authority does not lie in the word, not in the text, not in the Bible, but in the encompassing that is at once subjective and objective in original adoption, in free association with the Bible."[48] On the contrary, theological authority lies in submission to the Bible or to the Word of God in the Bible. It is in the biblical word that we hear the eternal word, and there can be no separation between form and content in this context.

Neither could I say with Gregory Baum that "the ground of truth on which a man stands is his own deep experience of life (in which God's Word addresses him). Man must build his life on his own convictions."[49] It is not our experience or our convictions that constitute the foundation for life in Christ but God's decisive action in the Jesus Christ of history, action that procures and effects our redemption and liberation. We can and will experience the effects of this redemption, but the authority for faith and life lies in the redemptive act itself, not in our experience. The ground of truth is the divine revelation given in the Bible. We should seek to bring our own convictions into accord with the Word. According to Baum, God is at work in human experience just as he is at work in the sacred history of the Bible. Truth, therefore, is attained in a dialectic between the Bible and human experience. In my view, the dialectic that brings us truth is between the Word in the Bible and a converted reason.

Truth is received from God through the Bible in the experience of faith. This experience marks a break with and judgment upon human experience as such. What we seek is the illumination and transformation of human experience by the Word of God. This Word is never encompassed by experience, but it breaks into experience, remolding and reshaping it. Even when we experience it, it remains something apart from and beyond our experience.

Baum follows in the footsteps of Schleiermacher, who saw truth in terms of intuitive depth awareness. Truth, however, is found not by gazing into ourselves but by looking to him who acted for our redemption in past history—the history mirrored and recorded in the Bible. This is why apostolic faith insists that salvation comes not from meditation on the self (as in Gnosticism) but from hearing the message from the mouth of a preacher (Rom 10:8-9; 1 Cor 1:21). Salvation comes not from a teacher who draws truth out of us (as in Plato and Socrates), but from the Jews (Jn 4:22), from God's decisive intervention in a particular history and a particular people.

Faith brings real knowledge but not univocal knowledge. We do not know literally the things of God, nor do we know merely symbolically. In revelation we are given not a symbolic awareness of God (as in Tillich) but an analogical knowledge that affords us a glimpse of the reality of God on the basis of his self-revelation in Jesus Christ. It is in the light of God's condescension in Christ that we discern both the congruity and incongruity between God and the human creature. Analogy gives us an approximate knowledge of God, but not a comprehension of his reality and working. It is a knowledge that can be expressed only in paradoxical and mythopoetic language.

To walk by faith means to walk in the light of the guidance of the church, in the light of conscience and in the light of Scripture. But most of all it means to walk in the uncreated light of Jesus Christ himself, which is reflected in the church, in Scripture and in conscience.

Paradoxically, to walk by faith also means to walk in the darkness, for the light and truth of Jesus Christ are hidden from all sight and understanding. John of the Cross spoke of a dark night of the senses and a dark night of the soul, which characterize the pilgrimage of faith. To walk in the darkness of these nights means to walk by faith alone, trusting only in the promises of God given in Scripture. "In order to say a little about this dark night, I shall trust neither to experience nor to knowledge, since both may fail and deceive; but, while not omitting to make such use as I can of these two things, I shall avail myself . . . of Divine Scripture; for, if we guide ourselves by this, we shall be unable to stray, since He Who speaks therein is the Holy Spirit."[50]

The truth of faith can be perceived only by the eyes of faith. It cannot be verified or established by experience. It can, however, be confirmed in our experiences, but this is a confirmation given by the Spirit himself to our experience. The confirming work of the Spirit consists not in proofs for the reality of God or for the inerrancy of the Bible but in fruits that he produces in us, fruits more discernible to others than to ourselves. Such workings and fruits can illumine our experience, but they cannot give rational certainty of the object of our faith.

In the last analysis, the truth of the gospel is self-authenticating and self-validating. It is a truth that speaks to the heart more than to the mind. It cannot be discovered by reason, but it can clarify the problems that reason confronts regarding the mystery of human existence. Once accepted, it makes sense of all our experience. Reason is a tool by which we search out the implications of faith for life and existence in the world. Our method, therefore, is faith seeking understanding, or understanding in the service of faith.

The authority of Scripture is demonstrated not by the scientific validation of its factual assertions but by its power to create and shape reality (Paul Achtemeier).[51] But this power is credible only to those who have actually experienced it, only to those who participate in it as believers and disciples. Non-Christians cannot be cajoled into believing in this reality by psychological pressure or by logical demonstration. But those outside the circle of faith can be invited to taste of this reality by people who speak in the spirit of love and holy boldness, people who manifest in their lives the fruits of the Spirit—joy, fidelity, peace, patience, self-control and kindness (Gal 5:22-23).

### Appendix F: The Wesleyan Quadrilateral

What Albert Outler has coined "the Wesleyan quadrilateral" is now being promoted in both evangelical and ecumenical circles as a live option in theological method. Donald Thorsen's book on the subject has contributed significantly to the burgeoning interest in Wesley in this area.[1] Clark Pinnock has declared that this method "if applied promises to reinvigorate classical theology in our time."[2]

The quadrilateral consists in Scripture, tradition, reason and experience, with the first given priority. Scripture is said to be the ultimate source of religious authority and church tradition the abiding resource. Reason and experience are criteria that support the claims of Scripture and tradition. Wesley's method has aptly been called a "transcendental empiricism," beginning with the data of sense experience and rising to a vision of God and the world that transcends experience.[3] Reason and experience can prepare the way for faith, but they can also validate and confirm the message of faith. For Wesley grace is everywhere at work convicting the consciences of men and women and opening their eyes and ears to God's truth pre-eminently revealed in Scripture.

Thorsen admirably shows that Wesley is a biblical, evangelical theologian because of his vigorous adherence to the priority of grace and the supreme authority of Holy Scripture. Yet he also recognizes that Wesley freely drew upon Enlightenment philosophy, particularly that of John Locke, which anchored religious certainty in empirical experience. Wesley was not a systematic theologian, so one can never be sure precisely where he stood on some of these questions. At the same time, he definitely believed that "religious belief is capable of rational assessment *and* rational justification."[4] For Wesley faith is not irrational or nonrational, for it presupposes a serious investigation of relevant evidence.[5]

My difficulty with the Wesleyan quadrilateral is that reason and experience are sometimes portrayed as independent criteria that can lead to a knowledge of God apart from faith. Wesley believed that even without the light of faith one can be convinced of the eternity and omnipotence of God, human immortality and a final judgment.[6] He is very clear, however, that such knowledge does not become salvific until it is united with the knowledge of God's redeeming work in Jesus Christ gained from Holy Scripture. While allowing a positive role for reason in laying the foundations of true religion, he is emphatic that this is reason "under the guidance of the Spirit of God."[7]

It is interesting to compare the Wesleyan *quadrilateral* with the *trilateral* of Charles Briggs, the defender of liberal values against rising fundamentalism in the late nineteenth and early twentieth centuries. For Briggs, Scripture, reason and church tradition all represent valid avenues to a knowledge of God,[8] conscience and religious experience being included under reason. According to Briggs it is possible simply by reason and religious feeling "to rise . . . into the higher consciousness of God."[9] Thus, he contends, a person can find religious certainty and salvation even apart from the mediation of Christ and Scripture. Moreover, the Bible and the church can never exert their full power until human reason "trained and strained to the uttermost" rises "to the heights of its energies" and reaches forth to the transcendent "with absolute devotion and self-renouncing love."[10]

In contradistinction to the above methods I propose a *unilateral* authority—divine revelation—but one communicated through various means. I see divine revelation received through Scripture and tradition and elucidated by reason and experience. Revelation does not so much proceed out of Scripture and tradition as descend into these earthen vessels. It is not based on reason or experience, but it employs reason and experience in making itself credible and effectual.

Reason and experience are not criteria alongside divine revelation but instruments by which revelation shapes human life. They do not validate or authenticate revelation but bear witness to it. Reason, experience and church tradition have a servant role in explicating and proclaiming the truth of God's self-revelation in Jesus Christ given in Holy Scripture. They do not determine the authority for faith, but through the light given by the Spirit of God they acknowledge this authority and celebrate it before the world.

Revelation has its ultimate source in the living God himself, but it is mediated through Holy Scripture, which becomes a conduit of revelation. The revealing act and truth of God in Jesus Christ is appropriated in the experience of faith—a critical component in the whole revelatory process. The church is the field where revelation advances in human history. Revelation might be likened to an electric current that lights up the earthen vessels that stand in its path, but these vessels have no power of their own to produce light.

This way of stating this interrelationship among the various modes of authority safeguards the crucial biblical and Reformation principle that it is God alone who saves and it is God alone who makes himself known. If we could know God on our own, then we would be partial saviors. We receive redemption rather than gain it, but once having received it we can try to understand it. We cannot procure God's redeeming grace, but we can serve it through lives of sacrificial service and words of praise and gratitude. To God alone belongs all the glory *(soli Deo gloria)*, but we can be instruments of his glory in bringing the good news of his redemptive action and mercy to a world afflicted by meaninglessness and despair.

# ·EIGHT·

# THE
# COMMUNICATION
# OF THE GOSPEL

---

Arise, O God, plead Your own cause.
PSALM 74:22 NKJ

---

No one can come to me unless the Father who sent me draws him.
JOHN 6:44

---

We must take care not so to embellish the gospel . . .
that it is quite lost, to defend it so well that it collapses.
Let us not be anxious, the gospel does not need our help;
it is sufficiently strong of itself.
MARTIN LUTHER

---

Many believe in the truth by human arguments,
but no arguments will convince the soul but such as are fetched
from the inward nature, and powerful work of truth itself.
No man can know God, but by God; none can know the sun,
but by its own light.
RICHARD SIBBES

---

It is hard to believe, not because it is hard to understand,
but because it is hard to obey.
SØREN KIERKEGAARD

---

From the time of its origin, the church has been divided on how to communicate the gospel to the unbelieving world. On the one hand, kerygmatic theologians have relied on a straightforward presentation of the law and gospel to penetrate the bastions of unbelief, without regard for the strivings for truth within secular philosophical systems. On the other hand, apologetic theologians have tried to argue the claims of faith with its philosophical critics on the basis of a criterion that both sides acknowledge. Apologetic theology is concerned to find a point of contact between faith and unbelief in order to counter unbelief, whereas kerygmatic theology is prone to deny a point of contact between divine revelation and human philosophy and culture.

Apologetic theology was conspicuous in the early church in the writings of the apologists, such as Justin Martyr, Lactantius, Athenagoras, Clement of Alexandria and Origen. At least some of these scholars treated Hellenistic philosophy as a steppingstone to the gospel analogous to the Torah of the Jews. A vigorous effort was made to win intellectuals to the faith by upholding Christianity as a superior morality or as the supreme wisdom. As a result Christian faith was transmuted into a philosophy of religion and agape was subordinated to the Greek eros. Grace came to be seen as "nothing else than the stimulation of the powers of reason existent in man," and revelation was regarded as "supernatural only in respect of its form."[1]

Some church fathers raised their voices against the biblical-classical synthesis forged by the apologists. Tertullian gave this stern rebuke: "What indeed has Athens to do with Jerusalem? What concord is there between the Academy and the Church? What between heretics and Christians? . . . Away with all attempts to produce a mottled Christianity of Stoic, Platonic, and dialectic composition! We want no curious disputation after possessing Christ Jesus, no inquisition after enjoying the gospel! With our faith, we desire no further belief."[2] Yet Tertullian himself proposed an apologetic defense of the faith based on the superior rationality and loftier morality of the Christian religion.

Irenaeus was one voice that consistently called into question the methodology of the apologists. He complained of those who asserted that the apostles "did . . . frame their doctrine according to the capacity of their hearers, and gave answers after the opinions of their questioners."[3] Jesus never addressed his hearers "in accordance with their pristine notions, nor did He reply to them in harmony with the opinion of His questioners, but according to the doctrine leading to salvation, without hypocrisy or respect of person."[4] Appealing to Isaiah 7:9, Irenaeus declared that faith, which is given by God, is necessary "to have a true perception of reality."[5] Wolfhart Pannenberg contends that Irenaeus found a point of contact with Greek philosophy in his notion of the incomprehensibility of God, but this can be questioned, for in Irenaeus only faith appreciates the full implications of the gulf between divinity and humanity.[6]

While Augustine emphasized the role of faith in coming to a true understanding of the mysteries of God, he nonetheless allowed for a rational defense of the faith as a possible preparation for a faith commitment. He was ready to appeal not only to divine revelation but to such natural reasoning as would attract those who do not share the faith. He believed that reason could make the existence of God as clear to our mind as the sun is to our eyes.[7]

Thomas Aquinas thought it possible to demonstrate by reason certain general truths relating to God and morality, but regarded it as a risky enterprise because we have no assurance that our hearers are ever brought closer to true faith in this way.[8] The only way to convince the unbeliever of the truth of the gospel is to appeal to Scripture.[9] The mysteries of the faith are beyond human imagination and are disclosed only through the outpouring of the Holy Spirit in conjunction with the preaching of the Word of God.[10]

It remained for the Protestant Reformers, especially Luther and Calvin, to call into radical question the biblical-classical synthesis introduced into the church by apologetic theology.[11] Luther in particular drew sharp lines of demarcation between faith as a gift of God and reason, which apart from faith is blinded by sin and in the service of sin. "Faith must believe against reason, against its own feeling and intuition, and against its understanding which grasps and admits the validity only of that which is empirical."[12] In marked contrast to the Augustinian tradition, Luther averred that fallen humanity does not seek for God but must be turned around by grace before genuine seeking can begin. "The true seeking after God, which moves man to dedication and obedience, follows upon the right understanding."[13]

As a kerygmatic theologian Luther was adamant that true faith comes by the preaching and hearing of the Word of God. Such preaching is an instrument of the Spirit of God, who alone can penetrate the hardened hearts of sinners. When we rely on our own wisdom and ingenuity to convince the sinner of the truth rather than on God's revealed Word, we are in danger of blocking and grieving the Holy Spirit. The gospel does not need our aid in its defense; it is quite capable of defending itself.[14] Our task is simply to introduce the gospel to our hearers in the confidence that the gospel by its own intrinsic power will convert and persuade.

Calvin's position was similar. "Scripture . . . ought not to be made the subject of demonstration and arguments from reason; but it obtains the credit which it deserves with us by the testimony of the Spirit."[15] "God alone is a sufficient witness of himself in his own word."[16] It is the responsibility of ministers of the gospel to herald the gospel and let the Spirit reach the minds and hearts of their hearers. Ministers are to act as the prophets and apostles who "boast not of their own genius, or any of those talents which conciliate the faith of the hearers; nor do they insist on arguments from reason."[17] Rather they "bring forward the sacred name of God" that alone can penetrate the hearts of sinners.[18] Calvin believed that once people become Christians, they are then able to confirm their faith by the internal evidences of Scripture and conscience and the external evidences of nature. But Calvin made it clear that these evidences are cogent only for those who are already in the church.

Protestant orthodoxy after the Reformation tended to revert to an apologetic stance. One could argue that more than Luther and Calvin the mentor of Protestant orthodoxy was Philip Melanchthon, who defined faith in terms of intellectual assent and contended that the Holy Spirit follows rather than brings faith.[19] Once faith is posited as a human possibility, the way is open for apologetics of the classical type. Melanchthon resuscitated the proofs for the existence of God, even claiming to be able to prove by natural reason that God is mighty as well as good. The Lutheran orthodox theologian David Hollaz went so far as to allege that reason apart from grace could accept the doctrine of the resurrection.[20] Rationalism was also ascendant in Reformed theology. Francis Turretin (d. 1687) argued that by natural reason one could know the power and existence of God, though not his grace and mercy. Before coming to faith one needed to be convinced of the divinity of the biblical witness, which was assured by such evidences as the Bible's antiquity and duration and the divinity of its authors.[21]

The Age of Enlightenment brought in its wake a new wave of apologetics designed to counter the critique of modernity. Yet in combating the spirit of the new age, Christian apologists unwittingly accepted the presuppositions of their adversaries and thereby undercut the theological basis on which faith rests. Bishop Butler could even say: "Let reason be kept to: and if any part of the Scripture account of the redemption of the world by Christ can be shown to be really contrary to it, let the Scripture, in the name of God, be given up."[22]

Many of the apologies of the eighteenth century were based upon an appeal to miracles, biblical prophecy and design in nature. By the end of that century rationalistic apologetics was increasingly called into question by the probing intellects of the time. Perhaps the most notable critic of apologetic theology was David Hume, who dealt a severe and possibly mortal blow to natural religion in England by his demolition of the proofs for the existence of God. William Adams, George Campbell and William Paley, among others, made valiant but generally futile attempts to answer Hume.

In the nineteenth century Schleiermacher epitomized a new kind of apologetics based not on arguments for the existence of God or on the credibility of the biblical miracles but on the viability of religion.[23] His goal was to convince the cultured despisers of religion that religion is necessary for a meaningful and exhilarating life. Yet he acknowledged that no one religion is final, for people apprehend the Infinite in different ways. While maintaining that Christianity is the highest of the religions, he looked forward to a time when the faith of the church would be supplanted by new and more vital religions.

Among the voices raised against rationalistic apologetics in the nineteenth century was Abraham Kuyper, a Reformed pastor in the Netherlands, who profoundly distrusted appeals to rational evidences in support of the faith: "Arguments for the truth of the Scripture never avail anything. A person endowed with faith gradually will accept Scripture; if not so endowed he will never accept it, though he should be flooded with apologetics. Surely it is our duty to assist seeking souls, to explain or remove difficulties, sometimes even to silence a mocker; but to make an unbeliever have faith in Scripture is utterly beyond man's power."[24] For Kuyper, testing God's revelation is a disingenuous attempt to get behind it to some more ultimate criterion. This then means that revelation and redemption are not the final word.

Tillich is perhaps the apologetic theologian par excellence, for his whole theology is oriented toward showing the inadequacies of modern systems of thought and pointing the searching intellectual to the answer that Christian revelation alone can give. "My whole theological work has been directed to the interpretation of religious symbols in such a way that the secular man—and we are all secular—can understand and be moved by them."[25]

Tillich championed what he called the method of correlation, the aim of which is to correlate the penetrating, creative questions of secular culture with the answer of Christian revelation.[26] The task he set himself was to build a bridge that would lead the outsider to see the necessity of faith in the power of the New Being for an integrated and meaningful life. All people, he contended, have a sense of alienation or estrangement from the source and ground of their being, and this can be used as a point of contact for the truth of the biblical revelation. We can show that faith in the power of the unconditioned can enable the alienated soul to be reunited with the center and ground of its being.

Apologetics has also been rampant in the circles of conservative evangelicalism. Benjamin Warfield claimed that Christianity can "reason its way to dominance."[27] He saw apologetics as a preparatory science conducted prior to theology. "Christianity makes its appeal to right reason, and stands out among all religions, therefore, as distinctively 'the Apologetic religion.' It is solely by reasoning that it has come thus far on its way to kingship. And it is solely by reasoning that it will put all its enemies under its feet."[28]

Edward John Carnell, who acknowledged the affinity of his approach with Tillich's, tried to find useful points of contact between the gospel and culture.[29] He variously appealed to the law of noncontradiction, the law of judicial sentiment and the law of love. He argued that Christianity is the most coherent of all religions, that it can pass the bar of reason without violating the law of noncontradiction. From this perspective, the Christian revelation is inherently consistent and makes sense of all human experience.

Francis Schaeffer's emphasis was on exposing the contradictions and inconsistencies in non-Christian systems of thought and thereby creating a sense of meaninglessness that can lead to faith. "We must tear away the atheist's defenses: rip off the roof, break down the walls, tear off his clothes and leave him naked against the blizzards of life without God until he sees his need of faith in the historical Christ."[30] This approach resembles that of Reinhold Niebuhr, who perceived creative despair as the soil of faith. It also has affinities with Emil Brunner's eristics, the method of attack on the world's illusions rather than the method of building upon the world's aspirations.

Schaeffer was adamant that no one believes without having examined the evidence and being satisfied intellectually that it is true. We must, therefore, show that the evidence gleaned from the senses fails to support the non-Christian system of thought but reinforces the Christian claim to truth. "Theistic presuppositions then can be presented as better accounting for and explaining those things over which the naturalist must stumble."[31] We seek to lead the non-Christian "from the façade of the outward to the reality of the inward,"[32] from a faith that is based on insufficient evidence to a faith that is rationally satisfying.

We can demonstrate that Christian theism is a more credible option than naturalistic humanism.[33]

Perhaps the most formidable advocate of an apologetic theology at the present time is Wolfhart Pannenberg, who holds that revelation must be demonstrable to natural reason without any special illumination by grace. He stoutly defends the Enlightenment stance that revelation must be open to "general reasonableness." Faith is not knowledge but trust on the basis of what historical reason is able to guarantee. Historical investigation can discover the revelatory character and significance of the Christ event, but faith is necessary for this revelation to have efficacy in our own lives. Yet we should not be expected to make the venture of faith until "we have settled whether the God of Jesus is able to shed light on the problems of our contemporary life, and whether the reality in which we live, and which we ourselves are, can therefore be shown to be determined by him."[34]

Karl Barth has been the foremost critic of apologetic theology in our century. He sees apologetics as "the attempt to establish and justify theological thinking in the context of philosophical, or, more generally and precisely, nontheological thinking."[35] Apologetics is based on a mutually acknowledged criterion with secular thought, but no general principle or natural knowledge can lead toward the Christian revelation, which is discontinuous with the thinking and strivings of sinful humanity. Once we base our case on some common ground with the secular mind, we have already lost half the battle. Christianity stands only on its own claim to truth and validity. Barth does not deny the apologetic dimension of theology, but this dimension must be integrated in the dogmatic task of announcing and explaining the contents of the biblical revelation. Apologetics as a preparatory discipline to dogmatics is suspect, but dogmatics with an apologetic concern is salutary, for in presenting the faith we must also strive to answer attacks upon it.

G. C. Berkouwer has also expressed misgivings about the whole apologetic enterprise. True to the tradition of Kuyper and Bavinck, Berkouwer rejects all a priori, preparatory verification of the gospel. The truth of God cannot be delivered into "the grasp of human, testing rationality."[36] Faith in Scripture "is not and cannot be a matter of logical arguments and conclusions furnishing proof comprehensible to the human mind. It is a matter of choice and trust."[37] Yet Berkouwer sees the need for a believing apologetics, one that addresses the truth claims of non-Christian systems of thought from the vantage point of faith.

In the light of this perduring division in the history of theology, we must be careful in trying to determine whether apologetics has a role in theology today. We must certainly, as Barth says, make a place for apologetics to the extent that we must prepare "an exact account of the presupposition, limits, meaning and basis of the statements of the Christian confession, and thus be able to give this account to any who may demand it."[38] We are called to answer those who demand a reason for our faith (1 Pet 3:15), but we must beware of seeking to ground faith in a reason outside the parameters of faith, in a criterion that may be acceptable to the philosophical mind but may be unwarranted in the light of the biblical witness.

Tillich is right that simply to throw the gospel at our hearers as if it were a stone cannot be the way the church fulfills its evangelistic mandate.[39] But to begin with the creative questions of our hearers rather than with the divine question to humanity in its fallen state of sin is also suspect as a way of doing theology. We must avoid both an apologetic accommodationism and a kerygmatic reductionism if we are to give a convincing and biblically faithful statement on the communication of the gospel to the unbelieving world of our time.

It will become evident that my sympathies are much closer to kerygmatic theology than to apologetic theology. I still definitely see a place for presenting truth claims as well as reciting the narrative of biblical history. In our disenchantment with rationalistic apologetics, we must not go to the other extreme of embracing a purely descriptive theology that is willing to make judgments on whether doctrines are normative for the believing community but remains silent on the question of whether these doctrines have ontological truth or universal validity.

## Revelation and Communication

When we speak of the communication of the gospel, we have in mind the miracle of God's self-revelation in Jesus Christ. Communication rests not on techniques or human strategies but on the divine initiative. I say this in opposition to a long history of evangelical revivalism that has often resorted to human technique to bend the human will. Charles Finney, for example, argued that "sinners are not converted by direct contact of the Holy Ghost"[40] but "by the influence of truth, argument, and persuasion." Indeed, he maintained that in our conversion we make use of our natural powers and are merely urged on by the Spirit of God. Calvin was more in line with the biblical position when he averred that we are converted not by our own strength but by "the hidden working and influence of the Holy Spirit."[41] "Certainly we do not turn, unless we are turned. It is not willingly or by our efforts that we turn; but it is the work of the Holy Spirit."[42]

The problem of human conversion must be understood in the light of the biblical affirmation that fallen humanity is both unable and unwilling to come to God in faith and repentance. Paul contends that "the mind that is set on the flesh is hostile to God; it does not submit to God's law, indeed it *cannot*" (Rom 8:7, italics mine). The prince of this world "has blinded the minds of the unbelievers, to keep them from seeing the light" (2 Cor 4:4). Our Lord declares that "no one can come to me unless the Father who sent me draws him" (John 6:44). The people of this world are "ever learning, and never able to come to the knowledge of the truth" (2 Tim 3:7 KJV).

Scripture speaks in this context not of physical inability but of moral inability. Because the human will is in bondage to the power of sin, we of our own power could not turn from the way of destruction even if we were intellectually persuaded that this was the right thing to do. Against Pelagius, Augustine rightly argued that our freedom is not annulled by sin but is so impaired that we are rendered incapable of extricating ourselves from the mire in which we are sinking.

Despite the quandary in which we find ourselves, we have the message of hope that God has chosen to deliver us from our bondage by condescending to meet us in Jesus Christ, by sending forth his Holy Spirit, who places us in contact with the resurrection power of Christ. Moreover, the Spirit chooses to work and speak through human acts and means. These divinely appointed means of grace are preaching, prayer, the Bible, the sacraments and the Christian life. God acts to save us, but in conjunction with our telling the story of salvation and our living out this story in fidelity and obedience. In order to come to a knowledge of God's grace, we must ourselves be beneficiaries of God's grace. In order to be resurrected from spiritual death, we need to be acted on by a power beyond ourselves, the power of divine grace.

The communication of the gospel entails prayerful searching and pertinacious wrestling with Scripture. It consists of much more than merely quoting Scripture. The presentation of the message of salvation involves the interpretation of Scripture, not simply its recitation. We have to discover the relevance of the Bible to the contemporary situation in order to speak and teach the Word of God with power and meaning, and this implies diligent study and fervent prayer.

The gospel is communicated when its emissaries faithfully proclaim the Word of Scripture to the world of sin and darkness. The gospel needs to be heralded more than defended. It needs to be announced and explicated but not recommended as if it were an item for sale.[43] It must be told more than taught (Brunner), though the truths of revelation should, of course, be taught. Indeed, the *didachē* (teaching) is a necessary supplement to the kerygma if our hearers are to know the full ramifications of God's self-revelation in Christ.

Revelation must be proclaimed but in an intelligent way. One must understand the words of the preacher before believing in the message. The gospel should be related to the cultural situation in which people find themselves, for in this way it takes on specificity and concreteness. It must be put in the language of the people. Our presentation must be as logically coherent as possible if our hearers are to understand.

Yet communication means more than making the message intelligible: it means making it knowable. But only the Holy Spirit can do that; therefore the success of our preaching effort rests on the One whom we proclaim and not basically on the way in which we proclaim. As Barth succinctly put it, "Man must receive . . . not only the Word of Christ, but also the Spirit by which it is known, or he will not know it at all."[44]

Communication of the gospel involves not simply the imparting of information but the transmission of meaning and power. Unless the truth we present is appropriated by the understanding and received by the heart, it falls short of being effectively communicated. Full appropriation of the truth involves assimilation as well as commitment.

To be effectual, truth must be spoken in the power of the Spirit. This point is brilliantly made by Nels Ferré:

All arguments in terms of experience, reason and expedience which the Christian offers the unsaved in any realm, even the social realms, are torn to shreds by the unwilling and chained spirit because overt context clashes against overt context and the natural man both prefers and is bound by his own defensive context of meaning. Therefore truth that is not spoken in the Spirit lacks the power of becoming translated, of moving with living meaning into the man who does not share it.[45]

There is a difference between conversation and communication, between impersonal contact and the encounter of minds, between association and dialog. In the event of communication persons become subjects to be cared for and enjoyed rather than objects to be manipulated and controlled. In association we have to do with the meeting of individuals; in dialog our concern is with the meeting of persons.

The communication of the Word of God means presenting the truth to our hearers in such a way that they can make an existential response. But our communication will not be effectual for salvation unless the response is positive. This is why the communication of the gospel necessarily entails a decision of faith. Effectual communication means more than simply giving our message serious consideration: it involves surrender, dedication and faith. In the act of faith and repentance one moves from being a spectator to being a participant.

Again, we must keep in mind that only God can make the human response positive. As Pascal declared, "We shall never believe, with an effective belief and faith, unless God inclines our hearts, and we shall believe as soon as he does so."[46] In a strict sense, only God converts. The prophet confesses, "Thou hast persuaded me, and I was persuaded" (Jer 20:7 ASV).

The decision of faith rests not on free will but on a liberated will, a will emancipated from its downward proclivity by conquering, irresistible grace. Once our inward eyes are opened to the measure of God's love for us, once our will is liberated for service to this love, we will inevitably believe, decide and obey. This is not to discount the impossible possibility of turning back to the way of sin and error after having once been enlightened, but we also have the scriptural assurance that God will not let us go, that he will pursue us even into the darkness, that we will be made to acclaim Jesus as Lord even in the perdition that we might create for ourselves.

The principal channel of God's redeeming action is the heralding of the gospel. According to Paul, "it pleased God through the folly of what we preach to save those who believe" (1 Cor 1:21). "So faith comes from what is heard, and what is heard comes by the preaching of Christ" (Rom 10:17). And in the words of 1 Peter: "You have been born anew, not of perishable seed but of imperishable, through the living and abiding word of God. . . . That word is the good news which was preached to you" (1 Pet 1:23, 25).

The primacy of the Word over symbolic acts and works of reparation is especially noticeable in the writings of Martin Luther. He insisted that Christ "should and must be preached in such a way that, in both you and me, faith grows out of, and is received from, the preaching. And that faith is received and grows when I am told why Christ came, how men can use and enjoy Him, and what He has brought and given me."[47]

A preacher is more than a herald of the gospel: he or she is an agent of reconciliation, a vehicle of divine grace. The one who proclaims is a servant of the Word of God and by the Spirit becomes a conveyor of this Word. We should heed these words of that redoubtable warrior of the faith, St. Vincent Ferrer: "When a preacher preaches the Word of God and is not concerned . . . how to flatter the listeners with sonorous phrases . . . but preaches only the Word revealed by God, it is not he who preaches, but the Holy Spirit in him, or Christ Himself."[48]

## Questionable Methods

When discussing the communication of the gospel we also need to be alert to questionable methods of communicating that actually subvert our best efforts. One of these is preaching at people, simply throwing out words without regard to the situation in which our hearers find themselves. This kind of preaching can be labeled abstractionism. Jacques Ellul gives an acerbic critique of such preaching: "To proclaim the word of God to men in the abstract, to people who are in a situation which prevents them from understanding it, means that we are tempting God."[49] Jesus condemns this approach when he warns us not to give dogs what is holy or cast our pearls before swine (Mt 7:6). The word must be proclaimed but at the right time and in the right place. We must make sure that our hearers are ready to pay attention to our words. If they will not listen, we must shake the dust from our feet and go elsewhere (Mt 10:14). In order to know that auspicious moment when Christ should be openly confessed, we need to pray for the word of wisdom and the word of knowledge (1 Cor 12:8).

In abstractionist preaching the gospel is not interpreted but simply repeated without any real grasp of its content. It is reduced to a gross simplification of a truth that is both profound and mysterious. No effort is made to relate the gospel to people's existential situation. More often than not, the truth proclaimed is not informed by love but delivered from a sense of duty.

Another questionable approach is focusing primarily on our own experiences. This is the peril of subjectivism, a temptation to which Americans seem to be particularly vulnerable. Paul warned against this when he said: "We do not preach ourselves, but Jesus Christ as Lord" (2 Cor 4:5 NIV).

This brings us to the question of whether illustrations have any place in sermons. In my opinion, they do have a place, but they must arise from an encounter with the text rather than be brought in from the outside to validate the text. We can draw on experience, but it is always experience seen through the lens of the text. There is a signal difference between theological illustrations and reminiscing or storytelling.

We are not to exclude personal experiences completely from our preaching, but our experiences must serve the Word rather than ourselves. Helmut Thielicke offers these words of wisdom:

> The witness not only confesses and declares his *message,* he also confesses and declares his *encounter* with the message. Consequently, he also speaks of himself, simply because of the fact that he stands up for the truth he is witnessing. But he can do this only if he communicates to his hearers the fact that he himself has experienced this truth.[50]

Indirectly we preach our experience by revealing the depth of our faith and love in our preaching. The credibility of the witness is almost as important as the credibility of the message. The ambassador of Christ should be characterized by zeal for the faith, humility and outgoing love. Personal testimonies are appropriate if they serve the message, if they give all the credit and glory to Jesus Christ. If they are designed to elevate the preacher and thereby lead away from the message, they then become obstacles to belief.

Arguments in defense of the faith can be still another form of spurious communication. Many of the preachers of earlier generations endeavored to buttress the gospel by presenting proofs for the existence of God or by appealing to the miracles of Jesus or to biblical prophecy. Some seek to prove the bodily resurrection of Christ to the person without faith, but such proofs invariably fall short of being solid demonstrations and often end by presenting false stumbling blocks to faith. Pascal was more sagacious:

Our religion is wise and foolish: wise, because it is the most learned and most strongly based on miracles, prophecies, etc., foolish, because it is not all this which makes people belong to it. This is a good enough reason for condemning those who do not belong, but not for making those who do belong believe. What makes them believe is the Cross. . . . And so St. Paul, who came with wisdom and signs, said that he came with neither wisdom nor signs, for he came to convert, but those who come only to convince may say they come with wisdom and signs.[51]

It is commonly said that in the early period of his ministry Paul sought to prove the faith. In his encounter with the Jews in Damascus (Acts 9:22) he refuted their arguments on the basis of Scripture. He did not appeal, however, to an outside criterion but to Scripture itself. Paul was here in accord with Barth's dictum that "the best apologetics is a good dogmatics." In his sermon to the Athenians (Acts 17:22ff.) the apostle took for his point of departure the altar to the unknown god. Yet he began to strike home only when he preached about the resurrection. We read that some believed but others mocked. When he arrived in Corinth he resolved that he would preach only Jesus Christ and him crucified. Did Paul deliberately alter his strategy because of the low number of converts at Athens? Barth may well be right that Paul was not giving an apologetic discourse at Athens but was presenting a theology of creation and redemption, beginning with the first and then leading to the second. Whatever the case, Paul became more deliberately kerygmatic after his experience at Athens.

The attempt of the preacher to destroy the intellectual framework of unbelief is also suspect as a means of leading people to Christ. Such a strategy involves exposing inadequacies and contradictions in alternative positions. This is the method of attack, or eristics, to use Emil Brunner's term. It is apologetics on the offensive, an approach discernible in Reinhold Niebuhr, Emil Brunner, Os Guinness, Francis Schaeffer and Cornelius Van Til, among others. Niebuhr tries to show in his sermons that the Christian interpretation is more adequate than alternative interpretations because "it comprehends all of life's antinomies and contradictions into a system of meaning."[52] We may rightly ask whether the criterion of the greater coherence of the biblical view of reality is more Hegelian than Christian.

Many of the eristical theologians see despair or vital anguish as the precondition of faith. They seem to agree with Sartre that "life begins on the other side of despair." One can also detect this existentialist motif in Ellul: "When man is bereft of every security, the reality of hope opens wide before him."[53]

Existentialist theologians often appeal to Kierkegaard, who spoke much about anxiety and despair in connection with coming to faith. Yet Kierkegaard drew an important distinction between sinking into despair by refusing to be the self that God intends and trusting in God out of the depths of despair. Facing up to one's despair, which is the conscious-ness of sin, leads to hope and salvation and is given only by the Spirit of God in the event of the awakening to faith.[54]

The words of the father who brought his child to Jesus to be healed are pertinent here: "I believe; help my unbelief!" (Mk 9:24). Do they not suggest that the admission of despair before God is the first step of faith and indeed flows out of faith? Despair of life is destructive, but despair of self as the source of repose may be creative if it is induced by an encounter with the living God.

This idea of two types of despair is also found in Paul when he con-trasts the sorrow of this world, which leads to death, and the godly sorrow that produces repentance and faith (2 Cor 7:10). Paul makes clear that godly sorrow is both the catalyst of faith and the fruit of a living faith in the Lord Jesus Christ.

Biblical preaching should aim for conviction of sin, but this becomes a possibility only when we are exposed to the mercy and judgment of God as set forth in the gospel and law. We can know our sin only when we have first been confronted with the depth of God's love for us re-vealed in Christ. Calvin again shows his remarkable biblical discern-ment: "The light of the Lord alone can open our eyes to behold the foulness which lies concealed in our flesh."[55]

There is a place in biblical preaching for exposing the unbelief in the world and the unbelief that still retains a foothold among Christians. Unbelief needs to be taken seriously, but the power of the gospel needs to be taken even more seriously. Indeed, it is only in the light of the gospel that we can begin to fathom the mystery of unbelief. There is even a place for offering a defense of the gospel in preaching (Phil 1:7, 16), but what is defended is articles of faith that flow from the gospel. The right way to defend the gospel is to bring the truth of the gospel to bear on our misunderstandings and rationalizations.

I definitely do not recommend the way of harmonization for communicating the truth of faith. In this approach the goal is to discover a point of identity between the message of faith and the values and beliefs of the culture. It is said that the message needs to be culturally embellished or buttressed by philosophy or psychology. Or it is alleged that the highest values or deepest insights of the culture already embody the truth of the gospel, at least implicitly. Thomas Altizer speaks of the need to be "authentically contemporary" and to make the symbols of faith "meaningful to the modern consciousness."[56] The theologian is therefore "called to the task of identifying the deepest worldliness of the world as a manifestation of faith and of seeking to engraft that worldliness into the existing forms of faith."[57] Karl Rahner considers culture as well as the Bible to be a legitimate source for theology. The person who questions is already surrounded by the answer, because God's grace is universal in its scope and outreach. Our task is to help our hearers find what they already see dimly.[58]

Against the harmonizers and syncretizers I maintain that culture is not a bona fide source of theology but the catalyzing material that theology uses in the application of the Word of God. Our task is to make the faith intelligible but not credible or palatable, for only the Spirit does that. Our aim is to clarify the gospel, to set forth its scandal without ambiguity, not to remove or mitigate this scandal.

The reason people find it difficult to believe the message is not simply ignorance of the universal Christ, who is everywhere pervasive in culture, but hardness of heart, which clouds their perceptions and weakens their will. This is made disturbingly clear by our Lord: "Why do you not understand what I say? It is because you cannot bear to hear my word. . . . He who is of God hears the words of God; the reason why you do not hear them is that you are not of God" (Jn 8:43, 47).

Finally, there is the method of correlation, by which we try to lead people in the culture to ask the critical questions of human existence and then show how these questions are answered by divine revelation. This is the way of synthesis rather than identity: here the aim is to subordinate the values and goals of the culture to the higher values given in the Christian revelation. This is the approach, as we have seen, adopted by Tillich, but we also find it in Emil Brunner, Hans Küng,[59] Francis Schaeffer, Carl Braaten and R. C. Sproul, among others.

As Christians who seek to be more fully biblical, we too can speak of correlation, but the correlation we aim for is between the message of the church and the revelation of God in Christ. Our primary concern is not with the probing questions of the culture but with the divine question that judges both our questions and answers (cf. Job 40:7; 42:4). The gospel does not so much meet human needs as challenge and transform them. It makes us more cognizant of our need for salvation even while it often denies our immediate instinctual needs.

The way to knowledge of God lies not in an analysis of the human condition or predicament but in an exposition of the gospel of God that includes a call to decision and conversion. Only as converted men and women can we understand the source and the depth of the cultural malaise in which we live. Only in the light of the gospel can we see both the light and the darkness in the culture, which account for its promise as well as its deviousness, its wisdom as well as its folly. Only as Christians do we see hope in culture; this hope does not belong to the culture, however, but to the God who creates and rules over culture. Only then can we preach the message of faith with intrepidity and confidence, knowing that all of life belongs to God, that all civilization is moving toward God not because of any intrinsic desire or proclivity but because of the power of the Spirit of God, who will not rest until all of humanity is brought into subjection to the lordship of Jesus Christ.

## A Biblical Alternative

Against the ways of apologetic accommodation and psychological technique, I propose the way of kerygmatic proclamation united with the labor of prayer and deeds of love. This approach appeals not to common ground with our hearers but to the sovereign grace of God.

The basic problem in evangelism is not just lack of knowledge of the gospel—it is lack of the will to believe. The core of human reluctance to embrace the gospel is volitional more than intellectual. What is required is the conversion of the will before one can become a believer and follower of our Lord Jesus Christ.

The key to effectual evangelism is the regenerating and liberating work of the Holy Spirit. It is the Spirit whose role is to convict and convince (Jn 16:8). Jesus said to Peter after hearing his confession of faith: "Flesh and blood has not revealed this to you, but my Father who is in heaven" (Mt 16:17). Paul insisted that no one can say that Jesus is Lord except by the Holy Spirit (1 Cor 12:3). It is only when the gospel comes to us not simply in word but in power and in the Holy Spirit that it brings full conviction of sin (1 Thess 1:5). "To transmit the Word is not enough," says Nels Ferré, "even when translated and transformed, because the hearer must somehow find *the power* of salvation, and then *the power* of acting within this new context of the Spirit. Truth is not only meaning but also power."[60]

Christian faith has its source not in human need but in divine grace. Religious need provides the occasion for faith, but the Holy Spirit united with the revealed Word of God is its creative source and ground. Faith is an inner awakening to the reality of Christ's love that alone can satisfy the deepest longings of the human soul.

Study of the Bible and the ongoing theological commentary on Scripture is certainly necessary for an intelligent proclamation of the message of faith, but in addition to study we need prayer and meditation. Silence is the soil of the Word; only when we are alone with the Word do we gain the depth of insight that enables us to preach with power and clarity. Yet silence is only a means to a higher end. Silence that does not give rise to speech is dumbness. Speech that does not grow out of silence is chatter.

Prayer evangelism will always play a vital role in the effectual communication of the gospel. Billy Graham wisely adjures the ministerial associations that sponsor his crusades to engage in the labor of prayer—understood as supplication and intercession—before the actual evangelistic meetings take place. Prayer in the power of the Spirit is the necessary seedbed of the Word as well as its crown and goal.

The heart of evangelism is sharing the story of Christ, the good news of how God took upon himself the sin and shame of the human race so that all who believe in him might be saved. Paul tells the Corinthian church, "We refuse to practice cunning or to falsify God's word; but by the open statement of the truth we commend ourselves to the conscience of everyone in the sight of God" (2 Cor 4:2 NRSV). By the "open statement of the truth" he means making known what God has done for us and the whole world in the person of Jesus Christ. The apostolic mandate is not to disguise the truth or even to buttress the truth but instead to declare the truth. This involves relating the message of salvation to our hearers by entering their situation but without being ensnared in their delusions and mythologies.

The distinction between life-situation and expositional sermons is artificial. We must give a faithful rendition of the Word but direct our message to a particular situation. Only then does it have lucidity and power. The message must be made intelligible and applicable to all of life.

We must speak at the right time and the right place. We should not cast our pearls before swine (Mt 7:6), but we should also not cast pearls until we ourselves have ceased to be swine. Paul said that he beat his body so that he might not be disqualified as a credible witness and servant of the Lord Jesus Christ (1 Cor 9:27).

The proclamation of the Word also entails warning our hearers of God's judgment. This means preaching the law of God as well as the gospel. But we should preach the law not before the gospel but with the gospel, for the gospel and law comprise a unity. To preach the whole counsel of God means to preach the truth in love. It means to preach bad news as well as good news. Yet we do not truly know the bad news concerning the human condition until we are awakened to the good news of what God has done for us in Christ. We do not really know our sin until we have been confronted by the cross. As Calvin put it, "Repentance is preached in vain, except men entertain a hope of salvation."[61]

If we are to preach the law, our sermons will necessarily be prophetic as well as kerygmatic. The law when united with the gospel brings the searchlight of God's truth to bear on human sin, but it also provides a guide for living out the Christian life. The law directs us to the gospel, but the gospel also directs us to the law, for faith involves a commitment to discipleship.

Finally, effectual communication of the gospel includes sharing the love of Christ with our fellow human beings through self-giving service. Word and deed go together, and if we have only words to give we are noisy gongs or clanging cymbals (1 Cor 13:1). Dwight L. Moody was doubtless correct that "churches would soon be filled if outsiders could find that people in them loved them when they came. This draws sinners! We must win them to us first, then we can win them to Christ. We must get the people to love us, and then turn them over to Christ."[62] Frank Buchman of the Oxford Group movement, who engaged in a fruitful ministry to the up-and-outs of society, gave this salutary advice to his fellow soul-winners: "First be good friends."[63]

The ministry of sacrificial deeds will involve bringing people into the koinonia (fellowship evangelism), identifying with their grief and affliction (incarnational evangelism), and assiduously interceding for them (prayer evangelism). Logos must be united with praxis if the word is to become more than words, if letter is to be united with Spirit and power.

While deeds play a significant role in the communication of the truth of revelation, they must always be related to and, in fact, grounded in this truth. Jesus gave this keen retort to the prince of darkness, "Man shall not live by bread alone, but by every word that proceeds from the mouth of God" (Mt 4:4). Acts of kindness can be means of grace only when related to the gospel message of salvation. We are not to keep hidden the good news of God's salvation and simply witness through Christian presence. Evangelical theology here resonates with the words of the psalmist: "I have not hid thy saving help within my heart, I have spoken of thy faithfulness and thy salvation; I have not concealed thy steadfast love and thy faithfulness from the great congregation" (Ps 40:10; cf. 1 Pet 2:9).

The integral relationship between proclamation and service is made clear in Jesus' instructions to his disciples: "Whenever you enter a town and they receive you, eat what is set before you; heal the sick in it and say to them, 'The kingdom of God has come near to you' " (Lk 10:8-9). Here we see that the announcement of the good news is accompanied by identification with our hearers in the situation in which they find themselves and by the demonstration of God's power through signs and wonders.

As servants of the Word we should strive to incarnate our message in the cultural situation—relating it to the problems and issues of the time. The content of our message must be the gospel, but the context is the secular society of every age. According to Bonhoeffer, "The word of the church to the world must therefore encounter the world in all its present reality from the deepest knowledge of the world, if it is to be authoritative."[64] Only in this way does the word take on concreteness and specificity.

## A Reappraisal of Apologetics
Does the apologetic concern still have a place in Christian faith and mission in the light of my criticisms of traditional apologetic theology?

To be sure, we must give reasons for our faith as well as proclaim it. All Christian proclamation has an apologetic side in the sense of meeting objections to the faith from outside the circle of faith. To choose preaching over apologetics may mean opting for laziness.

Yet I do not support apologetics in the sense of trying to vindicate the faith to unbelievers on the basis of a common criterion or point of contact with unbelief. We should strive to forge cultural and psychological points of contact with our listeners, but there can be no theological point of contact between the gospel and systems of unbelief. This is because the gospel is not a human idea or a projection of the imagination but a concrete word from God that must never be confused with the words of philosophers or theologians. The words of God are not our words, his thoughts are not our thoughts (Is 55:8). We, therefore, know his will and purpose only when he chooses to reveal it to us, and this will always stand in contradiction to our will and purpose. The event of God's self-communication to a world in darkness will invariably bring about a disruption of our thoughts, values and goals.

All people have a natural awareness of God, but this knowledge is sufficient only to condemn, not to save, not even to set us on the road to salvation. Because this knowledge is inevitably idolatrous, it constitutes a serious obstacle to the true understanding of God. The natural person does not receive the things of the Spirit of God and can only regard them as foolishness (1 Cor 2:14).

Apologetics understood as the conscious effort to convince the outsider of the truth of faith by logic or experience rests on the misconception of faith as a human possibility. In the tradition of liberal theology faith is seen as a potentiality within the human being that needs only to be brought to fruition by grace. It is based on the idea of the freedom of the will, which both Augustine and Luther roundly attacked. Luther acknowledged that we are free in the things below but not in the things above. We are not free before God *(coram Deo)*; therefore, to have fellowship with God we must be made free by divine grace.

The Anglican luminary Richard Hooker (d. 1600) thought it possible to apprehend the things of God by the light of natural reason that shines within. By contrast, Jonathan Edwards was emphatic that the natural person is both unwilling and unable to believe. Fallen humanity needs not greater knowledge but a stronger will.

Apologetics as a conscious effort to persuade or as a strategy of defense is suspect in the light of biblical anthropology. Yet apologetics in the sense of a reasoned advocacy of the faith can still have a role. As Christians we should be prepared to give reasons for our commitment to Christ rather than to the gods of culture. We need to wrestle with the unbelief of the age and think out the implications of the faith as over against unbelief. We should strive to integrate our faith with the whole of our experience in the world. We should try to see the truth of faith in the light of attacks upon it.

The overriding purpose of this refurbished apologetics is not to make the faith respectable or palatable in the eyes of the world but to help Christians understand their faith better. We cannot prove the superiority of the Christian world view over other world views, though we can make a case for its validity when we are asked to do so. But this case will be persuasive only to those who seriously seek for faith or who already have faith.

Karl Barth held that this kind of apologetics belongs to dogmatics. "Dogmatics too . . . has to speak all along the line as faith opposing unbelief, and . . . to that extent all along the line its language must be apologetic, polemical."[65] While Barth was convinced that a good dogmatics will have "an apologetic character," he did not mean that we therefore need "a second discipline." "Dogmatics must have the character of *intelligent witness.*"[66]

Once the gospel is accepted it can be shown to make sense of all our experience. Its authority and authenticity are confirmed in our experience, not so much by the arguments that we can amass for the faith but by the Spirit of God enlightening our minds to see the truth of faith in every aspect of our experience. In place of a rationalistic apologetic, I propose a revelational or what Berkouwer would call a "believing" apologetic. I still think it wise to maintain some distinction between dogmatics and apologetics, but a believing apologetic will flow out of dogmatics, indeed will be incorporated in dogmatics. One might well conceive of it as an extension of the dogmatic task, as is polemics. It will be dogmatics in conversation with the outside world.

My position is not far removed from that of Thomas Aquinas, though significant differences remain. As we have seen, Thomas affirmed apologetics as capable of persuading people of the existence of a divine power and of a natural or moral law. Yet with regard to the credibility of the Christian revelation, apologetic arguments have little efficacy. We cannot prove the God of revelation, though we can show that it is not unreasonable to posit the existence of a transcendent or divine power.[67] Yet he recognized that if an opponent "believes nothing of what has been divinely revealed, then no way lies open for making the articles of faith reasonably credible; all that can be done is to solve the difficulties against faith he may bring up."[68] He saw the place for arguments designed to make the divine truth known, but "this should be done for the training and consolation of the faithful, and not with any idea of refuting those who are adversaries. For the very inadequacy of the arguments would rather strengthen them in their error, since they would imagine that our acceptance of the truth of faith was based on such weak arguments."[69] Thomas did make a place for apologetics directed to the faithful, and here I can resonate with him. I have difficulty with his view that demonstrative arguments can of themselves persuade people of God's existence, but I agree that such arguments are of little avail in bringing people to faith.[70]

To some extent my position converges with that of Jürgen Moltmann, who argues that we should seek to prove the world from God rather than vice versa.[71] Yet Moltmann subtly brings the faith into alignment with a theology of revolution and, like the enlightened Marxists, reconceives transcendence in terms of the unfolding of the future.[72]

As I see it, apologetics is a supplementation to the sermon, not an introduction. Its aim is not to prove or validate the faith before the world but only to clarify the truth of faith in the light of attacks upon it. It is a venture in believing integration, which serves evangelism by illuminating the situation of our hearers. Apologetics in the sense of a critical examination of the cultural and philosophical situation shows us where to *aim* the fire of the gospel; it does not invite us to use the resources of the culture to buttress the gospel.

Is there any place at all for apologetics before faith? As has been amply shown, this question has been vigorously debated through the ages. A. B. Bruce maintained that apologetics "is a preparer of the way of faith, an aid to faith against doubts whencesoever arising, especially such as are engendered by philosophy and science. Its specific aim is to help men of ingenuous spirit who, while assailed by such doubts, are morally in sympathy with believers."[73] Evangelical conservatives have been attracted to the Augustinian apologetic, which holds that self-knowledge is prior to God-knowledge, that the right understanding of self prepares the way for the true understanding of God. According to Augustine, "No one believes anything unless he previously knows it to be believable."[74]

Francis Schaeffer here speaks for many conservatives: "Before a man is ready to become a Christian, he must have a proper understanding of truth."[75] In my view, this proper understanding is given only in faith. I agree with Schaeffer that in one sense knowledge is prior to faith. But this is knowledge of the gospel given through preaching, not knowledge of ourselves arrived at by existential analysis. Schaeffer seeks to give an "honest answer" to an "honest question." But are not most of our questions dishonest, even our questions as Christians?

There can be no common ground between Christian revelation and secular philosophy, but there is common ground between Christians and philosophers. We share a common humanity and a common sinfulness. We can, therefore, dialog in order to clarify our respective positions, though dialog as such cannot bring the unbelieving side closer to faith in Jesus Christ.

Yet arguments for the faith are not necessarily worthless, even to those outside the circle of faith. If we present our arguments in the spirit of love and in the context of the biblical revelation, we can intensify the hunger in the soul of the unbeliever for the truth of God. Of course, this depends on whether the Spirit is at work in our feeble witness to the truth of faith. Our arguments can succeed in silencing criticisms of the faith, but they cannot in and of themselves lead the outsider in a positive way to the gospel. They can sustain an interest in the gospel but not induce a decision. In this sense they are a delaying or rearguard action. They have mainly a negative role. They are not the breakthrough that many hope for, nor can they lay the foundations for this breakthrough.

For those who are earnestly seeking salvation, apologetic arguments have more value. They can help many to become "almost persuaded," though real conviction is brought about only by the Spirit in conjunction with the preaching or reading of the Word of God. One can seek only on the basis of prevenient or quickening grace. One can believe only on the basis of conquering or regenerating grace. The first grace becomes conquering grace when the end result is saving faith in God.

As witnesses to Christ and not as apologists per se, we can point to reasons that the Bible itself gives—miracles, signs, prophecy. In Acts 28 Paul tries to convince the Jews by the law and the prophets (vv. 23-24). Yet texts such as these must be treated with caution. Paul concludes his discourse by giving up on the Jews, citing the prophet Isaiah:

You shall indeed hear but never understand, and you shall indeed see but never perceive. For this people's heart has grown dull, and their ears are heavy of hearing, and their eyes they have closed; lest they should perceive with their eyes, and hear with their ears, and understand with their heart, and turn for me to heal them. (Acts 28:26-27)

Jesus performed many signs and wonders; yet they were manifestly ineffectual in bringing people to faith in his messianic message. In fact, he condemned seeking after signs as proceeding from an idolatrous heart. "This generation is an evil generation; it seeks a sign, but no sign shall be given to it except the sign of Jonah" (Lk 11:29).

To the outside world we can give justification for our decision for the faith, but we can offer no rationally compelling demonstration of the truth of faith. We can show where we stand, but we cannot induce the unbeliever to stand with us. We can give a witness to the truth of the gospel in the hope that the Spirit may be acting to move that individual to seek for the salvation that Christ alone provides.

Apologetics is of most use to those already in the faith, enabling them to understand and meet the questions of unbelief. An interpretation of the faith necessarily entails a reasoned defense of the faith. Yet while reason can clarify and illumine, it cannot establish the truth of faith. It can serve this truth but cannot of itself determine it.

Augustine put it well: "Understanding is the reward of faith. Therefore, seek not to understand that you may believe, but rather believe that you may understand."[76] While Augustine tried to hold apologetic and kerygmatic theology together, his overall emphasis was on the power of faith to inform and enlighten.[77] Our primary task is to lead people to faith so that they will understand rather than to help them understand so that they can then believe.

It is more helpful to speak of pre-evangelism than of apologetics. Schaeffer views apologetics as a form of pre-evangelism, but I would make a clear distinction between them. Pre-evangelism might be called functional apologetics, or still better, good-Samaritan service. We cannot make people open to the gospel, but we can help them to be open to us as persons. In healing and feeding the hungry, Jesus was engaged in pre-evangelism. He was disappointed that his hearers did not see the sign in the miraculous meal, the sign of his messianic identity as the Son of God (Jn 6:25-34).

General William Booth, the intrepid founder of the Salvation Army, had as his motto "soup, soap, and salvation." He rightly recognized that before our hearers will pay attention to our gospel they must be exposed to our love and care for them as persons. Love is the motivation in Christian service but evangelism is the goal.

In summary, apologetics should be seen neither before the gospel as its preparation nor after the gospel as an appendage, but as a vital factor in the gospel proclamation. It both accompanies the gospel and proceeds out of the gospel. Its purpose is to clarify the truth of the gospel in the light of attacks upon it, thereby bringing people a richer and wider understanding of the gospel. As an integral element in the gospel proclamation, it speaks to the world as well as to the church, but it is most helpful to the community of faith, which already assents to the truth of the gospel, yet stands in need of a deeper understanding of this truth. No longer is apologetics a propaedeutic device leading to the revealed truth of Scripture. Instead, it is a faithful explication of the gulf between faith and unbelief, one that introduces our hearers immediately to the claims of biblical religion.

Apologetics is not a preamble to but a servant of faith as faith seeks to win its way in the world. The aim is not to make the gospel palatable or credible to either church or world but to enable the preacher to render an intelligible message, understandable at least with regard to its form and language. Only the Spirit of God can make the message of faith credible or knowable, and this he does when we rely not on our own defense of the faith but on the power and wisdom of the object of our faith, namely, the living Word of God, the Christ of the gospel who speaks to people everywhere through the witness of his prophets and apostles, a witness that includes teaching *(didachē),* fellowship *(koinō-nia)* and sacrificial, loving service *(diakonia).*

## Religious Imperialism Versus Evangelism

The basic issue in Christian mission is religious imperialism versus evangelism. Religious imperialism is a kind of triumphalism, imposing the values and beliefs of a particular religious tradition upon those who belong to another tradition. Evangelism is simply telling the good news of what God has done for us and the whole world in the life, death and resurrection of Jesus Christ in the confident expectation that God will move and act among our hearers in his own way and time.[78]

Apologetics often proves to be a form of religious imperialism. In its traditional sense it means the attempt to compel the outsider by the force of reasoning to assent to the claims of religious faith. Classical apologetics, Douglas Clyde Macintosh notes with hearty approval, "sought to advance reasons for the faith to which the unprejudiced and reasonable outsider *would have to yield his assent*" (italics mine).[79] Apologetics in this sense is nurtured by hubris, for it harbors the temptation to show that we are superior thinkers to others.

Another manifestation of religious imperialism is proselytism, the concerted and sometimes audacious effort to win people over to one's own position or to one's church. It consists in working *on* people, not necessarily working *for* people. Proselytism engages in manipulation, whereas evangelism is the open confession and declaration of the faith to broken and despairing human beings, whose personal integrity is nevertheless respected.

Religious imperialism has for its goal submission to an external authority—a theological formula, a creed or a moral code. It is, therefore, associated with what Kant called heteronomy. Bonhoeffer has some harsh words for this kind of strategy: "Every attempt to impose the gospel by force, to run after people and proselytize them, to use our own resources to arrange the salvation of other people, is both futile and dangerous."[80]

Yet in our condemnation of religious imperialism we must not rush to include evangelism in our stricture, for the two are quite different. Evangelism means seeking the total well-being and conversion of sinful humanity by sharing the good news. I again agree wholeheartedly with Bonhoeffer: "To tell men that the cause is urgent, and that the kingdom of God is at hand is the most charitable and merciful act we can perform, the most joyous news we can bring."[81]

Markus Barth goes too far when he peremptorily rules out missions to the Jews.[82] He sets out to show that anyone who tries to convert a Jew to Christ is basically anti-Semitic. "Neither Jesus himself nor any other Jewish teacher has shown the slightest intention to impose faith on anyone."[83] While it is true that Jesus was not bent on imposing his faith, he was passionately concerned that people embrace the message of the kingdom that alone could give them hope and meaning in a chaotic world.

Evangelism is not simply sharing the story of the gospel but presenting the truth of the gospel, which no adversary "will be able to withstand or contradict" (Lk 21:15). The way to meet attacks of our opponents is to bring the searchlight of the gospel to bear upon the deceptions and myths that beguile a credulous world. Paul gives this eloquent description of Christian warfare that employs not the wisdom of the world but the power of the Word of God itself:

> The weapons with which we do battle are not those of human nature, but they have the power, in God's cause, to demolish fortresses. It is ideas that we demolish, every presumptuous notion that is set up against the knowledge of God, and we bring every thought into captivity and obedience to Christ. (2 Cor 10:4-5 NJB)

A. W. Tozer overstates the case when he regards "the witness of the church" as "most effective when she declares rather than explains, for the gospel is addressed not to reason but to faith."[84] The ambassador of Christ is called to give reasons for faith that challenge the mind as well as tantalize the soul. To be sure, these reasons belong to faith itself—the resurrection of Jesus Christ from the dead and the evidence of a regenerated heart. Evangelism employs explication as well as confession, but the first is always subordinated to the second.

To proclaim the gospel to a lost world entails calling for a decision that has eternal significance. The announcement of the good news is not enough, despite the impression sometimes given in Barthian circles. In our preaching we must seek for both conviction of sin and commitment to Christ.[85]

Humanity cries out not for solutions to metaphysical problems but for salvation from the dread reality of sin. Evangelism is the answer to this heartfelt cry and need. As witnesses and servants of Christ, we should not try to force our faith on others but share our faith in love, with the hope that the Spirit of God will so act upon our hearers that they will gratefully receive and acknowledge the truth we profess. Our motivation is compassion for a lost and despairing humanity, not the vain desire to build up a religious empire. Evangelism is not the imposition of a point of view but the overflow of a thankful heart. Our reliance is on the grace of God, not on our superior understanding (cf. Prov 3:5 NEB).

D. T. Niles has compared evangelism to one beggar telling another where to get food. While this imagery contains the truth that the Christian too is a sinner, it tends to neglect the fact that the Christian unlike others is engrafted into the vine, the source of spiritual nourishment (Jn 15:1-11). This person is a vessel of the indwelling Spirit of God and, therefore, does not simply point to Christ but radiates the love and joy of Christ. We not only tell others where to get food, but we also bring them food.

Evangelism is not a recruitment program for a particular church but confronting our hearers with the gospel call to decision. Our weapons are divine: "the helmet of salvation," "the shield of faith" and "the sword of the Spirit, which is the word of God" (Eph 6:13-17). It is with these weapons and not by counterarguments that we "destroy arguments and every proud obstacle to the knowledge of God" (2 Cor 10:5).

As heralds and ambassadors of the kingdom we hope for conversions and even seek them—but always in Christ. By our own power and wisdom we cannot induce conversions. Apart from God, we can do nothing (Jn 15:5), but we can be used by God. We can be instruments of the Spirit in his work of persuasion and conviction.

The object in evangelism is not mutual understanding nor simple togetherness nor a higher synthesis but repentance and faith, unconditional surrender to God. Our call is not for blind submission but for a rational decision that leads our hearers into a new horizon of meaning and service. It should be kept in mind, however, that we introduce people not only to Christ the Redeemer but also to a redemptive fellowship—the holy catholic church. Therefore, the evangelistic mandate entails socializing and civilizing as well as converting and baptizing.

The ultimate purpose of our preaching and teaching is to serve both the glory of God and the freedom of a reborn humanity. God is glorified when we are made free to believe in the gospel and to serve our fellow human beings in outgoing love, which the New Testament calls *agapē*.

Karl Barth has trenchantly observed that to preach the Word of God is a human impossibility.[86] This is because God's Word can never be a human possession. It can never be within human control, although it can make contact with human reason. I would add that the ideological slant that invariably compromises the biblical message also renders it highly unlikely that any human being will ever preach the pure Word of God. "Ideology" here refers to a social stance that is shaped by class interests, and will ipso facto distort our perception of life and the world. We can never be entirely free of ideology, but we can strive to rise above it. Despite these considerable limitations, people can still hear God's Word through our preaching, because God himself graciously deigns to speak and act as we resolutely bear witness to his judgment and mercy as we see these in Jesus Christ.

In our preaching we communicate both a message and an experience. Faith is both intellectual and experiential. We cannot fully know the reality of the gospel unless we experience this reality. Yet we must not stereotype this experience. Our focus should always be on the message, not on the kind of experience that this message might induce.

As Christians in the tradition of the Reformation, we must always bear in mind that God is his own persuader. He acts and speaks by the power of his Spirit. It is he who seeks out his sheep (Ezek 34:11), and he enlists us in his service, but he does not need us. Indeed, he is able to raise up children of Abraham even out of stones (Mt 3:9). All our strategies and programs are to no avail until God sends out his light and truth, which alone can bring us to his dwelling place (Ps 43:3).

We do not cooperate with God until our will has been turned around by the Spirit. "The sovereign work of the holy Spirit," Charles Spurgeon perceived, "must be done in and on the spirit of a man before that man can be saved."[87] Then we become covenant partners with God, though we are partners not in procuring salvation but in manifesting this salvation to others.

It is not free will but free grace that saves us. We respond to the message of the gospel but always through the power of the Spirit, not on the basis of our own power or capacity. In conversion we are mastered by God, but we are not hypnotized or pulverized. We are liberated by being overpowered. Our experience is one of freedom, not of euphoria. We become responsible agents, not automatons.

The fact that the human subject is active and responsible in conversion is attested in the story of Lydia: "The Lord opened her heart to give heed to what was said by Paul" (Acts 16:14). She herself believed and obeyed, but only because she had been enlightened and enabled by the Spirit of God, who was working through Paul's witness. Forsyth rightly says, "The true freedom of man springs from the holy sovereignty of God, which we only know in Christ, in redeeming action."[88]

Our seeking for salvation is itself a sign of our election by God (cf. Jn 6:44). Pascal acknowledged this biblical truth: "You would not seek me if you had not found me." John of the Cross wisely perceived that if we are seeking God, it is because God is seeking us even more.

It is well to recognize that genuine seeking for God is itself a means of grace (cf. Mt 7:7-8). We must seek with all our heart, but this is possible only through the working of the Spirit. Yet seeking for salvation is no guarantee that we will find salvation or that we will be kept in salvation. Seeking will end in belief only if the Spirit infuses us with his grace. The very power to believe is also a gift of the Spirit.

In evangelical preaching the call is not simply to seek for salvation but to accept Christ. Jonathan Edwards was ambiguous here, often giving the impression that our hearers are able to seek but cannot of themselves believe. My position is that one is made free both to seek and to believe by the outpouring of the Spirit. As Paul declared, "Where the Spirit of the Lord is, there is freedom" (2 Cor 3:17; cf. Jn 8:32, 36; Rom 8:2). Faith is the fulfillment of the gift of freedom. According to Karl Barth, a person can come to faith "only when he is overcome by God's Word and its Spirit of power; when he is resurrected and recreated by it for such an act." But Barth went on to say that this act "is genuinely and freely man's *own.*"[89]

The paradox of salvation in which God does all but in and through human decision and obedience is made palpably clear by Jonathan Edwards:

> In efficacious grace we are not merely passive, nor yet does God do some, and we do the rest. But God does all, and we do all. God produces all, and we act all. For that is what he produces, viz., our own acts. God is the only proper author and fountain; we only are the proper actors. We are, in different respects, wholly passive, and wholly active.[90]

That evangelism, the preaching of the gospel in all of its power and glory, is the cardinal means used by the Spirit to reach an unregenerate humanity is strikingly confirmed in the history of the church. It was not the apologists who converted the masses in the ancient Roman world but the itinerant evangelists. This is the verdict of a great many distinguished historians including Williston Walker, Frederick Foakes-Jackson, Gerhard Uhlhorn and Gustave Bardy. The last doubts whether educated pagans even read the apologetic works, and believes that most of those who did were merely reinforced in their prior conviction that Christians were the archenemies of all the ideas on which classical civilization was founded.[91] It can also be shown that apologists like Joseph Butler and George Berkeley in the eighteenth century scarcely made an imprint on the religious life of people at large. It was the evangelical preachers who reached the masses—George Whitefield, John Wesley and Howel Harris.

Today the gospel is being advanced on college (and sometimes high school) campuses by parachurch evangelistic associations such as Campus Crusade for Christ, Young Life, the Navigators and InterVarsity Christian Fellowship (which also employs apologetics). The great luminaries of apologetic theology—Paul Tillich, Wolfhart Pannenberg, Rudolf Bultmann, Harvey Cox, Reinhold Niebuhr—have had little, if any, impact on bringing alienated students and hostile critics of the faith to Christ.[92] Perhaps one reason is that their presentations have compromised the gospel by an often unwitting accommodation to modernity, and people will not believe until they hear a strong and certain sound (cf. 1 Cor 14:8). The influence of C. S. Lewis is another matter, and his relative success in reaching searching intellectuals for the gospel may be due to the fact that his apologetic defense is set in the context of a firm faith in the gospel and the reliability of the biblical witness.[93]

Both good-Samaritan service and a biblically oriented apologetics have a role in Christian mission, but their role is subordinate to that of preaching and hearing the Word of God, which alone is the means to a saving faith in Christ. Apologetics that leaves out the story of salvation may stir people's interest in religion, but it will not create a living faith in Jesus Christ.

The aim in our apologetics should be to make the Christian position intellectually viable to searching persons, especially those associated with the community of faith, but not intellectually palatable to the world of unfaith. We can silence criticisms of the faith and whet intellectual curiosity by our dogmatic and apologetic arguments, but what brings people to faith is finally hearing the story of salvation and seeing this story confirmed in the self-giving lives of those who embrace it (cf. Mt 5:16).

In contrast to the early evangelicals, latter-day evangelicals have been increasingly attracted to rationalistic apologetics, which tries to prove to the unbeliever by logic or experience the reality of God and the authenticity of the Christian revelation. John Warwick Montgomery is adamant that the starting point in Christian mission to the world "has to be the common rationality . . . which all men share. If we insist that non-Christians begin in our sphere of Christian commitment, we ask for the impossible and vitiate all opportunity of reaching them."[94] Such a position obviously denies humanity's total inability to believe or even to seek for the truth of God and thereby reveals its distance from the position of the Protestant Reformers Luther and Calvin.

The testimony of Kenneth Pike, a one-time active worker in InterVarsity Christian Fellowship and a former member of the board of directors of the Wycliffe Bible Translators, merits serious consideration:

> I have given up trying to reach the intellectuals by argument. Whenever I have tried to meet them on their own ground by beginning a discussion in which tentatively none of us assumed the existence of the personal nature of God and the validity of the Scriptures, I have failed to make much progress. . . . In order to come out with faith in God, the discussion must begin with God assumed.[95]

The Dutch Pietist William Brakel goes so far as to affirm:

> True, saving faith is not the act of the mind assenting to evangelical truth, but the trusting of the heart to be saved by Christ on the ground of His voluntary offering of Himself to sinners and of the promises to them that trust in Him. And we say also that *faith has its seat, not in the understanding, but in the will.*[96]

While containing much wisdom, this statement creates the misleading impression that faith is exclusively volitional and not intellectual as well. Faith is the commitment of the whole person to the living Christ, an act that entails our reason, our will and our feelings. The gospel is addressed to the mind as well as to our emotional and moral sensibilities. We are called to exercise our reason as well as to bring our will into submission to Christ (cf. Is 1:18-20).[97] The truth of faith is above reason but not contrary to reason.[98] The commitment of faith is not a blind leap in the dark but a personal commitment made on the basis of evidence that faith itself provides: the consistent witness of the New Testament that Christ rose from the dead, the experience of the majesty and mercy of the holy God, the restoration to freedom brought about by the Spirit of God and the fruits of the Spirit discernible in the lives of the saints.[99]

# ˙NINE˙

# THE̲O̲L̲O̲GY
# AT THE
# CR̲O̲SSR̲O̲ADS

---

Christianity can endure, not by surrendering itself
to the modern mind and modern culture, but rather by a break with it:
the condition of a long future both for culture and the soul is the
Christianity which antagonizes culture without denying its place.

P . T . FORSYTH

---

Forgiveness is for sinners; but there can be
no reconciliation with sin and false doctrine.

DIETRICH BONHOEFFER

---

The point is not to break off the dialogue or to retire
to the desert, but the word of God can be proclaimed only by
someone who places himself outside "the world," while staying
at the very heart of the questioning that goes on within it.

JACQUES ELLUL

---

It is time that the Christian reacquire the consciousness
of belonging to a minority and of often being in opposition
to what is obvious, plausible and natural for that mentality
which the New Testament calls . . . the "spirit of the world."
It is time to find again the courage of nonconformism, the capacity
to oppose many of the trends of the surrounding culture.

CARDINAL RATZINGER

---

N othing so characterizes the contemporary theological scene as
the erosion of transcendence. In the heyday of neo-orthodoxy,
transcendence was very much in vogue. Borrowing a phrase
from Rudolf Otto, Karl Barth described God as "the Wholly Other" and
reaffirmed Kierkegaard's "infinite qualitative distinction" between God
and humanity. Karl Heim tried to show that divine transcendence is not

in conflict with the latest discoveries in modern science.[1] Emil Brunner was adamant that fallen humanity stands in need of a divine mediator, since divinity lies not within but outside the self.[2]

Since the 1960s a new immanentalism has emerged, which is conspicuous in a number of theological movements ranging from process theology to feminist and liberation theologies. Liberation theology and the neo-idealism of Pannenberg locate transcendence in the future. God becomes the power of the future or the eschatological fulfillment of history. Process theology identifies God with the creative force or vital energy (élan vital) within nature and history. Existentialist theology conceives of God as the uncertainty of the future (Bultmann), the infinite ground and depth of all being (Tillich) or simply the power of being (Tillich). In the neomysticism associated with the New Age movement God is the pulsating creative force within nature and humanity. In feminist theology God is the Womb of Being, the Immanent Mother, or the Empowering Matrix (Rosemary Ruether).

What is striking about the new theological movements is their cavalier dismissal of supernaturalism and their penchant for either idealism or naturalism. As an alternative to classical Christian theism in which God is an all-powerful, omniscient being existing before all temporal processes, Pannenberg proposes a theology of universal history in which God is the power of the future.[3] Jürgen Moltmann endeavors to move beyond a trinitarian monotheism to a tritheistic panentheism. The end result of Tillich's theologizing has been to supplant supernaturalism with an "ecstatic naturalism" or "eschatological panentheism."

Even fundamentalism has not been able to stem the tide away from a supernaturalist world view. While still giving support to supernaturalism many conservatives are inclined to focus on the conceptual significance of the scriptural signs rather than on the living God to whom the signs point.[4] Some on the conservative end of the spectrum appeal to innate ideas as the source of our knowledge of God and envisage revealed truth as immediately accessible to human reason (Gordon Clark).

The classical idea of the utter transcendence of God is not without its defenders. Thomas Torrance, Helmut Gollwitzer, Jacques Ellul and Kenneth Hamilton have all sought to counter the trend away from transcendence toward immanence.[5] Conservative evangelicals like Carl Henry, Norman Geisler, John Warwick Montgomery and Ronald Nash have also stoutly affirmed the transcendence of God in the face of secularizing and naturalizing trends. What they give us, however, is a transcendence in ontology but not in epistemology, for they are confident that human reason can lay hold of the truth of divine revelation apart from special grace. Neo-Thomists like Gabriel Marcel, Étienne Gilson and Avery Dulles have also tried to maintain adherence to a supernatural God, even though at the same time they make a prominent place for natural theology.

## Four Options

In its attempt to meet the challenges of modernity, theology has made various responses. One has been to return to a past position in which continuity with the tradition of the church is beyond question. Here the strategy is to disengage ourselves from modernizing trends and retrieve a position that still has some credibility for a great number of people.

Another response has been to accommodate to secularity and seek a point of identity between the highest values of the culture and the message of faith. The focus is on finding points of convergence between Christian tradition and modern philosophy. A call is made to revise the Christian message in order to bring it more into harmony with prevailing beliefs and attitudes. Such an endeavor necessarily entails resymbolizing the faith, translating the metaphors of faith experience into new symbols that speak to the modern age.

A third option is to maintain the uniqueness of Christian revelation but try to bring it into dialog with modernity, showing how this revelation fulfills the deepest yearnings and strivings of humanity. This is the approach of correlation, in which the aim is to purify the cultural vision without negating it. The result is a mediating theology intent on building bridges between faith and reason, Christ and culture.

Finally, the approach of confrontation seeks a conversion of cultural values and attitudes in the light of divine revelation. Cultural images and symbols are not annulled but instead are subordinated to the abiding revelatory symbols of Scripture and tradition. The apologetic interest is present in all four options, but it is definitely muted in this last one. Here the overriding concern is not so much to persuade people of the veracity of faith as to call them to repentance for their lack of faith or for their idolatrous faith. Yet apologetics still has a place: to serve the proclamation of the message of faith by showing the antithesis between faith and unbelief, between enlightened reason and defective reason.

## Theology of Restoration

The first strategy is marked by the desire to return to older methodologies and theological formulations in the sincere belief that these past positions can still be viable alternatives to seekers after meaning and truth. A theology of restoration is noticeable in the Anglo-Catholic movement, in fundamentalism and neofundamentalism, and among the old Lutherans and Reformed. It is also present among Anabaptist sectarians and Roman Catholic traditionalists.

Carl Henry has rendered a valuable service in warning of the dangers of capitulating to modernity. All of us should heed his timely admonitions against abandoning the conceptual and propositional dimension of revelation for a faith-encounter theology. Yet Henry basically calls for a return to the rationalistic idealism of the early Enlightenment. His indebtedness to Gordon Clark is obvious. I also see in his theology the pervasive influence of Descartes and Leibniz, both of whom placed supreme confidence in human reason and logic.[6] In this approach we arrive at truth by beginning with universal principles and then proceeding to deduce particular conclusions.[7]

Not a few in this tradition are closer to the empirical rationalism of the later Enlightenment in which sense experience and induction figure more prominently in theological method. Here we can list Benjamin Warfield, Charles Hodge, J. Oliver Buswell, Jr., John Gerstner, Norman

Geisler, R. C. Sproul and John Warwick Montgomery. Like Clark and Henry, all these scholars identify revelation with the propositional content of the Bible.

In many cases the theology of restoration becomes an evangelical or Catholic rationalism in which revealed knowledge is seen as a supplement to natural knowledge. Revelation gives us new information about God, but it is still basically propositional or conceptual knowledge. Grace builds on and completes nature rather than annuls nature.[8]

Another possibility for a theology of restoration is fideism, in which revelation confronts natural reason as an absurdity. Here the emphasis is not upon its continuity but upon its discontinuity with human reason. Tertullian in the early church best illustrates this attitude, though even here one can discern a rationalistic apologetic strand. It is a negative apologetics, however, that tries to undermine alternative positions to faith rather than bring these positions into correlation with faith.[9]

A theology of restoration is inclined either to attack or to ignore the historical and literary criticism of Scripture. Its objective is to return to a precritical stance, which makes a place for textual criticism but tries to hold the fort against higher criticism. Though it may study the results of higher criticism, it does not permit these to contribute in any real way to its understanding of Scripture.

Restorationists strive not so much to convert modern culture as to displace it by another culture. Their goal is to create or promote a counterculture, as evidenced in the support of many of them for a Christian school system. The theology of restoration either detaches itself from modernity and withdraws into an evangelical or Catholic ghetto, or it attacks modernity but without seriously engaging in the debates of the modern age. It is ready to criticize but not always willing to listen, thus avoiding a real dialog by allowing itself to be challenged by modernity. The restorationist often resembles Don Quixote, who tilts at windmills, imagining them to be giants, while completely missing the real enemy.[10]

Modern fundamentalism is not only pre-Barthian but also pre-Kantian. It has yet to come to terms with Kant's insightful observation that human reason by itself can yield knowledge only of the phenomenal world, not of the noumenal realm, which concerns God, freedom and immortality.[11] Kant did not speak as an evangelical Christian, but his position reflects Luther's caution regarding the reliability of human reason in matters of ultimate concern.

While this general approach sometimes appears to pit Christ against culture, it also comes very close to a Christ-of-culture stance. H. Richard Niebuhr makes a convincing case that it can be justly placed in the latter category because of its tendency to absolutize or enthrone the values and ideas of the past.[12] In some conservative religious circles, Americanism and Christianity are practically identified.

A theology of restoration is evident in the International Council on Biblical Inerrancy and the No Other Gospel movement in Germany, associated with such luminaries as Walter Künneth and Peter Beyerhaus. Nostalgia for the past is only one characteristic of these and similar movements. There is also an earnest attempt to confront the adversaries of faith in the present with the philosophical and exegetical tools available for this kind of battle. Yet the articulation of orthodoxy that comes to us in the tradition of the church is still considered the model in our dogmatic and apologetic efforts. Past confessions of faith (such as the Westminster Confession, the Decrees of the Council of Trent and the Formula of Concord) or past systems of theology (such as those of Thomas Aquinas or Calvin) are not critically examined in the light of new truth that the Spirit brings to his church through God's holy Word. In a theology of restoration, apologetics is crucial, for the faith must be defended in the face of the inroads of modernity and secularism. Apologetics often takes the form of eristics, seeking to overthrow the bastions of unbelief by exposing the inner contradictions in non-Christian systems of thought (Francis Schaeffer, Cornelius Van Til). Theology invariably becomes philosophical theology or philosophy of religion. The defense of the faith is often a defense of rational theism rather than a convincing attempt to uphold the God of biblical revelation.

Those who are tempted to go the way of restoration need to ponder this trenchant admonition of P. T. Forsyth:

> Theology, if it is to be of real use to the preacher, must be modernized. It is fruitless to offer to the public the precise modes of thought which were so fresh and powerful with the Reformers, or the schemes so ably propounded by the dogmatists of the seventeenth century, and so severely raked by the Socinians.[13]

The truth in a theology of restoration is that we must stand in unmistakable continuity with the voices of the saints and prophets of the church of the past if we are to claim our position as authentically Christian. The great creeds and confessions of the church should be treated as road signs that can be exceedingly helpful on our faith pilgrimage so long as we see them only as road signs, not as our final destination. Truth in its finalized version is always before us, but this does not imply that the witnesses to truth that we hear from the past are necessarily unreliable or erroneous.

By all means, let us look to the Bible and to the confessions, even to theological systems of the past, for indications of God's will and purpose for ourselves and for the world; yet may we not remain with the testimonies of the past but endeavor to use them to recognize the will of God for the present, as we battle adversaries of faith today that were only hinted at (or perhaps not named at all) in past documents. The Word of God that comes to us now is the same Word that inspired the prophets and apostles of the Bible and the fathers and mothers of the church through the ages. Tradition must therefore not be blithely set aside but instead made concrete and relevant in the present by the illumination given by God to his people in all ages through the Holy Spirit. For it is his Spirit that convicts the world of its sin and leads the people of God into all truth (Jn 16:13).

### Theology of Accommodation

A quite different approach is found in those who see in secularism more promise than peril. They discern the Spirit of God at work in the secularizing process. Because we are living in a totally different cultural milieu than the people of the Bible or the early church, they argue, we should update or revise the language of faith so that it can still speak to our contemporaries with meaning and power. Rather than relying on the categories of Hellenistic philosophy to make the faith credible and relevant, the accommodationists prefer to use concepts and symbols endemic to our cultural and historical period.

In a theology of accommodation the paramount task is to find the underlying unity between secular and religious wisdom and thereby forge a vision of God and of the world that can elicit support from all quarters. H. Richard Niebuhr aptly designates this approach "Christ-of-culture," for the Christ it upholds is drawn from and shaped by the cultural ethos more than by the biblical revelation.

Schleiermacher is an outstanding example of accommodationist theology. He strove to "reconcile religion with the freedom of science and the beauty of life,"[14] to awaken the cultured despisers of religion to the truth "that religion is rooted in authentic human experience."[15] "True science is complete vision; true practice is culture and art self-produced; true religion is sense and taste for the Infinite."[16] For Schleiermacher the superiority of Christianity lies only in its supposed freedom from exclusiveness.[17]

The accommodationist strand so glaringly apparent in Schleiermacher is endemic to all liberal theology. Walter Rauschenbusch argued that "the Gospel, to have power over an age, must be the highest expression of the moral and religious truths held by that age."[18] According to Shailer Mathews, theology is best understood as "an extension of the forms of social experience to religious belief. . . . Its purpose is to make religious experience consistent with other experience, and so reasonable."[19] Bernard Meland regards culture as an important source of faith, for culture discloses God's working and encountering people through events, values and structures of the past.[20] He dissociates himself, however, from those who uncritically embrace the cultural ethos in order to make the faith relevant.[21]

A theology of accommodation is not restricted to liberal theology. It is present in a certain kind of fundamentalism where the revealed knowledge of Scripture is harmonized with the natural knowledge of God and morality. It is also discernible in the radical strand in neo-Catholicism (Rosemary Ruether, Mary Daly, Matthew Fox, Louis Evely, Gregory Baum, David Tracy). According to Tracy, the modern Christian theologian "believes that the Christian faith is at heart none other than the most adequate articulation of the basic faith of secularity itself."[22] We are urged to reflect on the great texts of Christianity because they stand among the classics of our culture.[23] Accommodationist theology is also apparent in syncretistic mysticism, which presupposes a point of identity between the experiencing subject and the ultimate that appears in religious experience or in the experience of the world as "religious" (Geddes MacGregor, Thomas Altizer, Gerald Heard, Paul Knitter, John Hick, Ewert Cousins, Raimundo Panikkar).

In this kind of theology apologetics becomes the earnest attempt to forge a new understanding of the world and God in dialog with contemporary philosophy. As Langdon Gilkey puts it, "If our religious symbols interpret and thematize natural and not supernatural experience, theology, as understanding of natural experience through *Christian* symbols, must be in direct correlation with philosophical reason as the means by which natural experience is analyzed."[24]

In accommodationist theology revelation no longer signifies a divine incursion into human history; instead, it is an awakening of the human subject to his or her own divinity or a breakthrough into a higher form of consciousness. For Gregory Baum, Christian revelation does not provide knowledge of the will and work of God but furnishes a new awareness of one's place in the world that leads to creative action.[25]

Accommodationists are intent on finding the Christ already present in non-Christian religions or even in secular movements. In their view the religious experience of non-Christians can even be used to purify and correct misconceptions and archaic notions in Christianity that form part of the baggage of any religion. Christian consciousness must be united with global consciousness if the Christian message is to speak to peoples of other cultures and religious backgrounds.[26]

It is not surprising that accommodationist thought seriously entertains the possibility of broadening the canon or even of creating a new canon. Rosemary Ruether audaciously asserts that "feminist theology must create a new textual base, a new canon. . . . Feminist theology demands a new collection of texts to make women's experience visible. . . . Feminist theology cannot be done from the existing base of the Christian Bible."[27] Drawing on goddess traditions, Gnostic writings, heretical Christian traditions and current feminist writings, she sets out to assemble a body of women-church lore that will serve as a new standard of authority in the church.

Ironically, as H. Richard Niebuhr keenly observed, even the Christ-against-culture approach is inclined to lapse into a Christ-of-culture stance, for it invariably enthrones the values of the counterculture. Frequently those who uphold the true faith are in reality defending the world view and social mores of an earlier period of history.

In this same connection Karl Barth has astutely perceived the close but ambivalent relation between Pietism and rationalism. Pietists, who are generally anticultural, often prepare the way for rationalism, because their authority is no longer a definitive revelation in history but an inner experience that calls for rational articulation and substantiation. For Barth, rationalism and Pietism are two sides of the same coin—trust in human cognition and experience.

Likewise Emil Brunner has recognized an incontestable similarity between fundamentalism and liberalism. In both movements the appeal is to the cognitive possibilities in the human subject rather than to the new reality in the Jesus Christ of history. Yet Brunner saw more hope in fundamentalism than in liberalism, for what is dissolved can no longer be restored, whereas what is frozen or hardened can be brought back to life by the Spirit.[28]

## Theology of Correlation
In the theology of correlation nature and culture no longer function as

the ruling norm for Christian truth but have their completion or fulfillment in Christ and his redemption. They do not constitute the criterion
of Christian truth, but they lead into Christian truth. H. Richard Niebuhr
terms this approach "Christ-above-culture."[29] It is characterized by a
positive attitude toward human culture. It proposes a synthesis of
theology and philosophy but with the latter subordinated to the former.
Unlike accommodationists, these persons discern the gap between
Christ and culture but do not regard it as unbridgeable.

Correlation theology is a mediating theology, bringing together the
creative questions of the culture and the answer of Christian revelation.
The answer is not derived from human existence (as in the second
approach) but lacks sufficient intelligibility apart from the probing questions that arise from the existential situation in which people find themselves. In this approach apologetics functions as a kind of philosophy
of religion that prepares the way for theology or serves as its precondition. It is based on the supposition that reason finds its goal and
fulfillment in revelation.

This third general position is reflected in the dualistic approach of
both Catholic and Protestant scholasticism, which endeavors to build
a supranatural structure on a natural substructure. When scholasticism
becomes wedded to sectarianism, however, we find it closer to restorationism than to a theology of correlation.

We can also discern this third approach in the "ecstatic naturalism"
of Paul Tillich, who while perceiving the dangers of a too facile harmon-
izing of revelation with the wisdom of culture nonetheless claims that
cultural insights point beyond themselves to revelation. Tillich acknowledges the basic affinity between his theological method and that
of Thomas Aquinas, the architect of the theology of synthesis.[30]

Tillich sees apologetics as permeating the whole of theology, for the
very raison d'être of theology lies in its endeavor to construct a synthesis of faith and culture. This is why he calls his position an apologetic
as opposed to a kerygmatic theology, which, he alleges, contents itself
with simply proclaiming the message of revelation and disdains the

necessary task of making the message credible and intelligible to the mind of the culture. Tillich assigns an important role to philosophy of religion understood as the investigation of the question implied in the human situation; indeed, he considers it a prerequisite for the explication of biblical and theological themes.

Hans Küng is another powerful advocate of a theology of correlation. Theology should aim, he says, for a "critical correlation" between the biblical message and the paradigm of the culture—the total constellation of convictions, values and patterns of behavior that tie a people together.[31] Küng is convinced that theology must now come to terms with a postmodern paradigm in which the emphasis is on humanization and liberation rather than technological growth and scientific achievement. Theology must adapt its message to this shift in cultural orientation if it is to be relevant in today's world.

According to Küng, the two sources of a critical ecumenical theology are "our present-day world of experience" and "the Jewish-Christian tradition" based on the experiences of God and Christ recorded in the Bible.[32] While the second has a certain theological priority, the first provides the horizon that sets the stage for theological thinking. The goal of faith is historical understanding in which the traditions of faith are reinterpreted in the light of the changing historical ethos.[33]

Like Tillich in his later years, Küng has been preoccupied with interreligious dialog and its implications for theology. Rejecting the way of syncretism, in which we uncover a common spirituality, he upholds instead the way of "synthesis in the face of all denominational and religious antagonisms."[34] But this synthesis will never be a finalized system, for a comprehensive vision can never be realized in history, which is always changing and always open to a new future. Küng is opposed to relativism but contends for a sense of relativity toward all human claims to absolute truth. He does not seek a "unified religion for the whole world, but peace among the religions as a prerequisite for peace among the nations."[35]

Other theological luminaries in the history of the church who share the hope of a creative synthesis or reconciliation between Christ and culture include Clement of Alexandria, Thomas Aquinas, Karl Rahner, Edward John Carnell, Wolfhart Pannenberg and Rudolf Bultmann.[36] These scholars do not intend to minimize the cleft between the gospel and world philosophies and ideologies; yet instead of categorically repudiating worldly wisdom, they endeavor to assimilate it in a Christian world view or faith perspective.

## Theology of Confrontation

In this last approach the gospel sharply calls into question the values and presuppositions of secular culture. The accent is not on the synthesis between faith and culture but on their antithesis. It is not correlation but diastasis that characterizes the relationship between the message of revelation and secular wisdom. The criterion of the gospel stands at variance with secular philosophical wisdom, because human reason is not only limited by finiteness but also tainted by the lust for power. Luther voiced the spirit of diastasis when he said: "Before faith and the knowledge of God, reason is mere darkness; but in the hands of those who believe, 'tis an excellent instrument. All faculties and gifts are pernicious, exercised by the impious, but most salutary when possessed by godly persons."[37]

The goal in this kind of militant theology is not synthesis or correlation but the conversion of culture and philosophy to the new values and transcendent perspective of the kingdom of God. The gospel is not added to what is already known; instead, it overturns human knowledge and calls us to break with our past orientation.

A theology of confrontation is primarily kerygmatic, not apologetic: its first concern is to make known the claims of the gospel without any desire to bring them into accordance with the preconceived wisdom of the culture. It is a theology of crisis rather than process. It sees humanity as the question and the gospel as the answer. But humanity can see itself as the question only in the light of the answer, which is given in revelation.

This approach might be termed "Christ-transforming-culture," for it advocates not flight or withdrawal but conquest on the field of battle. It places its hope not in human argumentation but in the power of the gospel itself to convict and transform. A theology of confrontation is ready and willing to enter the debates of the modern age, but it is not willing to bend its message to the spirit of the age. It utilizes the language of the times without abandoning the biblical language. Its method is singularly unlike that of restorationists, which is inclined to ignore modern issues and concentrate on issues of the past.

This kind of theology does not repudiate the culture so much as strive to harness it in the service of the gospel. It sees the kingdom of God extending into secular culture and bringing the principalities and powers under the dominion of Jesus Christ. The kingdom is not an island separate from the culture but a leaven that is at work in the culture transforming its values and attitudes. Bonhoeffer shares Luther's conviction that "the Kingdom is to be in the midst of your enemies," which is also where Christians are to be.[38] Ellul agrees: "The point is not to break off the dialog or to retire to the desert, but the word of God can be proclaimed only by someone who places himself outside 'the world,' while staying at the very heart of the questioning that goes on within it."[39]

The world is not the domain of Satan, though he has intruded into it as an alien force, but instead the theater of the glory of God (Calvin), the field in which the kingdom of God advances. The world and all its achievements belong to Jesus Christ, although the world in its sin refuses to acknowledge this fact and must therefore be brought into submission by the spiritual forces of righteousness.

The primary concern of this kind of theology is not so much to safeguard the purity of the church (as in the first approach) as to overthrow the principalities and powers that still hold the world in subjugation. It is to spearhead the kingdom of God in the world. The focus is not on the survival of the church or the defense of the faith but on the renewal of the world. There is, of course, more than one kind of theology of confrontation. Militant fundamentalism rushes to impose the gospel upon a free conscience and thereby transforms the gospel into a new law. In the approach of eristics we expend our energies in undercutting false systems of belief. But in the approach of witness we set before the world the claims of the gospel and allow the gospel to convict the world by its own persuasive power. The confrontation is not one that we consciously plan to bring about but one that becomes inevitable once the gospel is declared and heard by the savants of the culture. It is the gospel that occasions the confrontation, not human strategy or technique.

Among the theologians of the church who uphold this transformationist model are Calvin, Barth, Kuyper, and to a lesser extent Augustine, Ellul, Brunner and Bonhoeffer. One can even find many passages in Luther that resonate with this approach, though Luther's unremitting pessimism regarding human culture militates against the transformationist vision.

**Points of Conflict**
The extent of the differences between these four approaches—restoration, identity (or accommodation), correlation and confrontation—becomes much clearer when we compare them on some critical issues. One of these is the enigmatic relation between reason and revelation. The theology of restoration holds that reason prepares the way for revelation. In the theology of identity reason in effect becomes the surrogate of revelation. Revelation is conceived as the breakthrough of reason toward a new horizon of meaning. It consists basically in the expansion of reason by grace. Revelation means a new awareness of God and the world. Grace gives assistance to reason and is thereby an aid in the human quest for wisdom. In the theology of correlation reason finds its goal and fulfillment in revelation. Grace carries reason beyond itself to a higher reality.[40] Here we see the transcendence as well as the fulfillment of reason. Divine grace directs and fulfills the human quest. In the theology of confrontation reason is overthrown by revelation and placed on a new foundation. Grace brings about the conversion of reason but

not its negation, as in radical Pietism and mysticism. The emphasis is on "God's search for man," not "man's search for God" (Barth).

The first approach (which often lapses into rationalism) envisions philosophy of religion as laying the foundation for theology. Natural revelation becomes the precondition for special revelation. Or philosophy of religion is deemed the true theology. The second approach regards philosophy of religion as more inclusive than theology, since the former concerns the realm of knowledge whereas theology deals with the realm of myth and symbol (Hegel, Whitehead). The third portrays philosophy of religion as a preparation or introduction to theology. It is the handmaiden of theology, going before it to prepare the way. The fourth approach views philosophy of religion as a branch of theology, for reason is now in the service of revelation.

On the issue of apologetics, the first position tries to demonstrate that Christianity is the most coherent system of belief or the highest philosophy of religion. The second endeavors to find the point of identity between Christ and universal religious experience, setting out to forge a new vision as it draws upon the wisdom of secular thought. In the third approach the task is to expose the deficiencies in secular understanding in order to point the hearer to Christ, who fulfills as well as negates secular philosophy and universal religious experience. The fourth approach tries to answer and refute the questions of culture but only in order to silence criticism and thereby arouse curiosity. In our answer we make a determined effort to bear witness to the faith. Apologetics is not a prolegomenon to dogmatics but a branch of dogmatics.

On the subject of scriptural authority, the first view treats Scripture as a document of revelation, as a compendium of revealed truths. The second regards Scripture as a pictorial account of the religious experiences of a particular people, containing abiding religious insights or enduring ethical values. In the third approach Scripture is a record and witness to historical revelation that has its climax in Jesus Christ. Some in this category would practically identify Scripture and revelation; here it is possible to detect a convergence with the restorationist vision. In the fourth view Scripture constitutes the mystery of the unity of God's self-witness to humanity and humanity's witness to God. Scripture is not simply a pointer to revelation but the reservoir and conduit of revelation. There is nonetheless a firm conviction that the mystery of faith is inaccessible to reason, that the truth of revelation cannot be extracted directly from Scripture.

On the relation of Christ and culture, the first (restorationist) and third (correlationist) approaches envision Christ as transcending cultural values but at the same time fulfilling them. In the second view (identity) Christ embodies or epitomizes the highest values of the culture. In the fourth view (confrontationist) Christ challenges and judges these values.

With regard to the goal of happiness, the first position emphasizes eternal happiness. Classical mystical spirituality and evangelical Pietism urge believers to deny the pleasures of this world for the sake of the pleasures that are abiding. The second approach attempts to equate true happiness as the world understands it with what the New Testament calls blessedness. Only divine grace brings us this happiness, we are told, though this is what all people yearn for. In the third approach the higher happiness fulfills and supersedes worldly happiness. In the fourth approach happiness is not a valid goal at all, at least not an ultimate goal. The overriding passion of the person of faith is the glory of God, even if this should entail the surrender or renunciation of human happiness.

On the subject of justice, a Lutheran form of restorationism posits a disjunction between human justice and the spiritual righteousness of the kingdom. The two coexist in paradoxical tension, but one does not necessarily lead into the other. In the liberal theology of identity justice is practically equated with love. The final norm is sometimes spoken of as "justice-love."[41] In the theology of synthesis justice is fulfilled in love, or it prepares the way for the higher righteousness of the kingdom. In the theology of confrontation as found in Karl Barth, justice is a sign and witness of the perfect righteousness of the kingdom.

It is interesting how often the first and third approaches converge.

One reason could be that restorationism often leads to a return to scholasticism, which sought a synthesis between Christ and culture. But the restorationist looks back to a synthesis in the past that stands in conflict with present cultural aspirations. The third approach as represented by Paul Tillich and Hans Küng entertains the hope of a synthesis with present-day culture, but it can be shown that this leads directly into a theology of identity.[42] Tillich is probably closer in the last analysis to Schleiermacher than to Thomas Aquinas.[43] Restorationism, in my sense of the term, proves to be closer to sectarianism and a Christ-against-culture stance than to the vision of catholicity enunciated in Thomas Aquinas.

All of these, of course, are ideal types, and no one system or theologian is to be identified completely with any particular type. This typology could perhaps be reduced to two: a theology of identity and a theology of confrontation. The sectarian restorationist would be closer to the latter and the correlationist to the former. Yet I believe that the nuances of difference between all these types justify the typology. While I am obviously borrowing from H. Richard Niebuhr's typology of Christ and culture, the typology presented here is something new, for it pertains to issues much wider than faith and culture.

### Toward a New Kind of Confessional Theology

The real battle lines in the future will be between those who espouse a revisionist theology bent on updating theology and bringing it into greater harmony with contemporary experience, and those who uphold a confessional theology that witnesses to the claims of the gospel as presented in Scripture and church tradition. The third option—a sectarian theology that in effect enthrones a particular tradition in the church—is still a viable alternative but will have decreasing importance in the years ahead. Those who advocate the revisionist model emphasize the necessity to revise the language of faith, but, as some acknowledge and others deny, such an undertaking always involves a revision of the witness of Scripture.

Revisionists are concerned to reconstruct the tradition of faith in order to make it credible and palatable to its cultured despisers. Confessing Christians are committed to reaffirm the faith testified to in Scripture and tradition in the language of Scripture and the church. They recognize that we must also confess in the language of our day, but this language must be subordinated to and interpreted by what Barth calls the "language of Zion" or the "language of Canaan."

Some who favor a return to confessionalism are closer to a sectarian than to an evangelical catholic mindset. What I uphold is not confessionalism in the sectarian sense but a confessing church (à la Barmen), which will confess the age-old faith in the language of our day and address itself to the issues of our day but still maintain continuity with the tradition of the whole church. A confessional theology in the sense advocated here will go against the stream of the culture for the sake of the culture. A sectarian theology will do battle for the sake of the church or the elect, the gathered fellowship of true believers, not for the sake of the world for whom Christ died. Perhaps the principal dividing line is between modernist theology and evangelical theology, between one that is all too ready to come to terms with the modern mind and one that challenges and calls into question the modern mind. Or we can locate the dividing line between an eclectic or cultural theology on the one hand and a genuinely biblical theology on the other.

Confessional theology in the catholic sense will not be reactionary. It advocates not a return to the past but a critical reappropriation of the wisdom of the past. It espouses continuity with tradition but is willing to subject even church tradition to the judgment of the Word of God. It is evangelical and catholic but not sectarian or restorationist.

The confessional theology I uphold will be both conservative and radical (in the sense of going to the roots, *ad fontes*). Its theologians will respect and try to learn from the creeds and confessions in their own traditions, but instead of remaining with them, will aspire to go through them to a fresh articulation of the faith for our day.

## Discordant Voices

The distinguished Lutheran scholar Carl Braaten, who has roundly denounced theological alignments with cultural ideology, nevertheless
believes that the future of theology lies in a new synthesis of biblical
and cultural wisdom rather than in a theology based exclusively on the
claims of biblical revelation.[44] He acknowledges that "the death of natural theology has been welcomed by some theologians, because it allows them to concentrate on real theology, on a theology of the gospel
and the biblical narratives. However, the gains are perhaps short-term,
because it is only a question of time before a Bonhoeffer will arise and
call into question the meaning of God also for those who already believe—all those insiders."[45] Braaten concedes that there is much to be
said for "the heroic way" of Barth and Eberhard Jüngel:

> As a strategy for survival in the secular catacombs, it places theology
> *contra mundo* . . . against the world outside. It is diastatic rather than
> synthetic; it is traditional rather than modernistic; it is counter-cul-
> tural rather than culture-conforming; it focuses on the God of the
> prophets of old rather than the idols or the ideologies of today; it
> follows the story line of the gospel rather than the fads and fashions
> of culture; it takes all things captive to Jesus Christ rather than chase
> after the elemental spirits of this world.[46]

Like Pannenberg, Braaten considers this theology of the catacombs a
precarious strategy

> for the long march of history. It is an understandable retreat from the
> increasing alienation of theology from the natural, historical, psycho-
> logical, and social sciences. Theology crawls into its own shell, taking
> shelter from the chilly world of the university into the warm huddles
> of the church. However, such a strategy may actually be tantamount
> to an unbelieving surrender, implicitly agreeing with Nietzsche,
> Feuerbach and Marx that God is as dead as a dodo in the world of
> today; that God is leaving himself without any witnesses except those
> who are Christian; and that if God is to get back into the world, be-
> lievers will have to put him there, by Christianizing the world.[47]

Rejecting the way of the diastasis as enunciated by Barth and Kierke-gaard (and I would add Luther and Calvin), Braaten upholds the way of synthesis and correlation as advocated by Tillich and Pannenberg. These latter thinkers "have led the way to a recovery of understanding God in a broader sense, under the conditions of modern times, and within the context of the natural, historical, psychological, and social sciences." This "new style of natural theology" functions "as an updating of the Lutheran distinction between law and gospel, entailing the priority of the law of creation to the gospel of redemption."[48] In Braaten's view, there-fore, we begin with human culture and try to ascertain the glimpses of God and morality discernible in nature and culture apart from revelation, and then proceed to bring this rudimentary knowledge into dialog with the knowledge of Jesus Christ given in the biblical revelation, which does not destroy but fulfills the human quest for wisdom and meaning.

Braaten, it seems to me, has made a profound mistake by deciding to cast his lot with the theology of synthesis, as found in Tillich and Pan-nenberg. He refuses to admit that both of these towering thinkers have been led into irremediable compromises of the faith in their well-inten-tioned efforts to make the faith meaningful and credible to its cultured despisers. While Tillich has said many true things about justification, he has abandoned the idea of a supernatural God for a God who is the dynamic depth and energy of the universe. This is not biblical mono-theism but a neomystical panentheism. Similarly, Pannenberg in his extreme rationalism has ended in a naturalistic idealism that is closer to Hegel than to the biblical prophets.

One can in fact show that the real movers of history and culture have not been the apologists or self-styled Christian philosophers but the saints and evangelists of the church, who have not watered down the claims of the gospel to the level of cultural wisdom but have challenged the cultural consensus by calling for its conversion to the service of biblical revelation and the kingdom of God. Braaten misunderstands Barth when he denies or underplays the apologetic and cultural dimen-sions of Barth's theology. What Barth propounds is not an apologetic that leaves the fortress of faith to engage in struggle with the world on its own terrain but an apologetic that finds its security precisely in the fortress of faith and calls the world to unconditional surrender by acknowledging the authority of the fortress of faith over its own domain. For Barth theology is not simply descriptive, as in George Lindbeck and David Kelsey, but prescriptive, unabashedly presenting before the world the claims of the gospel, which shatters the wisdom of the world and calls for a life-and-death decision.

I am not urging a repristination of Barthian theology (some of Barth's conclusions are problematic), but I believe we need to take his way of doing theology over that of Tillich, Küng and Pannenberg (and I might add Edward John Carnell, Francis Schaeffer and Carl Henry).[49] We would do well to remember that it was Barth who successfully challenged the principalities and powers that lay behind the German Christian movement in the 1930s and the cold war ideology of the 1950s. Tillich stubbornly refused to lend his support to the Confessing Church in Germany in its struggle with a Nazified Christianity, advocating instead a third way that would include humanists and others arrayed against the Nazi state. The third way, the way of correlation or synthesis, finally becomes modernism, giving up the unique claims of the faith and embracing the wisdom of the world.

It is my profound conviction that in our day as in others we need to take the way of Athanasius, Irenaeus, Luther, Calvin, Kierkegaard, Forsyth and Barth over the way of Clement of Alexandria, Origen, Erasmus, Melanchthon, Schleiermacher, Ritschl, Troeltsch, Tillich and Küng. The church will advance only when it ceases to equivocate in its message and unashamedly confesses the truth of its gospel in the very midst of its enemies. I concur wholeheartedly with these prophetic words of P. T. Forsyth: "Christianity can endure, not by surrendering itself to the modern mind and modern culture, but rather by a break with it: the condition of a long future both for culture and the soul is the Christianity which antagonizes culture without denying its place."[50]

Schubert Ogden has made the dubious assertion that if the claims of

Christianity are true at all, "they are so only because or insofar as they are also warranted somehow by our common experience and reason, or, at least, our common *religious* experience and reason, simply as human beings."[51] Against this position I contend that the claims of Christianity are true because they rest on events that really happened, events that cannot possibly be synchronized or harmonized with ordinary human experience and reason; and because their credibility and veracity is confirmed in our hearts by the Spirit of God himself as he authenticates the message of faith in the church through the ages where the Bible is read and believed and where the faith is proclaimed in fidelity and love. Because human reason is in the service of sin apart from faith (Rom 8:7; 14:23), it needs to be shattered and transformed before it can lay hold of the mystery of the truth of the gospel, which is hidden from natural sight and understanding but becomes the glorious possession of those who break with the arrogance and pretension that presently cloud their reasoning and cry out for the salvation that God alone can and does provide in the person of his Son, Jesus Christ.

We are closest to God when we acknowledge our despair and need rather than boast of our capacity to understand and believe, but we cannot know our real despair and need until our inward eyes are first opened to the glorious grace and incomparable love that we see in the death and resurrection of Jesus Christ. It is not only faith that is a gift from God but the very condition to receive faith. We must never forget that the hope of the church rests not on its own strategies and wisdom but on the living God alone, who speaks and acts wherever his Word is faithfully proclaimed and wherever the prayers of his children are offered up in faith and repentance.

# Notes

### Foreword

[1]Emil Brunner, *The Word and the World* (New York: Charles Scribner's Sons, 1931), p. 18.

[2]See Adolf von Harnack, *What Is Christianity?* trans. Thomas Bailey Saunders (New York: Harper & Row, 1957); Walter Rauschenbusch, *The Social Principles of Jesus* (Philadelphia: Westminster Press, 1916), and *A Theology for the Social Gospel* (New York: Abingdon, 1917).

[3]My position on this question is closer to Barth in his neo-Calvinistic phase than in his later theology, when he made a bifurcation between Jesus Christ as the one Word of God and the Bible and the church as mere testimony to revelation, the Bible being the primary, and the church the secondary, testimony. One could argue that Barth in his final years returned to an earlier position, reflected, for example, in the Barmen Declaration.

### Chapter 1: Introduction

[1]Richard Rorty, *Philosophy and the Mirror of Nature* (Princeton, N.J.: Princeton University Press, 1979), p. 12.

[2]Theologians associated with narrative theology include George Lindbeck, Hans Frei, David Kelsey, Ronald Thiemann, Paul Ricoeur, Stanley Hauerwas, Garrett Green, James McClendon and Gabriel Fackre. Admittedly some of these theologians would insist on the normativeness of the biblical narrative, but it is generally an existential rather than an ontological normativeness that they have in mind. While readily acknowledging that the study of the Bible as narrative brings coherence and meaning to human consciousness, narrative theologians are conspicuously reluctant to concede that it yields an interpretation of reality that has universal validity. For an illuminating introduction to narra-

tive theology, see Garrett Green, ed., *Scriptural Authority and Narrative Interpretation* (Philadelphia: Fortress, 1987). Also see Terrence W. Tilley, *Story Theology* (Wilmington, Del.: Michael Glazier, 1985). According to Tilley the truth of the story lies in its ability to resonate with the whole of our experience and to lead us into authenticity and faithfulness (pp. 182-214).

[3]One might say that the Bible has a functional role in directing us to Christ, but it has an ontological basis and goal in that it opens us to a perspective on God and the world that is not simply psychologically enriching or spiritually fulfilling but metaphysically true.

[4]See Gabriel Fackre, *The Christian Story* (Grand Rapids, Mich.: Eerdmans, 1978), 1:19. To his credit, Fackre tries to hold together the concern for the "truth of the symbol" and the evocations of "symbolic truth" derived from the biblical narrative. For an able critique of Fackre and of narrative theology in general from the standpoint of "evangelical orthodoxy," see Carl F. H. Henry, "Narrative Theology: An Evangelical Appraisal," *Trinity Journal* 8, no. 1 (Spring 1987):3-19. See also the response to Henry by Hans Frei (ibid., pp. 21-24).

[5]According to van Buren the term *story* refers to "the concatenation of words, ideas, memories and hopes which Christians and Jews have used to remind themselves of who they are, whence they come and whither they are going." The purpose of this kind of narrative theology is "to recall us to the continuing pattern of the means of self-identification, education and self-perpetuation that have marked both the Jewish people and the Christian church." Paul van Buren, "The Jewish-Christian Reality," *Religion and Intellectual Life* 5, no. 1 (Fall 1987):84.

[6]See Ronald F. Thiemann, *Revelation and Theology: The Gospel as Narrated Promise* (Notre Dame, Ind.: University of Notre Dame Press, 1985).

[7]See Thomas F. O'Meara, *Romantic Idealism and Roman Catholicism* (Notre Dame, Ind.: University of Notre Dame Press, 1982), p. 3.

[8]See Alfred North Whitehead, *Modes of Thought* (New York: Macmillan, 1938), p. 67.

[9]While dogma has an ineradicable propositional dimension, it bursts through all propositional forms. It signifies the truth of what is expressed as opposed to the way in which it is expressed. Dogma must not be reduced to propositions as statements, but propositions can convey the truth of dogma. Because dogma speaks to the human heart as well as the human mind, it is best described as a propositional-existential truth. For a further discussion of dogma see pp. 119-23.

[10]It goes beyond the humanly rational but not the divinely rational, as opposed to Neoplatonism in which the One transcends the *Nous*.

[11]When Bonhoeffer accused Barth of revelational positivism, he probably had in mind reducing revelation to an objectified datum that could be grasped by

reason. Bonhoeffer's stricture applies better to some Barthians than to Barth himself. For Barth, revelation makes itself an object for our understanding, but it is never accessible to mastery by human reason. A neoliberal critique of Barth's alleged positivism of revelation is to be found in Simon Fisher, *Revelatory Positivism? Barth's Earliest Theology and the Marburg School* (New York: Oxford University Press, 1988), esp. pp. 306-44.

[12]See Cornelius Van Til, *The Defense of the Faith* (Philadelphia: Presbyterian & Reformed, 1955); E. R. Geehan, ed., *Jerusalem and Athens* (Philadelphia: Presbyterian & Reformed, 1971); and Ronald Nash, ed., *The Philosophy of Gordon Clark* (Philadelphia: Presbyterian & Reformed, 1968). For an incisive critique of presuppositionalism by three evidentialists see R. C. Sproul, John Gerstner and Arthur Lindsley, *Classical Apologetics* (Grand Rapids, Mich.: Zondervan, 1984), pp. 183-338. For a helpful introduction to various types of apologetic systems currently found in conservative evangelical circles, including rationalistic empiricism and presuppositionalism, see Gordon R. Lewis, *Testing Christianity's Truth Claims* (Chicago: Moody Press, 1976).

[13]According to Thiemann, "foundationalists all agree that knowledge is grounded in a set of non-inferential, self-evident beliefs which, because their intelligibility is not constituted by a relationship with other beliefs, can serve as the source of intelligibility for all beliefs in a conceptual framework" *(Revelation and Theology,* p. 158). Thiemann seeks for a nonfoundational theology in which we arrive at abiding beliefs through a rational analysis of the biblical narrative rather than by intuition or supernatural revelation.

[14]It should be noted that Thomas Reid (d. 1796) sought to combine intuitive certainty, which is absolute, with inductive investigation, which yields a high degree of probability. Copleston notes a shift to a more consistent or thoroughgoing empiricism in Reid's disciple Dugald Stewart. Frederick Copleston, *A History of Philosophy* (rpt. New York: Doubleday Image, 1985), 5:375-83. See also the helpful discussion in Jack B. Rogers and Donald K. McKim, *The Authority and Interpretation of the Bible* (New York: Harper & Row, 1979), pp. 235-40.

[15]See Sproul, Gerstner and Lindsley, *Classical Apologetics;* and John W. Montgomery, *Where Is History Going?* (Grand Rapids, Mich.: Zondervan, 1969). Modern evidentialist apologetics has its source in the early British empiricism of John Locke and Bishop Joseph Butler and in the ensuing Scottish Common Sense Realism. It should be noted, however, that both Locke and Butler held that intuitive knowledge is superior in clarity and certainty to purely sensible knowledge. For a brilliant critique of the evidentialism of the later Enlightenment as this bears upon modern evangelicalism, see George Marsden, "The Collapse of American Evangelical Academia," in *Faith and Rationality,* ed. Alvin Plantinga and Nicholas Wolterstorff (Notre Dame, Ind.: University of Notre Dame Press, 1983), pp. 219-64.

[16]See Arthur F. Holmes, *Contours of a World View* (Grand Rapids, Mich.: Eerdmans, 1983), pp. 51-53. Kant makes a case for the cohesive unity of our beliefs in a number of his writings. See *Kant's Kritik of Judgment,* trans. J. H. Bernard (London: Macmillan, 1892), pp. 262-429.

[17]It could also be designated as a *dynamic revelationalism,* not to be confused with a revelational objectivism in which revelation is turned into a datum or formula that can be mastered by reason. In the revelationalism I espouse, we begin neither with the will to believe nor with the probings of the understanding but with the living God personally addressing us in the moment of decision.

[18]In contrast to Kant, for whom certainty in a transcendent order has its basis in the moral law within, I ground this kind of certainty in faith in the living God who revealed himself in the life history of Jesus Christ, though it is continuously realized and experienced in moral obedience. I could just as well describe it as a spiritual certainty, since it is anchored in a personal relationship with the God and Father of our Lord Jesus Christ. But it is deepened through obedience to the commandment of God.

[19]See Holmes, *Contours of a World View,* p. 50.

[20]As I see it, ultimate reality is neither act (as in actualism) nor static essence (as in essentialism) but the living God of the Bible, who is being in action.

[21]See George A. Lindbeck, *The Nature of Doctrine: Religion and Theology in a Postliberal Age* (Philadelphia: Westminster Press, 1984).

[22]See Schubert M. Ogden, *On Theology* (San Francisco: Harper & Row, 1986). Ogden understands constructive theology as "critical reflection on the meaning and truth of thought and speech about God or about the meaning or structure of ultimate reality generally" (p. 125). He clearly believes that one can be validly engaged in the theological task without being committed to the answer of faith (p. 119). I discuss this issue further on pp. 108, 124.

[23]See Edward John Carnell, *The Case for Orthodox Theology* (Philadelphia: Westminster Press, 1959), pp. 124-25, 127-28, 132-33.

### Chapter 2: The Theological Malaise

[1]The dualistic bent of Kant's thought is evident in his contention that humanity is "destined for two quite different worlds, for the realm of sense and intellect, hence for the world of this earth; but then also for still another world, one we do not know, a realm of morals." From Kant's *Der Streit der Fakultäten,* quoted in Hendrikus Berkhof, *Two Hundred Years of Theology,* trans. John Vriend (Grand Rapids, Mich.: Eerdmans, 1989), p. 6. Berkhof tries to show that Kant did not intend a stringent dualistic outlook on reality (ibid., pp. 6-10).

[2]See further discussion of this point on pp. 250-52.

[3]Because God creates each person as a living being, both soul and body, no part of humanity, including the intellectual part, can be identified with the being of

God, who remains wholly other than what humans can conceive or imagine. At the same time, God endows human nature with intimations of his perfections, and this means that there can be an analogical relation between God and humanity, divine reason and human reason. Yet the unlikeness is greater than the likeness; this is why the living God can never be equated with the laws of thought or the spirit of humanity. See the provocative discussion in Emil Brunner, *The Christian Doctrine of God,* trans. Olive Wyon (Philadelphia: Westminster Press, 1950, rpt. 1974), pp. 137-50.

4See Søren Kierkegaard, *The Sickness unto Death,* trans. Walter Lowrie (Princeton, N.J.: Princeton University Press, 1941), p. 207.

5See Jacques Ellul, *The Technological Society,* trans. John Wilkinson (New York: Vintage Books, 1964), and *The Humiliation of the Word,* trans. Joyce Main Hanks (Grand Rapids, Mich.: Eerdmans, 1985).

6Quoted in William Barrett, *Irrational Man: A Study in Existential Philosophy* (New York: Doubleday Anchor Books, 1962), p. 206.

7See Russell Chandler, *Understanding the New Age* (Dallas: Word Books, 1988); Douglas R. Groothuis, *Unmasking the New Age* (Downers Grove, Ill.: InterVarsity Press, 1986); Karen Hoyt, ed., *The New Age Rage* (Old Tappan, N.J.: Revell, 1987); Elliot Miller, *A Crash Course on the New Age* (Grand Rapids, Mich.: Baker Book House, 1989); and Ted Peters, *The Cosmic Self: A Penetrating Look at Today's New Age Movements* (San Francisco: Harper, 1991).

8George Lindbeck, "Scripture, Consensus, and Community," *This World,* no. 23 (Fall 1988):22.

9Historicism has its genesis in such writers as Giovanni Vico, Leopold von Ranke and Wilhelm Dilthey. See D. W. Bebbington, *Patterns in History* (Downers Grove, Ill.: InterVarsity Press, 1979).

10Cited by Gerhard von Rad in his "Typological Interpretation of the Old Testament," trans. John Bright, rpt. in *A Guide to Contemporary Hermeneutics,* ed. Donald K. McKim (Grand Rapids, Mich.: Eerdmans, 1986), p. 33. From Ernst Troeltsch, *Über historische und dogmatische Methode* (1898), in *Gesammelte Schriften* 2:729ff.

11Gordon D. Kaufman, " 'Evidentialism': A Theologian's Response," *Faith and Philosophy* 6, no. 1 (Jan. 1989):43.

12Ismael Garcia, *Justice in Latin American Theology of Liberation* (Atlanta: John Knox Press, 1987), pp. 12-13.

13See John Hick, *God and the Universe of Faiths* (London: Macmillan, 1973), and *God Has Many Names* (Philadelphia: Westminster Press, 1982); John Hick, ed., *Truth and Dialogue in World Religions* (Philadelphia: Westminster Press, 1974); Raimundo Panikkar, *The Unknown Christ of Hinduism* (London: Darton, Longman & Todd, 1964); Paul Knitter, *No Other Name? A Critical Survey of Christian Attitudes toward the World Religions* (Maryknoll, N.Y.: Orbis Books, 1985); and

Leonard Swidler, ed., *Toward a Universal Theology of Religion* (Maryknoll, N.Y.: Orbis Books, 1987).

[14]See Hick, *God and the Universe of Faiths,* pp. 120-32. Knitter asserts a similar view in his *No Other Name?* p. 143.

[15]Lindbeck quotes approvingly the remark of the philosopher Richard Rorty: "What is most important for human life is not what propositions we believe but what vocabulary we use." Craig Dykstra, George Lindbeck et al., "Review Symposium," *Theology Today* 46, no. 1 (Apr. 1989):59.

[16]George A. Lindbeck, *The Nature of Doctrine: Religion and Theology in a Post-liberal Age* (Philadelphia: Westminster Press, 1984), p. 9.

[17]See David H. Kelsey, *The Uses of Scripture in Recent Theology* (Philadelphia: Fortress, 1975), p. 48.

[18]See the illuminating discussion of Barth's relationship to narrative theology in Luděk Brož, "The Present Task of Theology," *Communio Viatorum* 31, no. 1 (Spring 1988):1-30, esp. 23-24.

[19]Edgar McKnight, *Post-Modern Use of the Bible: The Emergence of Reader-Oriented Criticism* (Nashville: Abingdon, 1988). In propounding a "post-modern hermeneutics," McKnight draws upon the reader-oriented criticism of narrative theology and structuralism, showing the thread of continuity between the two: "Early Russian and Czech formalists and structuralists emphasized the dynamic relationship between textual form and content and historically constrained, and yet constantly changing, conventions and codes. The difference today is that we are conscious of the relational and dynamic nature of literature and its meaning and significance at the very time we are reading and criticizing the text" (p. 60). The unbridled relativism of this new approach is strikingly apparent: "The sacredness sponsored by the Bible . . . comes to be the result of a vision that provides an opening to transcendence by seeing in the Bible a model for a plurality of visions of multiform humanity" (p. 184).

[20]James W. Lewis, "On Wisdom and Strife," *Criterion* 27, no. 3 (Autumn 1988):13. Cf. John Cobb: "There is still . . . a feature of theology about which the university is rightly disturbed. Some theologians not only seek truth from the perspective of the Christian faith but also absolutize some features of that faith. That is, they take certain doctrines as beyond criticism or revision, and they affirm their acceptance of those doctrines not on the grounds of their plausibility or illuminating power but on the grounds of sheer authority or irrational decision. . . . There is a real question as to how much of this a university can tolerate in its graduate faculty. To exclude it altogether would be to refuse to hear what can be learned from those who at some point challenge the assumptions of the university itself. . . . But the dogmatic spirit is certainly a negative factor in weighing the suitability of anyone for university teaching." John B. Cobb, Jr., "Theology as Thoughtful Response to the Divine Call," in *The Vocation of the*

*Theologian,* ed. Theodore W. Jennings, Jr. (Philadelphia: Fortress, 1985), p. 107.

²¹Hans Küng, *Theology for the Third Millennium: An Ecumenical View,* trans. Peter Heinegg (New York: Doubleday, 1988), pp. 15-46.

²²See esp. Karl Barth, *Protestant Theology in the Nineteenth Century* (Valley Forge, Pa.: Judson Press, 1973).

²³See Donald G. Bloesch, *Freedom for Obedience* (San Francisco: Harper & Row, 1987), pp. 248-86.

²⁴In a prophetic editorial Paul R. Hinlicky presents a cogent case that America is now on the verge of a *Kirchenkampf.* He scores the rhetoric of the new political theology that has penetrated the church: "It is plainly totalitarian in its aspiration. It speaks of 'relationality' but holds in contempt the community of faith almost as much as the community of the family; it talks of 'inclusiveness' but rages against all who will not be mastered with that net; it speaks of 'empowerment' and produces bullies and petty tyrants who have learned the fine art of verbal terrorism. It wants not to hear of sin, death, and the power of the devil, but of innocence, vitality, and the immanent divinity of a gnostic humanity in a New Age. It cares not for divine redemption but pleads for human self-transformation." "Grace Alone," *Lutheran Forum* 23, no. 1, Lent (Feb. 1989):6.

## Chapter 3: Faith and Philosophy

¹Tertullian wrote: "The Son of God was crucified; I am not ashamed because men must needs be ashamed of it. And the Son of God died; it is by all means to be believed, because it is absurd. And He was buried, and rose again; the fact is certain, because it is impossible." Tertullian, "On the Flesh of Christ," in *The Ante-Nicene Fathers,* ed. Alexander Roberts and James Donaldson (Grand Rapids, Mich.: Eerdmans, 1950), 3:525.

²Küng rightly perceives an affinity between Augustine and Pascal. For both, "it is never a question of an irrational but always of a *rationally justifiable faith;* not rationalism, but rationality; not blind, but reasonable submission." Hans Küng, *Does God Exist?* trans. Edward Quinn (New York: Doubleday, 1980), p. 66.

³For Thomas a philosophical knowledge of God is a preamble to faith. It provides a rational foundation for unbelievers in their approach to Christianity, but it does not induce faith, which is a gift from God.

⁴Meister Eckhart, *Sermons and Collations,* in *Meister Eckhart,* ed. Franz Pfeiffer, trans. C. De B. Evans (London: John M. Watkins, 1956), 1:21.

⁵John of the Cross, *Ascent of Mount Carmel* II.9, in *The Complete Works of Saint John of the Cross,* trans. and ed. E. Allison Peers, rev. ed. (London: Burns Oates & Washbourne, 1953), 1:93.

⁶John Calvin, *Sermons on the Epistle to the Ephesians,* trans. Arthur Golding (rpt. Edinburgh: Banner of Truth Trust, 1973), p. 257.

[7]See Jaroslav Pelikan, *From Luther to Kierkegaard* (St. Louis: Concordia, 1950), pp. 49-75.

[8]Heinrich Heppe, *Reformed Dogmatics*, rev. and ed. Ernst Bizer, trans. G. T. Thomson (London: George Allen & Unwin, 1950), p. 7.

[9]Only the early Barth can justifiably be accused of being a fideist. Von Balthasar acknowledges the rational character of Barth's conception of faith: "Faith is supernatural and positive, but it is also in conformity with nature. It engages our natural capabilities, our mind and our will. It does not derive from our nature, but it is adapted to our nature and it perfects our nature according to the Creator's plan." Hans Urs von Balthasar, *The Theology of Karl Barth*, trans. John Drury (New York: Holt, Rinehart & Winston, 1971), p. 131.

[10]Wolfhart Pannenberg, *Basic Questions in Theology*, trans. George H. Kehm, 2 vols. (Philadelphia: Westminster Press, 1983), 2:102.

[11]Ibid., p. 54.

[12]Blaise Pascal, *Pascal: Pensées*, ed. and trans. A. J. Krailsheimer (Baltimore: Penguin Books, 1966), no. 423, p. 154.

[13]*A Karl Barth Reader*, ed. Rolf Joachim Erler and Reiner Marquard, trans. Geoffrey W. Bromiley (Grand Rapids, Mich.: Eerdmans, 1986), p. 30.

[14]It should be kept in mind that *theology* and *philosophy* in this context refer to ideal types, which no single system of thought exemplifies fully. The way I define theology is definitely at odds with the approach of liberal theology in which theology is transmuted into philosophy of religion.

[15]It is interesting that Hegel defined philosophy as "its time grasped in thought." G. W. F. Hegel, *Sämtliche Werke: Jubiläumsausgabe* (Stuttgart: Frommann, 1927-40), 7:35. Cited in Gerhard Ebeling, *The Study of Theology*, trans. Duane A. Priebe (Philadelphia: Fortress, 1978), p. 66.

[16]A case could be made that theology has more affinity with the analytic than the synthetic method. We do not arrive at revelation by synthesizing the various aspects of human experience. Yet we employ the method of synthesis when we seek to relate the various facets of revelation to one another and to the world in which we live.

[17]Torrance argues that theology is much more synthetic than analytic, "for it is an advancing and positive movement of thought in response to the Word of God, which cannot be finally analysed through any system of logical formalization, far less be contained in it." Thomas F. Torrance, *Theological Science* (London: Oxford University Press, 1969), p. 277. At the same time, there is an indisputable analytic element in theology as well. We do not analyze metaphysical first principles, however, but the fact of revelation. The analytic method in theology indicates an unfolding of what is already given in revelation. We adduce meanings from revelatory events rather than deduce conclusions from universal judgments.

[18]See Immanuel Kant, *Critique of Pure Reason,* trans. Norman Kemp Smith (New York: Modern Library, 1958), pp. 311, 318. See also the Kant translation in *The Great Thoughts,* ed. George Seldes (New York: Ballantine Books, 1985), p. 222.

[19]Alfred North Whitehead, *Process and Reality* (New York: Macmillan, 1941), p. 63. Elsewhere he says: "The appeal to reason is the appeal to that ultimate judge, universal and yet individual to each, to which all authority must bow." Whitehead, *Adventures of Ideas* (New York: Macmillan, 1933), p. 208.

[20]See Immanuel Kant, *The Philosophy of Kant: Immanuel Kant's Moral and Political Writings,* ed. Carl J. Friedrich (New York: Modern Library, 1949), pp. 187-208.

[21]In contradistinction to Paul Tillich, who also uses this typology, I contend that God is not the deepest within the self but the Creator Lord who infinitely transcends the self even while sustaining and renewing the self.

[22]See Emil Brunner, *The Christian Doctrine of God,* trans. Olive Wyon (Philadelphia: Westminster Press, 1974), pp. 159-74, 248-55.

[23]I here side with Thomas Aquinas over Duns Scotus, who held that we can have univocal knowledge of God, that being predicated of humanity is equivalent to being predicated of deity. On Duns Scotus's defense of univocity in our conceptualization of God see Frederick Copleston, *A History of Philosophy* (New York: Doubleday Image, 1985), 2:500-508.

[24]Universals are not independent of the mind of God but originate in the unity of the divine will and the divine mind. God cannot be comprehended in the light of the universal ideals of "the good, the beautiful and the true," but conversely these ideals gain their meaning only when our eyes are opened to the reality of God as truth, goodness and beauty in action. God cannot be subordinated to a universal moral law, but moral order has its genesis in the will of God, which is always above all that we can conceive to be the good or the beautiful or the true.

[25]Whitehead, *Process and Reality,* p. 521.

[26]Aristotle, *Poetics* 1451 b, IX.3. In *Aristotle's Theory of Poetry and Fine Art,* ed. and trans. S. H. Butcher (London: Macmillan, 1911), p. 35.

[27]In Marxism and Hegelianism truth is still impersonal. These systems deal with truth in terms of causality, not of the appearance of the completely new in history.

[28]See Martin Heidegger, *Being and Time,* trans. John Macquarrie and Edward Robinson (New York: Harper & Brothers, 1962), pp. 301-11.

[29]Emil Fackenheim, "The Historicity and Transcendence of Philosophic Truth," cited in Armand Maurer, *St. Thomas and Historicity* (Milwaukee: Marquette University Press, 1979), p. 37.

[30]Obviously my position here stands in contrast to that of Pannenberg, who,

leaning upon Hegel, falls into an idealistic philosophy of universal history capable of interpreting every aspect of experience. Nothing can be fully known until the Whole is complete and there is no more future bringing in ever-new things. The words of the prophets and apostles have the character of revelation only in anticipation of the whole of reality. Pannenberg holds that theology is the true philosophy, but he lays himself open to the charge of transmuting theology into a philosophy or world view. A Christian philosophy may claim too much, which would make it comparable to most other philosophies. Christianity is not so much a way of looking at life as a revelation from God. It is not a position arrived at through historical analysis or abstract reflection but an ultimate concern that has grasped us, a passion that comes to control and direct our thinking and being.

[31]Pragmatic philosophers like Rorty try to curb this philosophical hubris by seeking knowledge that is conducive to human edification and aesthetic enrichment rather than knowledge that explains the whole of reality. Rorty celebrates with Lessing the infinite striving for truth over possession of truth in its ultimacy. See Richard Rorty, *Philosophy and the Mirror of Nature* (Princeton, N.J.: Princeton University Press, 1979). It should be noted that pragmatists such as Rorty still provide for an understanding of the self and the world, not for the sake of conceptual mastery of reality (as in idealism), but for the sake of generating new meanings that expand the human horizon.

[32]Philosophy is inclined to reduce theology to anthropology, whereas theology sees anthropology in the light of the knowledge of God.

[33]Paul Tillich, *Systematic Theology* (Chicago: University of Chicago Press, 1951), 1:25.

[34]Paul Tillich, *Biblical Religion and the Search for Ultimate Reality* (Chicago: University of Chicago Press, 1955), p. 65.

[35]This is not to deny that philosophers are in contact with the true God, for all people are inescapably related to God, who is the source and goal of their being. Yet philosophers outside the circle of faith unwittingly construct a god of their own imagination on the basis of this universal awareness and felt need of God.

[36]See René Descartes, *A Discourse on Method, Meditations on the First Philosophy, Principles of Philosophy*, trans. John Veitch (New York: E. P. Dutton, 1934), p. 156.

[37]Alfred North Whitehead, *Religion in the Making* (New York: Macmillan, 1926), p. 50.

[38]Modern positivists (G. E. Moore, A. J. Ayer, Bertrand Russell, the early Ludwig Wittgenstein) hold that the primary concern of philosophy is the analysis of meaning or ipso facto the clarification of language. In this perspective metaphysics becomes descriptive rather than normative.

³⁹H. R. Mackintosh, *Types of Modern Theology* (London: Nisbet, 1949), p. 142.

⁴⁰Ibid.

⁴¹For a recent attempt to expunge metaphysics from theology, see Joseph S. O'Leary, *Questioning Back: The Overcoming of Metaphysics in Christian Tradition* (New York: Seabury-Winston, 1985).

⁴²See Anders Nygren, *Agape and Eros,* trans. Philip S. Watson (Philadelphia: Westminster Press, 1953).

⁴³This same biblical-classical synthesis appears in the conservative theologian John Piper, who holds that God's agape does not contradict eros but instead expresses it. The Christian motivation is defined as the pursuit of pleasure, which can be ultimately satisfied only in union with God. John Piper, *Desiring God: Meditations of a Christian Hedonist* (Portland, Ore.: Multnomah Press, 1986). See also Piper, *The Pleasures of God* (Portland, Ore.: Multnomah Press, 1991).

⁴⁴Whitehead, *Process and Reality,* p. 532.

⁴⁵See Donald G. Bloesch, "Process Theology and Reformed Theology," in *Process Theology,* ed. Ronald Nash (Grand Rapids, Mich.: Baker Book House, 1987), pp. 48-54.

⁴⁶Quoted in Emil Brunner, *The Mediator,* trans. Olive Wyon (Philadelphia: Westminster Press, 1947), p. 24. See J. G. Fichte, *Ausgewählte Werke* (Darmstadt: Wissenschaftliche Buchgesellschaft, 1962), 5:197.

⁴⁷Pannenberg, *Basic Questions in Theology,* 2:139.

⁴⁸For a penetrating discussion of how philosophical concepts are transformed in the New Testament, see Paul Tillich, *The Protestant Era,* trans. James Luther Adams (Chicago: University of Chicago Press, 1948), pp. 27-31.

⁴⁹While Pannenberg also warns against allowing philosophical concepts too determinative a role in shaping our theological understanding, he nevertheless betrays a conspicuous dependence on Hegel in his interpretation of truth and reality. See n. 30.

⁵⁰Martin Buber, *Eclipse of God,* trans. Maurice S. Friedman et al. (New York: Harper Torchbooks, 1952), p. 86.

⁵¹Jacques Ellul, *Living Faith,* trans. Peter Heinegg (San Francisco: Harper & Row, 1983), p. 148.

⁵²Ibid., p. 112.

⁵³Ibid., p. 144.

⁵⁴Carl Gustav Jung, *Psychology and Religion* (New Haven, Conn.: Yale University Press, 1966), p. 113.

⁵⁵John Macquarrie, *In Search of Humanity* (New York: Crossroad, 1983), p. 138.

⁵⁶See Hendrik Kraemer, *The Christian Message in a Non-Christian World* (London: Edinburgh House Press, 1938).

⁵⁷See Donald G. Bloesch, *Freedom for Obedience* (San Francisco: Harper & Row, 1987), pp. 16-47.

[58]Modern existentialist ethics eulogizes freedom, but it is a freedom severed from law, a lawless freedom (Sartre). It is not a freedom for obedience (as in Christian faith) but a freedom to realize one's own creative power. Or it is a freedom to realize the law of one's own being (Tillich).

[59]See John Dewey, *Theory of the Moral Life* (New York: Holt, Rinehart & Winston, 1960), p. 18.

[60]For a contemporary reaffirmation of humanistic ethics within a Christian context, see Albert Plé, *Duty or Pleasure?* (New York: Paragon House, 1987).

[61]Even the world-denying philosophy of Schopenhauer, which sees happiness as the negation of desire, acknowledges the supremacy of eros: "Eros is the first, the creator, the principle from which all things proceed." Arthur Schopenhauer, *The World as Will and Idea*, trans. R. B. Haldane and J. Kemp (London: Routledge and Kegan Paul, 1957), 1:425.

[62]Thomas Oden gives another point of view, arguing for the complementarity and union of agape and eros. Thomas C. Oden, *The Living God* (San Francisco: Harper & Row, 1987), 1:119-22. In a theology faithful to the Reformation, agape and eros cannot be fused or united, but eros can be made to serve agape by being transformed into something other than itself.

[63]George Berkeley, "Passive Obedience," in *Berkeley: Essays, Principles, Dialogues,* ed. Mary Whiton Calkins (New York: Charles Scribner's Sons, 1929), p. 432.

[64]See Frederick Copleston, *History of Philosophy* (New York: Doubleday, 1985), 6:36. These are Copleston's words.

[65]See ibid., p. 77.

[66]My position is here in accord with both Bultmann and Nygren. For Nygren's supportive comments on Bultmann's position on self-love, see Nygren, *Agape and Eros,* p. 101.

[67]Johann G. Fichte, *Reden an die deutsche Nation,* in *Sämtliche Werke* (Berlin: Verlag von Veit, 1846), 7(3):349. This is a paraphrase rather than an exact translation.

[68]Quoted in David Manning White, ed., *The Search for God* (New York: Macmillan, 1983), p. 321.

[69]Karl Jaspers, *The Great Philosophers: The Foundations,* trans. Ralph Manheim (New York: Harcourt Brace & World, 1962), pp. 164-65.

[70]Quoted in Copleston, *History of Philosophy,* 2:120.

[71]John Locke, *An Essay Concerning Human Understanding,* ed. Alexander Campbell Fraser (New York: Dover, 1959), 2:415-27.

[72]Norman L. Geisler, "Avoid *All* Contradictions: A Surrejoinder to John Dahms," *Journal of the Evangelical Theological Society* 22, no. 2 (June 1979):159.

[73]Ibid., p. 155.

[74]See the discussion of Gordon Clark in Gordon R. Lewis, *Testing Christianity's*

*Truth Claims* (Chicago: Moody Press, 1976), pp. 100-124.

[75]See further discussion of Kierkegaard on pp. 61-66.

[76]Jacques Ellul, *Living Faith,* pp. 123, 125. Cf. Ellul, *What I Believe,* trans. Geoffrey W. Bromiley (Grand Rapids, Mich.: Eerdmans, 1989), p. 306.

[77]Ellul, *Living Faith,* p. 125.

[78]Ibid., p. 113.

[79]Ibid., p. 111.

[80]Ellul is not an irrationalist, however, for he sees a modest role for reason both before and after faith. Reason can show the tenuous basis of commonplace opinions and thereby set the stage for faith. But faith itself requires a leap, for its object is outside the range of rational demonstration.

[81]Anselm, *Proslogium* I, in *St. Anselm: Proslogium; Monologium; An Appendix in Behalf of the Fool by Gaunilon; and Cur Deus Homo,* ed. and trans. Sidney Norton Deane (LaSalle, Ill.: Open Court, 1959), p. 7.

[82]Quoted in William Barrett, *Irrational Man: A Study in Existential Philosophy* (New York: Doubleday Anchor Books, 1962), p. 206. See Martin Heidegger, *The Question Concerning Technology and Other Essays,* trans. William Lovitt (New York: Harper & Row, 1977), p. 112.

[83]Augustine, *Epistolae* 120.2.8, in *An Augustine Synthesis,* ed. Erich Przywara (New York: Harper Torchbooks, 1958), p. 60.

[84]The truth of the gospel story is not simply an existential truth for the Christian but an ontological-historical truth whose impact is existential. We do not simply resonate with the experiences that form a part of this story, but we are persuaded that the events around which this story revolves actually happened.

[85]One can say that in faith we are more sure of whom we believe than that we believe. We are more certain of God's love for us than of our trust in him.

[86]Hegel is typical of the rationalist mentality. For him, in the final stage of philosophy "there is no longer anything mysterious about God." Buber gives this rejoinder: "Nothing mysterious indeed, except that what is here and now called God can no longer be for man that God which he encounters, both deeply mysterious and manifest, in his despairs and in his raptures." Buber, *Eclipse of God,* p. 20.

[87]Francis Schaeffer, *Whatever Happened to the Human Race?* in *The Complete Works of Francis A. Schaeffer* (Westchester, Ill.: Crossway Books, 1982), 5:382-83.

## Appendix A: Kierkegaard

[1]While Kierkegaard is commonly classified as a philosopher because he wrote mainly in this field, in the context of this book he should really be seen as a crypto-theologian, since his thinking was controlled by a passionate commitment to the God of the Bible. One might say that he was a theologian in the

guise of a philosopher, or a religious thinker who freely drew upon philosophy.
²Søren Kierkegaard, *Concluding Unscientific Postscript,* trans. David F. Swenson (Princeton, N.J.: Princeton University Press, 1944), p. 209.
³Kierkegaard was adamant that one cannot make the leap of faith by one's own power: "The last movement, the paradoxical movement of faith, I cannot perform, whether it is my duty or no, although there is nothing I would sooner do." *Fear and Trembling,* trans. Robert Payne (New York: Oxford University Press, 1939), p. 71.
⁴Kierkegaard is thinking not of the communication of propositional truths but of an existential communication—the transmission of the power of the new reality of Jesus Christ.
⁵Kierkegaard can say that "becoming a Christian is . . . the most fearful decision of a man's life, a struggle through to attain faith against despair and offense." *Concluding Unscientific Postscript,* p. 333.
⁶For Kierkegaard, it seems, insofar as the Christian is a sinner, the truth of faith will take on the character of offense and paradox. But in the eyes of God there is no paradox. The paradox lies in the relation of God's truth to sinful humankind.
⁷Thus he says: "God does not think, He creates; God does not exist, He is eternal. Man thinks and exists, and existence separates thought and being, holding them apart from one another in succession." *Concluding Unscientific Postscript,* p. 296. Kierkegaard's biblical moorings are more apparent in a discourse on prayer, where he defines the changelessness of God as perpetual concern for his people. See *Eighteen Upbuilding Discourses,* ed. and trans. Howard V. Hong and Edna H. Hong (Princeton, N.J.: Princeton University Press, 1990), p. 393.
⁸Quoted in Régis Jolivet, *Introduction to Kierkegaard,* trans. W. H. Barber (New York: E. P. Dutton, 1946), p. 201. Cf.: "Now there is in God, if one may so put it, the contradiction which is the source of all torment: he is love, and yet he is eternally immutable. So he cannot be changed—and yet he is love." *Søren Kierkegaard: The Last Years,* ed. and trans. Ronald Gregor Smith (New York: Harper & Row, 1965), p. 147. Also cf. "O Thou who art unchangeable, whom nothing changes! Thou who art unchangeable in love, precisely for our welfare not submitting to any change: may we too will our welfare, submitting ourselves to the discipline of Thy unchangeableness, so that we may, in unconditional obedience, find our rest and remain at rest in Thy unchangeableness." In *A Kierkegaard Anthology,* ed. Robert Bretall (Princeton, N.J.: Princeton University Press, 1947), p. 470.
⁹H. R. Mackintosh, *Types of Modern Theology* (London: Nisbet, 1949), pp. 259-60.
¹⁰Even when he views reason in a positive light, it does not yield a deeper

understanding of Christianity. "The problem is not to understand Christianity but to understand that it cannot be understood. That is the holiness of faith, and reflection is sanctified by being thus used." In *The Journals of Søren Kierkegaard,* ed. Alexander Dru (London: Oxford University Press, 1951), p. 261.

¹¹Søren Kierkegaard, *Fear and Trembling,* trans. Walter Lowrie (New York: Doubleday, 1941), p. 64. I prefer to say that faith begins when both our thinking and willing are turned around by divine grace. For Kierkegaard, it seems, faith is heterogeneous from human reason, even from the reason of an enlightened believer. See Harold V. Martin, *The Wings of Faith* (London: Lutterworth Press, 1950), pp. 84-87.

¹²While Kierkegaard was inclined to dismiss history as giving only approximation knowledge, he nevertheless insisted that the object of faith is the moment in time when "God became man." He could even describe this moment as "the fullness of time," but it has no organic relation to what comes before or after. Kierkegaard could not speak of a sacred history that prepared the way for the miracle of the Incarnation of Christ and equipped people of faith to bear witness to this miracle. Christ represents the disruption of history rather than its center or apex. The "moment" is a surd in history rather than the culmination of history.

H. R. Mackintosh gives a similar reading: "History gives no revelation of God; even from believing eyes its meaning is completely hidden; if meaning there be, only God can know it. Kierkegaard will not see the promised Kingdom of God looming through the past, beckoning into the future, finally triumphant over human failure. For him only two realities are luminously visible—the God-man and his own soul." *Types of Modern Theology,* p. 259.

¹³In one sense it could be said that reason is crucified in the decision of faith, since the whole person is crucified with Christ (Rom 6:6; Gal 2:20), and this includes our thinking as well as our willing. At the same time, it is not the structure of reason but reason in the service of a sinful will that is negated. It is not intelligence but the thinking person who is converted. For Kierkegaard, it often seems, reason is simply baffled by the supreme paradox rather than harnessed in the service of the truth that shines through the paradox.

¹⁴For Kierkegaard reason is "set aside" in the awakening to faith. *Philosophical Fragments,* trans. David Swenson and Howard V. Hong, ed. Niels Thulstrup (Princeton, N.J.: Princeton University Press, 1962), p. 76. Faith is a "happy passion," not a form of knowledge. It also cannot simply be reduced to an act of willing, though will is certainly involved. The possibility of faith lies neither in the ingenuity of reason nor in the power of the will. Yet once the condition is given, the miracle of grace, both reason and will can be employed in the service of faith. Reason's task, however, is a modest one: to show that we cannot understand.

[15]According to one interpreter, Kierkegaard even more than Luther was constrained to state the infinite requirements of the law before proclaiming the good news of God's love and grace in Jesus Christ. See Johannes Sløk, "Kierkegaard and Luther," in *A Kierkegaard Critique,* ed. Howard A. Johnson and Niels Thulstrup (New York: Harper & Brothers, 1962), p. 100.

[16]For Kierkegaard, coming to faith paradoxically involves both a despair of oneself as the ground and hope of human fulfillment and a will to be oneself as God intended. The consciousness of despair can bring one closer to salvation, but it cannot induce faith apart from the aid of the Eternal. See *Kierkegaard Anthology,* ed. Bretall, pp. 211, 341-71. I discuss this point further on pp. 228, 320.

[17]Cornelio Fabro, a Catholic interpreter, contends that Kierkegaard saw a *theologia naturalis* as the point of contact with the gospel, since in order to believe one must pass through the religion of immanence before one is ready to enter the domain of faith. Fabro here discerns a Catholic motif in Kierkegaard. Cornelio Fabro, "Faith and Reason in Kierkegaard's Dialectic," trans. J. B. Mondin, in *Kierkegaard Critique,* ed. Johnson and Thulstrup, pp. 190-94. The fact that Kierkegaard makes self-love the ground and condition for the love of neighbor likewise suggests an affinity to Augustine and Catholic mysticism.

[18]"The communication of Christianity must ultimately end in 'bearing witness,' the maieutic form can never be final. For truth, from the Christian point of view, does not lie in the subject . . . but in a revelation which must be proclaimed." In *Journals,* ed. Dru, p. 259.

[19]"Dialectics itself does not see the absolute, but it leads, as it were, the individual up to it." *Concluding Unscientific Postscript,* p. 438.

[20]There are passages in Kierkegaard's works that affirm the unity of the aesthetic, ethical and religious, but in his last years an ascetical orientation became ascendant, and he openly began to preach the negation of life.

[21]By "reasonable" I here mean sensible or sane. We should try to make the truth of faith intelligible.

[22]While a bona fide evangelical theology will always make a crucial place for paradox in the language of faith, it will give even more attention to the work of the Holy Spirit in his illumination of the mystery of God's self-condescension in Jesus Christ, so that faith will gain understanding even from a revelation that inevitably takes paradoxical form.

### Chapter 4: Theological Language

[1]Cited by John Garvey in "Truth Flashes," *Commonweal* 113, no. 22 (Dec. 26, 1986):677.

[2]See Patrick Grant, ed., *A Dazzling Darkness: An Anthology of Western Mysticism* (Grand Rapids, Mich.: Eerdmans, 1985), p. 223.

³Ronald H. Nash, ed., *The Philosophy of Gordon H. Clark* (Philadelphia: Presbyterian & Reformed, 1968), p. 68.

⁴Edward John Carnell, *Christian Commitment* (Grand Rapids, Mich.: Baker Book House, 1982), p. 135.

⁵Ibid., p. 138.

⁶Norman L. Geisler, "Theological Method and Inerrancy," in *Evangelicals and Inerrancy,* ed. Ronald Youngblood (Nashville: Thomas Nelson, 1984), p. 140. While Geisler does make a place for analogy, he sees it as close to univocity.

⁷See Paul Tillich, "The Religious Symbol," *Journal of Liberal Religion* 2, no. 1 (Summer 1940):13-33; and "Symbol and Knowledge: A Response," *Journal of Liberal Religion* 2, no. 4 (Spring 1941):202-6; Immanuel Kant, *On the Form and Principles of the Sensible and Intelligible World* (1770) 2.10, in *Gesammelte Schriften* (Berlin, 1902-42), 2:396. Also see Frederick Copleston, *A History of Philosophy* (New York: Doubleday Image, 1985), 6:199.

⁸See Sallie McFague, *Metaphorical Theology: Models of God in Religious Language* (Philadelphia: Fortress, 1982); and *Models of God: Theology for an Ecological, Nuclear Age* (Philadelphia: Fortress, 1987).

⁹Wolfhart Pannenberg, "Analogy and Doxology," in *Basic Questions in Theology,* trans. George H. Kehm, 2 vols. (Philadelphia: Westminster Press, 1983), 1:211-38. Some of his critics have complained that by admitting the equivocity of all language about God, Pannenberg undercuts "the propositional content and truth-value of theological language." Christoph Schwöbel, "Wolfhart Pannenberg," in *The Modern Theologians,* ed. David F. Ford (Oxford: Basil Blackwell, 1989), 1:269. Pannenberg, particularly in his recent writing, acknowledges that the Trinitarian names for God are not exchangeable. I address this issue on pp. 89-90.

¹⁰See the discussion in Winfried Corduan, *Handmaid to Theology* (Grand Rapids, Mich.: Baker Book House, 1981), pp. 104-5. Note that Corduan is a critic of catalogy.

¹¹Karl Barth, *Church Dogmatics,* ed. and trans. G. W. Bromiley and T. F. Torrance (Edinburgh: T. & T. Clark, 1964), 2(1):213. While Thomas Aquinas was much more prone to stress the limitations of analogy in giving us knowledge of God, Barth was insistent that through the grace of God analogy could yield real knowledge of the very nature and being of God. Whereas for Thomas, God's incomprehensibility seems to place God *beyond* our knowledge, for Barth it is precisely *in* our knowledge of God derived from revelation that we are confronted with his incomprehensibility and hiddenness. See George Hunsinger, "Beyond Literalism and Expressivism: Karl Barth's Hermeneutical Realism," *Modern Theology* 3, no. 3 (Apr. 1987):221-22. Also see David B. Burrell, *Aquinas: God and Action* (Notre Dame, Ind.: University of Notre Dame Press, 1979), pp. 3-11, 55-77, 162-75.

[12]Barth, *Church Dogmatics,* 2(1):195.

[13]Thomas F. Torrance, *Theological Science* (London: Oxford University Press, 1969), p. 150.

[14]Thomas F. Torrance, *The Ground and Grammar of Theology* (Charlottesville: University Press of Virginia, 1980), p. 167.

[15]Thomas F. Torrance, *Reality and Evangelical Theology* (Philadelphia: Westminster Press, 1982), p. 109.

[16]Thomas F. Torrance, *Transformation and Convergence in the Frame of Knowledge* (Grand Rapids, Mich.: Eerdmans, 1984), p. 317.

[17]For a helpful discussion of the capability of metaphor to generate new meanings, see Janet Martin Soskice, *Metaphor and Religious Language* (Oxford: Clarendon Press, 1987), pp. 64-66, 74.

[18]The reference here is to symbols in general, not to the biblical symbolic language of divine revelation whose truth is hidden even from the purview of intuition and mystical insight.

[19]Paul Ricoeur, *The Symbolism of Evil,* trans. Emerson Buchanan (Boston: Beacon, 1967), pp. 347-57.

[20]John Macquarrie, *God-Talk* (New York: Harper & Row, 1967), p. 202.

[21]Avery Dulles, *Models of Revelation* (New York: Doubleday, 1983), p. 143.

[22]Henry Nelson Wieman, *The Wrestle of Religion with Truth* (New York: Macmillan, 1927), pp. 223-26.

[23]Gilkey says to the contrary: "No theological interpretation of fundamental symbols can have meaning for us . . . unless it gives Christian shape to some *modern* ontology, expressive of our own being in the world." Langdon Gilkey, *Catholicism Confronts Modernity* (New York: Seabury Press, 1975), p. 103.

[24]Benedict de Spinoza, *The Political Works,* ed. and trans. A. G. Wernham (Oxford: Clarendon Press, 1958), p. 123.

[25]Gilkey, *Catholicism Confronts Modernity,* p. 101. Tillich writes that though archetypal symbols "grow out of the . . . unconscious," nevertheless, "like living beings, they grow and die." Paul Tillich, *Dynamics of Faith* (New York: Harper & Brothers, 1957), p. 43.

[26]Gilkey would be cautious in this area, however, opting for the reinterpretation of the symbol rather than its total abandonment.

[27]Torrance, *Reality and Evangelical Theology,* p. 27.

[28]See Paul Ricoeur, "Biblical Hermeneutics," *Semeia* 4 (1975):135-38.

[29]John Stuart Mill, *An Examination of Sir William Hamilton's Philosophy* (New York: Henry Holt, 1884), 1:130.

[30]Dulles contends that the church grasps the content of revelation by turning to "the symbolic sources of its own life," by "plumbing the depths of its own self-consciousness." "Adhering to the Christian symbols, as interpreted in the tradition and in the faith and praxis of the Church today, the theologian seeks to

retrieve the wealth of meaning and wisdom contained in the multiple sources that were at the disposal of earlier theologians." *Models of Revelation,* pp. 281, 283.

31Cited in Paul L. Lehmann, "The Direction of Theology Today," *Union Seminary Quarterly Review* 3, no. 1 (Nov. 1947):8. See Emil Brunner, *The Word and the World* (New York: Charles Scribner's Sons, 1931), pp. 6-7.

32George Hunsinger asks: "If the direct knowledge of faith is of itself as being grasped, then is the situation ultimately any different than in liberalism? Doesn't faith know only itself rather than God's objectively grounded Word?" "Conclusion: Toward a Radical Barth," in *Karl Barth and Radical Politics,* ed. Hunsinger (Philadelphia: Westminster Press, 1976), p. 216.

33Barth writes: "There is no reason why the dialectic theology should be *specially* capable of leading one up *to* a gate which can be opened only from within. If one should fancy that it possesses a special preeminence, at least in preparing the way for the action of God, let him remember that it and its paradoxes can do no more *to this end* than can a simple direct word of faith and humility." Karl Barth, *The Word of God and the Word of Man,* trans. Douglas Horton (Gloucester, Mass.: Peter Smith, 1978), p. 212.

34See James D. Smart, *The Divided Mind of Modern Theology* (Philadelphia: Westminster Press, 1967), p. 224. Smart argues against von Balthasar that the dialectical method remained with Barth, though the way of analogy became much more prominent.

35Karl Barth, "Fate and Idea in Theology," in *The Way of Theology in Karl Barth,* ed. H. Martin Rumscheidt (Allison Park, Pa.: Pickwick Publications, 1986), p. 60.

36Karl Barth, *Church Dogmatics,* 2(1):75.

37Thomas Torrance, *God and Rationality* (New York: Oxford University Press, 1971), pp. 187-88.

38See Jacques Ellul, *What I Believe,* trans. Geoffrey W. Bromiley (Grand Rapids, Mich.: Eerdmans, 1989), pp. 29-46. Dan Clendenin makes a powerful case that dialectic is at the very heart of Ellul's theology. Daniel B. Clendenin, *Theological Method in Jacques Ellul* (Lanham, Md.: University Press of America, 1987).

39Jerry H. Gill, *On Knowing God* (Philadelphia: Westminster Press, 1981), p. 134.

40See my discussion of this point on pp. 61-66.

41Jacques Ellul, *The Humiliation of the Word,* trans. Joyce Main Hanks (Grand Rapids, Mich.: Eerdmans, 1985), p. 25.

42Karl Barth, *Church Dogmatics,* trans. G. T. Thomson (Edinburgh: T. & T. Clark, 1936), 1(1):189.

43Ibid.

44Brunner frequently accused Barth of lapsing into objectivism. See Emil Brunner, *The Christian Doctrine of God,* trans. Olive Wyon (Philadelphia: Westminster Press, 1974), pp. 346-52.

[45]Cf. Henri Frédéric Amiel, a nineteenth-century Swiss philosopher: "The philosopher aspires to explain away all mysteries, to dissolve them into light. Mystery, on the other hand, is demanded and pursued by the religious instinct; mystery constitutes the essence of worship." In *The Great Thoughts,* ed. George Seldes (New York: Ballantine Books, 1985), p. 12.

[46]Gerald Heard, *Is God in History?* (New York: Harper & Brothers, 1950), p. 188.

[47]Hans Urs von Balthasar, *The Theology of Karl Barth,* trans. John Drury (New York: Holt, Rinehart & Winston, 1971), p. 207. He goes on to make this apt observation: "Heretical thought has a tendency to exclude things, to overlook certain aspects, and to end up as a definitive, apodictic system."

[48]See T. E. McComiskey, "Names of God," in *Evangelical Dictionary of Theology,* ed. Walter A. Elwell (Grand Rapids, Mich.: Baker Book House, 1984), pp. 464-68.

[49]See notes on Ex 3:13-14 in *The New Jerusalem Bible,* ed. Henry Wansbrough (New York: Doubleday, 1985), p. 85.

[50]See Leo G. Perdue, "Names of God in the Old Testament," in *Harper's Bible Dictionary,* ed. Paul J. Achtemeier (San Francisco: Harper & Row, 1985), pp. 685-86.

[51]See McComiskey, "Names of God," p. 467.

[52]Because it is our Lord Jesus Christ who reveals the name of God as "Father," this name has divine origin and sanction (cf. Jn 5:43; 12:28).

[53]See Robert W. Jenson, *The Triune Identity* (Philadelphia: Fortress, 1982), pp. 10-13.

[54]In the Bible a title applied to a person is a form of a proper name.

[55]See the notes on Ps 8:1 in *New Jerusalem Bible,* p. 821.

[56]Karl Barth, *The Christian Life,* trans. Geoffrey W. Bromiley (Grand Rapids, Mich.: Eerdmans, 1981), p. 115.

[57]While it is true that in the Old Testament "Father" as a personal name for God was more and more accepted, it was still used sparingly perhaps because of Israel's reservations toward images of God that could be interpreted as simply heightened human images. In later Judaism the Father image for deity was associated less with religious than with national and theocratic concerns. See Gerhard Kittel and Gerhard Friedrich, eds., *Theological Dictionary of the New Testament,* 9 vols., trans., ed. and abridged in one volume by Geoffrey W. Bromiley (Grand Rapids, Mich.: Eerdmans, 1985), pp. 807-10. For an illuminating and provocative discussion of the close relation between "Father" and "Yahweh" in the Old Testament see Willem A. VanGemeren, " 'Abba' in the Old Testament?" *Journal of the Evangelical Theological Society* 31, no. 4 (Dec. 1988):385-98, esp. 390-94.

[58]Athanasius and the Cappadocian fathers in their struggle against Arianism argued that God is father not in a general or universal sense, but in a personal

sense. See Catherine Mowry LaCugna, "The Baptismal Formula, Feminist Objections, and Trinitarian Theology," *Journal of Ecumenical Studies* 26, no. 2 (Spring 1989):240-47. It should be noted that the Arians preferred to call God "the Unoriginate."

[59]This point is cogently made by Claude Geffré, " 'Father' as the Proper Name of God," in *God as Father?*, ed. Johannes-Baptist Metz and Edward Schillebeeckx (New York: Seabury Press, 1981), pp. 43-50. Agreeing with Paul Ricoeur, Geffré points out that in the biblical perspective "we have to give a 'zero content to the figure of the father before daring to invoke God as 'Father.' This is what the prophets (Hosea, Jeremiah, the Third Isaiah) began to do. But in this case God the Father is no longer just the ancestor, the figure of the origin. He is the father of a new creation, a new covenant" (p. 44).

Geffré also ably shows how the concept of "Father" is deepened in the New Testament, where God is depicted as the Father of the wayward and impious as well as of the righteous (cf. the parable of the prodigal son). "Compared with the God of Israel the God of Jesus represents a revolution in so far as God is the God of grace before being the God of the law. Belonging to the chosen people does not guarantee salvation, only belonging to the kingdom to come does so. And since one has to enter it like a child, the privileged name with which to invoke God is henceforth to be that of Father" (p. 45).

[60]Already at the time of the exodus Yahweh adopted Israel as his son (Ex 4:22-23).

[61]Some scholars (such as Roland Frye) regard "Father" in reference to God as an appellative metaphor, one that names and does not merely describe. I agree with Alvin Kimel that one problem in calling "Father" a metaphor is that "it functions first and foremost as a term of filial address." Another problem is that the identification of God as Father is an event in the Triune life. (From a private letter from Alvin Kimel, Sept. 30, 1989.) My present inclination is to view Father, when used as a name for God, as an analogy sui generis. See Kimel's brilliant article against feminist language for God: Alvin F. Kimel, Jr., "The Holy Trinity Meets Ashtoreth: A Critique of the Episcopal 'Inclusive' Liturgies," *Anglican Theological Review* 71, no. 1 (Winter 1989):25-47. Also see Alvin F. Kimel, ed., *Speaking the Christian God: The Holy Trinity and the Challenge of Feminism* (Grand Rapids, Mich.: Eerdmans, 1992). In addition see Christian J. Barrigar, "Protecting God: the Lexical Formation of Trinitarian Language," *Modern Theology* 7, no. 4 (July 1991):299-310. Barrigar sees the current debate revolving about whether the Trinitarian symbols are proper names or indefinite descriptions (metaphors).

[62]Emil Brunner, *The Theology of Crisis* (New York: Charles Scribner's Sons, 1935), p. 31.

[63]For this reason idealism is necessarily hostile to the orthodox doctrine of the

Trinity. It seeks a God above the differentiated God of Trinitarian speculation. This idealistic-mystical orientation is conspicuous in the feminist theologian and hymnist Brian Wren, who writes: "Trinitarian doctrine has been elaborated with the male metaphors of Father and Son, plus the nonpersonal name Holy Spirit. These names are a signpost pointing into the clouds, not a nametag identifying a guest. To speak of God as She is not to add a new nametag, and thus give God conflicting identities, but to follow a different signpost into the cloud of mystery." Brian Wren, "Meeting the Awesome She," *Christian Century* 105, no. 5 (Feb. 17, 1988):159.

[64] *The Vocation of Man,* in *The Popular Works of Johann Gottlieb Fichte,* trans. William Smith (London: Trübner, 1889), 1:463.

[65] See Donald G. Bloesch, *The Battle for the Trinity* (Ann Arbor, Mich.: Servant, 1985), pp. 69-87.

[66] Robert P. Ericksen, *Theologians Under Hitler* (New Haven, Conn.: Yale University Press, 1985), p. 163.

[67] Rolf Ahlers, ed., *The Barmen Theological Declaration of 1934* (Lewiston, N.Y.: Edwin Mellen Press, 1986), p. 40.

[68] Ibid., p. 41.

[69] See Kurt Rudolph, *Gnosis: The Nature and History of Gnosticism,* trans. P. W. Coxon, K. H. Kuhn and R. M. Wilson, ed. R. M. Wilson (San Francisco: Harper & Row, 1983); Elaine Pagels, *The Gnostic Gospels* (New York: Vintage Books, 1981); and Karen L. King, ed., *Images of the Feminine in Gnosticism* (Philadelphia: Fortress, 1988). Rudolph makes this interesting observation: "For the gnostics bisexuality is an expression of perfection; it is only the earthly creation which leads to a separation of the original divine unity, which holds for the whole Pleroma." *Gnosis,* p. 80.

[70] Hans Jonas, *The Gnostic Religion* (Boston: Beacon, 1963), p. 332.

[71] See Luther H. Martin, "Jung as Gnostic," *Essays on Jung and the Study of Religion,* ed. L. H. Martin and James Goss (Lanham, Md.: University Press of America, 1985), pp. 70-79; Stephan A. Hoeller, *The Gnostic Jung and the Seven Sermons to the Dead* (Wheaton, Ill.: Theosophical Publishing House, 1982); and Carl A. Raschke, *The Interruption of Eternity: Modern Gnosticism and the Origins of the New Religious Consciousness* (Chicago: Nelson-Hall, 1980), pp. 143-54, 160-62.

[72] Dionysius the Pseudo-Areopagite, *On the Divine Names,* ed. and trans. C. E. Rolt (New York: Macmillan, 1957), p. 53.

[73] See Frederick Copleston, *History of Philosophy* (New York: Doubleday, 1985), 2:95.

[74] Nicholas of Cusa, *The Vision of God,* trans. Emma Gurney Salter (New York: Frederick Ungar, 1960), chap. 13, p. 58.

[75] David Tracy perceptively observes that every major religion is grounded in

certain root metaphors that redescribe the human situation, and any attempt to eliminate these metaphors or move beyond them is effectively to substitute one set of meanings for another. See his "Metaphor and Religion: The Test Case of Christian Texts," in *On Metaphor,* ed. Sheldon Sacks (Chicago: University of Chicago Press, 1978), pp. 89-104, esp. 104.

[76]Rosemary Radford Ruether, *Sexism and God-Talk* (Boston: Beacon Press, 1983), p. 11.

[77]Tertullian, among others in the early church, perceived the analogical character of Father and Son in biblical and theological discourse. "Whereas other analogical terms like Lord and Judge indicate a merely functional relation to the world, the names Father and Son point to an ontological relation of distinct persons within the godhead itself." Christopher B. Kaiser, *The Doctrine of God* (Westchester, Ill.: Crossway Books, 1982), p. 52. See Tertullian, *Against Praxeas* 9-10, in *The Ante-Nicene Fathers,* ed. Roberts and Donaldson, 3:603-5.

[78]Pannenberg acknowledges that "human religion uses a great number of words and symbols. All of them are extrinsic to the divine reality which they refer to, and therefore they are exchangeable." But "Jesus' way of relating to God was not external to the divine reality itself. That makes for its finality." See Wolfhart Pannenberg, *An Introduction to Systematic Theology* (Grand Rapids, Mich.: Eerdmans, 1991), pp. 31-32.

[79]Mary McDermott Shideler shares these words of wisdom: "It would be safer and more effective to retain the deeply rooted masculine image and enrich it by redefining it. Father, for example, can be returned to its essential meaning as the seminal, generative impregnator. Taking God as Father in those terms, we can see both creation and redemption as impregnations, and God's seminal acts as crucial for the conception and birth of new life in Christ. Yet the idea of God impregnating the world with his Spirit is entirely compatible with the nurturing tenderness that too often is associated only with the image of maternity." Letter in *Christian Century* 103, no. 21 (July 2-9, 1986):620.

Similarly Susanne Heine, while fully recognizing the maternal side of the biblical God, nevertheless opts for the name of "Father" for God. "So in the tradition which we have in its final form the biblical God is far from being deserving of the name mother. His masculinity is never in question, nor is the fundamental repudiation of the female deities in the pantheon of the neighboring peoples. . . . That the biblical God who has from of old been male also takes on maternal and . . . other feminine features, shows rather that he is 'all in all' and can assimilate qualities or modes of conduct which are distributed between different divine figures in a polytheistic religion. The maternal side of this God, too, is at the service of the strict monotheism of Jewish faith, even if it was not beyond dispute at all times." Susanne Heine, *Matriarchs, Goddesses, and Images of God,* trans. John Bowden (Minneapolis: Augsburg,

1989), pp. 29-30.

[80]On the ineradicable conflict between Hebraic and Canaanite conceptions of God see Ruether, *Sexism and God-Talk,* pp. 47-68; Gerd Theissen, *Biblical Faith: An Evolutionary Approach,* trans. John Bowden (Philadelphia: Fortress, 1985), pp. 64-81; and Heine, *Matriarchs,* pp. 41-73.

[81]Theissen, *Biblical Faith,* p. 80.

[82]Although the symbol of the Sky Father more nearly approximates the God of biblical faith than that of the Earth Mother, it should be recognized that even the former is woefully inadequate to convey the reality of the biblical God. The God of the Bible actually transcends this polarity, since he is neither simply "above" nor "beneath" but "over," "in," "through" and "around." In the early stages of Israel's history God was indeed thought of in terms reminiscent of the Sky Father, but in later tradition God was envisaged as utterly transcendent and, paradoxically, at the same time infinitely near. He is a God who cannot be encompassed by human reason or imagination. He is a Father who is completely unlike human fathers, for he is pure Spirit. Susanne Heine comments, "It is striking that in biblical texts talk of God is accompanied by negations. God is father but does not beget; God reveals himself but remains invisible; God is life, but not affected by death; God acts in history, but is transcendent ('in heaven'); one may not make an image of him (in the literal and metaphorical sense); he is creator, not created himself, he is 'wholly other.' " *Matriarchs,* p. 34.

[83]Theissen, *Biblical Faith,* p. 79.

[84]Most cultures and religions see the masculine and the feminine as indicative of realities broader and deeper than sexual differentiation. Yet there are palpable cultural differences in the way this kind of polarity is concretely understood. In the Bible the inseparable relation between masculine and feminine is depicted in God's love for his people (described in Hosea as the "wife" of Yahweh) and in Christ's love for his church (cf. Eph 5:21-33). Christ is the bridegroom, the provider, the enabler, and the church is the bride of Christ, the mother and nurturer of the faithful. The bridegroom seeks out the bride, and the bride answers the call of her beloved (cf. Song of Songs 1—2; Rev 19:7-8). It should be noted that the response of believers to their Savior will involve some initiative as well as receptiveness (cf. Rev 3:20-22).

[85]Roland Frye brilliantly argues that the motherly qualities of God in the Bible are to be placed in the category of simile rather than some more precise framework of meaning. "A simile or similitude does not posit a general association, but rather an association applied to some particular sense within an encompassing lexical meaning. The similes comparing God to a mother illustrate some phase of divine attitude or intent, as defined in the simile's context, but they are not and do not claim to be transparent to personal identity as are

predicating metaphors such as 'the good shepherd' or 'the Lamb of God,' and even more broadly God 'the Father' and Christ 'the Son.' " Roland M. Frye, *Language for God and Feminist Language* (Princeton, N.J.: Center for Theological Inquiry, 1988), p. 19.

86Quoted in *Insight* 3, no. 14 (Apr. 6, 1987):14-15. See Elizabeth Achtemeier, "Exchanging God for 'No Gods': A Discussion of Female Language for God," in *Speaking the Christian God*, ed. Kimel, pp. 1-16.

87It is important to note that the ways in which God relates to us as Father, Son and Spirit reflect distinctions within God himself. He not only relates to us in a triune manner, but he exists within himself as a Trinity. He is Father, Son and Spirit from all eternity. At the same time, as the Triune God he has a maternal as well as a paternal side: he receives and nurtures as well as creates and empowers. Yet even here the thrust of the biblical conception of God accentuates the paternal, even though it is indeed possible to speak of motherly qualities within God as well. The controlling symbolism is masculine, but it is not the exclusive symbolism. One must be careful not to contend for an ontological priority of the masculine over the feminine, though one may affirm a functional priority in that the initiation of action precedes the response to action. The Son is begotten of the Father and not vice versa.

88While Hosea is thinking of man in the generic sense, it is not unjustifiable to see this as an indictment of the pretensions associated with patriarchy and monarchy because it was the male patriarchs and monarchs who claimed to represent God to the people. It should be noted that Hosea is presenting a picture of God that sharply contradicts the domination model of patriarchy.

89This thesis is ably documented in Robert Hamerton-Kelly, *God the Father: Theology and Patriarchy in the Teaching of Jesus* (Philadelphia: Fortress, 1979).

90David Tracy, *Plurality and Ambiguity* (San Francisco: Harper & Row, 1987), p. 61.

91See Donald G. Bloesch, *Is the Bible Sexist?* (Westchester, Ill.: Crossway Books, 1982), pp. 61-83.

92Whitehead, *Process and Reality*, p. 532.

93See Gustavo Gutiérrez, *A Theology of Liberation*, trans. Caridad Inda and John Eagleson (Maryknoll, N.Y.: Orbis Books, 1973); Jon Sobrino, *Christology at the Crossroads*, trans. John Drury (Maryknoll, N.Y.: Orbis Books, 1978); Leonardo Boff, *Passion of Christ, Passion of the World*, trans. Robert R. Barr (Maryknoll, N.Y.: Orbis, 1987); and Ismael Garcia, *Justice in Latin American Theology of Liberation* (Atlanta: John Knox Press, 1987).

94It is not uncommon for feminist writers to denigrate Judaism, which they regard as incurably patriarchal. See, for example, Leonardo Boff, *The Maternal Face of God*, trans. Robert R. Barr and John W. Diercksmeier (San Francisco: Harper & Row, 1987), pp. 63-70, 237. Theologian Susanne Heine warns that "feminist literature, which sweepingly makes 'the Jews' and their allegedly martial God responsible for all women's suffering down the centuries, affords a powerful stimulus to antisemitism." Heine, *Matriarchs,* p. 166.

[95]McFague, *Metaphorical Theology,* p. 8.

[96]Ellul, *Humiliation of the Word,* p. 201.

[97]See notes in New Jerusalem Bible, p. 1249.

[98]Dulles agrees with Tillich that a symbol "opens up levels of reality which otherwise are closed to us . . . and also unlocks dimensions and elements of our soul which correspond to the dimensions and elements of reality." Dulles, *Models of Revelation,* p. 137. But this is to give a symbol a power that belongs only to the Spirit of God. For both Dulles and Tillich symbols would seem to have innate power, whereas in an authentic evangelical theology symbols have power only as they are used by the Spirit of God to direct us to Christ.

[99]Ellul, *Humiliation of the Word,* pp. 69-71. See Paul Ricoeur, "Manifestation et proclamation," in *Le Sacré,* ed. Enrico Castelli (Paris: Aubier, 1974).

[100]Ellul and Ricoeur here resonate with Torrance, who holds that whereas the Greek way of thinking was a kind of seeing, the Hebrew way of knowing was closer to "*listening* and *responding . . . serving* and *obeying.*" Thomas F. Torrance, *Theology in Reconstruction* (London: SCM Press, 1965), pp. 14ff., 20ff. For a criticism of Torrance's view see Geoffrey Wainwright, *Doxology* (New York: Oxford University Press, 1980), p. 463.

[101]Ellul, *Humiliation of the Word,* p. 70.

[102]Ibid., pp. 70-71.

[103]Ibid., p. 190.

[104]Martin Luther, *Luther's Works,* ed. Jaroslav Pelikan (St. Louis: Concordia, 1957), 22:306.

[105]Friedrich Heiler, *Prayer,* trans. and ed. Samuel McComb (New York: Oxford University Press, 1958), pp. 65-73, 296-346.

[106]Ellul, *Humiliation of the Word,* p. 101.

[107]Geert Groote, founder of the mystical Brethren of the Common Life, speaks of "leaving the Scriptures and external signs behind" as we make progress in the Christian life toward the perfection of faith and love. *Devotio Moderna: Basic Writings,* trans. and ed. John Van Engen (New York: Paulist Press, 1988), p. 113. Mystics seek to get beyond images because of their desire for a direct or immediate perception of God. Evangelical Christians are ready to discard artistic representations of God because they realize the danger of confusing the sign and the reality.

[108]Gerald Heard, *The Code of Christ* (New York: Harper & Brothers, 1941), pp. 132-33.

[109]Gregory of Nyssa, *The Life of Moses,* trans. A. J. Malherbe and E. Ferguson (New York: Paulist Press, 1978), p. 116.

110Gerald Heard, *A Preface to Prayer* (New York: Harper & Brothers, 1944), p. 51.

111See Donald G. Bloesch, *The Struggle of Prayer* (San Francisco: Harper & Row, 1980), pp. 72-77.

112In Schleiermacher we see a new mysticism, which focuses on identification with the joys of the world rather than detachment from its trials. God is envisioned as the Infinite in the finite rather than a self-contained Infinite beyond the finite.

113Friedrich Schleiermacher, *On Religion: Speeches to Its Cultured Despisers,* trans. John Oman (New York: Harper & Row, 1958), p. 150.

114Ibid., p. 139.

115See Wilhelm Herrmann, *The Communion of the Christian with God,* ed. Robert T. Voelkel (Philadelphia: Fortress, 1971).

116See Paul Tillich, *Systematic Theology* (Chicago: University of Chicago Press, 1957), 2:106-7.

117Ellul, *Humiliation of the Word,* p. 45.

118Ibid., p. 46.

119Ibid.

120Calvin's legacy should especially be noted in this connection. He issued a stern warning against visual representations of the sacred, maintaining that the Christian life depends on "God's mouth" and that we begin to see only after we have truly heard. See William J. Bouwsma, *John Calvin: A Sixteenth-Century Portrait* (New York: Oxford University Press, 1988), p. 158.

121Karl Barth, *Theology and Church,* trans. Louise Pettibone Smith (New York: Harper & Row, 1962), p. 317.

122Ibid.

123Ernst Benz, *The Eastern Orthodox Church,* trans. Richard and Clara Winston (New York: Doubleday Anchor Books, 1963), p. 18. Icons are regarded as "a kind of window between the earthly and the celestial worlds" (p. 6).

124Nicolas Zernov says that icons in Orthodox heritage were "not merely paintings. They were dynamic manifestations of man's spiritual power to redeem creation through beauty and art." Nicolas Zernov, *The Russians and Their Church* (London: Fellowship of St. Alban and St. Sergius, 1945), p. 107. And in the words of Vladimir Lossky: "An icon or a cross does not exist simply to direct our imagination during our prayers. It is a material center in which there reposes an energy, a divine force, which unites itself to human art." Vladimir Lossky, *The Mystical Theology of the Eastern Church* (Crestwood, N.Y.: St. Vladimir's Seminary Press, 1976), p. 189.

125In George P. Fedotov, ed., *A Treasury of Russian Spirituality* (Belmont, Mass.: Nordland, 1975), 2:451, 463-64.

126Ibid., pp. 445-46.

127I am not here advocating a "low church" as opposed to a "high church" service but instead pleading for the free movement of the Spirit even within the framework of a structured order of worship.

### Appendix B: On Meaning

[1]Jerry H. Gill, *On Knowing God* (Philadelphia: Westminster Press, 1981), p. 13. For his interpretation of the critical philosophy see pp. 19-52.

[2]Thomas F. Torrance, *God and Rationality* (London and New York: Oxford University Press, 1971), p. 205.

[3]Jacques Ellul, *The Humiliation of the Word,* trans. Joyce Main Hanks (Grand Rapids, Mich.: Eerdmans, 1985), p. 108.

[4]Ibid.

### Chapter 5: Toward the Renewal of Theology

[1]Pierre Teilhard de Chardin, *Christianity and Evolution* (New York: Harcourt Brace Jovanovich, 1971), p. 160.

[2]Schubert M. Ogden, *On Theology* (San Francisco: Harper & Row, 1986), p. 87.

[3]Ibid., p. 11.

[4]Ibid., p. 12.

[5]Langdon Gilkey, *Catholicism Confronts Modernity* (New York: Seabury Press, 1975), p. 115. Gilkey draws upon both process thought and Tillichian philosophy.

[6]See Rudolf Otto, *The Idea of the Holy,* trans. John W. Harvey (New York: Oxford University Press, 1958).

[7]Friedrich Schleiermacher, *On Religion: Speeches to Its Cultured Despisers,* trans. John Oman (New York: Harper & Row, 1958), p. 95.

[8]Wilhelm Herrmann, *The Communion of the Christian with God,* ed. Robert T. Voelkel (Philadelphia: Fortress, 1971), p. 225.

[9]James M. Gustafson, *Ethics from a Theocentric Perspective* (Chicago: University of Chicago Press, 1981), 1:235.

[10]See Edward Schillebeeckx, *Jesus: An Experiment in Christology,* trans. Hubert Hoskins (New York: Crossroad, 1981), and *Christ: The Experience of Jesus as Lord,* trans. John Bowden (New York: Crossroad, 1981).

[11]Reinhold Niebuhr, *The Nature and Destiny of Man,* 2 vols. (New York: Charles Scribner's Sons, 1951), 1:127.

[12]P. T. Forsyth, *Faith, Freedom and the Future* (London: Independent Press, 1955), p. 120.

[13]P. T. Forsyth, *The Preaching of Jesus and the Gospel of Christ* (Blackwood, South Australia: New Creation Publications, 1987), p. 82.

[14]Quoted in Bengt R. Hoffman, *Luther and the Mystics* (Minneapolis: Augsburg, 1976), p. 82.

[15]Martin Luther, *A Commentary on St. Paul's Epistle to the Galatians,* ed. and

trans. Philip S. Watson (London: James Clarke, 1953), p. 372.

¹⁶Gabriel Fackre, *The Christian Story* (Grand Rapids, Mich.: Eerdmans, 1987), 2:134.

¹⁷John Piper, *Desiring God: Meditations of a Christian Hedonist* (Portland, Ore.: Multnomah Press, 1986), p. 195.

¹⁸Wilhelm Herrmann, *Systematic Theology*, trans. Nathaniel Micklem and Kenneth A. Saunders (London: Allen & Unwin, 1927), p. 64.

¹⁹Adolf von Harnack, *History of Dogma*, 7 vols., trans. Neil Buchanan (New York: Russell & Russell, 1958), 1:17.

²⁰Carl E. Braaten and Robert W. Jenson, eds., *Christian Dogmatics* (Philadelphia: Fortress, 1983), 1:47.

²¹Richard A. Muller, *Dictionary of Latin and Greek Theological Terms* (Grand Rapids, Mich.: Baker Book House, 1985), p. 299.

²²See Ernst Troeltsch, *Der Historismus und seine Probleme* (Tübingen, Germany: J. C. B. Mohr, 1922); *Ernst Troeltsch: Writings on Theology and Religion*, ed. and trans. Robert Morgan and Michael Pye (Atlanta: John Knox Press, 1977); *Christian Thought: Its History and Application*, ed. Baron F. von Hügel (London: University of London Press, 1923; rpt. New York: Meridian Books, 1957); and Walter E. Wyman, Jr., *The Concept of Glaubenslehre: Ernst Troeltsch and the Theological Heritage of Schleiermacher* (Chico, Calif.: Scholars Press, 1983). For the Hegelian roots of historicism see T. Z. Lavine, *From Socrates to Sartre: The Philosophic Quest* (New York: Bantam Books, 1984), pp. 217-18.

²³Brian Gerrish, "From 'Dogmatik' to 'Glaubenslehre,' " in *Paradigm Change in Theology*, ed. Hans Küng and David Tracy, trans. Margaret Köhl (New York: Crossroad, 1991), p. 173.

²⁴See Charles E. Curran, *Moral Theology: A Continuing Journey* (Notre Dame, Ind.: University of Notre Dame Press, 1982); and *Toward an American Catholic Moral Theology* (Notre Dame, Ind.: University of Notre Dame Press, 1987).

²⁵Letty M. Russell, *Human Liberation in a Feminist Perspective: A Theology* (Philadelphia: Westminster Press, 1974), p. 289.

²⁶Francis Schüssler Fiorenza, *Foundational Theology: Jesus and the Church* (New York: Crossroad, 1984), p. 289.

²⁷P. T. Forsyth, *The Work of Christ* (London: Hodder & Stoughton, 1910), p. 46.

²⁸Ibid., p. 48.

²⁹Ibid., p. 177.

³⁰See Herman Bavinck, *Our Reasonable Faith*, trans. Henry Zylstra (Grand Rapids, Mich.: Eerdmans, 1956), p. 7.

³¹Fackre sees the symbolists as belonging to the category of "affective experientialism." *The Christian Story*, 2:150-56.

³²Avery Dulles, *The Survival of Dogma* (New York: Doubleday, 1971), p. 195.

³³Ibid.

[34]Theodore W. Jennings, Jr., *Introduction to Theology* (Philadelphia: Fortress, 1976), p. 2.

[35]Ibid., p. 82.

[36]Ibid., p. 81.

[37]George Rupp, *Culture-Protestantism: German Liberal Theology at the Turn of the Twentieth Century* (Missoula, Mont.: Scholars Press, 1977), p. 33.

[38]"The immediate object of theological cognition is the community's faith that it stands to God in a relation essentially conditioned by the forgiveness of sins." Albrecht Ritschl, *The Christian Doctrine of Justification and Reconciliation*, trans. H. R. Mackintosh and A. B. Macaulay, 3d ed. (New York: Charles Scribner's Sons, 1900), p. 3.

[39]Gustavo Gutiérrez, *A Theology of Liberation: History, Politics and Salvation*, trans. and ed. Caridad Inda and John Eagleson (Maryknoll, N.Y.: Orbis Books, 1973), p. 6.

[40]See Gordon D. Kaufman, *The Theological Imagination* (Philadelphia: Westminster Press, 1981), pp. 21-57, 263-79.

[41]Schillebeeckx, *Jesus*, p. 13.

[42]Thomas N. Finger, *Christian Theology: An Eschatological Approach* (Nashville: Thomas Nelson, 1985), 1:54.

[43]Ibid.

[44]Finger's eschatological contextual theology leads him to bring the faith into a partial harmonization with the ideological movement of modern feminism, to the extent that he can advocate calling God "She" as well as "He." Theology, he says, must let itself be challenged by "reality's openness to change, growth and the partially unknown." See Thomas Finger, "Donald Bloesch on the Trinity: Right Battle, Wrong Battle Lines," *TSF Bulletin* 9, no. 3 (Jan.-Feb. 1986):21.

[45]Patrick Granfield, " 'Christian Realism': An Interview with Reinhold Niebuhr," *Commonweal* 85, no. 11 (Dec. 16, 1966):320.

[46]Rudolf Bultmann, "The Problem of a Theological Exegesis of the New Testament," in *The Beginnings of Dialectic Theology*, ed. James M. Robinson (Richmond, Va.: John Knox Press, 1968), p. 252. Along these same lines Gabriel Fackre, who was deeply influenced by Reinhold Niebuhr, defines theology as the "ordered reflection that seeks to elaborate and render intelligible the faith of the Christian community." *The Christian Story* (Grand Rapids, Mich.: Eerdmans, 1984), 1:16. Both Niebuhr and Fackre stand closer to Schleiermacher than Barth in their theological method. Barth would say that the object of theology is neither human faith nor Christian faith but divine revelation that stands over and against the community of faith, that continually calls the faith-perspective of the community into question, that provides the absolute standard by which the community must reform and purify its faith. Fackre's divergence from Barth is conspicuous in vol. 2 of his *Christian Story*, where he

includes "the world" as a criterion for faith (see pp. 51-54).

⁴⁷Stephen Happel and James J. Walter, *Conversion and Discipleship* (Philadelphia: Fortress, 1986), p. 145. See Bernard J. F. Lonergan, *Method in Theology* (New York: Herder & Herder, 1972), p. xi.

⁴⁸Once we see Scripture in the light of its divine center and goal, we are then free to use both induction and deduction in the task of understanding the full import of the scriptural message.

⁴⁹See George A. Lindbeck, *The Nature of Doctrine: Religion and Theology in a Postliberal Age* (Philadelphia: Westminster Press, 1984), pp. 30-45.

⁵⁰Paul Tillich, *Systematic Theology,* 3 vols. (Chicago: University of Chicago Press, 1951), 1:8-9.

⁵¹Harnack, *History of Dogma,* 1:17.

⁵²Ritschl, *The Christian Doctrine of Justification and Reconciliation,* pp. 203-12, 398-99.

⁵³McKim reminds us that for the Reformers and their followers "faith is personal trust and relationship with God through Jesus Christ, not primarily assent to what the church says must be believed." Donald McKim, "Dogma," in *Evangelical Dictionary of Theology,* ed. Walter A. Elwell (Grand Rapids, Mich.: Baker Book House, 1984), p. 328.

⁵⁴Karl Barth, *Church Dogmatics,* trans. G. T. Thomson (Edinburgh: T. & T. Clark, 1936), 1(1):304.

⁵⁵There is, to be sure, a propositional element in revelational truth in that this truth is a claim that calls for our acceptance and obedience. But this is a claim that presses itself upon our unders tanding rather than a claim that has been reduced to an object of our understanding. It is an announcement of unfathomable grace that can only be received in gratefulness, not a general truth that is there to be assimilated into a conceptual system. It is a command that calls us into action, not a principle that is ever at our disposal.

⁵⁶Barth, *Church Dogmatics,* trans. and ed. G. W. Bromiley, rev. ed. (Edinburgh: T. & T. Clark, 1975), 1(1):269-70.

⁵⁷Avery Dulles, *Models of Revelation* (New York: Doubleday, 1983), p. 223.

⁵⁸Barth, *Church Dogmatics,* trans. Thomson, 1(1):306.

⁵⁹Emil Brunner, *The Christian Doctrine of God,* trans. Olive Wyon (Philadelphia: Westminster Press, 1974), p. 106.

⁶⁰I address this point further on pp. 136-38.

⁶¹Thomas F. Torrance, *Reality and Evangelical Theology* (Philadelphia: Westminster Press, 1982), p. 147.

⁶²Ibid., p. 135.

⁶³Hans Urs von Balthasar, "Truth and Life," in *Concilium* 21 (New York: Paulist Press, 1967), p. 90.

⁶⁴Gerald O'Collins, "Dogma," in *The Westminster Dictionary of Christian Theol-*

*ogy,* ed. Alan Richardson and John Bowden (Philadelphia: Westminster Press, 1983), p. 163. According to O'Collins, "All dogmas are doctrines, albeit of a particularly solemn kind, but obviously not all doctrines have reached or ever will reach dogmatic status."

[65]Ibid., pp. 162-63. O'Collins here cites the Vatican II statement *Dogmatic Constitution on Divine Revelation* 6.21.

[66]Karl Rahner, *Theological Investigations,* trans. Cornelius Ernst (Baltimore: Helicon Press, 1961), 1:149.

[67]Paul Althaus, *The Theology of Martin Luther,* trans. Robert C. Schultz (Philadelphia: Fortress, 1966), p. 8. Note that these are the words of Althaus.

[68]Ogden, *On Theology,* p. 19.

[69]*Calvin: Institutes of the Christian Religion,* ed. John T. McNeill, trans. Ford Lewis Battles, 2 vols. (Philadelphia: Westminster Press, 1960), 1:li.

[70]See the discussion of this issue on pp. 138-42.

[71]Quoted in Eberhard Busch, *Karl Barth: His Life from Letters and Autobiographical Texts,* trans. John Bowden (Philadelphia: Fortress, 1976), p. 100.

[72]From a lecture by M. Douglas Meeks of Wesley Seminary, Washington, D.C., given at St. Paul's United Church of Christ, Chicago, May 4, 1980.

[73]Ogden, *On Theology,* p. 64.

[74]Rosemary Radford Ruether, *Womanguides: Readings Toward a Feminist Theology* (Boston: Beacon, 1985), pp. ix-xi. Also see Ruether, *Sexism and God-Talk* (Boston: Beacon, 1983), pp. 38-41.

[75]Cited in *Presbyterian Journal* 31, no. 50 (Apr. 11, 1973):13.

[76]Philip Jacob Spener, *Pia Desideria,* trans. Theodore G. Tappert (Philadelphia: Fortress, 1964), pp. 103-15.

[77]See Jared Wicks, *Luther and His Spiritual Legacy* (Wilmington, Del.: Michael Glazier, 1983), p. 89. Cf.: "The true contemplation is that in which the heart is crushed and the conscience smitten." *Luther's Meditations on the Gospels,* ed. and trans. Roland H. Bainton (Philadelphia: Westminster Press, 1962), p. 135.

[78]Cited by Marshall Shelley, review of *Bring Forth Justice* by Waldron Scott, *Christianity Today* 25, no. 11 (June 12, 1981):62.

[79]See Friedrich Schleiermacher, *The Christian Faith,* trans. H. R. Mackintosh and J. S. Stewart, 2 vols. (New York: Harper Torchbooks, 1963), 1:97-101.

[80]Schleiermacher fervently supported the creation of the Prussian Union Church by Frederick William III in which Lutheran and Reformed distinctives were sacrificed for the purpose of a pan-Protestant church.

[81]Gregory Baum, foreword to Andrew M. Greeley, *The New Agenda* (New York: Doubleday, 1973), p. 16.

[82]Gilkey, *Catholicism Confronts Modernity,* pp. 65-66.

[83]Max Thurian, *Visible Unity and Tradition,* trans. W. J. Kerrigan (London: Darton, Longman & Todd, 1964), pp. 30, 32. Thurian has since converted to the Roman

Catholic church and has left the Taizé community.

84Rosemary Ruether, "Theology as Critique of and Emancipation from Sexism," in *The Vocation of the Theologian*, ed. Theodore Jennings, Jr. (Philadelphia: Westminster Press, 1985), p. 30.

85Schleiermacher, *On Religion*, trans. Oman, p. 175.

86Langdon Gilkey, "Theology as the Interpretation of Faith for Church and World," in *The Vocation of the Theologian*, ed. Jennings, p. 97.

87Ogden, *On Theology*, p. 140.

88I affirm this against Thiemann, whose doctrine of revelation is "not a foundational epistemological theory but an account which traces the internal logic of a set of Christian convictions concerning God's identity and reality." Ronald F. Thiemann, *Revelation and Theology: The Gospel as Narrated Promise* (Notre Dame, Ind.: University of Notre Dame Press, 1985), p. 70. Unlike some other narrative theologians, Thiemann contrasts "descriptive" with "explanatory" rather than with "normative."

89See Alfred North Whitehead, *Religion in the Making* (New York: Macmillan, 1957), p. 50.

90Brunner errs in this direction when he says: "This fight with modern thinking is the task, supremely, of theology; and since it is a fight more critical than any other the Church has to wage, the responsibilities of theology are now perhaps greater than ever before." Emil Brunner, *The Word and the World* (New York: Charles Scribner's Sons, 1931), p. 6.

91Cited in *The Catholic Worker* 46, no. 6 (July-Aug. 1980):8.

### Appendix C: Gospel and Kerygma
1See the discussion in Donald G. Bloesch, *Freedom for Obedience* (San Francisco: Harper & Row, 1987), pp. 126-49.

### Appendix D: Orthodoxy
1Schleiermacher located the essence of religion not in adherence to dogma but in "the feeling of absolute dependence." *The Christian Faith*, ed. H. R. Mackintosh and J. S. Stewart, 2 vols. (New York: Harper & Row, 1963), I:12-18.

2Karl Barth, *The Word of God and the Word of Man*, trans. Douglas Horton (Gloucester, Mass.: Peter Smith, 1978), pp. 200-207.

3Friedrich Schleiermacher, *On Religion: Speeches to Its Cultured Despisers*, trans. John Oman (New York: Harper & Row, 1958), p. 175.

4It should be noted that orthodoxy in the original Greek *(orthodoxia)* could mean either right opinion or right praise.

### Chapter 6: Natural Theology
1Boethius, *The Consolation of Philosophy*, trans. V. E. Watts (New York: Pen-

guin Books, 1986).

[2]For Anselm God is that than which no greater can be thought, and therefore must exist not only in idea but also in reality. See Anselm, *Proslogium* III, in *St. Anselm: Proslogium; Monologium; An Appendix in Behalf of the Fool by Gaunilon; and Cur Deus Homo,* ed. and trans. Sidney Norton Deane (LaSalle, Ill.: Open Court, 1959), p. 8. For a lucid discussion of Anselm's ontological proof see Frederick Copleston, *A History of Philosophy* (New York: Doubleday Image, 1985), 2:161-65.

[3]Barth makes a valiant but not wholly convincing case that Anselm's proof must be understood in the context of his method of faith seeking understanding, and therefore the validity of this proof can be established only in the community of faith. See Karl Barth, *Anselm: Fides Quaerens Intellectum* (Richmond, Va.: John Knox Press, 1960).

[4]See further discussion of this issue on pp. 214, 321.

[5]Bonaventure develops this argument in his *The Soul's Journey into God.* See Bonaventure, *The Soul's Journey into God, The Tree of Life, The Life of St. Francis,* trans. Ewert Cousins (New York: Paulist Press, 1978), pp. 51-116.

[6]Meister Eckhart, *The Essential Sermons, Commentaries, Treatises and Defense,* ed. and trans. Edmund Colledge and Bernard McGinn (New York: Paulist Press, 1981), p. 207.

[7]John of the Cross, *The Ascent of Mount Carmel* 2.16, cited in *A Dazzling Darkness: An Anthology of Western Mysticism,* ed. Patrick Grant (Grand Rapids, Mich.: Eerdmans, 1985), p. 102.

[8]Stephen Clissold, ed., *The Wisdom of the Spanish Mystics* (New York: New Directions Books, 1977), p. 41.

[9]*Calvin: Institutes of the Christian Religion,* ed. John T. McNeill, trans. Ford Lewis Battles, 2 vols. (Philadelphia: Westminster Press, 1960), 1.6.1, p. 69.

[10]Philip Melanchthon, *Loci Communes Theologici,* trans. Lowell J. Satre, rev. and ed. Wilhelm Pauck, in *Library of Christian Classics,* ed. John Baillie, John T. McNeill and Henry P. Van Dusen (Philadelphia: Westminster Press, 1969), 19:90.

[11]Hans Engelland, *Die Gewissheit um Gott und der neuere Biblizismus* (Munich: Kaiser, 1933), p. 66. Cited in Otto Weber, *Foundations of Dogmatics,* trans. Darrell L. Guder (Grand Rapids, Mich.: Eerdmans, 1981), 1:202.

[12]See Jaroslav Pelikan, *From Luther to Kierkegaard* (St. Louis: Concordia, 1950), pp. 24-75.

[13]Cited in Copleston, *History of Philosophy,* 4:161. Cf. Pascal, *Pensées,* ed. and trans. A. J. Krailsheimer (Baltimore: Penguin Books, 1966), 14.190, p. 86.

[14]Francis Turretin could describe natural theology as providing "a subjective condition in humans for the admission of the light of grace"; at the same time, unless humans are enlightened by the Holy Spirit they will fail to grasp the

significance of what natural knowledge yields and will invariably sink deeper into sin. See Timothy Ross Phillips, *Francis Turretin's Idea of Theology and Its Bearing upon His Doctrine of Scripture* (Ann Arbor, Mich.: University Microfilms International, 1986), pp. 212-14.

15According to Tillich, two structures were affirmed in orthodoxy—"the substructure of reason, and the superstructure of revelation. The biblical doctrines form the superstructure. What actually happened later . . . was that the mixed articles became unmixed rationally, and that the substructure of rational theology dispossessed the superstructure of revelation, drawing it into itself and taking away its meaning. When this happens, we are in the realm of rationalism or Enlightenment." Paul Tillich, *A History of Christian Thought,* ed. Carl E. Braaten (New York: Harper & Row, 1968), p. 279.

16Richard Sibbes, *The Complete Works of Richard Sibbes,* ed. Alexander Balloch Grosart (Edinburgh: Nichol, 1862-64), 1:246.

17John Locke, *An Essay Concerning Human Understanding,* ed. Alexander Campbell Fraser (New York: Dover, 1959), 2:431.

18Cited in Ronald Gregor Smith, *J. G. Hamann* (London: Collins, 1960), p. 57.

19Friedrich Schleiermacher, *On Religion: Speeches to Its Cultured Despisers,* trans. John Oman (New York: Harper & Row, 1958), p. 48.

20G. W. F. Hegel, *Philosophy of Nature,* ed. and trans. M. F. Petry (London: Allen & Unwin, 1970), 1:204.

21Beecher, cited in *The Search for God,* ed. White, p. 56.

22Robert Southey, "Written on Sunday Morning," in *The Poetical Works of Robert Southey,* 10 vols. (London: Longman, Brown, Green, Longmans & Roberts, 1853-54), 2:153.

23Søren Kierkegaard, *Concluding Unscientific Postscript,* ed. and trans. David F. Swenson and Walter Lowrie (Princeton, N.J.: Princeton University Press, 1944), pp. 220-21.

24John Macquarrie, *In Search of Humanity* (New York: Crossroad, 1983), p. 23.

25The traditional proofs for the existence of God continue to find favor in the circles of conservative evangelicalism. See Norman L. Geisler, *Knowing the Truth about Creation* (Ann Arbor, Mich.: Servant, 1989), pp. 83-110.

26Karl Barth, *The Word of God and the Word of Man,* trans. Douglas Horton (Gloucester, Mass.: Peter Smith, 1978), p. 197.

27Karl Barth, *The Epistle to the Romans,* trans. Edwyn C. Hoskyns, 2d ed. (New York: Oxford University Press, 1968), p. 225.

28*Karl Barth/Rudolf Bultmann Letters 1922-1966,* ed. Bernd Jaspert, trans. Geoffrey W. Bromiley (Grand Rapids, Mich.: Eerdmans, 1981), p. 65.

29See Robert P. Ericksen, *Theologians Under Hitler: Gerhard Kittel, Paul Althaus and Emanuel Hirsch* (New Haven, Conn.: Yale University Press, 1985); and Klaus Scholder, *The Churches and the Third Reich,* trans. John Bowden, 2 vols.

(Philadelphia: Fortress, 1988). Note that Karl Adam soon broke with the Nazis and became the target of Nazi students. Otto Weber and Friedrich Gogarten also moved away from their earlier positions.

[30]Scholder, *The Churches and the Third Reich,* 1:335.

[31]See Arthur C. Cochrane, *The Church's Confession Under Hitler,* 2d ed. (Pittsburgh, Pa.: Pickwick Press, 1976).

[32]Rolf Ahlers, *The Barmen Theological Declaration of 1934* (Lewiston, N.Y.: Edwin Mellen Press, 1986), p. 40.

[33]See Paul Tillich, *The Socialist Decision,* trans. Franklin Sherman (New York: Harper & Row, 1977).

[34]Paul Tillich, *On the Boundary* (New York: Charles Scribner's Sons, 1966), p. 41.

[35]Ibid., p. 64.

[36]Emil Brunner, "Nature and Grace," in *Natural Theology,* ed. John Baillie, trans. Peter Fraenkel (London: Geoffrey Bles, 1946), pp. 59-60. This book includes Karl Barth's "Nein."

[37]Ibid., p. 31.

[38]Thomas F. Torrance, *Transformation and Convergence in the Frame of Knowledge* (Grand Rapids, Mich.: Eerdmans, 1984), p. 291. Note that this is Torrance's interpretation of Barth.

[39]See Karl Barth, *The Christian Life,* trans. Geoffrey W. Bromiley (Grand Rapids, Mich.: Eerdmans, 1981), pp. 115-53; *Church Dogmatics,* 4(3a):139-65.

[40]*Karl Barth's Table Talk,* ed. John D. Godsey (Edinburgh: Oliver & Boyd, 1963), p. 75.

[41]"The Vatican Council 1869-1870," chap. 2, in *The Sources of Catholic Dogma,* ed. Henry Denzinger, trans. Roy J. Deferrari (St. Louis: B. Herder Book Co., 1957), pp. 443-44.

[42]Gregory Baum, foreword to Andrew M. Greeley, *The New Agenda* (New York: Doubleday, 1973), p. 16.

[43]See Hans Küng, *Does God Exist?* trans. Edward Quinn (New York: Doubleday, 1980), pp. 438-41, 442-77, 569-78.

[44]Timothy E. O'Connell, "Vatican II: Setting, Themes, Future Agenda," in *Vatican II and Its Documents,* ed. T. O'Connell (Wilmington, Del.: Michael Glazier, 1986), p. 244.

[45]Ibid., p. 247.

[46]J. Patout Burns, "Declaration on the Relation of the Church to Non-Christian Religions," in O'Connell, *Vatican II,* p. 118.

[47]Karl Rahner, *Foundations of Christian Faith,* trans. William V. Dych (New York: Seabury Press, 1978), p. 181.

[48]See Karl Barth, *Ad Limina Apostolorum: An Appraisal of Vatican II,* trans. Keith R. Crim (Richmond, Va.: John Knox Press, 1968).

[49]John E. Linnan, "Declaration on Religious Liberty," in O'Connell, *Vatican II,*

p. 177.

[50]Romano Guardini, *The End of the Modern World,* trans. Joseph Theman and Herbert Burke (New York: Sheed & Ward, 1956), p. 123. Guardini also freely confessed his indebtedness to both Augustine and Bonaventure.

[51]Romano Guardini, *The Last Things,* trans. Charlotte E. Forsyth and Grace B. Branham (Notre Dame, Ind.: University of Notre Dame Press, 1954), p. 58.

[52]Hans Urs von Balthasar, *The Theology of Karl Barth,* trans. John Drury (New York: Holt, Rinehart & Winston, 1971), p. 228.

[53]Ibid., p. 229.

[54]Ibid., p. 249.

[55]A good case can be made that the many allusions in the Psalms to the working of God in nature and history are always coordinated with and subordinated to the revelation of God to Israel in the form of the Torah. The paradigmatic nature psalm concludes with this significant observation: "He reveals his word to Jacob, his statutes and rulings to Israel: he never does this for other nations, he never reveals his rulings to them" (Ps 147:19-20 JB).

[56]Peter Craigie makes these perceptive remarks on Ps 19: "In the second part of the hymn . . . the poet draws out the paradox of 'inaudible noise.' On the one hand, there is no speech, no noise, from a literal or acoustic perspective (v. 3); on the other hand, there is a voice that penetrates to the furthest corners of the earth. The poet conveys something of the subtlety of nature's praise of God: it is there, yet its perception is contingent upon the observer. To the sensitive, the heavenly praise of God's glory may be an overwhelming experience, whereas to the insensitive, sky is simply sky and stars are only stars; they point to nothing beyond. In this hymn of praise, it is not the primary purpose of the psalmist to draw upon nature as a vehicle of revelation, or as a source of the knowledge of God apart from the revelation in law (or *Torah,* v. 7); indeed, there is more than a suggestion that the reflection of God's praise in the universe is perceptible only to those already sensitive to God's revelation and purpose." Peter C. Craigie, *Psalms 1-50,* Word Biblical Commentary 19 (Waco, Tex.: Word Books, 1983), p. 181.

[57]In Rom 2:5-16 Paul says that the righteous judgment of God will be revealed on the day of wrath, i.e., when Jesus Christ will be revealed to the whole creation. Cf. Rom 9:22-24; 1 Cor 1:7-8; 5:5; 2 Cor 1:14; 1 Thess 1:9-10; 2 Tim 1:18; 4:8; Rev 6:16-17.

[58]For Ellul's sagacious interpretation of this passage see his *To Will and to Do,* trans. C. Edward Hopkin (Philadelphia: Pilgrim Press, 1969), pp. 49-51.

[59]It is interesting that Bultmann inadvertently supports the KJV reading "comprehend" instead of "overcome" or "attack" in this passage. "Grasp here does not mean a simple 'understanding' . . . but the comprehension of faith." Rudolf Bultmann, *The Gospel of John,* trans. G. R. Beasley-Murray, R. W. N. Hoare and

J. K. Riches (Philadelphia: Westminster Press, 1971), p. 48.

[60]Hendrik Kraemer, *Religion and the Christian Faith* (London: Lutterworth Press, 1956), p. 355.

[61]See G. C. Berkouwer, *General Revelation* (Grand Rapids, Mich.: Eerdmans, 1955), pp. 137-54.

[62]G. C. Berkouwer, *The Conflict with Rome,* trans. David H. Freeman (Philadelphia: Presbyterian & Reformed, 1958), pp. 76-112.

[63]Bruce A. Demarest, *General Revelation* (Grand Rapids, Mich.: Zondervan, 1982), pp. 250-51.

[64]In *War: Four Christian Views,* ed. Robert G. Clouse (Downers Grove, Ill.: Inter-Varsity Press, 1981), p. 99.

[65]Millard J. Erickson, *Christian Theology* (Grand Rapids, Mich.: Baker Book House, 1983), 1:170-71.

[66]Ibid., pp. 171-73. For Erickson this appears to be only a theoretical possibility; if it happens at all it is very rare. J. N. D. Anderson presents a similar position in his *Christianity and Comparative Religion* (Downers Grove, Ill.: InterVarsity Press, 1977), pp. 100-107. Anderson is more forthright than Erickson in suggesting that non-Christians may indeed be saved if they remain true to the light that is within them. Other evangelicals who celebrate this "wider hope" include John Sanders in his *No Other Name* (Grand Rapids, Mich.: Eerdmans, 1992); and Clark Pinnock in his *A Wideness in God's Mercy* (Grand Rapids, Mich.: Zondervan, 1992).

[67]Norman L. Geisler, *Options in Contemporary Christian Ethics* (Grand Rapids, Mich.: Baker Book House, 1981), p. 33.

[68]Hendrikus Berkhof, *Christian Faith,* trans. Sierd Woudstra (Grand Rapids, Mich.: Eerdmans, 1979), pp. 74-77.

[69]P. T. Forsyth, "Revelation Old and New," in *Revelation Old and New: Sermons and Addresses,* ed. John Huxtable (London: Independent Press, 1962), p. 15.

[70]Jn 12:41 states that Isaiah saw the glory of Christ and spoke of him (cf. Is 6), but Isaiah himself did not know that the God of glory who confronted him was the Messiah of Israel who would later appear in the person of Jesus.

[71]Donald A. Hagner, *The Jewish Reclamation of Jesus* (Grand Rapids, Mich.: Zondervan, 1984), p. 179.

[72]Ibid., p. 192.

[73]The idea of law as a death-bringing agent and belief in the human being as an incorrigible sinner are not to be found in Rabbinic Judaism. The grace of God is affirmed but generally in congruity with human merit. See Hagner, *Jewish Reclamation,* pp. 191-207.

[74]Cited by Emil Brunner in *Justice and the Social Order,* trans. Mary Hottinger (New York: Harper, 1945), p. 5.

[75]See Jacques Ellul, *The Theological Foundation of Law,* trans. Marguerite Wieser

(London: SCM Press, 1960).

[76]Ibid., p. 28. Ellul's thesis can hardly be reconciled at this point with William Graham Sumner's *Folkways* (Boston: Ginn, 1906).

[77]Ibid., p. 120.

[78]Berkouwer, *General Revelation*, p. 205.

[79]Ibid.

[80]Ismael Garcia, *Justice in Latin American Theology of Liberation* (Atlanta: John Knox Press, 1987), p. 158.

[81]See esp. Brunner, *Justice and the Social Order*, pp. 98-109. Brunner takes pains to differentiate the Christian concept of relative justice from the Stoic concept of relative natural law (p. 273).

[82]Otto Weber, *Foundations of Dogmatics*, 1:210-12.

[83]Note that in the New Testament God causes his rain to fall on the just and unjust and his sun to shine on both good and evil (Mt 5:45; cf. Job 25:3; Jas 1:17).

[84]Jonathan Edwards, *A Treatise on Religious Affections* (Grand Rapids, Mich.: Baker Book House, 1982), p. 143.

[85]On the pagan character of the new natural theology see Nikos Kazantzakis, *The Saviors of God*, trans. Kimon Friar (New York: Simon & Schuster, 1960); Naomi Goldenberg, *Changing of the Gods* (Boston: Beacon, 1979); Monica Sjöö and Barbara Mor, *The Great Cosmic Mother: Rediscovering the Religion of the Earth* (San Francisco: Harper & Row, 1987); and Carol P. Christ, *Laughter of Aphrodite: Reflections on a Journey to the Goddess* (San Francisco: Harper & Row, 1987).

[86]Elizabeth Achtemeier, "Female Language for God: Should the Church Adopt it?" in *The Hermeneutical Quest*, ed. Donald G. Miller (Pittsburgh, Pa.: Pickwick Publications, 1986), p. 105.

[87]George Hunsinger, "Barth, Barmen and the Confessing Church Today," *Katallagete* 9, no. 2 (Summer 1985):23.

**Appendix E: Thomas F. Torrance**

[1]Thomas F. Torrance, *Reality and Evangelical Theology* (Philadelphia: Westminster Press, 1982), pp. 33-39.

[2]Thomas F. Torrance, *God and Rationality* (New York: Oxford University Press, 1971), p. 22.

[3]Torrance, *Reality and Evangelical Theology*, pp. 103-4, 107.

[4]Torrance tries to affirm God's initiative, but he sees this as the divine leading of the creature through the sign to the reality signified by it. In my understanding of the biblical view, divine reality enters into the sign from the beyond, adopting it as its earthly vehicle. For Torrance, it seems, the sign is a pointer to revelation rather than a bearer or carrier of revelation.

[5]Torrance, *Reality and Evangelical Theology*, pp. 31-34; *Transformation and*

*Convergence in the Frame of Knowledge* (Grand Rapids, Mich.: Eerdmans, 1984), pp. 287-301.

[6]Robert J. Palma, "Thomas F. Torrance's Reformed Theology," *Reformed Review* 38, no. 1 (Autumn 1984):22.

[7]Ibid.

[8]It has been suggested that Torrance prefers "natural theology" to a "theology of creation" because the latter makes no place for the Incarnation, and thus magnifies the distance between God and humanity. We would all agree that a theology of creation if left on its own is insufficient. From a conversation with Kurt Richardson of Southeastern Baptist Seminary, at the American Academy of Religion, Chicago, Nov. 22, 1988. Richardson was a student of Torrance.

[9]Karl Barth, "Fate and Idea in Theology," in *The Way of Theology in Karl Barth,* ed. H. Martin Rumscheidt (Allison Park, Pa.: Pickwick Publications, 1986), pp. 25-61.

Torrance does not totally exclude idealistic elements from his theology, since he sees the bipolarity of form and being perfectly united in Christ. Yet idealism as a philosophical system he regards as an adversary of Christian faith, whereas realistic philosophy he sees as a potential ally. He calls his position a "critical realism" that holds to "the inseparability of empirical and theoretical components in knowledge, i.e. with the indissoluble unity of being and form." *Space, Time and Resurrection* (Grand Rapids, Mich.: Eerdmans, 1976), p. 6.

Torrance demonstrates a remarkable capacity to appreciate what is valid in Schleiermacher's idealism while still calling it into question for failing to maintain God's objectivity. Torrance, "Hermeneutics According to F. D. E. Schleiermacher," *Scottish Journal of Theology* 21, no. 3 (Sept. 1968):257-67, esp. 263-64.

[10]Barth, "Fate and Idea in Theology," p. 47.

[11]James D. Smart, *The Divided Mind of Modern Theology* (Philadelphia: Westminster Press, 1967), p. 203.

[12]Torrance, *Transformation and Convergence,* pp. 285-87.

[13]See my earlier discussion of this point, p. 309, nn. 55-56.

[14]Smart, *The Divided Mind of Modern Theology,* p. 204.

[15]We should engage in dialog with the natural sciences as well as the philosophy of science and appreciate what they have to offer wherever possible, but this is quite different from making the truth of faith conform to a particular Weltanschauung.

[16]Note that Torrance opposes the typology of *Historie* and *Geschichte* as signifying the re-entrance of dualistic metaphysics into theological speculation. *Reality and Evangelical Theology,* pp. 79ff.

[17]Ibid., p. 39.

[18]We need to give more attention to Karl Heim's imposing attempt to relate

Christian faith and natural science. Heim's position stands solidly in the tradition of evangelical supernaturalism. See Karl Heim, *The Transformation of the Scientific World View*, trans. W. A. Whitehouse (London: SCM Press, 1953); *Christian Faith and Natural Science*, trans. N. Horton Smith (New York: Harper & Brothers, 1953); and *The World: Its Creation and Consummation*, trans. Robert Smith (Philadelphia: Muhlenberg Press, 1962).

## Chapter 7: Rethinking Theological Authority

[1]Tillich uses the word *theonomy* to describe the Christian position, as opposed to "autonomy" and "heteronomy." See his *Systematic Theology*, 3 vols. (Chicago: University of Chicago Press, 1951), 1:83-86. But he means by "theonomy" centering authority in the ground and depth of selfhood rather than in the Wholly Other, who confronts the human self from without before making his abode within. My position might better be designated as "Christonomy," since the emphasis is on the incarnate and living Christ who comes to humanity in its lostness as the truth that liberates as well as commands.

[2]In contradistinction to various existentialist theologians, I agree with Berkouwer that the subjective and objective poles of salvation are not equal, for the objective has truth and reality apart from the subjective appropriation of this truth. See G. C. Berkouwer, *The Triumph of Grace in the Theology of Karl Barth*, trans. Harry R. Boer (Grand Rapids, Mich.: Eerdmans, 1956), pp. 262-75.

[3]It seems that most narrative theologians see the biblical story as a linguistic community's self-identification. The story then becomes another "language game." Gabriel Fackre takes strong exception to this kind of reductionism. Personal letter, Jan. 5, 1989.

[4]We might say that God speaks to the soul in conjunction with external events. The events themselves are not self-interpreting.

[5]From *D. Martin Luthers Werke* (Weimarer Ausgabe, 1883ff.), 50:629-30. Cited in Jaroslav Pelikan, *The Christian Tradition: A History of the Development of Doctrine*, 5 vols. (Chicago: University of Chicago Press, 1984), 4:182.

[6]Karl Barth, *Theology and Church*, trans. Louise Pettibone Smith (New York: Harper & Row, 1962), p. 283.

[7]Huldreich Zwingli, *Selected Works of Huldreich Zwingli*, ed. Samuel Macauley Jackson (Philadelphia: University of Pennsylvania Press, 1901), pp. 85-86.

[8]See Paul Tillich, "What Is Wrong with the 'Dialectic' Theology?" *Journal of Religion* 15, no. 2 (Apr. 1935):127-45.

[9]In his early years Barth spoke of Jesus Christ as the one and only Word of God, but vol. 1 of his *Church Dogmatics* reflects a neo-Calvinism which unites the transcendent Word with the outward sign of Scripture and proclamation. Later he returned to his earlier stance that Jesus Christ is the one Word of God, and the Bible and the church constitute respectively the primary and secondary

witnesses to this Word. Yet even in this later stage Barth was insistent that the witness to revelation participates in the revelation itself and that we therefore have in the Bible and the church an echo and mirror of this one Word of God.

[10]The term *perichoresis* has been used in classical theology with regard to the interpenetration of the members of the Trinity. Barth suggests that the unity of the three forms of the one Word of God corresponds to the unity of the persons of the Trinity. See Karl Barth, *Church Dogmatics,* ed. G. W. Bromiley and T. F. Torrance, 2d ed. (Edinburgh: T. & T. Clark, 1975), 1(1):120-24.

[11]The Quaker theologian Robert Barclay posited an uncreated light within all humanity, though this light is not inherent in human nature. "Christ is in all men as a seed, a holy, pure seed and light from which he cannot be separated." In *Barclay's Apology,* ed. Dean Freiday (Elberton, N.J.: n.p., 1967), p. 90. In the Reformation view Christ is related to all people, but he dwells only in those who have faith.

[12]We might here speak of a mediated immediacy in that God's Word does truly come to us but through external signs and means.

[13]Concurring with Luther and Calvin in their conflict with the church of Rome, I maintain that the sacraments gain their power not from the performance of the rite as such *(ex opere operato)* but from the proclamation of the word, which illumines the meaning of the rite. On Luther's decisive break with sacramentalism see Lennart Pinomaa, *Faith Victorious,* trans. Walter J. Kukkonen (Philadelphia: Fortress, 1963), pp. 134-41.

[14]The apostolic writer may also have been thinking of the sacrament of the Eucharist when he speaks of the "blood." See the discussion by Amos Wilder and Paul Hoon in *The Interpreter's Bible,* 12 vols. (Nashville: Abingdon, 1957), 12:292-96.

[15]See Michael R. Watts, *The Dissenters* (Oxford: Clarendon Press, 1978), 1:191.

[16]*Barclay's Apology,* pp. 16, 42.

[17]See Charles S. Braden, *These Also Believe* (New York: Macmillan, 1949), pp. 403-20.

[18]Friedrich Schleiermacher, *On Religion,* trans. Terrence N. Tice (Richmond: John Knox Press, 1969), p. 245.

[19]Dietrich Ritschl, *The Logic of Theology,* trans. John Bowden (Philadelphia: Fortress, 1987), p. 69.

[20]Carl R. Rogers, *On Becoming a Person* (Boston: Houghton Mifflin, 1961), p. 23.

[21]Nicolas Berdyaev, *Truth and Revelation,* trans. R. M. French (New York: Collier Books, 1962), p. 68.

[22]Jerry L. Walls, *The Problem of Pluralism* (Wilmore, Ky.: Good News Books, 1986), pp. 81-82.

[23]Walls returns to a more classical and Wesleyan stance when he goes on to confess that we believe because God has revealed himself through the events

recorded in Scripture. Ibid., p. 82.

²⁴Quoted by L. Bruce Van Voorst, "Follow-up on the Küng-Rahner Feud," *Christian Century* 88, no. 34 (Aug. 25, 1971):999.

²⁵Roland H. Bainton, *Here I Stand* (New York: Abingdon-Cokesbury, 1950), p. 261.

²⁶Emmy Arnold, ed., *Inner Words* (Rifton, N.Y.: Plough Publishing House, 1975), p. 46.

²⁷Cited in Schubert M. Ogden, *On Theology* (San Francisco: Harper & Row, 1986), p. 54.

²⁸This is especially clear in Barth's *Church Dogmatics,* ed. G. W. Bromiley and T. F. Torrance, vol. 4, pt. 4 (Edinburgh: T. & T. Clark, 1969).

²⁹Quoted by Rudolf Bultmann, *Glauben und Verstehen,* 2 vols. (Tübingen, Germany: J. C. B. Mohr, 1954). Translated by Ogden, *On Theology,* p. 54.

³⁰The new life in Christ cannot be directly discerned by either ourselves or others, but it is indirectly apprehended by people who see the fruits of faith in our lives.

³¹Calvin was inclined to say that the gospel is ordinarily given through the Bible and church proclamation, whereas Luther tended to treat these as *necessary* means of grace.

³²See Robert Clyde Johnson, *Authority in Protestant Theology* (Philadelphia: Westminster Press, 1959), p. 191.

³³In his debate with John Eck in 1519, Luther declared that both councils and the church may err. Neither the church nor the pope can establish articles of faith, for these must come from Scripture. See James Atkinson, *Martin Luther and the Birth of Protestantism* (Atlanta: John Knox Press, 1981), p. 46.

³⁴Paul Tillich, *Systematic Theology,* 3 vols. (Chicago: University of Chicago Press, 1951), 1:45.

³⁵Ibid., p. 46.

³⁶I acknowledge that the experiential and cultural matrix in which we do theology will always color our interpretation of the truth of revelation, but it will also necessarily distort and blur this truth. The hermeneutical task is to be alert to the dangers of experiential and cultural distortion, and we are, therefore, challenged to rise above our place in history *(Sitz im Leben).*

³⁷This does not mean that Christ succumbed to the bias of history but that he was really tempted by it. As a real man in history he was capable of erring, but as fully imbued with the Spirit of God he most assuredly did not err in either life or teaching.

³⁸On how the hypostatic union between Christ and Jesus differs from other kinds of union see Heinrich Heppe, ed., *Reformed Dogmatics,* rev. Ernst Bizer, trans. G. T. Thomson (London: Allen & Unwin, 1950), pp. 431-32.

³⁹Hans Küng, *The Church,* trans. Ray Ockenden and Rosaleen Ockenden (New

York: Sheed & Ward, 1967), p. 174.

[40]Jean-Jacques Rousseau, *Émile,* trans. Barbara Foxley (New York: E. P. Dutton, 1957), 1:254.

[41]Fichte, *The Vocation of Man,* in *The Popular Works of Johann Gottlieb Fichte,* trans. William Smith (London: Trübner, 1889), 1:412. Cf. "The voice of conscience, which imposes on each his particular duty, is the light-beam on which we come forth from the bosom of the Infinite, and assume our place as particular individual beings; it fixes the limits of our personality; it is thus the true original element of our nature. the foundation and material of all our life." Ibid., p. 458.

[42]Cf. Forsyth: "A real authority . . . is indeed *within* experience, but it is not the authority *of* experience, it is an authority *for* experience, it is an authority experienced." P. T. Forsyth, *The Principle of Authority,* 2d ed. (London: Independent Press, 1952), p. 75.

[43]*Luther's Works,* ed. Jaroslav Pelikan (St. Louis: Concordia, 1963), 26:387.

[44]Forsyth, *Principle of Authority,* p. 55.

[45]Ibid., p. 328.

[46]*Thy Kingdom Come: A Blumhardt Reader,* ed. Vernard Eller (Grand Rapids, Mich.: Eerdmans, 1980), pp. 63-64.

[47]Cf. the NEB version of Ps 51:6: "Though thou hast hidden the truth in darkness, through this mystery thou dost teach me wisdom." Also cf. Job 12:22 (NASB): "He reveals mysteries from the darkness, and brings the deep darkness into light."

[48]Karl Jaspers, *Philosophical Faith and Revelation,* trans. E. B. Ashton (New York: Harper & Row, 1967), p. 336.

[49]Gregory Baum, "The Bible as Norm," *The Ecumenist* 9, no. 5 (July-Aug. 1971):77.

[50]John of the Cross, *Ascent of Mount Carmel,* in *The Complete Works of Saint John of the Cross,* ed. and trans. E. Allison Peers, rev. ed. (London: Burns, Oates & Washbourne, 1953), p. 11.

[51]Cf. Achtemeier: "The authority of Scripture is therefore demonstrated, not in the literary form in which it has been cast, as supporters of inerrancy would have it, but rather in its power to create and shape reality." Paul J. Achtemeier, *The Inspiration of Scripture* (Philadelphia: Westminster Press, 1980), p. 159. Achtemeier here refuses to call Scripture the Word of God, preferring to describe it as a witness to the Word of God. In contradistinction to my position, he rejects the analogy associating the two sides of Scripture with the two natures of Christ.

### Appendix F: The Wesleyan Quadrilateral

[1]Donald A. D. Thorsen, *The Wesleyan Quadrilateral* (Grand Rapids, Mich.: Zon-

dervan, 1990).

2A blurb on the back cover of Thorsen's book.

3Thorsen, *The Wesleyan Quadrilateral,* p. 191.

4Ibid., pp. 210-11.

5Ibid., p. 210.

6Ibid., pp. 189-90.

7Ibid., p. 176.

8Charles Augustus Briggs, *Inaugural Address and Defense 1891/1893* (New York: Arno Press, 1972), pp. 24-29.

9Ibid., p. 26.

10Ibid., p. 66.

### Chapter 8: The Communication of the Gospel

1Adolf von Harnack, *History of Dogma,* trans. Neil Buchanan, 7 vols. (New York: Russell and Russell, 1958), 2:225.

2Tertullian, "Prescriptions against Heretics," in *The Ante-Nicene Fathers,* ed. Alexander Roberts and James Donaldson (Grand Rapids, Mich.: Eerdmans, 1950), 3:246.

3Irenaeus, "Against Heresies," in *The Ante-Nicene Fathers,* ed. Roberts and Donaldson, 1:418.

4Ibid.

5Irenaeus, *Proof of the Apostolic Preaching,* ed. and trans. Joseph P. Smith (London: Longmans, Green, 1952), p. 49.

6Wolfhart Pannenberg, *Basic Questions in Theology,* trans. George H. Kehm, 2 vols. (Philadelphia: Westminster Press, 1983), 2:153-57. Von Balthasar gives this apt description of the theological method of Irenaeus: "He refutes by unmasking and, still more profoundly, by setting forth the truth. He does not seek to persuade by the use of syllogism; he lets the truth like the sun do its lighting and its warming." Hans Urs von Balthasar, *The von Balthasar Reader,* ed. Medard Kehl and Werner Löser, trans. Robert J. Daly and Fred Lawrence (New York: Crossroad, 1982), p. 384.

7See Eugène Portalié, *A Guide to the Thought of St. Augustine,* trans. Ralph J. Bastian (Chicago: Henry Regnery, 1960) p. 106. In Augustine, *Soliloquia* 1.6.12. Augustine was convinced, however, that reason cannot achieve its goal apart from the purification of the heart, which is possible only through grace.

8See *On the Truth of the Catholic Faith: Summa Contra Gentiles,* trans. and ed. Anton C. Pegis (New York: Hanover House, 1955), 1.9, pp. 77-78.

9Ibid., p. 77.

10Thomas Aquinas, *Commentary on Saint Paul's Epistle to the Ephesians,* trans. Matthew L. Lamb (Albany, N.Y.: Magi Books, 1966), pp. 126-29, 141-48, 242-43.

[11]This was not a complete break, however, for the Reformers retained such Hellenistic ideas as the impassibility of God and the immortality of the soul, which they tried to hold together with the biblical idea of the resurrection of the body.

[12]Quoted in Paul Althaus, *The Theology of Martin Luther,* trans. Robert C. Schultz (Philadelphia: Fortress, 1966) p. 57.

[13]Martin Luther, *Commentary on the Epistle to the Romans,* trans. J. Theodore Mueller (Grand Rapids, Mich.: Zondervan, 1954), p. 54.

[14]Barth quotes from Luther's *Fastenpostille:* "Thus conclude we that of God's Word can be no master or judge or any protector save God Himself. 'Tis His Word, and as He letteth it go forth without man's service and counsel, so will He hold and maintain it Himself for man's help and strength." *The Doctrine of the Word of God,* trans. G. T. Thomson (Edinburgh: T. & T. Clark, 1949), p. 33 n.

[15]John Calvin, *Institutes of the Christian Religion,* trans. John Allen, 7th American ed. (Philadelphia: Presbyterian Board of Christian Education, 1936), 1.7.5, p. 90.

[16]Ibid.

[17]Ibid., p. 89.

[18]Ibid.

[19]See Jaroslav Pelikan, *From Luther to Kierkegaard* (St. Louis: Concordia, 1950), pp. 24-48.

[20]Ibid., pp. 65-69.

[21]See Jack B. Rogers and Donald K. McKim, *The Authority and Interpretation of the Bible* (New York: Harper & Row, 1979), pp. 172-83.

[22]Joseph Butler, *The Analogy of Religion, Natural and Revealed, to the Constitution and Course of Nature* (New York: Robert Carter & Brothers, 1858), p. 224.

[23]See Friedrich Schleiermacher, *On Religion: Speeches to Its Cultured Despisers,* trans. John Oman (New York: Harper & Row, 1958).

[24]Abraham Kuyper, *The Work of the Holy Spirit,* trans. Henri De Vries (Grand Rapids, Mich.: Eerdmans, 1966), pp. 418-19.

[25]Paul Tillich, *The Future of Religions,* ed. Jerald C. Brauer (New York: Harper & Row, 1966), p. 29.

[26]Paul Tillich, *Systematic Theology,* 3 vols. (Chicago: University of Chicago Press, 1951), 1:30-31, 59-60, 64-66.

[27]W. Andrew Hoffecker, *Piety and the Princeton Theologians* (Phillipsburg, N.J.: Presbyterian & Reformed, 1981), p. 135.

[28]*Selected Shorter Writings of Benjamin B. Warfield,* ed. John E. Meeter, 2 vols. (Nutley, N.J.: Presbyterian & Reformed, 1973), 2:99-100.

[29]See Edward John Carnell, *The Kingdom of Love and the Pride of Life* (Grand Rapids, Mich.: Eerdmans, 1960), pp. 5-10. See also John A. Sims, *Edward John*

*Carnell: Defender of the Faith* (Washington, D.C.: University Press of America, 1979), p. 17.

[30]Cited by Gordon R. Lewis, "How to Share Christ with the Now Generation," *Eternity* 25, no. 9 (Sept. 1974):29, 36.

[31]Thomas V. Morris, *Francis Schaeffer's Apologetics: A Critique* (Grand Rapids, Mich.: Baker Book House, 1987), p. 116.

[32]Francis A. Schaeffer, *He Is There and He Is Not Silent* (Wheaton, Ill.: Tyndale House, 1972), p. 83.

[33]See Morris, *Francis Schaeffer's Apologetics,* pp. 109-21.

[34]Wolfhart Pannenberg, *The Apostles' Creed in the Light of Today's Questions,* trans. Margaret Kohl (Philadelphia: Westminster Press, 1972), p. 33.

[35]Karl Barth, *Ethics,* ed. Dietrich Braun, trans. G. W. Bromiley (New York: Seabury Press, 1981), p. 21.

[36]G. C. Berkouwer, *The Church,* trans. James E. Davison (Grand Rapids, Mich.: Eerdmans, 1976), p. 248.

[37]G. C. Berkouwer, *Holy Scripture,* trans. and ed. Jack B. Rogers (Grand Rapids, Mich.: Eerdmans, 1975), p. 279.

[38]Barth, *Church Dogmatics,* 4(3a):109.

[39]Tillich, *Systematic Theology,* 1:7. Tillich shows that he misunderstands Barth when he associates him with this kind of kerygmatic theology.

[40]Charles Grandison Finney, *Lectures on Revivals of Religion,* ed. William G. McLoughlin, Jr. (Cambridge, Mass.: Belknap Press/Harvard University Press, 1960), p. 53.

[41]John Calvin, *Commentary on the Book of the Prophet Jeremiah,* trans. John Owen (Edinburgh: Calvin Translation Society, 1854), 4:102.

[42]Quoted in Alexandre Ganoczy, *The Young Calvin,* trans. David Foxgrover and Wade Provo (Philadelphia: Westminster Press, 1987), p. 251.

[43]Cf. Barth: "The word of God is not for sale; and therefore it has no need of shrewd salesmen. The word of God is not seeking patrons; therefore it refuses price cutting and bargaining; therefore it has no need of middlemen. The word of God does not compete with other commodities which are being offered to men on the bargain counter of life. It does not care to be sold at any price. It only desires to be its own genuine self, without being compelled to suffer alterations and modifications. It would shine in its own glory to be snapped up of those who would not buy it, but who will accept it as grace, as a gift of grace, just as it is." Karl Barth and Eduard Thurneysen, *Come Holy Spirit,* trans. George W. Richards, Elmer G. Homrighausen and Karl J. Ernst (Grand Rapids, Mich.: Eerdmans, 1978), p. 219.

[44]Barth, *Church Dogmatics,* trans. Thomson, 1(1):222.

[45]Nels F. S. Ferré, *Christianity and Society* (New York: Harper & Brothers, 1950), p. 155.

[46]Blaise Pascal, *Pensées,* ed. and trans. A. J. Krailsheimer (Baltimore: Penguin Books, 1966), p. 138.

[47]*Reformation Writings of Martin Luther,* trans. and ed. Bertram Lee Woolf (London: Lutterworth Press, 1952), 1:368.

[48]Quoted in Domenico Grasso, *Proclaiming God's Message* (Notre Dame, Ind.: University of Notre Dame Press, 1965), p. 33.

[49]Jacques Ellul, *The Presence of the Kingdom,* trans. Olive Wyon (New York: Seabury Press, 1967), p. 141.

[50]Helmut Thielicke, *The Trouble with the Church,* trans. and ed. John W. Doberstein (New York: Harper & Row, 1965), p. 50.

[51]Pascal, *Pensées,* p. 290.

[52]Reinhold Niebuhr, *Faith and History* (New York: Charles Scribner's Sons, 1949), p. 165. See also p. 136.

[53]Jacques Ellul, *Hope in Time of Abandonment,* trans. C. Edward Hopkin (New York: Seabury Press, 1973), p. 204.

[54]For Kierkegaard faith and despair are polar opposites, yet they are dynamically related. Despair certainly sets the stage for faith, but it cannot induce faith. Faith does not so much rise out of despair as break through despair. The despairing person may indeed be moving toward faith as awareness of the reality of despair intensifies. In the depth of despair life appears futile and meaningless. Yet God can and does come to us in our despair and may use our despair to turn us in a new direction.

Eristical theologians are not wholly wrong in appealing to Kierkegaard, but they need to recognize his emphasis on grace as the source of all faith and consolation in God. Kierkegaard delineated the various types of despair in his *Sickness unto Death,* ed. and trans. Walter Lowrie (New York: Doubleday, 1954), but his basic contrast was between despair as an avoidance of facing one's limitations and the consciousness of sin, in which despair is surmounted. For helpful discussions of despair in Kierkegaard's thought, see Martin J. Heinecken, *The Moment Before God* (Philadelphia: Muhlenberg Press, 1956), pp. 183-224; and Hermann Diem, *Kierkegaard: An Introduction,* trans. David Green (Richmond, Va.: John Knox Press, 1966). See my discussion on pp. 61-66.

[55]John Calvin, *The Epistles of Paul the Apostle to the Romans and to the Thessalonians,* ed. David W. Torrance and Thomas F. Torrance, trans. Ross Mackenzie (Grand Rapids, Mich.: Eerdmans, 1960), p. 135 (on Rom 6:21).

[56]Thomas J. J. Altizer, *The Gospel of Christian Atheism* (Philadelphia: Westminster Press, 1966), p. 105.

[57]Thomas J. J. Altizer, "Theology's Response to the Challenge of Secularism," *Centennial Review* 11, no. 4 (Fall 1967):481.

[58]See Karl Rahner, *Hearers of the Word,* trans. Michael Richards (New York: Herder & Herder, 1969), pp. 101, 111-20; Karl Rahner, *Theological Investiga-*

*tions* (Baltimore: Helicon Press, 1969), 6:71-81; and Brian L. Horne, "Today's Word for Today: Karl Rahner," *Expository Times* 92, no. 11 (Aug. 1981):324-29. Rahner could be interpreted as belonging to the theology of synthesis as well as that of identity, since he seeks to bring the partial insights of the culture into coordination with the fuller insights of Christian revelation. In a way that sets him off from traditional Thomism he maintains that nature not only leads to grace but is permeated and upheld by grace. David Tracy is a more consistent proponent of a theology of identity, since he sees the answer as well as the question of faith already present in culture. See his *Blessed Rage for Order* (New York: Seabury Press, 1975), pp. 43-63.

59I consider this matter further on p. 261.

60Ferré, *Christianity and Society*, p. 157.

61John Calvin, *Commentaries on the Twelve Minor Prophets*, trans. John Owen (Edinburgh: Calvin Translation Society, 1846), 2:60 (on Joel 2:13).

62Quoted in Richard K. Curtis, *They Called Him Mister Moody* (New York: Doubleday, 1962), p. 135.

63See Garth Lean, *On the Tail of a Comet: The Life of Frank Buchman* (Colorado Springs, Colo.: Helmers & Howard, 1988).

64Dietrich Bonhoeffer, *No Rusty Swords,* ed. Edwin H. Robertson, trans. Edwin H. Robertson and John Bowden (New York: Harper & Row, 1965), pp. 161-62.

65Barth, *Church Dogmatics,* trans. Thomson, 1(1):31.

66*Karl Barth's Table Talk,* ed. John D. Godsey (Edinburgh: Oliver & Boyd, 1963), p. 62.

67Thomas was insistent that unbelievers cannot know the God of revelation. "Belief in God as descriptive of the act of faith is not attributable to unbelievers. In their belief God's existence does not have the same meaning as it does in faith. Thus they do not truly believe in God." *Summa Theologica,* trans. T. C. O'Brien (New York: Blackfriars/McGraw-Hill, 1974), II-II, 2.2, ad 3, 31:67-69. On what might be called the "Pascalian" side of Thomas's thought, see Victor Preller, *Divine Science and the Science of God* (Princeton, J.M.: Princeton University Press, 1967).

68*Summa Theologica,* trans. Thomas Gilby (New York: Blackfriars/McGraw-Hill, 1964), I-I, art. 8, 1:31.

69*Summa contra Gentiles,* ed. and trans. Anton C. Pegis (New York: Doubleday, 1955), 1.9, pp. 77-78.

70Dulles detects in Thomas's apologetics a certain ambiguity about what reason really means. "Is Thomas here speaking about what man could know in a hypothetical state of pure nature, or about his capacities in the present state of fallen and redeemed nature?" Avery Dulles, *A History of Apologetics* (Philadelphia: Westminster Press, 1971), p. 93.

71Jürgen Moltmann, *Theology of Hope,* trans. James W. Leitch (New York: Harper

& Row, 1967), pp. 90-91.

[72]Ibid., pp. 230-338. See also Jürgen Moltmann, *Hope and Planning,* trans. Margaret Clarkson (New York: Harper & Row, 1971), pp. 101-29, 155-99.

[73]Alexander Balmain Bruce, *Apologetics: Or, Christianity Defensively Stated* (New York: Charles Scribner's Sons, 1912), p. 37.

[74]Quoted in Peter L. Berger, *A Rumor of Angels* (Garden City, N.Y.: Doubleday, 1969), p. 96. From *De praedestinatione sanctorum* II.5.

[75]Francis A. Schaeffer, *The God Who Is There* (Downers Grove, Ill.: InterVarsity Press, 1968), p. 143.

[76]Augustine, *In Joannis Evangelium tractatus* 29.6, in *An Augustine Synthesis,* ed. Erich Przywara (New York: Harper & Brothers, 1958), p. 58.

[77]See Robert E. Cushman, "Faith and Reason," in *A Companion to the Study of St. Augustine,* ed. Roy W. Bettenhouse (New York: Oxford University Press, 1955), pp. 287-314.

[78]Forsyth was profoundly alert to the all too human tendency to control the processes of conversion by focusing on the malleability of the subject rather than on the invincibility of the object of faith: "Missions are seriously threatened because we have been trying to do more for souls than for Christ, and understanding them better than we do the Gospel. We can do less by winning people for Christ than by carrying home to them a Christ who wins them." P. T. Forsyth, *The Preaching of Jesus and the Gospel of Christ* (Blackwood, South Australia: New Creation Publications, 1987), p. 107.

[79]Douglas Clyde Macintosh, *The Reasonableness of Christianity* (New York: Charles Scribner's Sons, 1926), p. 2.

[80]Dietrich Bonhoeffer, *The Cost of Discipleship,* trans. R. H. Fuller (London: SCM Press, 1959), p. 165.

[81]Ibid., p. 188.

[82]Markus Barth, *Israel and the Church* (Richmond, Va.: John Knox Press, 1969), pp. 110-15.

[83]Ibid., p. 15.

[84]A. W. Tozer, *That Incredible Christian* (Harrisburg, Pa.: Christian Publications, 1964), p. 11.

[85]Karl Barth held that in our preaching we are not to call our hearers to make a decision. "A decision, if it is made, is a matter between the individual and God alone and is not a necessary element in preaching." Karl Barth, *The Preaching of the Gospel,* trans. B. E. Hooke (Philadelphia: Westminster Press, 1963), p. 10.

[86]Karl Barth, *The Word of God and the Word of Man,* trans. Douglas Horton (Gloucester, Mass.: Peter Smith, 1978), pp. 97-135.

[87]Cf. Spurgeon: "Unless God, the Holy Spirit, who 'worketh in us to will and to do,' should operate upon the will and the conscience, regeneration is an ab-

solute impossibility, and, therefore so is salvation. . . . In the salvation of every person there is an actual putting forth of the divine power whereby the dead sinner is quickened, the unwilling sinner is made willing, the desperately hard sinner has his conscience made tender; and he who rejected God and despised Christ is brought to cast himself down at the feet of Jesus." *The Treasury of Charles H. Spurgeon,* ed. Wilbur M. Smith (Westwood, N.J.: Revell, 1955), pp. 187-88.

[88]P. T. Forsyth, *Positive Preaching and the Modern Mind* (London: Independent Press, 1953), p. 43.

[89]Karl Barth, *Evangelical Theology: An Introduction,* trans. Grover Foley (New York: Doubleday Anchor Books, 1964), pp. 90-91.

[90]Jonathan Edwards, "Concerning Efficacious Grace," in *The Works of President Edwards,* 4 vols. (New York: Leavitt & Allen, 1857), 2:580.

[91]See Gustave Bardy, *La Conversion au Christianisme durant les premiers siècles* (Paris: Éditions Montaigne, 1949), p. 278. See also Aimé Puech, *Histoire de la littérature grecque chrétienne depuis les origines jusqu'à la fin du IVe siècle* (Paris: Société d'Édition "Les Belles Lettres," 1928-30), 2:231-32.

In contrast, Kenneth Scott Latourette maintains that the arguments of the apologists appealed to many. *A History of the Expansion of Christianity* (New York: Harper & Brothers, 1937), 1:127. A distinction should be made here between the appeal of an argument, which is within our natural powers, and the conviction of faith, which only the Holy Spirit creates.

[92]It was commonly said of Reinhold Niebuhr that he convinced intellectual agnostics of the validity of the Christian doctrine of sin, but they remained agnostic regarding the doctrine of God. This is not to deny that Niebuhr, Tillich et al. have reached a small number of outsiders, but the question remains whether such conversions were to evangelical Christianity or to a modernized and more often than not distorted version of the faith.

[93]For a fairly convincing appraisal of C. S. Lewis as an apologist whose basic appeal was to the "Christian vision" of reality rather than to rational proofs or empirical evidences, see Robert Holyer, "C. S. Lewis—the Rationalist?" *Christian Scholar's Review* 18, no. 2 (Dec. 1988):148-67. For a quite different assessment of Lewis, claiming that he unwittingly compromised the faith through his apologetic concerns, see John Beversluis, *C. S. Lewis and the Search for Rational Religion* (Grand Rapids, Mich.: Eerdmans, 1985).

[94]John Warwick Montgomery, "Once Upon an A Priori," in *Jerusalem and Athens,* ed. E. R. Geehan (Nutley, N.J.: Presbyterian & Reformed, 1971), p. 391.

[95]Kenneth L. Pike, *With Heart and Mind* (Grand Rapids, Mich.: Eerdmans, 1962), p. 94.

[96]Quoted in Abraham Kuyper, *Work of the Holy Spirit,* p. 391.

[97]My position is not quite the same as that of the skeptic Franz Overbeck, who

influenced the early Karl Barth: "A strong faith relies on itself and holds reason at bay. When a faith becomes feeble and calls on reason for aid, it renders itself superfluous." See Robert B. Luehrs, "Franz Overbeck and the Theologian as AntiChrist," *Katallagete* 4, no. 4 (Summer 1973):19. I acknowledge that the truth of faith confounds reason, for it is too great for reason to take it in. Yet this truth at the same time enlightens reason and enlists reason in its service. Faith relies not on itself but on its object, the living Word of God, which brings reason into conformity with its goal and purpose.

[98]It could be said that faith contradicts the direction of human reasoning but not the structure of human reason. It opposes reason in the service of the sinful will, but it affirms reason in the service of divine revelation.

[99]It should be noted that these are reasons that appeal more to the heart than to the intellect. It is neither logical necessity nor historical probability that leads us to believe in the gospel but instead existential need rekindled by the flame of the Spirit of God as we are confronted by the reality of the risen Christ speaking to us in the word of Scripture and church proclamation.

### Chapter 9: Theology at the Crossroads

[1]See Karl Heim, *God Transcendent,* trans. Edgar Primrose Dickie (London: Nisbet, 1935). Also see p. 313, note 18 (above).

[2]Emil Brunner, *The Mediator,* trans. Olive Wyon (Philadelphia: Westminster Press, 1947).

[3]See Wolfhart Pannenberg, *The Idea of God and Human Freedom,* trans. R. A. Wilson (Philadelphia: Westminster Press, 1973), pp. 108-10. He rejects the idea that the revelation of God is "a supernatural event which breaks into history perpendicularly from above"; rather "it is the theme of history itself, the power that moves it in its deepest dimension." Pannenberg, *Basic Questions in Theology,* trans. George H. Kehm, 2 vols. (Philadelphia: Westminster Press, 1983), 1:xv. In his *Systematic Theology* he speaks in almost Hegelian fashion of the world process as "the history of God." In contrast to Moltmann he wishes to reinterpret rather than jettison the concept of monotheism. *Systematic Theology,* trans. Geoffrey W. Bromiley (Grand Rapids, Mich.: Eerdmans, 1991), 1:327-36.

[4]See the discussion in Thomas F. Torrance, *Reality and Evangelical Theology* (Philadelphia: Westminster Press, 1982), pp. 17-19.

[5]See esp. Kenneth Hamilton, *Revolt against Heaven* (Grand Rapids, Mich.: Eerdmans, 1965).

[6]Henry is not, however, uncritical of Descartes and Leibniz. See Carl F. H. Henry, *God, Revelation and Authority* (Waco, Tex.: Word Books, 1976), 1:305-8, 314-19.

[7]For an astute analysis of the evangelical rationalism of Henry, Clark, Geisler,

Carnell and others, see Nicholas F. Gier, *God, Reason and the Evangelicals* (Lanham, Md.: University Press of America, 1987).

8James Oliver Buswell argued that divine revelation confirms and validates the laws of reason rather than contradicts these laws. Revelation and reason are essentially compatible, grace and nature are basically congruent. *A Systematic Theology of the Christian Religion* (Grand Rapids, Mich.: Zondervan, 1962), 1:15. For an illuminating discussion of evangelical rationalism in America see David F. Wells, "An American Evangelical Theology: The Painful Transition from *Theoria* to *Praxis*," in *Evangelicalism and Modern America*, ed. George Marsden (Grand Rapids, Mich.: Eerdmans, 1984), pp. 84-88.

9Today Jacques Ellul best represents the anticultural spirit of Tertullian.

10The continuing Calvinist attack on Arminianism and the Arminian counterattack illustrate this Quixotian mentality.

11It is, of course, a mistake to remain with this Kantian dichotomy as much liberal and existentialist theology has done; knowledge of the noumenal realm is then reduced to symbolic awareness or mystical insight, which eludes conceptual articulation. As Christians we must affirm that the noumenal has entered into the phenomenal in the person of Jesus Christ and confronts us on the plane of the phenomenal, bringing us real knowledge of transcendent reality previously hidden from human sight and understanding.

12See H. Richard Niebuhr, *Christ and Culture* (New York: Harper & Brothers, 1951). Niebuhr's other categories are "Christ-above-culture," "Christ-and-culture-in-paradox" and "Christ-transforming-culture."

13P. T. Forsyth, *Positive Preaching and the Modern Mind* (London: Independent Press, 1953), p. 168.

14A free translation by William A. Dyrness from Dilthey's *Leben Schleiermachers* in Dyrness, "The Pietistic Heritage of Schleiermacher," *Christianity Today* 23, no. 6 (Dec. 15, 1978):17. See Wilhelm Dilthey, *Leben Schleiermachers* (Berlin: Walter de Gruyter, 1966), 1(2):33-35.

15Woodrow A. Geier, " 'Schleiermacher as Contemporary': A Consultation," *Christian Century* 85, no. 14 (Apr. 3, 1968):435.

16Friedrich Schleiermacher, *On Religion: Speeches to Its Cultured Despisers*, trans. John Oman (New York: Harper & Row, 1958), p. 39.

17For a brilliant critique of Schleiermacher's cultural Christianity from a neo-Reformation perspective, see H. R. Mackintosh, *Types of Modern Theology* (London: Nisbet, 1949), pp. 31-100. For a more positive and comprehensive analysis of Schleiermacher's theological contribution, see Martin Redeker, *Schleiermacher: Life and Thought*, trans. John Wallhausser (Philadelphia: Fortress, 1973).

18Walter Rauschenbusch, "The New Evangelism," in *American Protestant Thought: The Liberal Era*, ed. William R. Hutchison (New York: Harper & Row,

1968), p. 109.

[19]Shailer Mathews, *The Atonement and the Social Process* (New York: Macmillan, 1930), p. 25.

[20]See J. J. Mueller, *What Are They Saying About Theological Method?* (New York: Paulist Press, 1984), pp. 46-55. Also see Bernard E. Meland, *Faith and Culture* (New York: Oxford University Press, 1953).

[21]Bernard E. Meland, "A New Morality—But to What End?" *Religion in Life* 35, no. 2 (Spring 1966):191-99.

[22]David Tracy, *Blessed Rage for Order* (New York: Seabury Press, 1975), p. 10.

[23]Avery Dulles is severely critical of Tracy's "revisionist" stance, calling it a "latent heresy" that treats the Christian story as the "supreme fiction." He also finds Tracy guilty of capitulating to secularity: "Nowhere does Tracy suggest that Christian revelation might challenge or correct the basic secular faith or transvalue its implicit values. Wherever a conflict appears between Christian commitment and the faith of secularity, it is the former rather than the latter which must be revised." Dulles, *The Resilient Church* (New York: Doubleday, 1977), pp. 67-68, 78.

[24]Langdon Gilkey, *Catholicism Confronts Modernity* (New York: Seabury Press, 1975), p. 160. Gilkey's cultural Christianity is evident when he says that theology "should set in its own terms the best ideals of the culture that it is in," but he warns that theology should never simply advocate cultural ideals. Gilkey agrees with Tillich that theology should also be "a prophetic critic of church and culture." See Joseph L. Price, "The Ultimate and the Ordinary: A Profile of Langdon Gilkey," *Christian Century* 106, no. 12 (Apr. 12, 1989):383.

[25]In Gregory Baum's foreword to Andrew M. Greeley, *The New Agenda* (New York: Doubleday, 1973), p. 16.

[26]Ewert Cousins gives this tribute to Raimundo Panikkar: "When Christian consciousness opens to global consciousness, a new type of systematic theology can be born. This new theology calls for a new kind of theologian with a new type of consciousness—a multi-dimensional, cross-cultural consciousness characteristic of mutational man." In *Toward a Universal Theology of Religion,* ed. Leonard Swidler (Maryknoll, N.Y.: Orbis Books, 1987), p. 47.

[27]Rosemary Radford Ruether, *Womanguides: Readings Toward a Feminist Theology* (Boston: Beacon, 1985), pp. ix-x.

[28]Emil Brunner, *The Divine-Human Encounter,* trans. Amandus W. Loos (Philadelphia: Westminster Press, 1943), p. 170. It is to be noted that the dominant typology that Brunner works with in this book is objectivism and subjectivism, which are more inclusive than fundamentalism and liberalism.

[29]Niebuhr, *Christ and Culture,* pp. 116-48.

[30]See Paul Tillich, *Systematic Theology,* 3 vols. (Chicago: University of Chicago Press, 1951), 1:65-66. Donald Keefe makes a persuasive case that despite their

many differences, Tillich and Aquinas share a commitment to a theology of correlation. Donald J. Keefe, *Thomism and the Ontological Theology of Paul Tillich* (Leiden, the Netherlands: E. J. Brill, 1971).

[31]Hans Küng, *Theology for the Third Millennium: An Ecumenical View,* trans. Peter Heinegg (New York: Doubleday, 1988), pp. 166, 211.

[32]Ibid., pp. 166-68.

[33]Ibid., p. 112. Küng also insists that the changing historical ethos be assessed and critiqued in the light of the abiding standard of faith—the gospel of Jesus Christ. At the same time, he hastens to add that we do not have this standard except in the web of historical relationships and interpretations.

[34]Ibid., p. 237.

[35]Ibid., p. 253.

[36]The conservative evangelical theologian R. C. Sproul also champions the theology of synthesis, openly acknowledging his indebtedness to Thomas Aquinas. See R. C. Sproul, "Does Christian Education Compromise Excellence?" *Eternity* 38, no. 9 (Sept. 1987):64.

[37]*The Table Talk of Martin Luther,* ed. Thomas S. Kepler (New York: World Publishing, 1952), p. 49.

[38]Dietrich Bonhoeffer, *Life Together,* trans. John W. Doberstein (New York: Harper & Brothers, 1954), p. 17.

[39]Jacques Ellul, *Living Faith,* trans. Peter Heinegg (San Francisco: Harper & Row, 1983), p. 277.

[40]Cf. Küng: "Every man is thus summoned, in believing trust, to go beyond the world and its time into another, eternal dimension." Hans Küng, *Does God Exist?* trans. Edward Quinn (New York: Doubleday, 1980), p. 683.

[41]See *Presbyterians and Human Sexuality 1991* (Louisville, Ky.: Office of the General Assembly, Presbyterian Church USA, 1991), pp. 9, 23.

[42]Küng approaches a theology of identity when he sees a convergence between faith seeking historical understanding and historical understanding seeking faith. *Theology for the Third Millennium,* p. 112.

[43]While it is true that in his systematic theology Tillich seeks to distance himself from Schleiermacher's theology of identity, he nevertheless regards Schleiermacher as his spiritual father. See Nels F. S. Ferré, "Tillich and the Nature of Transcendence," in Nels F. S. Ferré et al., *Paul Tillich: Retrospect and Future* (Nashville: Abingdon, 1966), p. 11.

[44]Despite his espousal of a mediating theology, Braaten continues to view Barth as a source of renewal for the church today. While both Tillich and Braaten occasionally distance themselves from the goal of synthesis, their overall effort approaches synthesis, as this is delineated in H. Richard Niebuhr's typology.

[45]Carl E. Braaten, "Let's Talk About the 'Death of God,' " *Dialog* 26 (Summer 1987):212.

[46]Ibid., p. 213.

[47]Ibid.

[48]Ibid., p. 214. Also see Carl E. Braaten, *Justification: The Article by Which the Church Stands or Falls* (Minneapolis: Fortress, 1990), pp. 56-60.

[49]I here find myself in agreement with Bernard Ramm in his *After Fundamentalism* (San Francisco: Harper & Row, 1983).

[50]Forsyth, *Positive Preaching and the Modern Mind,* p. 89.

[51]Schubert M. Ogden, "Sources of Religious Authority in Liberal Protestantism," *Journal of the American Academy of Religion* 44, no. 3 (Sept. 1976):409.

# Name Index

Kaufman, Gordon D., *28, 115, 277, 302*
Kazantzakis, Nikos, *159, 311*
Keefe, Donald, *326-27*
Kehm, George H., *289*
Kelsey, David, *271, 273, 278*
Kepler, Thomas S., *327*
Kierkegaard, Søren, *26, 57-58, 61-66, 76, 79, 148, 151, 158-59, 212, 228, 250, 270-71, 277, 280, 285, 287-88, 306-7, 318, 320*
Kimel, Alvin F., Jr., *293, 297*
King, Karen, *294*
Kittel, Gerhard, *151, 292, 307*
Knitter, Paul, *29, 258, 277-78*
Kraemer, Hendrik, *52, 161, 283, 310*
Krailsheimer, A. J., *280, 306, 320*
Küng, Hans, *12, 31, 52, 149, 156-57, 200, 230, 261, 267, 271, 301, 308, 315, 327*
Künneth, Walter, *255*
Kuyper, Abraham, *217, 219, 264, 318, 323*
Lactantius, *213*
LaCugna, Catherine Mowry, *293*
Lamb, Matthew, *317*
Latourette, Kenneth Scott, *323*
Lean, Garth, *321*
Lehmann, Paul L., *291*
Leibniz, Gottfried Wilhelm, *21, 60, 253, 324*
Lessing, Gotthold Ephraim, *28, 282*
Lewis, C. S., *248, 323*
Lewis, Gordon R., *275, 319*
Lewis, James W., *25, 31*
Lindbeck, George, *23, 25, 28, 30, 118, 132, 271, 276-78, 303*
Lindsley, Arthur, *275*
Linnan, John E., *308*
Locke, John, *57, 147, 209, 275, 284, 307*
Lonergan, Bernard, *118, 156, 303*
Lossky, Vladimir, *299*
Lowrie, Walter, *277, 287, 307, 320*
Lubac, Henri de, *156*
Luehrs, Robert B., *324*
Luther, Martin, *14, 31-32, 36, 55, 57-58, 95, 97, 109, 124, 129-30, 134, 146, 195-96, 198, 201, 203, 212, 214-15, 224, 235, 248, 255, 262-63, 270-71, 280, 288, 298, 300-301, 304, 306, 313-16, 318, 320, 327*
McClendon, James, *273*
McComiskey, T. E., *292*
McFague, Sallie, *69, 93, 289,*

*298*
MacGregor, Geddes, *258*
Macintosh, Douglas Clyde, *242, 322*
McKim, Donald K., *275, 277, 303, 318*
Mackintosh, H. R., *45, 63, 283, 286-87, 302, 304-5, 325*
McKnight, Edgar, *30*
McLoughlin, William G., Jr., *319*
McNeill, John, *124, 304, 306*
Macquarrie, John, *52, 71, 116, 149, 281, 283, 290, 307*
Marcel, Gabriel, *252*
Marquard, Reiner, *280*
Marsden, George, *275, 325*
Martin, Luther H., *294*
Marx, Karl, *269*
Mathews, Shailer, *257, 326*
Maurer, Armand, *281*
Meeks, M. Douglas, *304*
Meeter, John E., *318*
Melanchthon, Philip, *146, 215, 271, 306*
Meland, Bernard E., *177, 257, 326*
Metz, Johannes-Baptist, *293*
Mill, John Stuart, *75, 290*
Miller, Donald G., *311*
Miller, Elliot, *277*
Moltmann, Jürgen, *237, 251, 321-22, 324*
Montgomery, John Warwick, *21, 248, 252, 254, 275, 323*
Moody, Dwight L., *233, 321*
Moore, G. E., *282*
Mor, Barbara, *311*
Morris, Thomas V., *319*
Mueller, J. J., *326*
Muller, Richard A., *301*
Müntzer, Thomas, *194*
Nash, Ronald, *68, 252, 275, 283, 289*
Newman, John Henry, *194*
Nicholas of Cusa, *88, 294*
Niebuhr, H. Richard, *189, 255, 257, 259-60, 267, 325-27*
Niebuhr, Reinhold, *109, 117, 173, 186, 205, 218, 227, 247, 300, 302, 320, 323*
Niemöller, Martin, *152*
Nietzsche, Friedrich, *27, 269*
Niles, D. T., *244*
Nygren, Anders, *283-84*
O'Collins, Gerald, *123, 303-4*
O'Connell, Timothy E., *308*
Oden, Thomas, *284*
Ogden, Schubert, *23, 108, 124, 126, 132, 271, 276, 300, 304-5, 315, 328*
O'Leary, Joseph S., *283*
O'Meara, Thomas, *156, 274*
Origen, *18, 213, 271*
Otto, Rudolf, *108, 250, 300*
Outler, Albert, *208*

Overbeck, Franz, *323*
Pagels, Elaine, *294*
Paley, William, *216*
Palma, Robert J., *312*
Panikkar, Raimundo, *29, 258, 277, 326*
Pannenberg, Wolfhart, *37, 48, 57, 69, 89-90, 214, 219, 247, 251, 262, 269-70, 280, 281-83, 289, 295, 317, 319, 324*
Pascal, Blaise, *37, 43, 57, 143, 146, 156, 158-59, 224, 226, 246, 279-80, 306, 320, 321*
Pauck, Wilhelm, *306*
Peers, E. Allison, *279*
Pegis, Anton C., *317*
Pelagius, *221*
Pelikan, Jaroslav, *280, 298, 306, 311, 316, 318*
Perdue, Leo G., *292*
Peters, Ted, *277*
Phillips, Timothy R., *307*
Pike, Kenneth L., *248, 323*
Pinnock, Clark, *208, 310*
Pinomaa, Lennart, *314*
Piper, John, *110, 283, 301*
Plantinga, Alvin, *275*
Plato, *41, 44, 54, 56, 156, 166, 179, 207*
Plé, Albert, *284*
Plotinus, *42, 44, 156*
Portalié, Eugène, *317*
Preller, Victor, *321*
Price, Joseph L., *326*
Priebe, Duane, *280*
Protagoras, *40*
Przywara, Erich, *159, 285, 322*
Puech, Aimé, *323*
Quinn, Edward, *279*
Rad, Gerhard von, *277*
Rahner, Karl, *52, 123, 149, 156, 194, 200, 229, 262, 304, 308, 320, 321*
Ramm, Bernard, *328*
Ranke, Leopold von, *277*
Raschke, Carl A., *294*
Ratzinger, Joseph Cardinal, *250*
Rauschenbusch, Walter, *257, 273, 325*
Redeker, Martin, *325*
Reid, Thomas, *21, 275*
Richardson, Alan, *304*
Richardson, Kurt, *312*
Ricoeur, Paul, *71, 74, 96, 273, 290, 293, 298*
Ritschl, Albrecht, *45, 114, 119, 150, 271, 302-3*
Ritschl, Dietrich, *192, 314*
Robinson, James M., *302*
Robinson, John, *125*
Rogers, Carl R., *193, 314*
Rogers, Jack B., *275, 318-19*
Rorty, Richard, *16, 273, 278, 282*
Roszak, Theodore, *27*

## Subject Index

# Scripture Index

230.01
B 652
c.3

125 400

Lincoln Christian
University Library

3 4711 00231 1605